To Faye—
With All My Love

The record of the Intelligence Unit is merely the
composite result achieved by its Special Agents.

ELMER IREY

by Hank Messick

G. P. PUTNAM'S SONS   *New York*

SECRET FILE

SECRET FILE

Books by Hank Messick

PREFACE

THE secret files of the Intelligence Division of the Internal Revenue Service are protected by law and by fear. Only the President of the United States has authority to release certain information relating to income tax returns. Other data not legally restricted are virtually classified because they reflect on powerful politicians who have life and death power over jobs and budgets.

In 1950-51 the Kefauver Committee made the most penetrating probe ever conducted of the links between organized crime and politicians. The investigation was successful largely because the President signed an executive order giving the committee the right to examine income tax returns and other information in the files of the IRS. Yet following the probe the committee's records went into the National Archives to remain inaccessible for fifty years. Much valuable information that never became part of the public record of the committee was lost to those who deal with the problem of organized crime and corruption today.

Added to the legal and political difficulties of obtaining information from those secret files is a tradition dating back to

1919, when the Intelligence Division was created. Assigned first to "police" Treasury agencies, the men of the new unit became known as silent investigators. Publicity wasn't wanted. This tradition carried over as the men of Intelligence found themselves saddled with the duty of enforcing the nation's tax laws. Since this country depends largely on a system of voluntary compliance, policy seemed to indicate the less publicity given tax evaders, the better. In those innocent days it was naïvely assumed that most Americans needed no threat of prison to make them pay their fair share.

The Federal Bureau of Investigation, hampered by no such restrictions and led by men who knew the value of a public image, began making the headlines. Director J. Edgar Hoover picked his targets carefully. While he chased bank robbers such as Ma Barker and Pretty Boy Floyd, the men of Intelligence wrestled with Al Capone, Waxey Gordon, and Huey Long. Later, the FBI defended the country against the Reds, real and alleged, while Intelligence continued its not always popular task of making everyone—big and small—pay taxes.

While little is said of it today, there was a time when the Intelligence Division bitterly resented the publicity given the FBI. Competition was keen; had the FBI not avoided the problem of organized crime with determination, the basic conflict would have become more apparent. Again and again it was left to the Intelligence Division to build income tax cases against gang lords, murderers, political bosses, and other criminals who apparently were otherwise untouchable. Yet the grumbling of special agents had little influence in Washington, and the policy of silent service continued.

Not until Senator Edward Long of Missouri—for reasons detailed in Chapter 20—began a bitter attack on the wiretapping practices of the Intelligence Division did policymakers begin to wonder. They knew, as did the men in the field, that the FBI had conducted a hundred taps for every one used by the IRS. Yet such was the FBI's prestige, built up deliberately over the years, that Senator Long decided it would be safer to attack the IRS. Tax collectors have never been popular, and over the years, almost no attempt to inform the American people of their achievements had been made. The FBI so dominated the public consciousness that even a tax case was often automatically credited to Hoover's men.

Senator Long failed to achieve his purpose, but he did tremendous damage to the IRS public image—such as it was— and to the morale of the men in the field. Aware of this, the top brass in Washington decided the time had come to take countermeasures. Nineteen sixty-nine, the fiftieth anniversary of the Intelligence Division, offered a perfect excuse to obtain publicity, to boast of past achievements, to set the record straight. Perhaps a book could be written if the right author were found.

In 1966 I had been called to testify before Senator Long's subcommittee. The Senator had not been happy with my performance. Unlike most of the other witnesses, I didn't seem to understand that my purpose there was to tie yet another can to the tail of the IRS. I concluded my testimony by telling the Senator for the record: "Right now, I think organized crime considers you the best thing since Prohibition."

As a newspaper reporter working in some of the nation's hot spots and later as a researcher on organized crime for the Ford Foundation, I had met and worked with special agents of the Intelligence Division for years. They, the men in the field, knew and trusted me, as I knew and admired them. Unhappily, my contacts in Washington were "shipped out" in a vain effort to appease the unappeasable Senator Long. Their successors had every reason to be cautious.

So when in 1967 I began research on a book about Michael "Trigger Mike" Coppola, I got no cooperation from Washington. Mike had been a high-ranking Mafia figure for decades. His income from assorted rackets was at least $1,000,000 a year —in cash. He lived like a king on Miami Beach, apparently so well insulated that no law enforcement agency could touch him. Yet the Intelligence Division, overcoming amazing handicaps, made a case against him when all other agencies, including the FBI, had failed and sent him to prison. I wanted to tell the story of Mike's rise and fall, but my formal request for a look at the secret files on Coppola was firmly, if politely, rejected. I utilized other sources, got the material I needed, and wrote the book. Commissioner of Internal Revenue Sheldon S. Cohen wrote a short introduction for *Syndicate Wife*. Shortly thereafter, the high brass apparently having recognized the value to the Intelligence Division of such a book, I was asked if I would like to write a history of its fifty-year war against organized crime.

I was interested, if skeptical. To write a good book that would do justice to the subject would require access to the secret files of the Intelligence Division. On no other basis could it be done. I was assured of cooperation. The FBI, it was pointed out, had on more than one occasion opened its files to friendly writers. I would be granted the same privileges.

Still skeptical, I accepted the assignment. Soon my cynicism seemed justified. From the Public Information Office of the Internal Revenue Service poured a steady stream of information, but most of it was newspaper clippings, copies of court decisions, and other data of "public record" nature. I protested, explaining that I had been promised case files. Again came assurances —the files were being "screened" to make sure I was given nothing prohibited by law. In due time I would receive the "hard" information.

The year 1968 was full of political suspense. Would President Johnson seek reelection? If not, who would be the Democratic nominee? Did the Republicans have a good chance?

This uncertainty had a bearing on my project. Any change in the status quo would almost inevitably mean a new commissioner. He might oppose the book project as a matter of principle. Or his political friends might object. No one could be sure, so in the tradition of bureaucracy, a decision was made to delay until the political skies cleared.

At the heart of the problem was the fact that crime and politics go hand in hand. One cannot explain the Capones, the Lucianos, the Lanskys, or the Costellos, without explaining the Huey Longs, the Tom Pendergasts, the Nucky Johnsons, or the Bernard Goldfines. Indeed, it is even necessary if one is to be honest and objective, to touch on the careers of such men as Harry Truman, Lyndon Johnson, and Richard M. Nixon.

Thus even in my frustration, I could understand why the boys in the national office were having second thoughts about the book. They had selected me, I was sure, because they be-

10

lieved I could and would say things that they could not say. The problem was how to give me the material I needed while avoiding responsibility for what I would write.

At one point, when it seemed the Democrats would retain power, I was asked to delete a planned chapter on Huey Long. The Kingfish was long dead, but his son was Majority Whip in the United States Senate and a powerful man. Conceivably, he might take offense if he thought a federal agency had helped smear his father.

Later, after the Republicans won, I received a suggestion that the chapter on Bernard Goldfine might annoy Republicans. After all, Goldfine had been close to men who were close to Eisenhower and Nixon.

I made no promises and continued to press for the material I had been assured I would receive. Time was running out; other obligations were waiting. Yet although my filing cabinets were becoming full, I still had not received any information from the secret files.

To solve the crisis, I went to the men I knew and trusted—the men of the Intelligence Division. I also went to Commissioner Cohen. What kind of battle followed in the highest levels of the IRS I can only guess at, but it resulted in an unprecedented victory for those who believed the public had a right to information about their silent investigators.

The secret files I wanted were loaded into an automobile and brought to the Intelligence Division's field office in Fort Lauderdale, Florida. A specially selected special agent and a representative of the Public Information Office rode shotgun. The records were considered too valuable to be trusted to the mails.

In Fort Lauderdale the records remained in custody of the IRS, but I was permitted free access to them as long as I needed. Many were so old the ink had faded. It almost cost me my eyesight to read them. Since so much time had been wasted, I was forced to work night and day. Only the knowledge that I had been given a unique opportunity kept me going, for a writer given the opportunity to mine the rich lode of intrigue and adventure that is the history of the Intelligence Division of the Internal Revenue Service is confronted with an embarrassment of riches. There is too much deserving material for one book or a dozen to encompass. Much of the data with which I was supplied—correspondence, memos, case records—had never been made public. In addition, the material in the book is drawn from literally hundreds of sources: court records; files of Senate and House committees; interviews with special agents and with gangsters; Justice Department data; police departments from coast to coast; newspapers and magazines. Combined with basic information provided by the Intelligence Division, they complete a pattern.

The completed manuscript was checked for factual errors by a team of special agents in Washington. Somewhat to my surprise, they questioned only one item—a date. Research proved I was right, however. Yet doubts about possible political repercussions remained, scarcely to be allayed by the Republican victory in November. Commissioner Cohen resigned, and after a long interim period, Randolph Thrower of Atlanta was appointed to succeed him.

But I had the facts I needed. For their selection, as well as for any conclusions drawn from them, I take full responsibility. If any public official or politician is offended by them, he should direct his anger at me. No laws have been violated, and no reputations have been unfairly tarnished. I have written the truth as collected by men who were interested only in the truth.

The truth, unhappily for some, is complex. Unlike the legends of La Cosa Nostra, the true story of organized crime fits into no simple theory, no easy story line. No one ethnic group can be blamed, no single secret society. Organized crime is so intermingled, so interwoven with the political and economic life of this country that to simplify is to be dishonest. For this reason, I feel this book has a unique value. In our free enterprise system, the primary goal is to make money. The Intelligence Division, alone of all agencies, has been concerned with how that money was made, what happened to it, and who got what. Only from its secret files can the real story be derived, and I have been fortunate to be the first to examine those files.

Had I simply tried to glorify the Intelligence Division as writers have glorified the FBI, I would have had fewer problems. Instead, I got the facts and let them speak for themselves. This is what the special agents of Intelligence have done for fifty years. I'm well content to follow their example.

HANK MESSICK

Fort Lauderdale, Florida

CONTENTS

CONTENTS

Illustrations follow page 192.

PROLOGUE

STRICTLY speaking, it was none of Richard E. Jaffe's business when in July, 1959, he spotted a familiar-looking white Cadillac in front of his car. Nevertheless, he played a hunch and followed it. Some months later the United States was $8,000 richer, and a syndicate accountant was dead.

Jaffe, a special agent assigned to the Miami office of the Internal Revenue Service's Intelligence Division, suspected the car ahead of him belonged to Charles "the Blade" Tourine—one of the many Mafia figures who found Miami Beach a comfortable place to live and work. His suspicions were confirmed when he approached close enough to see the license tag on the Cadillac. 1WW 8643 was the number of Tourine's car.

Three men were in the car. A young man with black hair and a round face was at the wheel. An elderly man was on the right. In the middle was a man who greatly resembled Tourine. The Caddy was headed for the Seventy-ninth Street Causeway, that narrow strip of land connecting Miami Beach with Miami. Along that strip the bosses of organized crime had invested millions in nightclubs, motels, and apartment houses.

Suddenly the driver veered sharply to the left, leaving the

17

special agent no time to follow. As quickly as traffic permitted, Jaffe made a U-turn but was unable to locate his quarry. A search of the immediate area was unproductive, so the special agent shrugged and returned to the causeway. As he passed the Isle d'Capri, a property of the Cleveland Syndicate, he found himself smiling. Directly ahead was the same Cadillac. The man who resembled Tourine had been dropped during the short detour.

Fully aware that a good agent makes the most of his luck and earns the rest, Jaffe followed cautiously as the gangster's car continued across the causeway and stopped at last in the parking lot of the Little River Bank & Trust Company in Miami. The two men went inside the bank. A second later a guard began locking the door. It was exactly 2 p.m. Only by showing his credentials did Jaffe gain admittance.

The men he had followed were standing by a desk in front of the safe-deposit boxes. The older man was apparently filling out an application form of some kind while the younger chatted with a woman employee. Jaffe watched as each man handed the woman a $100 bill. She took it to a teller and received change. At least part of the money was returned to the men along with a safe-deposit box. The men carried the box into a booth and closed the door. After apparently putting something into the box, they emerged from the booth and entered the vault. A minute later they left the bank emptyhanded.

Again the special agent produced his credentials and interviewed the woman. The two men had rented a box under the names of Jack Cohen and Sam Kay. Jaffe recognized the jest implicit in the use by the younger man of the name, Sam Kay. In syndicate circles the real Sam Kay was an almost legendary moneyman, who had been plotting international deals long before the driver of the Cadillac was born.

Asked about the exchange of money, the woman explained that "Cohen" gave her a $100 bill in payment of the box rental. "Kay" had produced another and asked for change. Jaffe secured copies of the application form and the receipt for the box rental. After thanking the puzzled woman, he returned to his office. A check of the picture file confirmed another suspicion— "Kay," the younger man, was Tourine's son. Around Miami

18

Beach he was known variously as Chuck White and Charles Delmonico.

The episode, while intriguing, seemed of no immediate value. The Intelligence Division operates on a specific case basis, and while Jaffe and his superiors would have enjoyed peeping into the mysterious safe-deposit box, they had no legal "handle" with which to justify such a peep. The special agent wrote a memorandum for the files and turned to the case in hand.

Months passed. One day Jaffe was having coffee with Revenue Officer Martin Berkman. It seemed that Berkman had been handed a tough one. A delinquent taxpayer's account had been transferred from New York and assigned to him for collection. The taxpayer had filed income tax returns showing he owed $8,000, but he had neglected to include a check. For weeks Berkman had been trying to locate some assets to satisfy the debt, but the effort was futile. Who was the insolvent taxpayer? Why, Charles Delmonico, son of Charles the Blade.

Memory stirred Jaffe. He found the memo he had written in July. Berkman glanced at it and grinned broadly. Within an hour he served a lien against the contents of the box at the Little River Bank & Trust Company. Within two hours he received a call from an attorney representing Delmonico. The attorney promised to bring in his client and a certified check the next morning. He kept his word, and the lien was released.

Still curious, special agents followed Tourine's son when he left the IRS office and went to the bank to clean out the safe-deposit box. They noted that he was joined by Benjamin Berkowitz, an accountant long associated with Tourine. Meanwhile, informants reported the underworld grapevine was buzzing with rumor and surmise. How had the Feds discovered that Sam Kay was a pseudonym for Delmonico? Had someone squealed?

Sometime later the syndicate's decision was apparent. The body of Berkowitz was found slumped at his desk in his plush office near the Seventy-ninth Street Causeway. He had been shot through the heart. Bay Harbor Island police, cooperative as usual, called it a suicide and closed the case without investigation. In high syndicate ranks, a different story was accepted:

Tourine had been part owner of the Casino de Capri in Havana under a franchise granted Mafia members by syndicate boss Meyer Lansky. The Capri, along with other casinos, had closed early in 1959, after Fidel Castro came to power and booted out Lansky. Berkowitz, the trusted accountant, had been given custody of much of the casino's cash. After all, Tourine—a typical Mafia hood—couldn't read or write. Allegedly, Berkowitz had gambled on his boss' ignorance and used some of the money for personal investments that had gone sour. In an effort to conceal the loss, he—according to underworld gossip —tipped the IRS about the safe-deposit box in the belief its entire contents would be seized. However, the tax boys wanted only the money due the government, and the plot failed.

Thus, according to syndicate logic, Berkowitz deserved death on two counts.

No tears were shed for the dead accountant by Jaffe and his associates as they reconstructed the story. As for Delmonico, he was to cross Jaffe's trail in still another connection. The special agent was involved in a complicated probe of Michael "Trigger Mike" Coppola, a high-ranking member of the Mafia, whose unreported income was estimated at $1,000,000 yearly in cash. A key witness was Coppola's ex-wife, who was concerned, among other things, with the future of her daughter by an earlier marriage. Trigger Mike had introduced the beautiful girl to such swains as Charles Delmonico. To protect her daughter, as well as obtain revenge, the ex-wife broke the code and talked. Coppola went to prison.

This one episode combines many of the elements that have made the special agents of the Intelligence Division so effective and so feared: attention to small details; an understanding of human nature; the ability to wage psychological warfare; and, finally, a capacity for inspiring confidence in persons who don't even trust themselves.

1

SILENT INVESTIGATORS

THERE are some today who look back with longing to a dim and distant past when the United States was a second-rate power and its citizens were free to become robber barons in the sacred name of free enterprise.

In youth all things seem possible.

Prior to the adoption of the Sixteenth Amendment to the Constitution in 1913, the principal income of the federal government was obtained from customs duties and excise, or indirect, taxes. A happy situation, yes, but no longer a realistic one. And so, on March 1, 1913, the first income tax law became effective.

By today's standards the fiscal medication was mild indeed. The surtax imposed provided for a rate of 1 percent on income of more than $20,000, with a maximum of only 6 percent. Three years later, with war raging in Europe, still higher rates were applied. When the United States entered the war on April 6, 1917, still more money was needed. The income tax rates were again increased, and the excess-profits tax feature was added. Citizens were asked to pay a surtax of 1 percent on net incomes of $5,000 and up to 63 percent on net income above that figure. In a seven-year period, internal revenue collections increased from $344,424,453.85 in 1913 to $5,407,580,-251.81 in 1920.

The growth of the Bureau of Internal Revenue, as the agency assigned to collect taxes was then known, was of necessity equally rapid. Personnel increased from about 4,000 in 1913 to more than 14,000 in 1919. Inevitably in such an expansion some of the new employees proved incompetent and dishonest. Since the American system of taxation was then, and remains, largely voluntary and dependent on public confidence, the need for an internal police agency became apparent.

On July 1, 1919, the Intelligence Unit of the Bureau of Internal Revenue was born.

The unit was the brainchild of the Commissioner of Internal Revenue, Daniel C. Roper, who prior to his appointment had served as First Assistant Postmaster General. In that capacity he had become acquainted with the work of the Post Office Inspection Service—then, as now, an elite group concerned with the investigation of fraud in the use of the mails and with the elimination of dishonest employees. Why not create a similar outfit in Internal Revenue, where the opportunities for graft were even larger?

Roper's special assistant, a former Post Office clerk named Joseph Callan, suggested the new unit be built around a nucleus of experienced Post Office inspectors. Reluctantly the Postmaster General agreed that Roper could have "six men of his own choosing but no more."

The job of selecting the six men was handed to Elmer Irey, a thirty-one-year-old Post Office inspector stationed at Lynchburg, Virginia, and a former colleague of Callan's. Irey was lured away from his old job by the challenge of the new—and an increase in salary to $2,500 a year.

Irey, who was to become a legend during his long tenure, deserves much of the credit for creating and developing an organization composed of efficient, dedicated men. However, his first selections were perhaps his best decision. Aided by his assistant, W. H. Woolf, he chose wisely and well. Frank Frayser, Everett Partridge, Hugh McQuillen, Arthur Nichols, Her-

22

bert E. Lucas, and Arthur Smith were tapped. Of these six, all but Smith remained with Irey and assumed responsible roles in the growing organization.

Thanks to the romantic illusions a naïve America cherished during World War I about spies, "intelligence" had become a popular word. "Special Intelligence" should, therefore, be even more favorably received, and the new unit was so designated. The order creating the unit specified its duties as the investigation of such charges against Internal Revenue employees as extortion, solicitation or acceptance of a bribe, embezzlement, aiding in the prosecution of a claim against the government, and official or moral misconduct. Almost as an afterthought, another function was added: the investigation of attempts to defraud the government of taxes due. In a very short time the latter assignment was to become the primary objective, but in those days most people assumed that citizens would willingly, if not cheerfully, pay their just dues in full.

The first case dampened some of the optimism. It involved a conspiracy between two certified public accountants and an Internal Revenue inspector, and it came within days after the Special Intelligence Unit was created. The two accountants, doing business as Sterling Accounting and Audit Company of New York City, made a practice of calling on firms having large incomes. The Internal Revenue inspector was in a position to supply the names of prospects and to follow through on any deals arranged. The taxpayers were offered a "foolproof" scheme to reduce the amount of taxes required. In return, the accountants asked for 20 percent of the amount saved. The plot required the deliberate destruction and falsification of records, as well as the cooperation of the crooked inspector in accepting the fraudulent returns.

Adolph Pricken, vice-president of Coastwise Warehouses, Inc., one of the firms approached, reported the solicitation and agreed to cooperate in the probe. Pretending to go along with the deal, he paid off in marked money, which was soon recovered from the persons of the conspirators. Meanwhile, the records of Sterling Accounting were seized and examined. Proof of fraud in 115 cases involving firms and individuals was found, and more than $1,000,000 in taxes were recovered. The Intelli-

23

gence Unit had proved its worth in record time. If any doubts remained, they were quickly set to rest by the Underwood case.

Garnett Underwood was a tax consultant in Washington. The Intelligence Unit received information he had proposed a deal to a wealthy oil operator whereby all evidence relating to a proposed assessment of taxes in excess of $1,000,000 would be destroyed. In return, Underwood wanted $160,000.

It was obvious that to consummate such a scheme, the cooperation of a high-placed Internal Revenue employee would be necessary. A special agent presented himself to Underwood as the oilman's attorney to arrange the details. After considerable negotiations, Underwood produced the oilman's tax returns and asked for his money. Instead, he was arrested on the spot by the bogus attorney. Still trying to make a deal—this time to stay out of prison—the tax consultant identified his silent partner as Earl C. Rickmeier, assistant chief of personnel for Internal Revenue. Rickmeier, it developed, had been promised $45,000 of the loot.

Both men were indicted, and both pleaded guilty to the charge of embezzling government documents. They were sentenced to twenty-one months in federal prison.

Scores of similar cases followed, and much progress was made in cleaning up the parent organization. Before the task could be completed, however, Irey's silent investigators—as the men of Special Intelligence dubbed themselves—were confronted with a new and truly impossible mission. They were asked to police the men who were supposed to stop America from drinking alcoholic beverages.

To Irey's credit it must be said that both he and his boss, Commissioner Roper, did everything they could to avoid the assignment. Enforcement of the Volstead Act belonged properly, they argued, to the Justice Department. Justice had other ideas, however, and a unique duel was fought in the cloakrooms of Congress. It is a common assumption by students of political science that every government agency, large or small, seeks constantly to grow at the expense of rival agencies. Nevertheless, early in 1920, both Treasury and Justice declined the opportunity and sought to saddle the other with the responsibility. Justice proved to have the best lobbyists, if not the best investigators, and Roper immediately resigned. Later, after Repeal, he returned to public service as Secretary of Commerce.

Ironically for Irey, if the decision could have been delayed a year, Justice would have wanted the job. For in 1921 the Ohio Gang moved into Washington under the nominal leadership of President Warren G. Harding, and one of the most corrupt eras of American history began. The Justice Department and its Bureau of Investigation, as the FBI was then known, was taken over completely, and a working alliance was formed with bootleggers. Millions in graft were collected by such men as Jesse Smith and Gaston B. Means, and the young men who were shortly to become leaders of organized crime were put into orbit. Their only foes then—and their most effective foes later—were the men of Special Intelligence. From 1920 to 1928, when Justice finally took over the task, Irey's men were responsible for firing 706 prohibition agents and prosecuting 207 more. To eliminate corruption completely was impossible—even President Harding had his personal bootlegger, and everyone in Washington knew his name—but a final breakdown of law and order was prevented.

Despite the impossible nature of their assignment, the men of the Special Intelligence Unit—understaffed and underpaid —went doggedly about their duties. No target was too small and none too large. The first major scandal of the Harding administration involved a Congressman and the Acting Commissioner of Internal Revenue.

Key to the scandal, and to many that followed, was a piece of paper known as a permit for withdrawal. When Prohibition began, there were thousands of cases of good liquor stored in warehouses across the country. Many were immediately shipped to the Bahamas, later to be smuggled back during the third phase of the illegal liquor business—rum-running. Plenty remained, however, to make profitable the first phase—diversion. Under law, the liquor and alcohol in storage could be released for medicinal purposes or for such things as the manufacture of hair tonic. To obtain such releases, a permit for withdrawal was necessary.

Millard West was introduced to President Harding by Representative John Langley of Kentucky, a state where much liquor was stored. On the recommendation of Langley, West was appointed Acting Commissioner of Internal Revenue. Almost his first official act was to sign permits of withdrawal authorizing the release of 4,000 cases of bonded whiskey to the Congressman. Investigation revealed that West received $100,000 for the chore. As Irey put it, in a masterpiece of understatement, "It then became the Intelligence Unit's unpleasant duty not only to arrest a Congressman but to indict our own boss." Ultimately, the boss went free, but Langley ended up in prison.

New York City was another hotbed of activity. In probing the situation, special agents picked up $11,580 in bribes, which they used as evidence, while making ninety-four arrests of prohibition agents and liquor dealers. Turning to Philadelphia, the Intelligence Unit found a conspiracy involving William C. McConnell, state prohibition director. In the first three months in office, McConnell issued 215 fraudulent permits for withdrawal covering 315,567 gallons of whiskey and 239,650 gallons of alcohol. McConnell was removed from office and indicted. Irey noted that if he had not been exposed, "he would have released all the whiskey in distilleries in Pennsylvania to the bootlegging trade within a year at the rate he was then authorizing withdrawals."

The same pattern was found in Milwaukee. Investigation resulted in the indictment of the assistant chief of the Prohibition Bureau, a prohibition director, a chief prohibition inspector, the prohibition agent in charge, a prohibition inspector, a deputy collector of Internal Revenue, a bank president, a prominent attorney, and fifteen liquor dealers. It was established that approximately 100,000 gallons of booze had been illegally sold and $110,000 in bribes paid to officials.

Even worse was the situation in Cleveland, where one of the nation's major crime syndicates was in process of formation and the Ohio Gang had its base. A total of 112 persons, including some top state officials, were indicted, but the hoods of Cleveland were undismayed. The city became a center of production during the second phase of the business, the manufacture of rot-gut liquor, and was a major port of disbarkation during the rum-running period that followed. Huge illicit distilleries, among the largest ever found, were located in Cleveland long after Prohibition officially ended. With the profits of bootlegging in their pockets, members of the Cleveland Syndicate went on to establish the country's largest gambling empire. Moe Dalitz, one of the charter members of the syndicate, later played a key role in a weird series of events that took the heat off Las Vegas in 1968.

In return for dropping suits against the FBI for illegal wiretapping, Dalitz, as part of a Justice Department "deal," was let off the hook on a tax evasion charge.

The immense profits of the illegal liquor traffic were well illustrated by the case of the day laborer who became a millionaire in four months—September through December, 1920. Under the system then in effect, a distillery receiving permits for withdrawal was required to telegraph the number of the permit to the prohibition director. When the director sent word the permit was legitimate, the whiskey could be released. It looked like a foolproof plan, but Edward Donegan, a New York day laborer, found a way to beat it.

Bootleggers were offered forged permits by Donegan with the assurance they would be approved by the director. Because of this assurance, he was able to charge as much as $20 per case. A girl employee in the director's office whose duty it was to verify permit numbers was the key to success. She assured the distilleries the permits were genuine.

Special agents were unaware of the operation and stumbled on it by accident. In connection with an unrelated investigation, they visited Donegan's apartment at the McAlpin Hotel in New York City. Suspecting the worse, Donegan offered them $6,500 to lay off. Now it was the special agents' turn to become suspicious. They arrested Donegan for attempted bribery and searched his apartment. Almost 100 telegrams addressed to the director requesting that permit numbers be verified were found. Donegan, still trying and convinced that every man had his price, simply raised his offer to $25,000.

The search of the apartment also revealed the presence of two women from the director's office. They were arrested. Bail for the three was set at $250,000, a figure Donegan had no trouble in meeting. It came from a safe-deposit box. Somewhat

27

curious, the Intelligence men got a search warrant and examined the box. It contained $500,000. Investigation disclosed that in the four-month period he had operated, Donegan had deposited $1,653,797.25. He could hardly be blamed for quitting his job as a day laborer, agents agreed.

The "Great Mouthpiece," William J. Fallon, defended him on the various charges, and for once Fallon's genius failed. On appeal, his case was argued by John W. Davis, later a Presidential candidate, but ultimately Donegan went to prison.

An even more fantastic figure was George Remus, "king of the bootleggers." A Chicago attorney, Remus quickly recognized the opportunity Prohibition offered and moved to Cincinnati, which was the geographic center of the distilling industry of three states. He bought protection on the local level and dealt personally with Jesse Smith, the "collector" of the Ohio Gang in Washington. Smith received more than $250,000 from Remus by assuring him there would be "no ultimate conviction" if ever he got into trouble.

How well Remus' protection functioned was discovered by William J Mellin, a pioneer wiretapper who worked for all Treasury agencies on loan from the Special Intelligence Unit. In the course of his long career, Mellin eavesdropped on every hood of note and even tapped the private line of President Franklin D. Roosevelt just to prove it could be done. Remus, however, frustrated him.

In October, 1920, Mellin was ordered to go to Columbus, Ohio, and register at a hotel under an assumed name. Shortly thereafter he was driven to Cincinnati and signed into another hotel. Ten days passed as he sat around Fountain Square waiting for instructions. When at last they came, he was told to bug Remus' hotel suite. The first step was to tap his telephone. Mellin so arranged it that whenever Remus received a call, the telephone in the agent's adjoining room also rang. Listening in, he soon learned the bootleg king was planning a short trip. While Remus was away, Mellin planted a microphone behind a bureau and ran the connecting wires through the wall to his own room. Two stenographers were sent in from Washington —the tape recorder had not been perfected—and they wrote down every word that was said in Remus' suite.

Much was being said, for Remus had many visitors. On one day alone forty-four men dropped in with outstretched palms. Many of them were prohibition agents or deputy federal marshals. Remus paid them an average of $1,000 each. Later he was to estimate he spent a total of $20,000,000 for protection while selling $70,000,000 in liquor over a two-year period.

The Special Intelligence Unit had no authority to arrest Remus or anyone else for simply violating liquor laws. It could act, however, if there were evidence of conspiracy involving Prohibition Bureau personnel, and it was to obtain such evidence that Mellin was assigned the case. It did not take long to get the evidence.

According to Mellin, he took his findings to a federal official in Cincinnati. The official was not on Remus' payroll, but he was acutely aware of the influence of the Ohio Gang and the impending election of President Harding. After considering the situation, he told Mellin: "Son, there's times when a man has to be practical in this business. It's only a few weeks to election and the information you've dug up is political dynamite. Go back to New York and forget it."

Mellin went instead to Washington "and squawked," but with the political climate such as it was, not even Irey could help him. Ultimately, however, the Intelligence men applied such pressure that unbribed prohibition agents from other states were sent to Cincinnati to raid "Death Valley," the carefully guarded supply depot Remus maintained outside the city. The raid diverted Remus' attention from a new project he had just begun in St. Louis and gave Mellin's colleagues a new opportunity.

The new scheme involved the purchase of the Jack Daniel Distillery Company's bonded warehouse at St. Louis and the subsequent milking from it of more than 40,000 gallons of good whiskey. Remus maintained that he had planned to replace the whiskey with alcohol to keep up the proof and thus fool inspectors. However, when the 891 barrels were examined, all but one had been refilled with less expensive water. Remus claimed he was "doublecrossed by that greedy St. Louis crowd."

The probe resulted in the indictment of thirty-nine men and the subsequent conviction of twenty-four of them. Among

29

those going to prison were several high-ranking officials, including the Collector of Internal Revenue for St. Louis. Several others were important business and political figures. The Intelligence Unit was later to return to St. Louis on other cases, among the most important being one that sent Frank "Buster" Wortman to prison.

Remus, meanwhile, found his world collapsing. His "friend" Jesse Smith was mysteriously dead in Washington, and the stink of Teapot Dome was in the air. Despite the bribes to the Ohio Gang, he went to prison for his activities in "Death Valley." While he was there, his part in the Jack Daniel case became known, and a warrant was awaiting him upon his release. Also waiting were divorce papers. It seems that Mrs. Remus, to whom the king of the bootleggers had assigned power of attorney, as well as stock and cash totaling many millions, had fallen in love with a federal agent—a Department of Justice man. Heartbroken, for he had truly loved Imogene whom he had married, appropriately enough, as it turned out, in the sin city of Newport, Kentucky, Remus made bond and hurried to Washington, where he made a full confession in the Jack Daniel case.

Feeling somewhat better, Remus returned to the million-dollar palace he had built for Imogene on Price Hill in Cincinnati. The place had been looted. Priceless paintings, Oriental rugs, even the solid-gold doorknobs were gone. Mrs. Remus had made a clean sweep. Eventually, the distraught ex-millionaire trailed his wife's car into Eden Park and fatally shot her. Brought to trial for murder, he made an emotional plea on Christmas Eve to the jury.

"I have served in ten jails for the violation of one law," he said, "and felt every heartache in the annals of human suffering, but if you as members of the jury believe it is your duty, send me to the electric chair. To you and yours I wish a merry Christmas and a happy new year."

The jury required only nineteen minutes to find Remus not guilty by reason of insanity. A Cincinnati newspaper editor commented in print:

> He did his bit, and threw a fit.
> Had he been poor, the electric chair for sure.

Cincinnati underwent a thorough housecleaning that sent hundreds of hoods to the safety of "Little Mexico" across the Ohio River in Covington and Newport, Kentucky. Lieutenants of Remus ruled there, taking advantage of the corruption their former boss had created, until 1940, when the Cleveland Syndicate moved in and took over. The cleanup of the area became the first objective of Robert F. Kennedy when he became Attorney General in 1961, and in that bitter battle the Intelligence Division played a key role. Some of the men still active had begun their careers under Remus.

Organized crime has deep and hardy roots.

The episode of George Remus was only one of hundreds, as Irey and his men sought to keep prohibition agents honest in the face of overwhelming temptation. To add to their troubles came a demand from Assistant United States Attorney Mabel Willebrandt that something be done about Rum Row—that system of ships outside the legal reach of the Coast Guard to which rum-runners brought liquor from Canada, the Bahamas, and Europe. Bill McCoy, who prided himself on smuggling quality booze, devised the scheme, and the squadron of ships became more or less permanent fixtures off the coasts of such cities as Boston, New York, New Orleans, and San Francisco. "Retailers," representing the developing liquor syndicates, bought liquor from the ships, hauled it ashore, cut it several times with water, and sold it in thousands of speakeasies to thirsty or sensation-seeking citizens.

In vain Irey protested that Rum Row was not his assignment, but the lady knew how to handle her man. A few snide remarks about the Treasury Department reminded Irey of a sneer made earlier by William J. Burns, chief of the Bureau of Investigation. "Intelligence, bah," Burns had said, and now Irey was ready to make him eat his words.

The biggest Rum Row was then operating off San Francisco, and to that city the Intelligence chief dispatched his ace undercover man, Mike Malone. Mike was destined to become as much a legend as Irey himself, but his true name was a closely guarded secret until his death in 1960. Writers who described his adventures called him Pat O'Rourke, and few of his colleagues ever saw him.

31

Mike was an Irish-American with a unique ability to look like an Italian, a Frenchman, or anyone else his role required. Crooks from Al Capone on down gave Mike their confidence and respected him even after discovering, to their sorrow, he was something more than they suspected.

In San Francisco, Malone opened a "real estate office" but let the word pass that he was a hood on the lam from Chicago with money to invest in the liquor traffic. Soon he was ready to make his first buy from Rum Row. Elaborate plans were made to take out several Treasury agents, disguised as punks, to a mother ship and load a supply of Canadian booze into a speedboat. As soon as the transfer was completed and marked money passed, Mike would fire a flare into the air, and Coast Guard boats lurking nearby would close in on the ship.

The raiders were stationed at their posts on time, but Mike didn't appear. He was in jail. The local sheriff had concluded he was a prohibition agent and ordered him arrested. In jail, Mike found another Intelligence Unit special agent who had been picked up on the same grounds. Mike turned on all his charm and finally convinced the sheriff he was not a federal officer but a crook. Thereupon the local representative of law and order released him.

The expedition was reinstated, and this time it went off without a hitch. The bootleggers were shocked, but one recovered long enough to boast the raiders had arrived too late. He had just sent a bank money order, he said, for $75,000 to the Canadian exporters in Vancouver. It so happened the Treasury Department had a $400,000 lien against the company. Mike went to the nearest telephone. When the letter containing the money order reached the border, Intelligence agents armed with a search warrant intercepted it. Later, when five of the Canadians aboard the mother ship jumped bail, another $100,-000 was collected.

Back in Washington, Irey was pleased. Not only had his men demonstrated Rum Row could be beaten, but they had made a tidy profit on the venture. That was as far as he could go in that direction, confronted as he was with a minimum of men and a maximum of problems demanding attention. Let the lady from Justice call on her own resources now that the trail had been blazed. At her disposal was that very efficient organization headed by J. Edgar Hoover, which was now called the Federal Bureau of Investigation.

Chicago was one city asking for aid. A new United States Attorney, George E. Q. Johnson, was being financed by a group of businessmen called the Secret Six, and all concerned wanted fast action. Johnson's first attempt had been spectacular, to say the least, but a bit unproductive. He had been given a small task force of "fresh, unspoiled prohibition agents." In Irey's words:

"The agents swooped down on unsuspecting Chicago, their eyes blazing and their guns in hand. The chief of this new group led his men through miles of popping photographer's flash guns as he rounded up dozens of illicit backroom ginmills and bathroom alcohol stills. He even knocked off a few breweries. These melodramatics began to pall somewhat when one of the agents shot a man who was guilty of that dangerous American crime of being an 'innocent bystander.' The agent had to go into hiding in the Federal Building, sleeping and eating in an Assistant United States Attorney's office until his victim disappointed the critical Chicago press and recovered from his wound."

Millions of Americans who learn history by watching television can be pardoned for not recognizing in Irey's words a description of the Untouchables and their heroic chief, Eliot Ness. The name, it will be remembered, was given the group for allegedly refusing a bribe. The silent investigators of the Special Intelligence Unit had been supplementing the government's revenue with bribe money for years, but in the belief that convictions were more important than headlines they had said little about it. The "passion for anonymity" continued over the years and hardened into policy. Some special agents began having second thoughts, however, when they discovered newspapers were blandly crediting their exploits to the much better-known FBI.

Ness, it should be mentioned, later became public safety director of Cleveland, where once again he made many headlines but did little to curb the growing power of the Cleveland Syndicate. Yet today it is common practice to report that special

33

Justice Department task forces are patterned after Ness' Untouchables. So much for the ability of television to create legends.

U.S. Attorney Johnson, belatedly recognizing his mistake in selecting Ness, turned to Irey. A dozen special agents were sent to Chicago to work under A. P. Madden, the special agent in charge. They moved quietly, exploring the Windy City, studying the relationship between crime and politics, and setting the stage for the big push to come. Two things made a meaningful push possible. The Prohibition Bureau had at last been given to the Justice Department, and Intelligence was freed of its time-consuming and largely futile attempt to keep that agency honest. Equally important, a minor bootlegger had provided a court test that gave the Intelligence Unit a new and powerful weapon against bootleggers and all other racketeers.

Manley Sullivan was only a small-time automobile dealer in sleepy South Carolina, yet because he supplemented his income by selling bootleg whiskey on the side, he left his mark on legal history and made possible the conviction of thousands of bigger crooks in years to come.

The case began in March, 1922, when Sullivan refused to file a tax return on his income of $10,000. He argued that since much of the money came from bootlegging, it was nontaxable. Furthermore, he said, to report such income would violate his rights against self-incrimination under the Fifth Amendment.

When the presiding judge rejected the argument, Sullivan was found guilty of a misdeameanor and promptly appealed. His attorneys argued the case before the Fourth Circuit Court of Appeals. They pointed out that Congress could not have intended to make gains from crime taxable and thus put legitimate and illegitimate transactions on the same footing. Public policy demanded, they said, that gains from criminal transactions should be regarded as "beneath the contempt of the law for purposes of taxation." For good measure, they again advanced the plea of self-incrimination.

On October 19, 1926, the appeals court rejected the argument that criminal profits should not be taxed but reversed the decision on the grounds that the defendant was indeed protected by the Fifth Amendment. This time the government appealed, and the case of the minor bootlegger went to the Supreme Court. The ubiquitous Mrs. Willebrandt helped argue the matter. On May 10, 1927, a decision reversing the Fourth Circuit's opinion was handed down.

The High Court confirmed that criminal profits could be taxed in these words: "We see no reason to doubt the interpretation of the [Revenue] Act, or any reason why the fact that a business is unlawful should exempt it from paying the taxes that if lawful it would have to pay."

The defense of self-incrimination was rejected in one sentence: "It would be an extreme if not extravagant application of the Fifth Amendment to say that it authorized a man to refuse to state the amount of his income because it had been made in crime."

The court added: "It is urged that if a return were made the taxpayer would be entitled to deduct such illegal expenses as bribery. This by no means follows but it will be time enough to consider the question when a taxpayer has the temerity to raise it."

The Special Intelligence Unit now had the green light to move against organized crime. Irey signaled his men to begin the Battle of Chicago.

2

AN AMERICAN MUSSOLINI

IN a "confidential document" circulated among the personnel of the Intelligence Unit—the word "special" had been dropped as superfluous—Elmer Irey listed "protection" as a successful bootlegger's most essential requirement. And, he added, protection was divided into two classifications: "First—a corrupt alliance with dishonest politicians and police. Second—the ability to withstand competition of other bootleggers by maintaining a gang of so-called 'strong-armed' men."

In an amazing interview granted Cornelius Vanderbilt, Jr., on the eve of his 1931 trial for income tax evasion, Al Capone made this statement: "Graft is a byword in American life today. It is law where no other law is obeyed. It is undermining this country. The honest lawmakers of any city can be counted on your fingers. I could count Chicago's on one hand."

Irey, who once described Scarface Al as "just a big fat man in a mustard-colored suit," did not often agree with the gangster, but on the subject of graft and corruption they were in accord. And today, when "law and order" serves Presidential candidates as a campaign slogan, the opinions of Irey and Capone still have great validity. Organized crime in the second half of the century has become too sophisticated to need gangs of "strong men" to beat back rivals, but a "corrupt alliance with dishonest politicians and police" is more essential than ever. Yet most Americans, be they officials or private citizens, still shun the truth and, instead, blame the rising crime rate on everything from the Supreme Court to the teachings of Dr. Spock.

It was Capone's misfortune that he achieved his power before the National Crime Syndicate divided up the country and eliminated—save for localized civil wars within the Mafia— much of the violence that amounted to birth pains during Prohibition. For it was the bloody gang wars in Chicago, rather than the bootlegging or the corruption, that at last aroused public opinion. Despite the legends that have since pictured Capone as the boss of Chicago and perhaps the country, the gangster who saw himself as an American Mussolini had to fight a continuing battle with other hoods throughout his career. It was a war he never won. At the height of his power he controlled no more than one-fourth of the nation's second largest city, and at one stage he was forced to retreat to such suburbs as Cicero in order to survive. Al learned early that it is easier and cheaper to capture a small town near a large city than it is to dominate, to the degree needed, a metropolis. Other gangsters over the years applied the lesson throughout the country.

To fight his battles in those days of direct action, Capone indeed needed "a gang of so-called 'strong-armed' men" as primitive as himself. Their personalities, restrained only by the fear of the "Big Fellow," caused Al much unnecessary trouble on and off the streets of Chicago. According to one story widely accepted in Miami, it was the antics of Capone's entourage that won for him the enduring enmity of President Herbert Hoover.

Capone was the first of thousands of gangsters to discover the delights of the Miami area and often vacationed there in his plush home on Palm Island in Biscayne Bay. Always he brought along a group of hoods, who slept late each morning and enjoyed themselves late each night. Local inhabitants tolerated the situation as they tolerated all the crooks who followed. Capone, after all, was a big spender, and he brought publicity to the area. His mansion was a tourist attraction.

Hoover, however, was not so tolerant. One night while relaxing on Biscayne Bay, he was awakened from an untroubled sleep—the Depression would soon go away, and business would turn the corner—by shouts, screams, and pistol shots. Capone's boys, a little drunker than usual, were doing some target practice, and competition stirred much excitement. Even the "broads" were screeching. Then and there Hoover decided that Capone had to go. The man was a menace.

That Hoover wanted action Irey had reason to know. He was called one day to the office of Secretary of the Treasury Andrew Mellon and asked if he knew about the President's so-called medicine-ball cabinet. Hoover, it seemed, was a believer in the value of physical exercise as a stimulus to thought and each day convened his trusted advisers to plan the affairs of the nation while tossing medicine balls about. Mellon informed Irey that a ritual had developed. As soon as the ball started moving, the President would ask: "Have you got that fellow Capone, yet?" The session would end with a reminder: "I want that man Capone in jail."

Irey could take a hint as well as the next man.

In reality, Irey had begun a full-scale probe of Chicago long before Hoover's dreams were disturbed in the Magic City, as Miami likes to be called. Following the Manley Sullivan case, which established that illegal income was taxable, a special task force was set up in the Intelligence Unit to strike at top racketeers. There were fewer than 100 agents in the unit at the time, and the diversion to special assignment of a group of its best men presented problems. Irey was later to grumble out loud about the assignment and wonder why the Justice Department—which under law had to prosecute—didn't order "the famous FBI" to do the job. Nevertheless, there is every reason to suspect Irey and his dedicated men welcomed the task now that they had a legal hook on which to hang the mobsters.

The preliminary probe had explored the background of Chicago crime in some detail. Long a lusty, wide-open city, Chicago had known vice lords and crooked politicians for many decades. The series of events that brought Capone to power began with Big Jim Colosimo sometime in the 1880's.

Jim was ten years old when his father brought him from Italy, and he adjusted quickly to the American way of life. Beginning as a newsboy and bootblack in the Levee, that infamous red-light district of the South Side, he soon became an accomplished pickpocket and pimp. Reaching maturity, he became an extortionist for the Black Hand, as the Mafia was then known and squeezed much money out of his fellow Italian-Americans. After several narrow escapes from arrest, he turned to honest employment as a street cleaner and soon organized his colleagues into a "social and athletic club." When he proved he could deliver the votes of the members, he was made a precinct captain by that well-known alderman Hinky Dink Kenna. Public servants such as precinct captains were virtually immune from arrest, and Colosimo took full advantage. In 1902 he married a successful madam and took charge of her brothel. Expansion followed, and by 1910 Big Jim was wealthy, respected, and overworked. In what was perhaps one of the most important events in the history of organized crime, he imported his nephew from New York to serve as his general manager. The nephew was Johnny Torrio—a man Irey was later to describe as "the smartest of all the hoodlums" and "the father of modern American gangsterdom."

Torrio was a native of Naples—a fact that automatically excluded him from membership in the Mafia, which was then a strictly Sicilian society. Later, after first Torrio and then Capone rubbed out many of the "Mustache Petes," the boys of the Honored Society—the real name of the organization—relaxed the rules to permit selected Italians to join. Nevertheless, Capone at the height of his power held only the rank of a *capo decina*—head of ten—in the Chicago chapter.

Growing up in Brooklyn, Torrio became a saloonkeeper and a manager of prizefighters. The sport, as now, was largely controlled by gangsters, and many hoods from Morris Kleinman to Mickey Cohen got their start in the squared—and usually fixed—circle.

Upon coming to Chicago in 1910, Torrio proved his executive ability and soon branched out into gambling. By 1919 he had scores of gambling joints, many located in the back rooms of cigar stores. To assist him, he had already imported a young punk from back home in Brooklyn. In his apprenticeship the punk had picked up a distinctive scar, so it was only logical he become known as Scarface Al Capone. While trying him out, Torrio tested his abilities by installing him as bouncer of one of his suburban brothels. Young Al—he was only twenty-three —proved so capable he was promoted to manager of the Four Deuces, a combination whorehouse and gambling joint where Torrio maintained his offices. Later Al's brother, Ralph "Bottles" Capone, took over the post.

The stage was set, and events were helped along when Big Jim fell in love with Dale Winters, a young and respectable musical comedy actress. To get her, Colosimo had to divorce his wife and marry her. During the long courtship, the diamond-studded gang boss—he wore a diamond on every finger, as well as in his shirt, his belt, and suspender buckles— had neglected business. Torrio assumed more and more power, and by May, 1920, his uncle was no longer needed. Frankie Uale, who called himself Yale because it had a certain Ivy League touch, was blamed for the killing. Yale had just arrived from Brooklyn, where his reputation as a gunman was so well established that Frankie gave his profession as "undertaker" when routinely arrested after any important murder. Irey, however, credits Capone with the killing.

Torrio took over in name, as well as fact. An oddity in the underworld in that he neither smoked nor drank and enjoyed a quiet evening at home listening to music with his wife, he nevertheless won the respect of the hoods because of his brains. Violence had its uses, and Johnny didn't hesitate to use bullets when logic failed; but for the most part his was the voice of reason. In 1924 he called together all his rivals and proposed that Chicago be divided into spheres of influence. Each man would have his territory clearly defined and would be boss within that territory. Later Torrio was to propose the same plan on a national scale and see it adopted by such men as Lepke, Meyer Lansky, and Charles "Lucky" Luciano.

While all the rackets were operating in the territories, the most profitable, of course, was the beer and liquor trade. Torrio had made bootlegging the first order of business after the death of his uncle and organized it in a very efficient manner. To strengthen his hand in dealing with rivals in Chicago, he had captured most of Chicago's suburban cities. Climax of that drive came in the fall of 1923, when he sent Capone at the head of a small army of hoods to seize control of election machinery and guarantee the success of his handpicked candidates. Cicero was to remain a syndicate-controlled city—despite its modern boast that it was the "best-lighted town in America" —until forty years later, when after a series of Intelligence Division raids on gambling joints, Cook County Sheriff Richard B. Ogilvie sent deputies in to patrol the streets. A Republican and one of the best sheriffs Cook County has ever known, Ogilvie could move against the Republican dynasty Torrio and Capone had installed without being accused of playing politics. On the basis of his record, he was elected governor of Illinois in 1968.

In any case, Cicero was captured by Capone under Torrio's orders, and it was from a position of strength that Johnny was able to propose an end of gang war. Agreement was reached, and an uneasy peace existed for some months. It ended when Dion O'Banion, the famous florist and boss of the North Side, got restless and tried to be cute. He sold one of his breweries to Torrio for $500,000. Exactly twenty-four hours later the brewery was raided by Police Chief Morgan Collins, who arrested twenty-eight hoods, including Torrio, and turned them over to the United States Attorney, who, he said, had promised "prompt cooperation." Torrio dipped into his pockets and made bail, but he was more than a little annoyed. When he got proof that O'Banion had helped arrange the raid, his patience, for which he was famous, was suddenly exhausted.

Mike Merlo, head of the Mafia in Chicago, persuaded Johnny to wait. Merlo was that rare exception among Mafia hoods. He took literally the Honored Society's rules about helping members instead of killing them and was much loved by the Italian community. As a result, he was one of the few Mafia leaders of the period to die peacefully in bed. His death came on November 8, 1924, some six months after the brewery raid. Angelo Genna replaced him as *capo,* and two days

41

later O'Banion was shot down in his flower shop. Torrio, still out on bail, attended the funeral, which was among the most elaborate in Chicago's history.

O'Banion had friends, however, and the peace Torrio had so long sought was immediately broken. Warfare broke out, and bodies littered the streets again. Torrio was among those shot. The bullets were smeared with garlic to make them poisonous, but Johnny pulled through eventually. Capone set up guards around the hospital and moved into his boss' room to prevent yet another attempt.

Upon release from the hospital, Torrio decided discretion was the better part of valor. He withdrew his appeal and went to prison to serve nine months in safety. In October, 1925, his sentence expired. Capone was already ruling that section of Chicago Johnny had conquered, and his power was made official by Torrio, who decided to travel for his health. Eventually he returned to New York. Most officials and writers assumed he had retired to enjoy the quiet life his millions made possible. It was not until ten years later that Irey learned the truth—Torrio, the mastermind, was bigger and busier than ever.

Capone, his bloodstained crown perched uneasily on his head, carried on, meanwhile, in Chicago. The violence never stopped, but the money rolled in faster than ever.

Irey's special squad took a quick look around Chicago and decided that whereas Al was smart—having been trained by Torrio—his brother, Ralph, was stupid. It was decided to begin work on Bottles in the belief groundwork could be prepared for attacking his big brother. Al, so investigators discovered, had never bothered to file an income tax return. It was Irey's hope that during the probe of Bottles, Al would not realize that under Internal Revenue policy any taxpayer who on his own volition came in and paid up would not be prosecuted.

The investigators selected Ralph largely because he had unwittingly given them a handle. It developed that back in the pre-Sullivan decision days a young revenue agent—a member of the Collections Division of Internal Revenue—had developed a hobby of persuading gangsters that it was their patriotic duty to pay taxes. One day in 1926, Eddie Waters, the agent, appealed to Ralph Capone. Bottles, who had perhaps emptied a few too many, complained that filling out the forms was just too much work.

Waters decided to be helpful. "Tell me what you made," he said, "and I'll fill it out for you."

Impressed by this show of kindness, Ralph listed $15,000 for 1922 and 1923 and $20,000 for the following two years. He gave his business as "gambler."

The enterprising revenue agent raced back to his office and filled out four delinquent forms. According to the figures, Bottles owed $4,065.75. When Waters brought the returns back to the bar, Ralph signed with a flourish and promptly forgot them. He also forgot to pay the tax bill. Later, when threatened with a tax lien against his racehorses, he offered a compromise. He was broke, he said, but if Uncle Sam would settle for one grand, he would borrow the money and pay up. When asked, he put the offer in writing. It was rejected. Irey ordered a probe to discover just how broke a Capone could be.

Special Agent Archie Martin became interested in some records seized in a raid on a gambling joint allegedly owned by Oliver Ellis. After a little discreet pressure, Ellis talked discreetly and admitted he maintained an account in a small bank under an assumed name. A check drawn on that account in favor of a James Carroll was investigated and found to be closed. Another account was found, however, that was opened with the exact amount in Carroll's account when it was closed. Eventually the second account had been closed, and the balance had apparently been transferred to another account under another name. The trail went on and on. Ultimately, to no one's surprise, it was proved that all the accounts belonged to Bottles. Combined, the various accounts had accumulated $1,751,840 from 1924 to 1929.

The bankers were ready to swear Capone had never been inside the bank. The money, they explained, was brought in by a messenger boy accompanied by a bodyguard who it developed, usually guarded Ralph's body.

It was now possible to prove that Bottles was loaded with cash at the very moment he so unwisely signed a statement saying he was too broke to pay more than $1,000 on his admitted tax bill. Irey's men dusted off an old Civil War statute originally designed to trap war profiteers for attempting to "cheat, swindle and defraud" the United States. An indictment was easily secured, and on October 8, 1929, Bottles was arrested in full view of dozens of his pals as he strode proudly in to watch a prizefight.

In a fifteen-day trial, the high spot of which came when someone stole Ralph's hat from the courtroom and then returned it after serious second thoughts, Ralph was found guilty and sentenced to a three-year prison term and a $10,000 fine. Greatly puzzled, he was led away muttering, "I don't understand this at all."

When appeals were made and rejected, Bottles went to jail. Meanwhile, the Civil Division of Internal Revenue moved into action. Bottles was assessed $12,289.59 for taxes due for the years 1922 through 1925 and $87,217.35 for the years 1926 through 1928. Time passed. Bottles got out of jail, but he seemed in no hurry to settle his bill. Several times offers in compromise were tendered, and in 1949 Bottles offered to pay $25,000. He was indicted in 1952 in connection with the offer on the grounds he knowingly made a false statement, but the indictment was dismissed when the court held he had qualified the falsehood.

The truth about the inevitability of death and taxes seemed at stake. To some officials it seemed death would come before the taxes could be collected. An effort was made in 1954 to bring the case to judgment by serving a summons and complaint on old Bottles, who had been living since 1941 in a mansion constructed by his brother near Mercer, Wisconsin. For some reason, the Justice Department was unable to get the legal papers served. On April 30, 1954, the chief of the Intelligence Division was notified that a secret court order had been issued appointing a special agent of the Intelligence Division to try. Inasmuch as the papers could only be served when Bottles came into the jurisdiction of the Northern Judicial District of Illinois, the Intelligence Division could only watch and wait. New special orders were issued from time to time, the eleventh in the series coming on March 7, 1958. Special

Agent George L. Wilson was given the assignment. Wilson was told the FBI would notify him when Capone entered his jurisdiction.

The break came on April 2. Bottles was reported driving south from Milwaukee in a 1955 Buick, white over black. The FBI was tailing him. Wilson headed out immediately in a radio-equipped car and picked up the procession. It was discovered Capone's car was registered to R. J. Capper of Mercer, a name Bottles had used before.

The federal agents, using a variety of cars, continued to follow the aging gangster down Highway 42A into Illinois. Curious about his business, they made no move to interfere. When he stopped in North Riverside for gas, they got a good look and reconfirmed the identification. Bottles was wearing a blue suit and a gray hat—the color the boys had favored in the old days. In Lyons, Illinois, he pulled into a large parking area in a forest preserve, parked, and got out to enter a late-model black Oldsmobile. The agents were too far away to see the occupant of the Olds, with whom Capone conferred for fifty-five minutes, but FBI agents followed it after Bottles returned to his own car.

It was soon apparent the business that had brought him to Illinois was finished. Bottles headed home. Via radio, quick plans were made. At Touhy Avenue in Niles—a suburban Cook County town—Bottles stopped for a red light. Federal agents were in a car directly in front of him. Another car closed in from the rear, boxing in Capone. Special Agent Wilson leaped out of still another car and ran up beside the bottled Bottles. Opening the right-hand door, which observation had shown to be unlocked, he leaned across the front seat, flashed his badge, and asked, "Mr. Capone?"

"No," said Bottles, defiant to the end.

Ignoring the reply, Wilson continued: "I'm serving you with a copy of a district court order and complaint."

Bottles said nothing. Wilson placed the folded documents in his lap Capone picked them up and tossed them on the seat beside him.

"Okay?" questioned the special agent, still trying to win an acknowledgment. Capone said nothing. Wilson closed the door and returned to his car. It was 3:40 P.M. The light turned green, and the lead car turned right, giving Bottles a free road. Sixteen minutes later he stopped for another light. Wilson, still following with several witnesses, who had observed the whole affair closely, noticed that Capone at last picked up the papers and was reading them.

The next day an affidavit of return of service was filed with the clerk of the federal court, and the four-year effort to force Bottles into court was finished.

On September 28, 1959, the long legal battle came to an end. A U.S. district court ruled: "There is due and owing from the defendant, Ralph J. Capone, to the United States of America up to and including September 25, 1959, the sum of $210,715.75."

The interest and penalties that had accumulated since 1928 had dramatically increased the original debt. Bottles who twenty-five years earlier had considered it too much work to fill out income tax returns had reason to reconsider that opinion in 1959.

Brother Al had not been so hard to convince. Neither had others of the Chicago Syndicate.

On the day after Ralph's conviction in 1929 the Chicago Collector of Internal Revenue was astonished to find a long line of hoods waiting outside his office. Many of them had been considered nothing but bums, but they knew otherwise, and they didn't know how much the Intelligence Unit knew. So they came in droves to voluntarily pay more than $1,000,000 in back taxes in the hope of avoiding the fate that had befallen Bottles.

President Hoover was pleased but far from satisfied. He still wanted the Big Fellow, and pressure mounted on Irey to get him. The chief decided to play his ultimate weapon—undercover man Mike Malone. The genial Mike decided the best approach was to join Capone's gang. The Secret Six, that group of Chicago businessmen, provided an expense fund with no questions asked, and Mike was able to buy a wardrobe even Scarface might have envied—everything from a white hat to purple shirts to checked suits. Whether he also bought some of the silk drawers Al favored is one detail left unrecorded by Intelligence Unit historians. His clothes bore Philadelphia labels and laundry marks, and Mike steeped himself in the lore of the mobs that ruled the City of Brotherly Love. One of his tutors was Max "Boo-Boo" Hoff, who, like many other gangsters, had come to admire Mike after being arrested by him.

Arriving in Chicago by train, Malone called the local Intelligence office and notified his colleagues he had arrived. Then he took a cab to the Lexington Hotel and registered as Michael Lepito.

Al had returned his headquarters to Chicago after a stint in Cicero made necessary by the unexpected defeat of Mayor Big Bill Thompson. With Thompson's return to office, Capone came back to town and settled at the Lexington, where his gang occupied the sixth, seventh, and eighth floors. So impressive was Mike's appearance he was given Room 724, next to chief bodyguard Phil D'Andrea.

Playing the role of a hood on the lam, Malone sat around the lobby for days. He passed time shooting dice and reading the newspapers in public. In private he wrote many letters, which he mailed to Philly, where friends mailed them back. When it became apparent some of his letters were being opened, he could feel a sense of progress. Soon he was invited to play cards with some of the boys, who began enjoying his sexy gossip about Philadelphia. Yet Mike was always discreet, willing to listen politely when Capone's punks tried to match his stories but never asking questions that betrayed more than a casual interest. He became acquainted with such notables as Machine Gun Jack McGurn; Jake "Greasy Thumb" Guzik and his brother, Sam; Paul "the Waiter" Ricca; Louis "Little New York" Compagna; and Frank "the Enforcer" Nitto, better known as Nitti. Murray "the Camel" Humphreys wandered in and out, as did Sam "Golf Bag" Hunt. While men of Sicilian extraction were in the majority, almost every nationality was represented. Jake Guzik, for example, was treasurer, and his nickname resulted from a green stain that came from counting cash.

Mike learned that despite the bloody reputation of Chicago hoods, killers were imported from New York or St. Louis to

47

perform hits. Occasionally, however, when the Big Fellow had a personal interest, he would take a hand. According to the gossip, Al enjoyed inviting a group of the boys to a banquet. When the champagne had done its work and everyone was relaxed, Capone would step behind the unsuspecting hood marked for death and knock out his brains with a baseball bat. Such episodes were considered good for discipline, and jolly good fun as well.

While Malone was slowly working himself into the confidence of the boys at the Lexington, another Intelligence Unit special agent was poring over records seized in various raids around Chicago. Frank J. Wilson, later to become chief of the Secret Service, was a patient man, and ultimately in the mass of records he found checks signed by Nitti and Guzik. They represented profits from gambling joints.

Special Agent Nels Tessem, something of a human computer, began tracing the Nitti-endorsed check. The trail led to the Schiff Trust & Savings Bank, where officials insisted they had never heard of Nitti. Unperturbed, Tessem sat down and made a complete set of books for the day the $1,000 check cleared the bank. He discovered the bank's totals were exactly $1,000 short. Convinced he was on the right track, he demanded to see the general ledger of the bank and supporting documents. There he found a long list of checks credited to the Enforcer. Ultimately, after considerable pressure, bank president Bruno Schiff admitted he had personally arranged to clear Nitti's checks and deliver cash without showing the gangster's name in the usual way.

Bankers have always been essential to organized crime. In years to come, the National Crime Syndicate learned to get control of existing banks and form new ones for its purposes. Ultimately it came to rely heavily on the numbered accounts of banks in the Bahamas, Switzerland, and Panama, but in Capone's day the tricks of the trade were just being developed.

Nitti, who sported the type of mustache later made famous by Adolf Hitler—gangsters have always admired dictators—got wind of the probe and disappeared. A secret grand jury indictment charging the Enforcer with accumulating almost $750,000 in a three-year period during which he filed no income tax return was secured, and the hunt began for the gangster. Meanwhile, Wilson turned to Greasy Thumb.

Handwriting experts concluded that much of Guzik's money had been handled for him by a bank cashier named Frank Ries. By the time that was established, Ries also had vanished. He was located in St. Louis, and after Wilson and Tessem pointed out a few facts concerning his life expectancy—more than one Capone witness had been murdered—Ries agreed to talk if given protection. He "spilled his guts" on September 18, 1930, and by November 19 Greasy Thumb had been indicted, convicted, and packed off to prison for five years. With funds supplied by the Secret Six, Ries and a special agent took a trip to South America. The Intelligence Unit, for which everything had so far been but a prelude, wanted him alive to testify again.

Over at the Lexington, the boys were shocked and apprehensive. Malone, by now accepted, reported their reactions and kept eyes and ears open for a clue to the missing Nitti. After hearing much talk about the Capone stronghold of Berwyn, a suburb where some of the married hoods lived, Mike went out one morning to check some addresses with the local postmaster. He spotted a very pretty woman who looked very much like Mrs. Nitti, and he followed her around for hours as she visited the grocery store and a beauty parlor. After that she took a long drive into the country. Did she simply want to taste the fresh air, or was she routinely checking to see if she had a tail? Mike decided the second theory was the most logical. Six hours after he first spotted her, Mike followed the mysterious beauty to an apartment house on Clinton Avenue in South Berwyn.

Surveillance followed. The problem was to discover the number of the apartment. After several days Mike pushed the empty car used by Mrs. Nitti—for now he had no doubts —in front of a fire hydrant and turned in an alarm. Firemen rushed to the scene, and having nothing else to do when they arrived, they checked out the ownership of the car. Mike was able to discover it belonged to a Mrs. Belmont in Apartment 3D.

Malone was watching from across the street a few days later as a raiding party led the elusive Enforcer out of the building. He returned to the Lexington, where his friends were still insisting the Feds would never get Al. He was too smart. Solemnly, Mike agreed.

When the case came to trial, the Enforcer pleaded guilty, paid a $10,000 fine, and went off to prison for eighteen months. Some years later, when again trapped by the Intelligence Unit, he took even more dramatic action—he killed himself.

Capone apparently did not share the confidence of his flunkies. In the summer of 1930, accompanied by an attorney, he called on Frank Wilson and explained he wanted to pay Uncle Sam anything he owed. The lawyer did most of the talking, but upon departing, Al advised the special agent "to take care of yourself."

Other conferences followed, and at last the syndicate attorney admitted the gangster had an income, but it never amounted to more than $100,000 a year. When Wilson seemed impressed, the attorney put the statement in writing. The document, which pictured Al as the sole support of his widowed mother, contained an admission that Capone was a member of an organization that kept no records and, from which, Al received one-sixth of the profits.

The statement helped disprove the idea that Al was smart.

Meanwhile the probe into Capone's real income continued. According to Irey, Al spent more than $100,000 a year on racehorses and silk drawers alone, so there was reason to believe additional funds could be found. And eventually the sharp-eyed Wilson found them. While checking old records seized in a raid in 1926 on the Hawthorne Smoke Shop, (tobacco stores were traditional fronts for handbooks operating in the back room) the special agent found an entry: "Frank paid $17,500 for Al." There were other references to Al. Again handwriting experts were called on, and the identity of the bookkeeper was established. Leslie Shumway was the name, but Leslie had vanished. Aware that underworld figures who can add were in demand at mob-controlled racetracks, Wilson played a hunch. Racing follows the sun—at that time of year Florida had the action, in Tropical, Hialeah, and Gulfstream parks, in that order. It was Hialeah's turn, so the special agent went down to Miami and, sure enough, found his man at the $2 window. Again the type of reasoning that had convinced Ries was employed, and soon Shumway was talking. He confirmed that Capone was the "Al" on the books, and he estimated the total gambling profits of the "smoke shop" at $587,721, in the twenty-two-month period he had worked there.

On March 13, 1931—two days before the statute of limitations would have barred prosecution for 1924—Shumway testified before a federal grand jury. Then he took a trip, financed once more by the Secret Six. The indictment was kept secret pending additional investigation, and in May another indictment was handed down, charging evasion for the years 1925 through 1929. Al was alleged to have evaded payment of $215,030.48, over the six-year span. Three hours after the indictment was made public, a cheerful Capone surrendered, posted $50,000 bond, and went home to the Lexington Hotel.

Mike Malone expressed the sentiments suitable for the occasion, listened to the excited chatter, and strolled down to the nearest pay telephone to report that five gunmen had been imported from New York to kill A. P. Madden, the special agent in charge, Irey and, of course, Wilson. The reasoning, according to Mike, was that if the three top men were bumped off, no one else would have the guts to prosecute.

The three men marked for murder took precautions. Four days later Mike reported that signals had changed. The gunmen had gone home. Shortly thereafter, a suave young man called on Joseph H. Callan in New York. Callan, now in business, was the former special assistant to the Commissioner of Internal Revenue and was the man who in 1919 selected Irey to form the Special Intelligence Unit. The visitor came to the point: "If Irey's boys let Capone off without a jail sentence, I'll give you one and a half million dollars in cash."

The bribe was beginning to replace the bullet, but Callan was the wrong man to test. Yet not everyone on the federal team was confident. Juries were always unpredictable, and a jury asked to convict the Big Fellow might be unable to withstand the tremendous pressure Al was sure to exert. The word from the mob that Al would accept a thirty-month sentence had an appeal. "Better be safe than risk being sorry" went the argument, and information got back to Capone that the deal was set. He decided to give himself a party—and Mike Malone was invited.

Mike wouldn't have been human if he hadn't considered the possibility that his undercover role had been discovered and that the party was planned to give Al some batting practice. Yet he decided to attend, taking the precaution of carrying an extra gun. It was customary to check all "iron" at the door, but two-gun men were rare. Mike got in with his weapon.

Al was in good spirits. His old friend Johnny Torrio was on hand and was being introduced as the caretaker who would handle things while Al "was away." All went well until Mike choked on some spiced steak and began coughing. The coughs shook his gun out of the concealed belt holster into his lap. Had it fallen to the floor and been spotted, Malone's career would have been abruptly ended.

At the last minute, the Department of Justice, which years before had assigned Capone to Intelligence, got into the act with 5,000 separate indictments against Capone for bootlegging violations. Judge James H. Wilkerson promptly dismissed them as worthless.

On June 16, 1931, Capone—convinced his deal was set—appeared before Judge Wilkerson and pleaded guilty. A newspaper broke the story of the deal on the same day. Capone's attorneys requested a delay to permit Al to arrange his affairs. This was a mistake—it permitted the judge time to read the newspaper account of the alleged deal.

Court reconvened on June 30, and Judge Wilkerson made a brief announcement: "It is utterly impossible to bargain with a federal court."

Hastily, Capone's attorneys changed their plea. The trial was set for October 5. Shortly before that date, Malone at the Lexington discovered the boys were pulling a final fast one. They had secured the jury list and were busily offering bribes and threats to the prospective jurors. Again Judge Wilkerson crossed them up. On the morning of the trial he ordered the regular panel of jurors available to other courts be substituted for the 100 men originally summoned to try Capone.

On the fourth day of the trial, Mike Malone came out of hiding. He had learned that Phil D'Andrea, his neighbor at the Lexington and Al's bodyguard, was carrying his gun to court. During the noon recess, Mike and Special Agent Jim Sullivan shoved D'Andrea into a side room and frisked him. Phil went to jail, and later, after Capone had been sentenced to eleven years in prison and $80,000 in fines and costs, the bodyguard was given six months for contempt.

In Washington, when news of the verdict arrived, an incredible thing was reported. According to reliable sources, a harried Herbert Hoover smiled.

3

SIDEWALKS OF NEW YORK

THE Intelligence Unit found itself famous after the conviction of Al Capone. Its silent investigators became the new folk heroes of America, and its chief, Elmer Irey, was suddenly a celebrity. Unaccustomed to the role, Irey learned the hard way to watch his words.

Even as Capone was being led out of the Chicago courtroom, a reporter asked Irey: "When are you going after the New York mob?"

"I'm leaving for New York tonight," replied Irey, little realizing that next day's headlines would proclaim a new drive against crime by the "Giant Killers."

In reality, the battle against organized crime had already begun in New York, as well as several other cities. In Cleveland, for example, a probe was under way into the complex affairs of a rum-running syndicate which had controlled Lake Erie from Detroit to Buffalo. It centered on Morris Kleinman, who, with partners Moe Dalitz, Louis Rothkopf, and Sam Tucker, had formed a working alliance with Mafia elements of the region. Such men as Frank and Tony Milano, Al Polizzi, Joe Massei, and Peter Licavoli saw the wisdom of cooperation.

54

By speedboat, barge, and airplane, liquor crossed Lake Erie from Canada in an ever-increasing flood. The Cleveland Syndicate, as it came to be known, soon worked out an arrangement with the Big Seven in New York, largely through friendship with Meyer Lansky. At intervals when a shortage developed in the Midwest, booze from New York would be purchased. Occasionally, shipments went East from Cleveland to relieve the situation there. The friendships made during the period helped pave the way for the National Crime Syndicate and made possible many joint gambling ventures in the future.

The probe of Kleinman was begun by Revenue Agent Alvin Giesey in 1931, following newspaper stories that fingered Kleinman as the head of the smuggling ring. It developed that Kleinman had banked $1,673,554 in 1929 and 1930 and had neglected to file income tax returns for either year. Special Agent W. E. McElveen was assigned to the probe. Kleinman, confronted with the evidence, admitted his guilt, but his attorneys insisted he had been promised immunity. A conference was held in Washington on December 19, 1932, with Irey sitting in. Kleinman's attorneys quoted Maurice Maschke, Republican boss of Cleveland, as saying a "no prosecution" promise had been given him on behalf of Kleinman. Franklin D. Roosevelt had just been elected President, however, and Republican politicians were no threat. On February 3, 1933, Kleinman was indicted. He disappeared for six months before surrendering in August. On November 27 he was sentenced to four years in prison and a $14,000 fine.

Kleinman served his time and rejoined the syndicate. His guilty plea had protected his partners, who, while he "was away," entered into a joint venture with Lansky in New York to operate huge illicit distilleries. Gambling, however, soon became the principal preoccupation of the Cleveland boys, and their casinos sprouted across the nation and the Caribbean as well. The Intelligence Unit battled them again in years to come. Much of their success could be attributed to Giesey, the revenue agent, who so impressed the syndicate after Kleinman's conviction that they hired him as an accountant. He served it long and well after quitting his job with the IRS.

Another case occupying the Intelligence Unit's attention was in St. Paul, Minnesota, where Leon Gleckman had won the title of the Al Capone of the Northwest.

Gleckman, although president of the Republic Finance Company, had never filed a tax return before 1928. In that year, following the Manley Sullivan decision, he went to the office of the United States Attorney and said he had learned that income from illegal liquor transactions was taxable. When this was confirmed, he promptly filed returns for 1925 through 1927, showing a net lump income of $15,000 for each year. He continued to pay thereafter.

The Intelligence Unit's attention was drawn to Gleckman on September 24, 1931, when he was kidnapped and held for $200,000 ransom. He agreed to pay off on the installment plan and was released after a down payment of $5,000. Shortly thereafter the reputed head of the kidnapping ring was murdered, and Gleckman made no more payments.

Mike Malone was dispatched to St. Paul as an undercover agent, and a long investigation began. It was climaxed on November 22, 1933, when Gleckman was indicted for allegedly evading taxes on $366,522 in unreported income for the years 1929 through 1931. The investigation proved Gleckman controlled several rackets in St. Paul by means of protection purchased from city officials. The scandal enabled reformers to overthrow the corrupt political machine.

The first trial began on April 24, 1934. One of the jurors was Bernard A. Fuchs, an accountant at the Federal Land Bank. Previously he had done some work for the city and was known to Mrs. Rose Harper, a city employee. After Fuchs' selection as a juror, Mrs. Harper called his home that night and asked him to come by her office the next morning before going to trial. He complied, and she asked him to help Gleckman. When he agreed, she gave him a pint of liquor, $20, and a promise of $300 more. The liquor was consumed by the jurors during their deliberation. Fuchs was unable to win over three of the jurors, and on May 19 a mistrial was ordered. The next day Mrs. Harper and Alexander "Jap" Gleckman, the defendant's brother, drove to Fuchs' home and paid him the

56

promised $300. Later other "loans" were arranged for Fuchs through Gleckman's finance company.

On November 12, 1934, the second trial began. Fuchs was asked to influence a woman juror who worked at the same bank. He went to the trial and, when observed looking fixedly at the woman, was asked or ordered to leave the courtroom. Malone did not get a chance to testify after defense counsel stipulated "that foundation did not have to be laid." On November 28 the unfixed jury found Gleckman guilty, and he was sentenced to eighteen months in prison and a $10,000 fine. Fuchs turned state witness, and Gleckman and his brother were found guilty of two counts of contempt as well.

Another case was closer home. For many years Jimmy La Fontaine operated gambling houses in and near Washington, D.C. His most elaborate joint was a three-story brick and clapboard house on Bladensburg Road just across the state line in Maryland. Like gamblers elsewhere, La Fontaine closed down the casino during sessions of the local grand jury and during the Maryland racing season. He estimated his income since 1914 at $800,000 a year and said he kept "several hundred thousand" in the house to pay off gambling debts. Many of his best customers were high Washington officials during the years Republicans and their businessmen allies ruled.

President Hoover was still in office, however, when William H. McReynolds, head of the Bureau of Efficiency, asked Irey to investigate the seemingly untouchable gambler. The probe didn't take long. La Fontaine opened his books and admitted he had paid no taxes prior to 1927 because he thought illegal income was immune. He agreed to plead guilty to one count and to pay $206,651 in back taxes.

The indictment was returned at Baltimore on November 19, 1931. That afternoon La Fontaine went into court and pleaded guilty to tax evasion for the year 1926. A second count covering 1925 was dropped. On December 5 he was sentenced to nine months in prison and a $1,000 fine. A postponement was granted, however, when, with tears in his eyes, the sixty-three-year-old gambler pleaded for an opportunity to play Santa Claus to his two adopted nieces. When he went to prison after Christmas, he served only fifty-six days. The judge decided his health was bad and modified the sentence.

The outcome was not likely to convince anyone that crime doesn't pay, but the Intelligence Unit had the satisfaction of knowing it had ventured where no one else had dared to tread.

Other cases were demanding attention, but New York had a certain priority. The drive there was originally aimed at racketeers who preyed on legitimate business, though it was soon broadened. The pattern of syndicate evolution was similar in its early stages to that of Chicago—liquor diversion and then home manufacture. Mafia leaders rose and were killed; gangs developed along ethnic lines. With the advent of rum-running, however, events in New York came to resemble more closely those in Cleveland. A smooth working relationship evolved between the bosses of the two port cities, and it was carried over into the final phase of Prohibition—the manufacture of alcohol in huge illicit distilleries. This intercity cooperation prepared the way for the National Crime Syndicate, and joint ventures became the rule, rather than the exception.

Arnold Rothstein was the Johnny Torrio of New York. A pioneer and a teacher, he gave many of the hoods who later were to be targets of the Intelligence Division their start, and he showed them the techniques necessary to make crime a big business. Shylocking, sports betting, stock market swindles, the smuggling of diamonds and narcotics—all these and more were developed by Rothstein, who, nevertheless, is remembered today primarily as the man who fixed the 1919 World Series.

It was Rothstein who made rum-running a big industry along the East Coast. The idea was brought to him by Irving Wexler, better known as Waxey Gordon. Previously he had served Rothstein as a labor goon—breaking strikes in the garment center or defending strikers, all according to which group paid Rothstein the most. With Waxey was Big Maxey Greenberg of Detroit, who wanted to borrow $175,000 to go into rum-running on a large scale. The meeting took place on a Central Park bench. Rothstein listened, asked for time to think, and next day proposed a grander scheme than either Waxey or Maxey had conceived. The liquor would be bought in England and brought over by the shipload. Rothstein would arrange distribution.

Plans worked as they usually did when made by Rothstein. His European agent, Harry Mather, bought 20,000 cases of scotch, found a ship, and sent the cargo on its way. A fleet of small speedboats met the ship offshore and brought the booze to land, where a fleet of trucks was waiting on Long Island. Rothstein had made all arrangements with the Coast Guard and police. A motorcycle escort protected the convoy on its way to a warehouse.

Ten crossings were made without incident, and the profits were enough to dazzle the best brains of the underworld. Then came trouble. The Coast Guard cracked down on its men, and an unbribed commander was stationed at the Montauk Point headquarters on Long Island with specific orders to seize Rothstein's ship, which even then was making its eleventh voyage. The Brain, as Rothstein was known, received a timely tip, however, and the ship was diverted to Cuba and its cargo sold —sold to Rothstein, who managed to get it from Cuba in small boats.

The gambler didn't believe in pressing his luck. Moreover, it was now apparent that rum-running would become too large a business for one man, however smart, to handle. A loner by nature, Rothstein enjoyed keeping control of an operation. Then, too, he had other interests, and they required much of his attention. Calling in Gordon and Greenberg, Rothstein settled his accounts with them. Both men were to continue in the business with Waxey as boss. Ultimately Waxey was to become the Intelligence Unit's number one New York target.

Rothstein, meanwhile, had turned to another phase of the liquor business. John T. Nolan, who was to become infamous as Legs Diamond, was Rothstein's bodyguard before Prohibition. Late in 1921 he became ambitious. As Rothstein had foreseen, hundreds of gangsters had begun smuggling liquor. No strong leader or group of leaders emerged, however, so it was every man for himself. Legs, a thin but handsome young man with white hair, saw possibilities in the situation. He wanted to become an outlaw among outlaws. Why bother to smuggle in liquor, pay off the cops, and invest great chunks of capital when it was simple enough to hijack the cargo after it arrived? However, Legs needed money for trucks, for warehouses, and perhaps for local protection. He also needed an easy way of disposing of the booze. Rothstein was the answer to both problems, and he was willing. Such a scheme was indeed better than smuggling—he got good whiskey at bargain prices, and other people took the risks.

Legs proved to be a cunning, yet savage hijacker, and his reputation attracted such young men on the make as Arthur Flegenheimer and Charles Luciana. Flegenheimer was later to become known as Dutch Schultz and was to branch out into other fields, such as narcotics and numbers. Many people wondered about his uncanny business ability and his political alliance with Tammany Hall. A deputy sheriff's badge was one of the minor rewards of that arrangement. Yet it was not until Dutch was murdered that the truth came out—the brains behind him belonged to Johnny Torrio, late of Chicago.

Luciana became known as Lucky Luciano and in time more powerful than Dutch. He was one of the "new breed" who, after a bloody purge of the Mafia, helped form the National Crime Syndicate. In the process it became necessary to knock off Schultz.

All that was for the future, however. Legs Diamond, backed by Rothstein, robbed and killed for three years. He grew to enjoy killing and became drunk with power. Eventually, Rothstein decided to withdraw his protection. As usual, his decision was based on economics. Times had changed once more. Out of chaos had emerged a degree of order. Big Bill Dwyer, boss of the Irish Mob, had become the biggest smuggler and thus the chief target of Legs' hijackers. He wanted to strike back, and Rothstein gave his consent. The first attempt late in 1924 failed, but the message was clear to everyone. Legs' gang fell away fast, and Legs truly became an outlaw among outlaws. That he outlived Rothstein by almost three years is a tribute to his cunning and to the poor marksmanship of New York gangsters.

The end of Legs Diamond as a power in the underworld marked the beginning of a new era. Legs had operated only because Rothstein had influence with the politicians who could to a large extent control the gangsters. Slowly, however, the situation reversed itself. The gangster became the boss.

A bitter battle for control of Tammany Hall developed with the death in 1924 of Boss Charles F. Murphy. His successor lacked the ability to ride the tiger and became boss in name only. A struggle for power arose between James J. Hines and Albert C. Marinelli—and it reflected a similar battle in the underworld between the Irish and the Italians. For many years, the Irish had dominated both crime and politics in New York, but a flood of Italian immigrants in the early part of the century slowly altered the power balance. Natural allies of the Italians were the Jews, who fled in increasing numbers from Russian persecution and found themselves bucking the entrenched Irish in their new homeland.

Behind Hines ranged the old-timers, the independents, led by Dwyer—Owney "the Killer" Madden, Vannie Higgins, and Larry Fay, who organized the milk racket. Behind Marinelli was the Mafia, led by Joe "the Boss" Masseria and his principal lieutenant, Lucky Luciano.

Hines won the early stages of the battle, primarily because the Mafia was in a constant state of civil war. *Capi* in various cities killed to get power and continued to kill to keep it. Rivals began bringing in troops from other cities and this led to vendettas on a larger scale. To end the slaughter, it was agreed to appoint a *capo de capi re,* an overall boss who could settle intercity disputes without unnecessary bloodshed. This plan, while sound in theory, simply moved the conflict to a higher level. Now all *capi* intrigued for the top job. Masseria killed his way to the post and was immediately challenged by Salvatore Maranzano, and a bigger war than ever broke out.

Luciano blamed much of the trouble on the "Mustache Petes," the old-timers of the Mafia. He resented their loyalty to the old ways which emphasized personal honor—or what passed for it—over the greater good of the society. Most of all, he became enraged at the thought of the profits that were going to the Dwyers and the Maddens through default.

Other young Italians shared his feelings, and they found a similar viewpoint among young men of Jewish descent. Louis Buchalter, known simply as Lepke, was one of these allies, and

61

the Bugs and Meyer Mob was another. It was headed by Meyer Lansky and Benjamin "Bugsy" Siegel. The two partners had already won for themselves a reputation as cunning, ruthless killers and hijackers.

With the aid of the Bugs and Meyer Mob, Luciano moved to end the civil war. In Chicago, Al Capone offered to fly in a small army to help if needed. It wasn't. Lucky arranged for Masseria to be murdered, a fairly simple assignment since he had the boss' confidence. Maranzano took over and immediately ordered a new purge. This time Lucky had to call on Bugs and Meyer for help, and they lived up to their reputation. With Maranzano out of the way, a purge of Mustache Pete's followed, and the Mafia was "Americanized." In place of the *capo de capi re,* a commission was set up to arbitrate intercity disputes. Murders and vendettas continued as a matter of course but never threatened to get out of hand. Luciano ruled in New York and was able to mobilize Italian political power as never before. In short order, he took the Mafia into the Combination, which in turn became the Eastern Syndicate with control from Boston to Miami. To such logical men as Lucky and Lansky, an alliance with combinations in other cities seemed in order, and by 1934 the National Crime Syndicate was a reality.

Rothstein was mudered long before the change he had foreseen was completed. For a short time, he acted as a middleman between the forces of Hines and Marinelli, serving both sides as a political fixer and arbitrator. Only a man of genius could have occupied such a position, and even Rothstein, for all his confidence, surely realized the end was inevitable. On November 4, 1928, he was fatally wounded on the third floor of the Park Central Hotel. Exactly why he was killed remained a mystery officials did not try to solve. It seems safe to assume, however, the same forces that required Rothstein's death were responsible for the murder almost thirty years later in the same hotel of Albert Anastasia. Albert, asserting the right of a Mafia member to kill and steal, defied the syndicate and tried to muscle in on Meyer Lansky.

In the interval between Rothstein's death and the rise of the Combination, two of Rothstein's pupils achieved wealth and power. In 1931, when a reporter asked Elmer Irey about the New York mob, Irey was thinking primarily of Waxey Gordon and Dutch Schultz. The two men were competitors. Dutch had the best political clout in his alliance with Hines of Tammany Hall. Gordon had been forced to operate his breweries in New Jersey, where he had a working arrangement with politicians. Financed and to a large degree guided by the invisible Johnny Torrio, Dutch expanded all over the place. In the numbers racket he found a business as lucrative as liquor and promptly cut himself in for one-fourth of Jose Enrique Miro's business. It wasn't a bad deal for Miro in that he got use of Dutch's attorney, J. Richard "Dixie" Davis, and the friendship of Jimmy Hines. Dutch also devised new ways to rig the racket and thus increase profits for everyone. However, when Irey's men began probing Schultz's empire, they quickly settled on Miro as a point of attack.

Miro, a Puerto Rican by birth, worked as a stoker on the steamship which brought him to Harlem. A numbers racket was operating there under the control of Ciro Terranova, a nephew of Ignazio Saietta, who as Lupo the Wolf had been an early leader of the Mafia. Terranova was more concerned with the artichoke racket—he was known as the Artichoke King—than with numbers, and Miro was able to move into the field and develop it into a big business.

The daily number was obtained from the reports of the New York Clearing House. Newspapers carried the necessary figures. Three-digit numbers were used. The first two digits were taken from the total of all bank clearings for the preceding day, with the formula calling for the last two digits in the thousands of the total. Thus, if the clearing should total $8,351,-089, Miro would post 51. To that he would add the last digit in the thousands of the clearing house balance at the end of the preceding day. If the balance totaled $483,255, he would extract the 3—making the winning number 513. In an age where literally everyone played the stock market and dreamed of becoming a Mellon or a Morgan, such a financial formula seemed perfectly natural.

After the stock market crash of 1929, however, Dutch Schultz introduced the pari-mutuel "handle" at racetracks he owned as a substitute. A lot of people who had lost faith in banks and bankers didn't realize that Dutch owned the racetracks and employed Otto Biederman, better known to Broadway as Abbadabba, to make the pari-mutuel handle reflect the number that had received the least play from the suckers.

Miro employed a small army of "writers," or collectors, who ranged the streets of New York's East Side writing bets and collecting dimes and quarters. The racket was aimed at the poor man and woman whose only chance to get ahead was the possibility of hitting the winning number and collecting at 600 to 1. Enough people won to keep the dream alive and the bets coming. The writers were permitted to keep 20 percent of all they collected. After paying off the few hits, the rest of the money went on to a central controller, who checked the records, which usually took the form of an adding-machine tape.

Even with Schultz taking one-fourth, Miro was still able to deposit $233,317 in 1928, $283,427 in 1929, and $566,409 in 1930. He put the money into ten different bank accounts.

The Intelligence Unit's probe into Miro's income coincided with an investigation into New York's magistrate courts by Judge Samuel Seabury. The Seabury inquiry was ordered by Governor Franklin D. Roosevelt, as were two more that followed. Roosevelt, his eye on the 1932 Presidential nomination, was on the spot. The public was demanding reform, yet an honest investigation would enrage Tammany Hall. It is a testimonial to Roosevelt's courage, and perhaps to his political wisdom, that he chose to listen to the people.

Irey's men turned over much of their findings to Seabury's staff, which was attempting to discover why so many cases involving the lottery were dismissed in the minor courts. Miro, backed up by attorney Dixie Davis, was of little help. For reasons not clear to anyone, however, he denied ownership of three of his bank accounts. Proof was presented that he indeed owned the accounts, and Seabury ordered Miro to jail on a perjury charge. He promptly posted $15,000 bail, but his troubles were just beginning.

A federal grand jury was called into session. Hugh McQuillen, head of the Intelligence Unit's special New York squad, presented evidence. Judge Seabury was also a witness.

The grand jury was advised by United States Attorney George Z. Medalie, aided by his first assistant, Thomas E. Dewey. Medalie was formerly an attorney for Arnold Rothstein. Dewey, who was to quickly become a special prosecutor for a New York grand jury and then district attorney, governor, and almost President, was virtually unknown at the time. With Miro, he began to build his reputation at the age of twenty-eight.

Miro was indicted on income tax evasion charges just two days after appearing before Judge Seabury. The indictment superseded one returned on May 15, 1931—the day Dewey took office as First Assistant United States Attorney. Two months after the second indictment, Dewey had his first conviction. Evidence presented included the fact that Miro kept Tammany district leader Jimmy Hines and Dutch Schultz supplied with silk shirts. When Dutch was asked about them, he made a classic reply: "Only queers wear silk shirts."

Dixie Davis, speaking for Hines, called the evidence "political mud." Miro, who received three years in prison and a $15,000 fine, didn't say anything.

At Roosevelt's direction, Seabury continued his investigations despite tremendous pressure from Tammany and other party leaders in and around New York. The alliance between gangster and politician was exposed again and again, and tales of police corruption sickened even the most hardened newspaper reader. Countless cops, it seemed, had little tin boxes filled with cash stowed away at home, and many were the explanations of where the money came from. One such cop was Vice Squad Detective James Quinlivan, who credited his wealth to tips given him by a drunken jockey. The Intelligence Unit proved he banked $80,000 in one year, in addition to the cash he kept at home. Investigation revealed he owned a speakeasy which he kept supplied with booze by raiding rival establishments and confiscating their liquor. With Dewey prosecuting, Quinlivan got three years in prison.

Inevitably, Seabury's probe led to New York's genial mayor, James J. Walker. To an admiring public and to many reporters, Mayor Jimmy was a friendly, dapper extrovert, who perhaps was too kindhearted to crack down on the crooks around him. That legend still persists despite the fact that Seabury

65

found almost $1,000,000 credited to Walker in a secret account at a brokerage house. Walker replied with a defense that was to become standard for hoods and politicians alike: The investigation was just a Communist plot to discredit him. Roosevelt was not impressed, however. Following his victory at the Democratic National Convention, the governor decided to hold a hearing to determine if Walker should be removed from office. It began in August—with much of the country watching to see if the Democratic nominee would buckle under the intense pressure of the Tammany Tiger. Roosevelt did not buckle, and on September 1, Walker resigned. In retrospect, some observers, who had warned Roosevelt to go easy, admitted that the Walker hearings had been a tremendous political asset.

The continuing pressure by Seabury on the politicians was coordinated with pressure on the hoods from the Intelligence Unit. Probes of Waxey Gordon and Dutch Schultz were under way. Meanwhile, both men were at each other's throats over which one would control the beer that, with Roosevelt's election, was about to become legal. The potential demand was greater than the breweries available to either man could supply. Instead of joining forces, they started fighting. Or, at least, Dutch did.

Beer became legal on April 1. On April 13, Gordon climbed out of a window of the Carteret Hotel in Elizabeth, New Jersey, and escaped with his life from a crew of Schultz's killers. Maxey Greenberg, who, with Waxey, had gone to Rothstein in 1920 to borrow money for rum-running, was not so lucky. He was in the next room with Max Hassell. Dutch's boys stuck a pistol up his ear as he lay sleeping and blew off the top of his head. Hassell was also killed.

The Intelligence Unit had dealt with Hassell in 1928, when he pleaded guilty to an indictment for income tax evasion. He paid $150,000 in back taxes and a fine of $2,000 but apparently considered it a bargain under the circumstances. A new case was pending against him when he was murdered. When police found the key to a safe-deposit box on Hassell's body, Irey became interested and assigned Special Agent Edmund J. Wrigley to investigate. A court order was necessary before officials of the Elizabethport Banking Company would open the box. Inside was found $213,500 in cash and a $50,000 promissory note signed by two bankers. Later the federal government collected $170,000 of the total for overdue taxes.

Bill Mellin, the Intelligence Unit's busy wiretapper, played a key role in the New York probe. As early as 1927 he tapped Rothstein's phone only to discover the Brain talked in code. One day Mellin met his quarry on the street.

"I like to see you out in the open like this, Bill," said Rothstein. "I know I'm safe using a telephone."

The murder of Rothstein caused Mellin to switch his taps to Gordon and Schultz. Dutch was wary but not so smart. While talking on the phone, he would tap against it with a metal pencil. The technique made it hard for the tappers to hear, but just as hard for the person Dutch was calling. Twice Schultz became so angry he tore out his phone and threw it on the floor.

Ultimately, the Dutchman got smart. Mellin discovered his target had set up new headquarters in a coalyard on the banks of the Bronx River. Patiently, the tapper traced Dutch's phones to a connection box on a pole nearby. He tapped into the box and ran a line to a rented apartment. All seemed set once more, and Mellin settled down to listen. Suddenly, at noon the next day his tap was cut off.

Deciding Dutch had discovered the tap, Mellin hid near the pole and watched. At noon on the following day two free-lance tappers known to Mellin appeared. They inspected the box. Obviously, they had found the tap the day before and disconnected it. Mellin responded to the challenge. At daybreak next morning he drilled "hair-fine holes into the back of the terminals on Dutch's line." A special wire, almost invisible, was employed to make the new tap. The solder used to fasten the wires was "less than a fly speck."

An entire squad of federal agents was assigned to the new tap. Each day for two months they heard the alleged experts hired by Schultz phone in at noon to report that everything was "all okay." They also learned Dutch paid each man $25 a day for the service. Confident now that his line was free, Schultz even quit rapping his phone with his pencil, and the listeners heard many interesting conversations. Only attorney Dixie

67

Davis remained cautious. The listeners heard him scream one day: "You are the most stupid bastard I ever saw. I already told you never to mention names on the telephone."

The job done on Waxey Gordon was Mellin's most complicated. So many of Waxey's friends and relatives were tapped it was necessary to set up a switchboard to handle the traffic. The moment one of them picked up his phone, a light glowed on the switchboard, which was set up in a vacant apartment on the top floor of a house. Much information of value was obtained. By the time the Intelligence Unit was ready to present its evidence to a federal grand jury, however, both Dutch and Waxey had gone into hiding, and Waxey's men were being mowed down by Dutch. According to Irey, it was decided Gordon should have priority only because it appeared he might not live long. "We wanted him before Dutch got him simply because it is extremely difficult to collect back taxes from gangster's estates," said Irey. Few left keys to safe-deposit boxes as Max Hassell had done. On April 23, 1933, the still-missing Waxey was indicted on four counts of tax evasion.

The case against Gordon involved the Eureka Brewery, a New Jersey corporation at Paterson which was allegedly owned by four men. Two of them were murdered. Shortly thereafter Gordon appeared in Paterson and took charge. He was later to maintain he was acting for the real owners, Hassell and Greenberg, but this was easily disproved.

Sales of Eureka beer amounted to more than $2,000,000 a year. The money was traced to two banks, where it was deposited under a series of fictitious names. The Intelligence Unit was able to show that with the funds, Gordon bought expensive cars and generally lived like a king. At a time when he was reporting income of only $8,125, he paid rent of $6,000 on an apartment. The apartment contained a bar costing $3,600 and a library with $3,800 worth of books. At the trial, Dewey proved that none of the books had ever been opened.

Before Waxey could be tried, however, it was necessary to find him. Irey gave the assignment to his ace undercover man, Mike Malone. Mike soon learned that Waxey was hiding somewhere in the Catskill Mountains of upper New York. Special Agent Joe Harvey accompanied Malone on a visit to the moun-

tains. They scouted around for a week or two before learning
that an old buddy of Gordon's ran a boardinghouse near Bethel.
They were also informed that some visitors had recently become speedboat happy and were annoying local residents by
tearing around on White Lake late at night. No one saw the
men or the boat in the daytime.

Adding two and two, Mike decided to take a look at the mysterious sailors. Late one night he and Harvey went on a scout-
ing expedition. As they approached the cottage where the
men lived, Mike slipped into a mudhole and fell. Instantly,
every light in the cottage went out. It was confirmation enough.
Honest citizens don't react in that manner.

The next day the special agents, reinforced with four state
troopers, made an official visit and found three men asleep.
The cottage was a small arsenal. Mike recognized Waxey and
pocketed the pistol beside the bed before awakening him.

"This is nonsense," said the gangster. "I ain't Waxey Gordon.
I'm William Palinski. I'm in the tobacco business." He kept
on arguing until the usually patient Malone had enough.

"Look, Waxey," he said, "you oughtn't to keep saying you're
William Palinski and walk around in silk drawers that have I.
W. embroidered on them. I. W. means Irving Wexler, Waxey."

Dewey prosecuted, and the case was airtight. Waxey insisted
his wealth was achieved in 1910, when he won $100,000 bet-
ting the horses. Dewey wondered why, if that were so, Waxey
had later found it necessary to become a pickpocket. The jury
required only forty minutes to convict, and the judge gave Gordon ten years in prison and a $20,000 fine.

The conviction so delighted the press, Irey noted, "that for
days it failed to refer to us as 'G-Men' or F.B.I. agents."

Gordon served his time and was released only to become
involved during World War II in the black market. He got
caught diverting 10,000 pounds of sugar to a distillery and
went back to prison. In a sense, however, he was lucky. Had
not the Intelligence Unit sent him to safety behind bars, the
killers of Dutch Schultz surely would have caught up with him.
And had they failed, the even more deadly guns of the National Crime Syndicate would have mowed him down.

It was the syndicate that at last brought Schultz out of hiding. The body was organized in 1934. Composed of men of all ethnic backgrounds, it was dominated by Luciano, Lekpe, Lansky, and Bugsy Siegel. The country was divided into territories with existing combinations largely confirmed in power. Since Dutch was "away" at the time, the syndicate saw no deed to cut him in. Instead, they divided up his rackets. Trigger Mike took charge of the numbers. Lepke got the garment industry racket. Abner "Longie" Zwillman took over the beer business formerly controlled by Gordon and Dutch and became known as the Al Capone of New Jersey. Luciano got a little of everything, including the brothels. The Cleveland Syndicate got Dutch's racetrack near Cincinnati and renamed it River Downs.

And so it went. No one worried about Dutch. He had been under federal indictment since 1933. If he reappeared, which was considered unlikely, he would but follow Waxey to prison.

For once the syndicate was wrong. Angry over the loss of his empire, Dutch suddenly reappeared. Dixie Davis pulled some legal miracles and got the case transferred to Syracuse, New York. On April 15, 1935, Schultz arrived in town declaring to one and all that he was a "victim of persecution." He had never done anything wrong except make a little beer. His many arrests since 1919 were not his fault either, he declared. He just happened to be available when the police wanted to pick up someone to make their record look good.

Perhaps the citizens from whom the trial jury was chosen bought the argument. Or perhaps there were other reasons. At any rate, to the surprise of both Irey and the syndicate, the jury was unable to agree on a verdict, and a mistrial resulted. Once again, Davis got the case moved—this time to the little border town of Malone, where the citizenry was even more naïve. Dutch went all out to prove he was a good fellow and a harmless one. The technique, perfected by practice, was even more successful in Malone than it had been in Syracuse. The jury acquitted him, leaving both the syndicate and the Intelligence Unit on the spot.

Irey's men recovered first and soon secured a new indictment. Dutch and two of his lieutenants, Frank J. Ahearn and Henry Margolis, were awaiting trial when the syndicate made all legal questions involving Dutch very much moot. Faced with a choice of giving back Dutch's purloined rackets or killing him, the decision was easy. On October 23, 1935, Schultz was burned down in the Palace Chop House in Newark, New Jersey. According to Irey, information was received to the effect that Luciano personally supervised the execution. Three associates, including Abbadabba Biederman, died with Dutch.

Ahearn and Margolis were eventually brought to trial. Apparently deciding the time for fun and game was over, they pleaded guilty. Each was fined $20,000 and sent to prison for a year and a day.

Ultimately, Dewey quit federal service but continued his drive against the mob in the capacity of special prosecutor and later as district attorney. The Intelligence Unit continued to help him. When at last Jimmy Hines was brought to trial for his part in the numbers racket, the widow of Schultz appeared as a witness. A small blonde, she had married the gangster when she was eighteen after a two-year career as a hatcheck girl. She told of a series of meetings between Hines and her husband from 1932—the year of her marriage—to 1934. Dutch was a good provider while he was in hiding, she said. He sent her money by courier.

Hines went to prison, and Dixie Davis became one of the all too few gangster attorneys to be disbarred. Early in 1939 a referee in bankruptcy awarded Mrs. (Schultz) Flegenheimer $10,000—money Dutch had invested in a Yonkers brewery. It was disclosed that the syndicate hoods who gunned down Dutch also cleaned out his wallet. The United States was not so lucky as Mrs. Dutch.

Back in 1931, New York police arrested Dutch on some minor matter. He produced a roll containing $18,600 and offered it to the officers. According to police legend, one of them became so angry he tried to ram the wad down Dutch's throat. The other officer prevailed on him to turn it in to the police property clerk. There it remained for a while. The federal government claimed it was due the money for back taxes and argued its case in federal district court. By then the money had disappeared, presumably returned to Dutch. The court upheld the government, and the city—which, naturally enough,

71

didn't want to make up the deficiency out of its own coffers—appealed. The Second Circuit Court of Appeals ruled the property clerk was not an agent of the city, and therefore, the city was not responsible for the missing cash.

Irey had other things to worry about. The "heat" in New York was beginning to cause the big boys of the syndicate to seek greener fields. As Dewey continued to apply pressure on the state level, the big dispersal began. With syndicate members in every city ready to help, the New Yorkers began expanding into virgin territory: Miami, New Orleans, Los Angeles, and Las Vegas.

With help from the Intelligence Unit—much of it coming from Bill Mellin's wiretaps—Dewey convicted Lucky Luciano for his part in the commercial prostitution racket and sent him to prison. The hunt began for Lepke, boss of Murder, Inc.—the enforcement arm of the syndicate, which had developed out of the old Bugs and Meyer Mob. Ultimately, Lepke surrendered to J. Edgar Hoover, who had no use for him. Hoover turned him over to the Federal Narcotics Bureau, which, after convicting him for the narcotics business he had fallen heir to after Rothstein's murder, turned him over to Dewey, who sent him to the electric chair for murder.

Yet Irey knew the syndicate could grow new heads as fast as old ones were chopped off. The war against the syndicate had just begun.

4

CRIME CIRCUS

M URDER was not a federal crime in 1932, nor is it today unless the killer is stupid enough to knock off his victim on a federal reservation. Yet the Intelligence Unit was asked to interrupt its pursuit of gangsters and other non-taxpaying citizens to help solve the kidnap-murder of Charles Augustus Lindbergh, Jr.

Al Capone was responsible.

The son of the "Lone Eagle" vanished from his crib in his parents' home near Hopewell, New Jersey, on the night of March 1, 1932. Al at that time was still in Cook County Jail awaiting the outcome of his appeal. On March 10 the highly paid columnist of the Hearst press Arthur Brisbane informed the world that if Capone were freed, he could restore the child to his parents.

Obviously Brisbane didn't consider tax evasion a serious matter, having settled a case against himself by coughing up approximately $250,000.

On March 11, 1932, A. P. Madden, special agent in charge of the Chicago office of the Intelligence Unit and one of the men who "got" Capone, wrote a letter marked "Personal" to his chief, Elmer Irey. It began:

> Several days ago, I was told that the Capone organization proposed to use Mr. Thomas J. Callaghan, the Operative in Charge of the Chicago office of the United States Secret Service, in an effort to temporarily release Al Capone from the Cook County Jail.
>
> It appears that the principal motive back of the proposal was to give Capone an opportunity to use such resources as he might have in an effort to solve the Lindbergh kidnapping. It appeared to be the consensus of opinion of various important members of the Capone organization that if Al did succeed in furnishing valuable information in the Lindbergh case, some move would be made to reduce his sentence.
>
> I inquired as to whether or not the proposal might be based largely on a plan for escape if Capone should be released from jail. The best information I was able to procure was that if there is any plan for him to escape it is just now regarded as of less importance than the plan for him to procure information that might result in leniency in the end.
>
> When I had learned of these things I took them up with the office of the United States Attorney. I did not know that Mr. Callaghan had already made one visit to the jail. However, upon my informing the office of the United States Attorney as to what I had learned, I was advised that Mr. Callaghan had then had one conference with Capone lasting forty minutes. I am now informed that he has made three or four visits to the jail. United States Attorney Johnson is evidently quite disturbed over accounts appearing in Chicago papers last night and this morning indicating that Capone may be the last resort of the Lindbergh family and of agencies of the law to solve the kidnapping case. . . .
>
> It is my judgment, and it is the judgment of the United States Attorney and of his assistants with whom I have conferred, that Capone could be useful only if the kidnapping was perpetrated by underworld characters or characters having underworld connections. Even if that were the situation, there is reason to believe that Capone, under an

eleven-year sentence, has necessarily lost much of his influence. In other words, there are undoubtedly many prominent individuals in the underworld who would pay no attention to instructions from him. . . .

Madden's letter continued with information about a Robert Conroy who, along with Fred Burke, Gus Winkler, and "Crane Neck" Neugent, was currently considered responsible for the St. Valentine's Day massacre of seven members of the George "Bugs" Moran gang. He added that Conroy "is a man who can adjust himself to almost any conditions. Necessarily, he is very much at home in dealing with desperate criminals. On the other hand, it is asserted that he makes a very good appearance, that he is affable, and that he is very much given to reading good literature."

The letter continued:

> Several days ago, when some of the members of the Capone organization concluded that Al Capone might be helped through a solution of the Lindbergh kidnapping, a determined effort was made to locate Conroy. I am advised that an ex-convict operates a florist shop on South Michigan Avenue. . . . That location is a congregrating place for criminals affiliated with the Capones. The telephone numbers are given as Wabash 0579 and Wabash 0580. I am told that those phones were, and perhaps are, being used for local and long distance calls in an effort to ascertain the whereabouts of Conroy. . . . I know that Frank Rio, one of Capone's principal lieutenants, has been trying to find Conroy from another location. It is said that Rio is communicating with Capone in jail, in spite of the guards that have been stationed there by the United States Marshal, and all the indications are that Capone himself has concluded that Conroy is a very promising prospect. . . .
>
> I am sending a photograph of Conroy herewith. I am told that the photograph is an excellent likeness except that when Conroy was here last summer he looked somewhat heavier than he appears to be in the photograph.
>
> I am advised that there is a man in the east, presumably a New York Italian, named Charles Lucky (spelling of

last name uncertain) who has more influence among the criminal Italians than Al Capone ever had. It is said that Lucky is Capone's boss and the boss of all the other Italians engaged in important violations of the law. The thought was expressed that Lucky, in view of his great influence, could do more in the Lindbergh kidnapping case, if anything could be done at all, than Capone could do. I do not recall that I ever heard of Lucky,* but I presume that he is as influential as he is reported to be. If this particular kidnapping is an underworld crime, perhaps means could be devised to communicate with Lucky and to get his cooperation if that has not already been done. . . .

I am told that Jack Guzik, within the past year, invested about $60,000 in a project at or near Miami, Florida. Other members of the Capone organization are said to be interested in the same project, but it is stated that William Dwyer of New York controls. It is asserted that Dwyer has many excellent underworld connections. I presume that a plan could be made to "reach him," but I do not know what the prospects for accomplishing anything would be. Perhaps he is already doing what he can.

History proved that Madden had good information. The "project" near Miami turned out to be Tropical Park racetrack. Almost ten years passed before its true ownership was estabished. A partner of Dwyer—who was, of course, the Big Bill Dwyer of rum-running days—was Owney "the Killer" Madden. Dwyer took no active part in the Lindbergh investigation, but Owney Madden's services were used—but not by the Intelligence Unit. The "Charles Lucky" referred to as Capone's boss, was, of course, Lucky Luciano.

Brisbane's story about Capone's eagerness to help came to the attention of Lindbergh, who immediately called Secre-

* This astonishing lapse points up one of the biggest problems in fighting crime in this country: the lack of a central intelligence agency to make available facts to agents and newspapers. Madden was an expert on Chicago; it is possible that a New York special agent would not have known who Frank Nitti was. Cases in the IRS and the FBI were worked on a specific case basis, and an agent had little knowledge of what other agents in his own city knew. Lucky was a public figure in New York. Every city, unfortunately, makes heroes out of its personalities and, indeed, tries to give them overall power.

Madden's ignorance of Lucky was no less appalling than, as we shall see, the fact that New York agents wasted years by presuming Costello was the big boss.

tary of the Treasury Ogden Mills to discuss the offer. Mills, in turn, ordered Irey to go to Hopewell and talk to Lindbergh. Irey recommended that Capone's offer be rejected and promised to aid in any way possible. Lindbergh was still hopeful the baby could be found alive. He assured Irey that he might call on him later.

Madden and Frank J. Wilson, both Capone experts, were ordered to New York to search for Conroy. Mike Malone was also assigned to the case, and headquarters were set up in a quiet New York club. Meanwhile, new ransom notes had been received, and Dr. John F. Condon, the eccentric Jafsie, was nominated as the go-between. The price had gone up to $70,000. Madden and Wilson insisted that as much of the money as possible be in gold certificate $50 bills which were easily recognized. The serial numbers were listed. The box containing the money was carefully made of a dozen kinds of wood, and samples were kept. Special string and paper were also used. Jafsie delivered the money and talked the mysterious "John" into reducing the price. Unhappily, the $20,000 he saved constituted most of the $50 gold certificates upon which such high hopes had been placed. Greater disappointment followed. The baby, according to John, was on "boad [*sic*] Nelly" out at sea. Irey went along on the fruitless search. No such boat was found.

On May 11, 1932, a body identified as the Lindbergh baby was found near Hopewell. Immediately President Hoover made public a statement directing all government agencies having investigative services to place themselves at the disposal of the State of New Jersey, which had primary jurisdiction in the probe. Secretary Mills quickly ordered Irey to cooperate and added:

> The three government departments having investigation services should at once coordinate themselves under the direction of the Department of Justice and through this agency offer themselves to assist the police of New Jersey in every way possible. You will, accordingly, see that, in so far as your bureau is concerned, this case is treated as a live one for an indefinite period. You will further get

in touch with Mr. Hoover of the Department of Justice, who is charged with responsibility of coordinating the activities of the Federal services.

Irey obeyed. On May 18, Hoover called a conference of the cooperating agencies and stated it was the opinion of the Department of Justice that the actual direction of the investigation should be left in the hands of the New Jersey authorities. Consequently, he said, he was assigning a special agent of the Bureau of Investigation (the FBI) to act as liaison officer between his office and the New Jersey state police. Meanwhile, he continued, the Intelligence Unit officers should be withdrawn from the case.

Irey had no choice but to obey. Madden returned to Chicago, and Wilson was granted annual leave. Six days later signals were changed. Wilson was recalled from leave and told that Lindbergh had again asked Secretary Mills for help from the Intelligence Unit. A rather delicate problem existed. Irey had no desire to get into a battle with the FBI, but orders were orders. Mills discussed the situation with President Hoover, who ordered Irey and Wilson to confer with J. Edgar Hoover "in the most diplomatic manner" and work out a solution.

The FBI head said he was aware of Lindbergh's request and had already ordered his liaison man to withdraw from Trenton. Irey suggested that Wilson be assigned to work under Hoover and promised he would be "practically divorced" from the Intelligence Unit during the assignment. Hoover declined and told Irey to carry on as he was doing before the Department of Justice was ordered to act as coordinator. Irey immediately ordered Special Agent Wilson back to New Jersey.

If there was confusion on the federal level, it was nothing when compared to the chaos that existed in New Jersey. Not only did Lindbergh largely control the probe, but every politician, private investigator, gangster, and crackpot in the country tried to get into the act—and many of them did. All sorts of subplots developed. Some were exotic, and some were merely efforts at extortion; but none could be overlooked. Countless man-hours were wasted investigating them.

Irey's men were shocked to learn that three gold-carat gangsters had been given an okay by Lindbergh to explore the underworld. Two of them were minor-league—Salvatore Spitale and Irving Bitz—but Owney "the Killer" Madden was bad news in any ball park. A native of Leeds, England, Owney gained his nickname as boss of the Gophers, one of the many street gangs that terrorized New York before World War I. He was a crack shot with a revolver and handled such weapons as the slingshot, brass knuckles, and the blackjack with the skill of an artist. Police credited him with five murders before they were at last able to send him to prison. He got out in time to become a rum-runner with Big Bill Dwyer in 1923. His Cotton Club was one of the most famous night spots in New York. Ultimately, however, he proved unable to adjust to the changing times and fell out of favor with the emerging Combination. The Lindbergh case represented a last chance for Owney to regain prestige. When he failed to make an important contribution, he retired in exile to Hot Springs, Arkansas, and built up a carefully controlled gambling empire that endured for decades.

Owney should not be blamed for his failure to solve the case since his assignment involved penetrating the spirit world. Colonel Henry Breckinridge, Lindbergh's chief adviser, was lured to Somerset, New Jersey, by a couple who promised they had information. The couple proved to be Peter Baritella and a woman, known as Mary Magdalene, who claimed to be a medium. She promptly went into a trance and moaned something about the original ransom note being left on the windowsill in the nursery—a fact that had been kept secret. She also told Breckinridge he was wasting his time at the Lindbergh home and should go to his office next morning. When a new ransom note arrived at Breckinridge's office next morning, the episode was taken more seriously. Owney the Killer, having sent many men to the spirit world and thus presumably with influence there, was ordered to investigate. Later, when Wilson was told of the affair, he assigned Mike Malone. Mike joined the spiritualistic church presided over by Baritella but eventually concluded that Owney had frightened off the spirits. The probe, as did so many, ended in a blank wall.

79

Another big gangster getting considerable attention was Abner "Longie" Zwillman, a member of the Big Seven and the so-called Al Capone of New Jersey. Longie offered a huge reward for the kidnapper, and the public applauded. Cynics observed, however, that the heavy concentration of police and sensation seekers in the vicinity of Hopewell was interfering with the movement of Zwillman's liquor convoys through the area and causing perfectly innocent crooks to be picked up and questioned.

Another weird interlude was provided by Murray Garsson, then Special Assistant Secretary of Labor, who sent word to Lindbergh he could solve the case in twenty-four hours. Lindbergh, ready as always to seize any straw, telephoned his wife and told her to greet Garsson, who would arrive in the middle of the night. Mrs. Lindbergh, who was expecting a child, got up and dressed.

Garsson arrived at 3 A.M., carrying a large portfolio. So large was it that some of the women in the house thought it must contain the missing baby—the body had not been found at this stage. He opened the portfolio and took out a number of files. An interview with all the servants was the first demand. The servants were awakened. Garsson, who talked in a very overbearing and melodramatic way, told Mrs. Lindbergh to go upstairs and walk around so he could determine if her footsteps could be heard in the living room. She obeyed but, upon descending, was told to do it again. He had been so busy talking he had neglected to listen. When someone pointed out the upstairs was carpeted, Garsson dismissed the matter and demanded to see the basement. He poked around in the furnace as Mrs. Lindbergh watched, then probed the cesspool.

Twice more, each time late at night, Garsson returned. On the third visit he announced plans to take the servants into custody. A series of hurried calls to the White House and to the Secretary of Labor finally brought Garsson instructions by telephone to discontinue his activities.

Irey commented later: "I'm pleased to report that I eventually got Garsson fired."

A few years later Garsson and his partner, Congressman Andrew J. May of Kentucky, were sent to prison for hanky-panky in war contracts. During the Kefauver Committee investigation, it was learned that Frank Costello used May and Garsson to install slot machines in the Newport-Covington area of Kentucky. However, Costello, when questioned, denied it, although admitting he knew Garsson.

Despite all the false leads and strange coincidences that marked the case, Special Agent Wilson never forgot Bob Conroy, the man Capone had selected as his candidate. Eventually, the Intelligence Unit office in Miami discovered that early in 1932 Conroy and a blond woman who posed as his wife had spent some time in the Magic City. They left in February, well before the kidnapping. No new lead was found until August, when New York newspapers reported a couple had been found dead in an apartment near Broadway on West 102d Street. Police identified the bodies as Robert and Rosemary Sanborn, and called it a murder-suicide—the man having first shot the woman and then himself. A counterfeiting plant, as well as some high-quality bogus bills, was found in the apartment.

Wilson and his colleagues made a routine check of the case. The fingerprints from the dead man matched those on file for Conway. An anonymous note added new interest: "Check activities of Robert and Rosemary Sanborn in Lindbergh case. Keep quiet until convinced. 221."

More interest developed when it was learned that Conroy's death in New York was known to the Capone gang in Chicago before the news was published. Yet no one involved in the case recognized pictures of Conroy or the woman who died with him. Her true identity was not established, and she was given a pauper's burial. Conroy, a veteran of World War I, was given a military funeral.

Just another of the many mysteries surrounding the Lindbergh kidnapping was the Conroy episode, yet it was Capone's interest in Conroy that brought the Intelligence Unit into the case. One of the routine phases of the probe concerned Dr. Condon. Wilson learned the elderly man had for twenty-five years been principal of a New York school. He decided to check the possibility that the kidnapper or some of his associates may have been a former student of Jafsie's, so Wilson obtained a card index of 50,000 students. All were checked for criminal

81

records. Quite a few were found, and their pictures were submitted to Dr. Condon to see if any resembled the "John" to whom the ransom money had been paid. No luck.

Word came through an informant in Detroit that Waslov Simek was the kidnapper. Simek had earlier been convicted of attempted extortion when he threatened to kidnap the baby of Edsel Ford. Upon his release in 1925 he had been deported to Czechoslovakia. A number of pictures of Simek were obtained and included in a file of others. Dr. Condon was asked if any resembled "John." Unhesitatingly, he picked Simek and said, "Boys, you are hot. I want to see that man." Yet he wouldn't definitely state Simek was "John." Since it was the first time he had indicated the investigators were getting close, there was great excitement.

The investigation of Simek covered several months, and the trail seemed to grow hotter. It was learned that the ex-convict had fled Czechoslovakia after being charged with arson. Russia was his next stop, and once again he got into trouble. Patiently Wilson reconstructed the movements of the international criminal—from Russia to India to South America. And then, about a year before the kidnapping, he reached Santo Domingo in the Caribbean.

Once more the dead end. In Santo Domingo, Simek had found work with a public service corporation which required him to make readings of certain instruments each day and write a report. Written reports by Simek were found for the day of the kidnapping.

Was it just a coincidence that the American consul at Budapest, Hungary, sent an urgent cablegram asking if the body found near Hopewell was beyond doubt the Lindbergh child? If not, said the consul, an investigation should be made in the town of Uzsok in Czechoslovakia. Hungarian police insisted the Lindbergh baby was alive and well in that town.

Since Lindbergh had identified the body of his own son, the men of the Intelligence Unit had little reason to question the assumption that the Lindbergh baby was dead. Yet some officials insisted the decomposed body was beyond identification when found. The legend persists that Charles Augustus Lindbergh, Jr., still lives in a remote village in Czechoslovakia.

Since the body found was cremated, there seems little chance of proving anything.

Finally, more than two years after the baby vanished, the case broke wide open. A ransom bill was passed to an alert gas station attendant and was traced to Richard Bruno Hauptmann. Irey later was to maintain Hauptmann could have been found in two months at the most, if a suggestion made by Special Agent Madden had been followed. Madden had suggested the handwriting on the ransom notes be checked against drivers' license files in the Bronx County Courthouse. The notes were written in such an unusual style as to make it easy to recognize similar writing. Yet at the time Madden had no authority. His suggestion was greeted with approval—and quickly ignored.

With Hauptmann's arrest, the Intelligence Unit jacketed a new case and proceeded to investigate the suspect for income tax evasion. Special Agent William E. Frank was assigned the job. Using Hauptmann's records, Frank was able to establish that the subject owned or had spent exactly $49,950.44 more than he had earned since coming to America. This totaled up to just $49.56 less than the $50,000 ransom Dr. Condon had given "John."

The three-ringed circus that surrounded the case from its beginning did not end with Hauptmann's conviction. Harold Hoffman, who became governor of New Jersey after the crime, conducted his own bizarre probe and delayed the execution of the convicted man to do it. Finally, however, Hauptmann was electrocuted on April 3, 1936, and it became necessary for the governor to distribute a reward of $25,000 promised earlier by Governor A. Harry Moore.

Hoffman discovered that although the reward had been offered, the legislature had neglected to provide the money to pay it. He managed to get an appropriation passed and then was confronted with the question of who should receive the money. In a statement issued on January 10, 1938, the stubborn governor clarified his position in these words:

> My views on this crime, the case, and its challenge to
> society are generally well known. There have been many

misrepresentations of this position, so I must today re-
iterate my belief that more than one person was involved
in this crime, that the case has not been completely solved,
and that the action of enforcement agencies in closing the
investigation with the conviction of Hauptmann, is highly
reprehensible. I believe that even some of those who will
share in the reward, particularly the so-called "identification witnesses," were either mistaken or untruthful. There
are official records not produced at the trial which support
this statement and which I intend subsequently to give to
the public.

After having blown off some steam, the governor continued:

As I announce my decision, I wish to express my ap-
preciation of the cooperation of Mr. Elmer L. Irey, Chief
of the Intelligence Unit of the Bureau of Internal Revenue;
Special Agent in Charge A. P. Madden, and Mr. Frank
J. Wilson, Chief of the Secret Service. . . . [Following
the conclusion of the case, Wilson had left the Intelligence
Unit to become head of its sister agency.] The part played
by these men in bringing about the arrest and conviction
of Hauptmann is reflected in official letters from Colonel
Lindbergh and others. Colonel Henry Breckinridge, personal representative of Colonel Lindbergh, in a letter to
Mr. Madden stated: "Had it not been for Mr. Irey, you,
and Mr. Wilson, I think Hauptmann still would be at
large. . . ."

Noting that Irey had stated that officers of the Intelligence
Unit "could not, and certainly would not, under any circumstances, participate in the distribution of any of the reward,"
the governor proceeded to divide it among the individual witnesses. In the process, he also bestowed caustic criticism on
some of them.

So ended the Lindbergh case—one that Irey and his men
had no business entering. While many questions remain unanswered even today and doubts still exist, there seems no excuse
not to agree that without the presence of the Intelligence Unit,
the mystery would be greater than ever. The Crime of the Century it was called, and had not Irey and his men kept their

cool while everyone else was losing theirs, it would have been known, perhaps, as "the most bungled case in history."

One of the many opportunists who saw in the Lindbergh kidnapping a chance to profit was a character out of the Harding scandals of the twenties. Gaston B. Means, con man extraordinary, had served as a collection agent for the Ohio Gang, which put Harding in the White House. He cheated gangster and government alike, passing on much of the loot to Jesse Smith. Among those who paid Means for protection was George Remus, king of the bootleggers, who was assured there would be "no ultimate conviction."

Means went to prison for some of his activities during the period and, having time on his hands, wrote a best seller, *The Strange Death of President Harding*. It was his thesis that the President was murdered in a largely successful effort to protect his reputation from the scandals that were about to break. Some observers saw some validity to the theory, but by then Means' reputation as a liar was so great it was impossible to separate any truth from the mass of fiction.

Means appeared early in the Lindbergh case and persuaded Mrs. Evalyn Walsh McLean, proud possessor of the Hope Diamond, that he could recover the baby by means of his knowledge of and contacts in the underworld. Shortly thereafter he told her he had been in touch with the kidnappers, who now wanted $100,000. Mrs. McLean, excited to be so deeply involved in such an interesting intrigue, gave him the money. Means, making sure she continued to be excited, led her on a merry chase before her attorney found out what was going on and called the FBI. Means was sentenced to fifteen years in prison.

The Intelligence Unit was soon to have another reminder of the Ohio Gang and its freebooting ways. On November 2, 1934, Robert H. Jackson, then assistant general counsel for the Bureau of Internal Revenue, wrote a memo to Irey asking for aid in collecting taxes from principals involved in that most famous of scandals, the Teapot Dome case.

"In order to carefully prepare the case for trial," Jackson wrote, "it is the belief of this office that the most effective results may be accomplished by having an experienced Special Agent assigned to the case to become very familiar with the entire situation and make such personal investigations as he can, and possibly direct investigations in other parts of the country as may be deemed necessary."

Teapot Dome, Wyoming, was one of three tracts of oil-bearing land set aside in 1909 for future use of the United States Navy. When Harding became President in 1921, there was much excitement over the "Yellow Peril," meaning Japan. There was also great concern about the "Red Peril," meaning Russia, but no one found an easy way to exploit the latter danger. The President was told that the Navy must be ready to fight Japan and should have its oil out of the ground and in storage depots. Secretary of the Interior Albert B. Fall persuaded Harding to transfer the oil reserve land from the custody of the Secretary of the Navy to his department. He promised to see the oil would be pumped out promptly and stored.

Once he had authority, Fall, secretly and without competitive bidding, leased the Teapot Dome reserve to Harry F. Sinclair's Mammoth Oil Company. The reserve at Elk Hills, California, was similarly leased to Edward L. Doheny's Pan-American Petroleum Company.

Prior to the transfer, a group of oilmen gathered at the Hotel Vanderbilt in New York and worked out a deal. E. A. Humphreys, owner of the Mexia oilfields, agreed to sell more than 33,000,000 barrels of oil to the newly formed Continental Trading Company, Ltd., of Canada for $1.50 a barrel. Continental, it developed, resold the oil to Sinclair, James O'Neill, Robert W. Stewart, and Harry M. Blackmer at $1.75 a barrel. The man fronting as president of the dummy corporation was supposed to divide the ultimate profit of $8,000,000 among the four oilmen after deducting a 2 percent commission for his trouble. Scandal broke, however, and it became necessary to do away with Continental after only profits of slightly more than $3,000,000 had been realized. The loot was invested in Liberty Bonds and cut up as planned. Blackmer received approximately $763,000, O'Neill approximately $800,000, Stewart approximately $759,000, and Sinclair approximately $757,000.

What did this little deal have to do with Teapot Dome? After a long Senate investigation it was discovered that Secretary Fall, the obliging boss of the Interior Department, received $260,000 in Liberty Bonds from Sinclair for his aid in arranging the lease of the oil reserve. Doheny, who had received the lease for the Elk Hills reserve, was equally kind—he "lent" Fall $100,000 in cash without asking for interest or security.

Fall was ultimately convicted of accepting a bribe and went to prison. For some reason not easily understood in terms of conventional justice, Sinclair and Doheny were acquitted. However, Sinclair served two terms in jail for contempt of the Senate. Blackmer and O'Neill departed for France. The scandals went on and on, coming to the public in bits and pieces and doing little to destroy the belief of most citizens that what was good for businessmen was good for the country. Calvin Coolidge succeeded Harding and was, in turn, followed by Herbert Hoover. It was not until a Democratic President was elected that an effort began to collect taxes from the men who had profited so greatly from the scandals.

Irey assigned Special Agent Everett Partridge to the complex case. It was discovered that Carl H. Pforzheimer, a New York stockbroker, had been an associate of Blackmer's. When Pforzheimer realized he was under investigation, he paid $1,393,910 to cover additional taxes and penalties due on his 1921 and 1922 returns. Blackmer also settled up, paying an additional $3,669,784.

A total of $1,331,229 in back taxes and penalties was assessed against Sinclair, Stewart, and the estate of O'Neill. Compromise offers were rejected, and the cases went into court under orders from Secretary of the Treasury Henry Morgenthau to fight them out to the end. In the end the United States collected $602,123 for its trouble.

While efforts were under way to collect from Sinclair, a rather nasty spin-off developed. Two revenue agents offered to get Sinclair's assessment reduced to $30,000 if he would pay them $37,500. A Sinclair attorney reported the offer. Irey, who was hell on tax evaders, hated corrupt federal officials even more. He assigned special agents of the Intelligence Unit to do what in 1919 the unit had been created to do—get the goods on dishonest personnel.

A special agent was in the attorney's office when one of the revenue agents showed up to conclude the deal. The entire plot to reduce the assessment was reviewed. Sinclair's attorney, as had been prearranged, handed over a $10,000 "down payment," and the bribe taker went happily on his way. Other special agents were waiting outside to grab him. They found the bribe neatly tucked away in the man's straw hat. Both revenue agents were indicted and dismissed from service.

Other matters of high finance during this period included the case of Charles E. Mitchell, former chairman of the board of the National City Bank and a former director of the Federal Reserve Bank of New York. During the gay days of the twenties and the great bull market, Mitchell had been regarded as one of the "lords of creation," to employ the term coined by Frederick Lewis Allen. He was indicted on March 24, 1933, less than two weeks after Roosevelt became President, and charged with reporting a net loss of $88,000 for the year 1929 and paying no taxes when, according to the indictment, he had a net income of $2,823,405. Evasion of $1,860,000 for the year 1930 was charged in a second indictment.

The case was historic, coming as it did when all the banks in the country had just been closed and being the first criminal prosecution of a so-called stock loss case. The practice of claiming losses through the "sale" of stock was a common one. In Mitchell's case he had "sold" the securities to his wife.

Despite the fears of some members of the financial world, the American people were not yet ready for revolution. A jury heard the evidence and on June 22, 1933, found Mitchell innocent on both charges. Nevertheless, a civil case was pushed centering on the tax year 1929. Some legal questions of interest were raised, one of them being whether the not guilty verdict in the criminal case prevented the application of fraud penalties in the civil case. The Commissioner of Internal Revenue's decision that Mitchell owed $728,709 in taxes and $364,-354 in fraud penalties was upheld by the Board of Tax Appeal. The circuit court of appeals, however, ruled the tax bill was okay but reversed the decision on the fraud penalties. Ultimately, the Supreme Court on March 7, 1938, overturned the court of appeals' decision and agreed the fraud penalties applied.

It was a left-handed victory for the Intelligence Unit, and it resulted in the collection of many millions of dollars in additional revenue. It also led to the closing of some large loopholes in the Internal Revenue laws.

In years to come, organized crime discovered the stock market and used it in a variety of ways. Blazing the trail was none other than that old mastermind Johnny Torrio, who suddenly reappeared as a "legitimate" businessman. Understandably, Elmer Irey was curious.

5

SYNDICATE SUPERMAN

ON May 25, 1935, a memorandum was sent from the Washington office of the Alcohol Tax Unit—one of the several Treasury agencies now under the overall command of Elmer Irey—to the New York field office. The memo was short and to the point:

> This office has information to the effect that one John Torrio, alleged to be a notorious gangster during the prohibition era, is now financially interested in the importing firm of Prendergast and Davies Co., Ltd., New York City. This company is also a wholesale liquor dealer. A list of the officers has been secured from the Federal Alcohol Control Administration but fails to reveal this individual as of record.
>
> This is furnished you for your information and such investigation as may be desirable.

A routine message, but one that was destined to rock organized crime to its foundations.

Little was known of the activities of Torrio since the trial of Al Capone. In February, 1926, he had departed on an around-the-world cruise with his wife but had stopped in Honolulu and purchased a home there. Returning to the United States in 1928, he had shuttled between his mother's home on Long Island and his brother-in-law's residence in St. Petersburg, Florida. It was generally assumed he was in retirement, enjoying the millions he had made in Chicago.

Prendergast & Davies was the biggest corporation of its kind in New York. Its business ran into millions of dollars every month, for it had exclusive rights on the products of several nationally known distillers and importers. Its delivery truck was as familiar a sight as the postman at the door. The possibility that Torrio was connected with such a respectable company seemed remote indeed, but Irey's men had learned never to rule out anything as impossible.

Beginning routinely at the beginning, the agents found that three men—Jerry Baum, Herbert C. Heller, and Allen N. Bernstein—incorporated the company in November, 1933— just a month before Repeal. Baum was a dabbler in various businesses; Heller and Bernstein were investment brokers. The three of them put up $22,500 each to start the company.

Repeal on December 5, 1933, brought block-long queues of merchants to the doors of Prendergast & Davies. All were eager to pay almost any amount for five cases of whiskey. One hundred cases was worth a small fortune. Three days after Repeal, the partners had a disagreement. Bernstein wanted to move slowly, while Baum insisted the tremendous demand could be met. When Bernstein refused to agree, Baum bought him out with $17,500 in cash and $5,000 in two certified checks. The money came from a William Slockbower, who took Bernstein's place in the company.

The agents decided to call at the offices of Prendergast & Davies, 601 West Twenty-sixth Street, to see if perhaps Slockbower was the elusive Torrio. The offices were plush and smelled of success. Thick carpets hushed the movements of the many employees. At the rear of the eleventh-floor suite was a huge storeroom filled with liquor to the ceiling. A special freight elevator carried orders to the ground.

General manager Sam Borden greeted the agents and expressed shock at the quaint notion Torrio had anything to do

91

with the business. He offered them free access to the books of the company and even the correspondence files. Torrio's name did not appear anywhere.

Two weeks later the agents returned, bringing with them a newspaper picture of Torrio. It had appeared in the Chicago papers following Johnny's narrow escape from the guns of his rivals. The agents had studied it well, noting the high forehead; the large ears, nose, and mouth; and the thin, straight lips. While waiting in the reception room for Borden to see them, they spotted Torrio talking to a group of liquor salesmen.

"Who is that man?" was the first question asked of Borden. The manager shrugged and smiled.

"Just a fellow named McCarthy who is in and out a lot," was his careless answer.

The agents then asked to see Slockbower. Investigation revealed he was listed as a warehouse superintendent at a salary of $150 a week, in addition to being a part owner and a member of the board of directors. Prior to investing in the liquor company, he had been a railroad clerk for twelve years at a salary of $124.50 a month. Where had his money come from?

Borden wanted to be helpful, he said, but, unhappily, Mr. Slockbower had departed only the day before for a two-week stay in Canada. The liquor agents thanked him politely and went straight from his office to the apartment in White Plains where Slockbower lived. They had learned earlier the owner of the building was John Torrio.

The building superintendent's wife was very helpful. Where was Mr. Slockbower? Why, at his office at Prendergast & Davies. Hadn't he gone on a trip to Canada? Of course not. She had seen him leave for work that morning. Moreover, Mrs. Slockbower had told her a few minutes ago that she was preparing pork chops and sauerkraut for her husband's evening meal.

Angry now, the agents rushed back to Prendergast & Davies to confront Borden. The smile faded, and a flush turned his face to an ugly purple, as the agents demanded to see the mysterious Slockbower. Borden promised to have him in his office two days later. He kept his word. A perspiring Slockbower was waiting when the agents arrived. With him was the man who looked like Torrio. Borden formally introduced him as John McCarthy, and the agents began to question him. When "Mc-Carthy'" insisted he had no connection with the company, they asked him to leave the room while they interviewed Slock-bower. Angrily, "McCarthy" replied: "I will not allow you to question my brother-in-law without my being present."

"Did you marry Mr. Slockbower's sister?" asked the agents.

"No," said "McCarthy." "Mr. Slockbower married Miss Torrio, my sister."

And the Fox, as Torrio was known, was out of the bag at last. The agents soon terminated the interview and left. More investigation was needed before a serious effort to question Torrio could be made.

The probe continued for months and was far from complete when in April, 1936, a rumor was heard that Torrio was planning to visit Europe. Recalling his last cruise, when he spent thirty months in Honolulu, the agents decided to stop him. The probe had satisfied them that if Torrio was not violating the liquor laws, he was violating internal revenue laws. A warrant was obtained for his arrest, and Torrio was lured into the White Plains post office and arrested without dramatics. Quickly he was arraigned and held under $100,000 bond. His attorneys attempted to get the bond reduced but failed, and Torrio posted a cash bond of $100,000 and went free. His trip to Europe had to be abandoned, however.

United States Attorney Lamar Hardy, whose duty it was to prosecute the case, studied the investigative files and became worried. He invited Hugh McQuillen, special agent in charge of the Intelligence Unit's New York squad, to lunch and confided that the alcohol tax case "was worthless for prosecution." Would the Intelligence Unit please take over and try to save the U.S. Attorney's office some embarrassment by making an income tax case against Torrio?

McQuillen and his boss, Irey, were entirely willing. The case was jacketed, and Special Agent James N. Sullivan was assigned. Sullivan had worked in Chicago and knew Torrio. For eighteen months Sullivan and his men worked night and day.

Records of Prendergast & Davies were seized, and the story

of Torrio's venture into legitimate business was reconstructed. In the first months, Slockbower had dumped $67,000 of Torrio's money into the business, permitting the accumulation of a large stock of liquor. Harry Bernstein, who had operated as an agent in Canada during Prohibition, was hired as sales manager. He proved too crude, however, for legitimate business and was soon fired. Before leaving, however, he had frightened the remaining two partners, Heller and Baum, into withdrawing from the company. Now Torrio was in complete control. Hoods who had learned the ropes during Prohibition were installed in key positions, but, all agreed, Torrio ordered them to operate as legitimate businessmen should.

Investigators learned that Torrio wanted a liquor czar to stop price-cutting, and his candidate was none other than ex-Mayor Jimmy Walker. Later they learned why.

Business grew rapidly. Torrio's price was right, deliveries were prompt, and adjustments were made to keep customers happy. Small wholesalers pressed for cash learned they could borrow money from Torrio. He gave more than they asked, but when they couldn't repay it on demand, he stepped in and absorbed their businesses. Six wholesalers were swallowed up in this manner, and Prendergast & Davies became the largest wholesaler in the state.

Millions of dollars rolled in, but it was a check for $109 that trapped Torrio. The check was one of many listed in the company's records and wouldn't have attracted attention if it hadn't been for the fact that the name J. Weinstein had been written alongside an erasure in the ledger column indicating the source of the check. A drop of ammonium sulfide was applied to the erasure. Slowly the initials J. T. appeared. Did they represent John Torrio? It seemed very possible.

The careful, necessarily tedious job of checking that followed was a superb example of the thoroughness and doggedness of the Intelligence Unit. Special agents examined 60,000 ledger sheets at the bank upon which the check had been issued before discovering that a J. Connolly of Brooklyn had drawn the check. He was the operator of a bar and grill. When questioned, Connolly admitted he gave the check to an L. Jacobs in payment for a delivery of bootleg whiskey.

An air of mystery had been added to the check because it had bounced twice, once for insufficient funds and once for improper signature. After the second bounce it had been taken to a New York bank and certified to the account of a J. Kent.

Connolly knew Jacobs only as an occasional source of whiskey, but a description was obtained, plus the helpful data that he lived "somewhere in Brooklyn." Queries were sent out to police, bartenders, and tavern owners. Eventually one of those contacted remembered that Jacobs used to have an office in a Brooklyn theater building. There a home address was found, but Jacobs had moved three years earlier. A canvass of the neighborhood disclosed the information that Jacobs still bought gasoline at a certain service station. The attendant knew Jacobs—he sold the station bootleg whiskey, and it sold him gas.

A few days later, waiting special agents watched Jacobs clatter up in an old car for some gas. He was presented with a subpoena and decided to talk. He had turned over the check, he said, to his source of supply in payment of a bill he owed. The supply source, in turn, had refused the check and told Jacobs to take it to the office of J. Weinstein, who was the accountant for the "Big Mob."

Now the problem was to locate "J. Kent," who had certified the check with funds in his Manhattan bank. A teller at the bank finally admitted Kent was, in reality, Jimmy La Penna. And everyone knew that La Penna had worked for the Big Seven, the combine of rum-runners which in the latter days of Prohibition controlled smuggling along the entire East Coast.

More puzzled than ever, the special agents began a hunt for La Penna. The trail led to Baltimore, where it was discovered he had obtained a permit to operate a small rectifying plant called the Lord Fairfax Company. He had operated until Alcohol Tax Unit men spotted loads of alcohol going in his back door at night. They had raided the place and seized his books, which were now turned over to the Intelligence Unit special agents.

Back in New York with the books, the special agents found that La Penna had kept complete records of his Prohibition era activities and carried them to Baltimore. After three entries of $50,000, $5,000, and $35,000 appeared the initials J. T.

And suddenly the investigators knew that their long, thankless search had not been in vain: Johnny Torrio had not retired after his adventures in Chicago. If their evidence could be believed, he had been part of the Big Seven.

La Penna was finally found living in Brooklyn with his sister. He had fallen on hard times. When asked who was meant by "J. T.," La Penna said he was. Then why the initials? "J. T." meant "Jimmy took it," said Jimmy La Penna. Everyone had a good laugh and bored in. Finally, La Penna admitted the truth. "J. T." did mean Johnny Torrio.

Once Torrio's part in the Big Seven was established, the special agents were able to reconstruct what had happened. Upon his return from Honolulu in 1928, Torrio had entered the rum-running business in partnership with Frank Zagarino of New York and Daniel Walsh of Providence, Rhode Island. Competition was heavy and sometimes expensive. Torrio, alert as always to the value of cooperation, suggested a combination be formed even as he had done in Chicago. The leading bootleggers agreed, and while the group became known as the Big Seven, it actually had as many as a dozen members. Charles "King" Solomon of Boston was generally considered the leader of the combine, but only because Torrio wanted no one on the outside to know of his role. Solomon controlled smuggling in Massachusetts and had created an efficient organization which included such men as Hyman Abrams, Mario Ingraffia, Joe Linsey, and Louis Fox.

Other leaders included Abner "Longie" Zwillman of Newark, New Jersey, Dutch Schultz, Walsh, Zagarino, and Joe Adonis, who headed the Broadway Mob. Cooperating was the so-called Reinfeld Syndicate which brought liquor from Canada to the Rum Rows of Boston and New York. So complete was the control of the Big Seven that it was possible to determine the exact amount of liquor to be permitted a member at a given time. Prices were fixed, and no one was allowed to undercut those prices. Central offices were set up where customers could place their orders. Graft was centralized as well.

The Bugs and Meyer Mob was hired to protect shipments from hijackers. Meyer Lansky and Bugsy Siegel, however, were soon taken into the Broadway Mob and came to be equal partners with Adonis and Frank Costello.

All this was happening at a time when Lucky Luciano was attempting to "Americanize" the Mafia. In Chicago, Al Capone, who was some sort of relative to Lucky, became angry at Torrio because he joined forces with the Combination instead of with Luciano.

Torrio, meanwhile, had become a partner in the numbers racket of Dutch Schultz. As a necessary subsidiary, he formed the Greater City Surety and Indemnity Company—a bonding company to write bonds for the small punks who were occasionally arrested. Schultz had a piece of that business as well, and so did Dixie Davis, his attorney. Key to the success of the numbers racket was the friendship of Tammany district leader James J. Hines. For payments as high as $1,000 a week, Hines prevented police from interfering with the racket. Following Schultz's murder, both Hines and Dixie Davis had been sent to prison by Dewey for their part in the racket. Davis became cooperative and talked freely about Torrio's behind-the-scenes role.

Although it was no official concern of the Intelligence Unit, it was now possible to see a bloody pattern which answered many unsolved murders. For as Repeal approached, strange things had happened to some members of the Big Seven. King Solomon in Boston had been first to die, shot down in January, 1933. Then Torrio's old partner, Danny Walsh of Providence, was kidnapped. He had $34,000 on his person when he vanished. Another $40,000 in ransom was paid, but Walsh never reappeared. Word on the underworld grapevine had his body dumped at sea. Al Lillian of New Jersey was knocked off as well, and there were dozens of other violent deaths among aspiring lieutenants.

The murders coincided with the rise in power of the Broadway Mob. Luciano, Adonis, and Costello, in combination with Lansky, Lepke, and Sam "Red" Levine, had formed an alliance and were taking over all the rackets. Torrio, already making plans to control legal liquor in New York, recognized the realities and joined the Combination. Those among the Big Seven who opposed were eliminated.

And now the dying words of Torrio's ex-partner, Dutch Schultz, took on new meaning. Dutch had lingered for hours with a police stenographer at his bedside taking down every garbled word. Asked during one of his more coherent moments who shot him, Dutch gasped: "The boss himself."

Later during another lucid moment, Schultz was asked: "What did the big fellow shoot you for?"

"Him . . . John? . . . Over a million—five million dollars."

It now appeared obvious that the boss—John—was Johnny Torrio. Was the murder of Schultz the price he had to pay for entry into the Combination? No one could say. However, few investigators doubted that once accepted, the brains of Torrio were put to use by Lansky and his friends. In later years, when more information about the formation of the National Crime Syndicate in 1934 came to light, Torrio was generally credited with being the man who brought gangsters from across the nation into the loose but lasting alliance.

Meanwhile, the Intelligence Unit found itself with a rather sticky problem. Back in 1931, Special Agent Charles W. Clarke audited Torrio's finances for the years 1917 to 1930. As a result, early in 1933 Johnny offered $100,000 in full settlement of his civil and criminal liability, and it had been accepted.*

Now, however, it was discovered that while the $100,000 compromise was being considered, a deputy collector in the New York office of Internal Revenue, contacted Torrio about a possible loan on some property in Maryland. The official was William H. Boyd. Mano, Inc., a real estate holding company owned completely by Torrio, issued two checks to Boyd's daughter totaling $3,363.12. The Baltimore bank holding first and second mortgages on the property was paid in full about February 16, 1933. And Boyd recommended Torrio's compromise offer be accepted.

Boyd had been transferred to the Department of Justice when the probe of his dealings with Torrio and other gangsters began in October, 1933. Boyd made some admissions to the

---

* The statute of limitations in criminal cases involving evasion and failure to file is six years. However, if fraud is established, civil assessments, plus penalties and interest, but not jailing or fining, can be made for any period beyond that time.

special agents and agreed to meet with them later to give full details. He failed to keep the appointment. A Maryland state trooper sent to investigate found his body hanging in his Piney Point summer home—the property that had been involved in his "refinancing" transaction with Torrio.

Shortly after the investigation of Prendergast & Davies began in May, 1935, Torrio—shrewd as always in knowing when to run—sold his stock to Mrs. Anne Feinberg of Boston for $283,-110. This represented a profit for Torrio of $109,110 over what he had paid the original stockholders.

The first indictment charging an attempt to evade income taxes for the years 1933 and 1935 was returned on September 4, 1937. On June 6, 1938, after new evidence was found, several superseding indictments were secured. Still more information brought additional sealed indictments superseding the earlier ones on February 3, 1939.

Some of the new information came from Al Capone, serving his time at Alcatraz Prison. He was visited there by Assistant United States Attorney Seymour Klein and gave a long deposition, which, while of little value as evidence, contained leads of great importance. Scarface Al put the finger on his erstwhile friend and leader without a qualm, excusing his violation of the underworld code by claiming Torrio had first violated it when he had joined Dutch Schultz instead of Lucky Luciano.

An even more valuable witness was Dixie Davis, the disbarred attorney for the late Dutch. Davis was lent to the United States Attorney by District Attorney Dewey at a time when Dixie was waiting to testify against Tammany district leader James J. Hines. Guards were placed outside the windows of the grand jury room while Davis testified and on the street outside the building. It was Davis who first revealed the relationship between Torrio and William H. Boyd. Among other things, Davis gave details of a midnight meeting between Torrio and Dutch Schultz in a coalyard on 138th Street. At that meeting plans for a bonding company were worked out.

Trial of Torrio began on March 29, 1939. Torrio was accused of reporting income of $18,000 in 1933 when he should have reported $145,262; of reporting $19,441 in 1934 when his income was actually $74,932; and of listing income of $43,-

874 in 1935 when it really was $96,129. He had paid a total of $11,420 in taxes for the three-year period. The government charged he should have paid an additional sum of $98,668. The application of the 50 percent fraud penalty brought his total debt to $148,002.

Of course, the Intelligence Unit was under no illusion that the income charged to Torrio included all his profits, but they were prepared to prove the income they listed.

Witness after witness appeared to tell of Torrio's connections with the Big Seven. Robert Kamm revealed he was the private pilot of the missing Danny Walsh and related how he flew Walsh from Providence to a house near Farmingdale, Long Island, to meet with Torrio. At the session, he said, Torrio disclosed he had decided to bottle the syndicate's liquor in plain bottles from Chicago because the "fancy bottles broke too much." Thomas W. Murray testified that he was a radio operator, whose job it was to communicate with incoming ships and warn them if the coast was clear. It was necessary to move his little radio station often, he said, to keep ahead of the Coast Guard, which was hunting for it. He listed one occasion when his warning came too late. The rum ship *Josephine K* was off Sandy Hook ready to meet a barge for unloading. Murray was in the process of radioing a warning that the Coast Guard was patrolling the area when suddenly the connection was broken. He went to the Douglas Hotel in Newark and told Torrio, who ordered him to check the barge office. He obeyed and learned the ship had indeed been seized by the Coast Guard and the captain killed in an exchange of bullets.

The highlight of Torrio's trial came, however, when Special Agent Jim Sullivan took the stand. Assistant United States Attorney Klein handed him the books of Prendergast & Davies and remarked: "I call your particular attention to the signs of eradication."

Instantly, Torrio's attorney, Max D. Steuer, objected, but the books were shown to the jury. Then Sullivan leaned across the rail and dabbed the page in question with ammonium sulfide. The odor of rotten eggs filled the room as the letters J. T. appeared as if by magic, and it became necessary to open the

100

windows. Torrio softly pounded his knee with his clenched fist.

By the time the jurors finished looking at the books the chemical had dried and the letters had begun to fade. When the record was passed to the defense table, the letters were gone. Steuer objected violently.

"I see no letters," he shouted. Neither could the judge. Sullivan repeated the experiment, and Steuer was silenced at last. Sullivan proceeded to explain the fateful history of the $109 check.

When court recessed for the day, Steuer requested a conference with the prosecuting attorneys. He told them Torrio would be willing to plead guilty if assured of a sentence of no more than three years in prison and a $10,000 fine on each of the three counts of the indictment. For reasons not readily apparent, the prosecutors agreed.

Reporters gathered on Monday, April 10, 1939, ready for new sensations as the trial reopened. The sensations were not long delayed as Steuer announced his client desired to change his plea to guilty. Torrio's brother-in-law, William Slockbower, and James La Penna, did the same thing. Judge John W. Clancy called the three defendants to the bench and asked them individually if they desired to plead guilty. Torrio lowered his head and whispered. Reporters straining to hear his words were disappointed. A mistrial was declared in the cases of two other defendants charged with Torrio—Louis V. La Cava, who had been a strong-arm goon under Capone in Chicago, and John D'Agostina, a minor punk.

Two days later, court reconvened to pass sentence. Steuer talked for two hours in virtually a whisper. He pictured Torrio as a man whose early environment had contributed to his life of crime but who, in his more mature years, had turned to legitimate business. Because of his past history, Steuer said, it was necessary that Torrio conceal his interest in Prendergast & Davies. Calling the conspiracy to evade taxes a "stupid business," Steuer said Torrio was willing to release the $100,000 cash bond posted upon his arrest to settle his civil liability. Mrs. Torrio had created quite a stir the day she appeared at the

Federal Building in 1936 and presented astonished officials with ninety-seven $1,000 bills and $3,000 in smaller denominations. The government slapped a lien against the money and still held it.

Steuer didn't say anything about it, but the Intelligence Unit knew he had received another $100,000 to represent Torrio at the trial.

Klein spoke only briefly, noting that all the defendants were elderly men. Judge Clancy accepted his recommendation and imposed a sentence of thirty months on the first count of Torrio's indictment, five years on the second, and two years on the third. He suspended the latter two terms and placed Torrio on probation for five years following the completion of his sentence. The other defendants got off even easier—Slockbower getting a suspended sentence of one year and La Penna getting nine months followed by probation for five years.

Nevertheless, Torrio's conviction marked the end of an era. Organized crime had become a vital force in American life. Many of its pioneer leaders such as Schultz, Capone, Luciano, Rothstein, and Torrio were dead or in prison, but such leaders as Lansky, Costello, Siegel, and Adonis in New York were allied with such men as Moe Dalitz, Sam Tucker, and Big Al Polizzi in Cleveland, with Joe Massei and Peter Licavoli in Detroit, with Frank Nitti and the remains of the Capone gang in Chicago. Other gangsters in Boston, Philadelphia, Newark, St. Louis, Minneapolis-St. Paul, Kansas City, New Orleans, and Los Angeles were part of the general organization that made up the National Crime Syndicate. The Miami-Miami Beach area was being developed, and soon Bugsy Siegel would discover Nevada. The future of Arizona was being charted by a combined New York-Cleveland task force.

Torrio and Rothstein had each made a unique contribution to the empire of crime. Rothstein had led the way in organizing the individual rackets while Torrio had put them on a businesslike basis and arranged interstate cooperation. Luciano had helped by—with aid from Lansky—"Americanizing" the Mafia to the point where it could find an uneasy place within the National Crime Syndicate. Lansky, graduating quickly from the role of enforcer, had demonstrated the value of cooperation by joining with the Cleveland Syndicate in the Molaska Corporation. At a time when Torrio was planning to take over the legal liquor industry, Molaska operated the largest illicit distilleries ever found. The joint venture continued well into 1937, after which both Lansky and his Cleveland allies turned to illegal gambling on a huge scale. If any man could be said to be Torrio's successor, it would be the man once known as Johnny Eggs—Meyer Lansky.

Into the shadows retreated Torrio after his release from Leavenworth Prison on April 15, 1941. During his probation period it was possible to keep a check on his movements, but after that he vanished. No one needed to feel sorry for him, however. On December 19, 1939, he estimated his net worth at $500,000. His wife stated that Torrio owned real estate in Brooklyn, Florida and Honolulu, as well as bonds and mortgages.

On July 25, 1944, New York police were stirred into activity by an anonymous letter alleging that Costello, Adonis, and Torrio were backing Empire State Agency, Inc., a bonding company. A probe led to the revoking of the firm's license, but no evidence relating to Torrio was found.

Following the revelations of the Kefauver Committee in 1950-51, a new drive on crime was launched by federal agencies. Almost automatically, the name of John Torrio was placed in the "racketeer category," but nothing was developed. Elmer Irey in 1948 summed up the situation in a very few words: "If Johnny is retired, I know he's retired in comfort. If he's in action, I know he's the biggest gangster in America today. If he's dead, I'll bet he died with his boots on."

New York Police Department records show that Torrio, after living for several years in Cincinnati—his wife, Ann Jacobs, was born in Covington, Kentucky—returned to Brooklyn in 1954 and died there on April 16, 1957.

6

THE SECOND LOUISIANA PURCHASE

THE forced resignation of Mayor Jimmy Walker and the continuing scandals involving gangster-infested Tammany Hall prepared the way for the Fusion ticket headed by Fiorello LaGuardia—the "Little Flower." He took the oath of office in Judge Seabury's home on January 1, 1934, and immediately ordered the arrest of Lucky Luciano.

Lucky's arrest didn't stick; it was only a publicity stunt by a master politician who knew that where crime is concerned, the public is easily persuaded to accept the appearance of action in lieu of the reality of accomplishment. The new mayor followed through on this plan by seizing and dumping into the bay several hundred of Frank Costello's slot machines.

Nevertheless, the combination of LaGuardia's words, Intelligence Unit investigations, and prosecutions by Dewey created the "big heat" in New York and stimulated the National Crime Syndicate to search for unexploited territory. An essential to expansion was a corrupt local or state government and the most obvious one at the moment was the domain of the Kingfish—Huey Long. Louisiana was the property of Long, and Huey's influence extended far beyond its borders. He had

104

ambitions to be President, and no longer was the possibility considered a joke. Money was needed, however, and although the income from graft was tremendous, Long was always eager to listen to new schemes. He met Costello at the New Yorker Hotel and worked out a deal to install slot machines in New Orleans early in 1935.

"Dandy Phil" Kastel, an early associate of Arnold Rothstein's, was put in charge of the slot machine venture. Meyer Lansky, who was casino boss for the syndicate, saw possibilities in the area and, with Kastel and Costello, later developed the plush Beverly Club just outside New Orleans. Among the local men cut in on the assorted rackets was Carlos Marcello. Long, of course, was to get his share of the loot.

The rise of Long from an obscure country lawyer to a position of national influence has been told many times and needs no repetition here. He was elected governor in 1928 and, after having arranged things to his liking, moved on to Washington as the Senator from Louisiana. Puppets, who hardly dared go to the bathroom without his permission, kept things under control back home.

The Intelligence Unit became interested in Long years before Costello and Lansky organized gambling on behalf of the syndicate in New Orleans. Elmer Irey was all too aware of the relation of crime to politics. During the probe of the Capone empire in Chicago, special agents had found time to convict Lawrence C. O'Brien and Gene G. Oliver. O'Brien, for many years a member of the legislature, operated a trucking concern which worked exclusively on city contracts. He contended unsuccessfully that as a state representative working for the city, he didn't have to pay taxes. Oliver, a member of the Chicago Board of Assessors, was an important political figure who said he handled a lot of other people's money. Both men were sent to prison in 1930. Thus, it was that reports reaching Irey from Louisiana had a familiar ring. The flood of letters, many of them anonymous, grew larger in 1931 and by 1932 constituted the bulk of Irey's mail. Long's henchmen were stealing $100,-000,000, said the complaints. Why couldn't the Intelligence Unit do something?

By mid-1932 Irey had ordered Archie Burford, special agent

in charge of the Dallas office, to go over to Louisiana and make a preliminary investigation. A few weeks later Burford reported that all the complaints were justified—and then some. Long's gang not only was stealing everything in sight but wasn't paying taxes on the loot. Irey responded by sending Burford back to Louisiana with 32 special agents out of the 200 men in the Intelligence Unit.

It didn't take the Kingfish very long to discover what was going on. He paid a personal visit to Commissioner of Internal Revenue David Burnet and warned him of the dangers of investigating a United States Senator. However, it was still 1932, and a Democrat such as Long carried little influence with the Republican administration, which had enough problems of its own. Following Roosevelt's election, however, Secretary of the Treasury Mills ordered Irey to suspend the probe, write a full report, and let the incoming Democrats handle the politically prickly catfish.

Irey obeyed. The special agents were ordered back to their regular jobs, and Burford prepared a long report which, in Irey's words, "left no doubt the Intelligence Unit was confident it could convict Long and his gang and hoped it would receive orders to do so." The report was turned in to Roosevelt's first Secretary of the Treasury, William H. Woodin, and the long wait began.

It was August, 1933, before there was even a whisper from the new administration, and it was Carter Glass, the Senator from Virginia, who inspired it. Glass called Irey to his sickbed and demanded: "Haven't you got that son of a bitch from Louisiana yet?"

Irey explained he was still waiting for orders. Glass promised he would receive them. But it was a query, not a command, that came next. Commissioner of Internal Revenue Guy Helvering, Irey's immediate boss, informed him that the White House wanted to know why Long was being investigated.

"Isn't it a job for the FBI?" asked Helvering, obviously hoping he could pass the buck and arrange for J. Edgar Hoover to go fishing for the Kingfish. Irey wasn't much help.

"It sure is a job for somebody," he replied.

Again there was silence. Long had helped Roosevelt win the

106

Democratic nomination, thereby creating a political debt. However, the Washington grapevine buzzed with rumors that Roosevelt was alarmed at Long's "Every man a king" program in a country still gripped by economic depression. So Irey waited in hope.

Woodin was succeeded by Henry Morgenthau, Jr., as Secretary of the Treasury in January, 1934. Burford's report was almost a year old. Three days after taking office, Morgenthau sent for Irey.

"Get your men back on the Louisiana job," commanded the new Secretary, "and let the chips fall where they may."

In Morgenthau, Irey had found a man after his own heart. Dedicated and determined in his opposition to crime and corruption, he backed the Intelligence Unit all the way. Much of the success of Irey's men in the next ten years was possible because of Morgenthau's unfailing support. And Morgenthau was close to the President; if muscle were needed, he could get it. Years later, Morgenthau's son became United States Attorney for the Southern District of New York and carried on the fight against organized crime in the same spirit.

Burford was again given the job of ramrodding the probe, and it was decided to use the technique that had worked against Capone—knock off the lieutenants first and then close in on the Kingfish. Mike Malone was called in and told to see if he could penetrate the Long gang as he had done the Capone mob. An entire floor of the Masonic Building in New Orleans was rented as headquarters, and it was guarded night and day.

Malone was assigned to concentrate on Seymour Weiss. Obviously a man of influence, Weiss had risen from barbershop manager to owner of the Roosevelt Hotel in a very short time. Some unkind people attributed his good fortune to the fact that earlier he had helped Long out of a sticky situation. The Kingfish had been accused of stealing $6,000 earmarked for the entertainment of a convention of governors. He said he gave the money to Weiss, who accounted for some of it and said the rest was spent for pleasures so exotic he didn't want to describe them publicly. Everyone knew, or thought he knew, what was meant—the French Quarter in the heart of New Orleans was famous for its strippers and experienced prostitutes.

The matter was dropped, and Weiss drew much praise for his discretion.

Malone checked into the Roosevelt Hotel, where he posed as a radio executive interested in buying or building a radio station. He even filed an application with the Federal Communications Commission for a permit. The FCC had been asked to ignore it. Inevitably, Malone became acquainted with Weiss. Inevitably, as soon as Long's lieutenant heard Mike gripe about federal red tape, he offered to help cut it. Inevitably, the man Weiss steered Mike to said he could take care of everything for $5,000. Mike managed to stall and, as usual, soon found himself accepted. Before long he was playing cards with the Kingfish himself.

A bad moment came one day when Louis La Cava suddenly appeared in the lobby where Malone was sitting. La Cava had been a Capone hood in Chicago and was later to be indicted with John Torrio in New York. He recognized Mike instantly.

"Hello," he roared in greeting, for even the hoods liked Malone. "Whatta you doing down here? Investigating Huey Long's taxes?"

Mike took La Cava for a long ride in an automobile. Exactly what he told him remains a secret between the two men, but it was effective. La Cava returned to the hotel, checked out, and left town. Mike continued his undercover role, reporting Long's men were confident that regardless of the evidence—and of that there was plenty—no jury composed of Louisiana citizens would indict or convict the Kingfish.

Irey, all too aware that a dishonest or incompetent prosecutor can so bungle a good case that not even a grand jury composed of persons of utmost integrity can return an indictment, began looking for a suitable attorney to present the evidence. Citizens of New Orleans had long memories going back to the military government that ruled their city during Reconstruction days, and Irey knew a Northerner would have little chance. He carried the problem to Secretary Morgenthau, who took it, and Irey, in to see the President.

Any sense of gratitude Roosevelt felt for Long had died months before. The Senator from Louisiana had led a successful fight against United States entry into the World Court, and harassed the administration at every opportunity. Roosevelt reached the conclusion soon to be voiced by Secretary of the Interior Harold L. Ickes that Long suffered from "halitosis of the intellect." When Irey's problem was presented, he immediately ordered Morgenthau to "see that Mr. Irey gets the type of lawyer he wants."

This was interdepartmental meddling at top level. It was the Department of Justice's job to prosecute tax evaders and all other alleged violators of federal law, not the Treasury Department, under which Irey and the IRS operated. Yet not only did the President approve Irey's request, but when a reluctant Dan Moody—ex-governor of Texas—was nominated by Irey, Roosevelt personally charmed Moody into taking the job. As Irey put it, "when the meeting was over, Moody would have indicted Sam Houston if FDR wanted him to."

Moody decided to test the water before diving in. State Representative Joseph Fisher was indicted for not paying income taxes on graft he had received from Long's multimillion-dollar road-building program. Mike Malone warned, however, that it wasn't a fair test—the "boys" had decided to let Fisher take a rap, and his acquittal or conviction meant little. The real showdown would come when someone on a higher level was indicted.

As usual, Malone proved correct. Fisher was found guilty on April 26, 1935, and was sentenced to eighteen months in prison. The easy conviction persuaded Irey and Moody to go after the Kingfish next. The big problem was not one of evidence—there was plenty of that—but rather the kind of evidence that would disillusion the people of Louisiana who for so many years had been brainwashed into believing Long was a friend of the poor and a foe of the vested interests.

Special Agent Burford had the answer—the Win or Lose Corporation. Long and several cronies set up the outfit in 1934 and invested nothing in it. Yet it earned $347,937 in 1935. Part of the profit came when Long's stooge O. K. Allen, who served as governor, blackmailed two gas companies into paying $320,000 under threat of passing a bill increasing taxes on natural gas. The money officially was in payment for twenty locations in a gas field which the companies had earlier refused

109

to buy. Burford reasoned the "little people" might lose some of their affection for the Kingfish when they realized the much-publicized tax increase had been called off as a result of the deal.

The decision to indict Long for his part in the Win or Lose Corporation was made in a hotel room in Dallas on September 7. Moody agreed to go before the federal grand jury the following month and present the evidence. He didn't. On September 8, 1935, Long was assassinated in the Capitol at Baton Rouge. Mystery still surrounds the event. Dr. Carl Weiss—no relation to Seymour—was blamed, and Long's bodyguards filled him with bullets even as Huey fell. The theory has been advanced that the Kingfish was killed by his own men, who thought his death would take the federal heat off them. Indeed, he might have survived the wound had proper medical techniques been employed—but they weren't.

The King was dead, but his machine still functioned. Great confusion existed, and gamblers who had not been part of the Long-Lansky-Costello monopoly blossomed out all over New Orleans with handbooks and casinos. Yet where federal prosecution threatened, their lines held firm. At an emergency meeting in Hot Springs, with Owney Madden as host, a new alliance was formed.

More confident than ever, Irey and his men proceeded. Abe Shushan, president of the New Orleans Levee Board, was indicted. He had collected a commission on every cubic yard of dirt that had been used to fill the swamp between huge Lake Pontchartrain and New Orleans. The Intelligence Unit charged he had accepted $525,732 in bribes and paid taxes on none of it. Irey considered it the strongest case of all. Only Mike Malone was pessimistic.

Again Mike proved right. The jury acquitted Shushan, perhaps as a sentimental gesture in memory of the departed leader. Wild confusion greeted the verdict as friends of the gang cheered and smashed the cameras of newsmen.

"We Intelligence Unit men were a sick lot," said Irey.

Worse was to come. Fifteen other defendants had already entered pleas of guilty or *nolo contendere* (no contest) when

110

the Justice Department abruptly announced it was dropping all the remaining cases.

New Orleans newspapers called it the Second Louisiana Purchase. Irey took the unprecedented step of disagreeing openly with the decision, but for once, even Morgenthau was unable to help. It was election year, and strange as it sounds in retrospect, many people were predicting that the country would go Republican.

Some insight into the situation was provided in 1953, when *The Secret Diary of Harold L. Ickes* was published. Under the date of October 30, 1935, Ickes wrote about a conversation with James Farley, Roosevelt's campaign manager.

"I referred to Huey Long's assassination and the situation in Louisiana," Ickes said. "He [Farley] told me that he was keeping his hands off in Louisiana because whichever faction won would be friendly to the Administration. He has no apprehension now over that state. Then he made the significant statement that if Huey Long had lived, as a candidate for President he would have polled six million votes. . . ."

Crime and criminals take a back seat when Presidential politics are involved. Before Long's death, prosecution; after his death, neutrality.

If Morgenthau could do nothing about the criminal cases that had gone out the window, he could and did order civil suits pushed all the way. By the time a special section of the Board of Tax Appeals could be set up the election was over, and Roosevelt had been returned to office in a landslide. Every person whose criminal case had been dismissed by Justice as "too weak" pleaded guilty and paid the amount demanded by Internal Revenue. Needless to say, fraud penalties were included. Even Shushan, who had been acquitted, paid up. Treasury collected more than $2,000,000 in taxes and penalties. For the Intelligence Unit it was vindication of a sorts.

Irey was still angry, however. He bided his time. Crooks being what they were, a new opportunity was sure to come in a state where graft and corruption had become a way of life.

The third Louisiana investigation began a few months later when Rufus W. Fontenot, Collector of Internal Revenue at

New Orleans, told Irey about J. Monroe Smith. Long, angry because his alma mater had refused him an honorary degree, had deliberately created a rival—Louisiana State University —and put Smith in as its president. Now, according to Fontenot's information, Smith was spending money like water and selling stock he didn't own under fictitious names for as much as $130,000. Yet he hadn't bothered to file income tax returns.

Special Agent Burford had been promoted and reassigned, so Irey gave charge of the third probe to Special Agents Frank W. Lohn and James M. Cooner.

Investigation revealed that while Dr. Smith was an able man with a PhD from Columbia University, it was his actions as dean at Southwestern Institute that had recommended him to Huey. It seems that Dean Smith sold three cows belonging to the school and reported to the trustees that the cows died of anthrax. Such academic antics convinced Long that Dr. Smith was qualified to run LSU, in which the Kingfish had invested $10,000,000 of state funds.

Smith's first assignment was to build up a football team and a band to accompany it. Like many an old grad, Huey felt a winning football team was more important than high scholastic standards, and he desperately wanted to see the Green Wave of Tulane fall before his handpicked warriors. Sparing no expense, Smith developed teams of professional quality and a band to match.

The Intelligence Unit also learned that after Long's death, Dr. Smith decided that in view of the general insecurity, he'd better get together a nest egg for his old age. The wheat market appealed to him, but he lacked capital. However, the university had plenty of stocks and bonds, so he began using them as credit for his brokerage dealings. He was singularly unsuccessful and soon found himself in the traditional predicament of the embezzler—using more and more bonds in the hope of making a killing that would allow him to cover up. The special agents discovered that about $1,000,000 worth of LSU bonds were missing. It didn't take long to discover the use Smith had made of them. In the process they found evidence he had received $45,000 in kickbacks from crooked contractors employed by the university.

The special agents also discovered that Smith had raised his salary from $15,000 to $18,000 by writing up minutes of a board meeting that never occurred. He probably got the idea from the episode with the cows.

Secrets were hard to keep in Louisiana, so it isn't surprising that Dr. Smith discovered he was about to be indicted. In June, 1939, he suddenly resigned and took off for Canada. Shortly thereafter he surrendered and told Louisiana by radio that he would not be made "the goat." Perhaps this annoyed the boys—or frightened them—for suddenly state grand juries began indicting him on everything except murder and spitting on the sidewalk. According to Irey, he set some sort of a record by being indicted on an average of once every two days for two months.

Now the old adage that honest men profit when crooks fall out began working. An old Long crony, James A. Noe, was miffed because he had failed to be selected as Long's successor. He began writing affidavits to columnist Drew Pearson—500 of them in all—in which he charged the Long machine with stealing millions of Works Progress Administration (WPA) funds. In line with this, another comment from Harold Ickes' diary is interesting. Ickes disclosed that on July 15, 1935, President Smith of LSU called on him to ask for federal funds for the university. "I told him," Ickes said, "that some people believed that this wasn't so much an educational institution as it was a political institution. He announced that he took great exception to that statement and I told him that was his privilege." The funds were refused.

Richard W. Leche had succeeded Long in the capacity of governor, with the consent of the gang, by playing records of Long's speeches in the 1936 campaign. Noe simmered awhile and then released his flood of affidavits. One of them claimed WPA workers and material had been used to build a house for, among others, Governor Leche. The governor resigned, changed his mind long enough to order Doc Smith arrested again, and resigned once more.

Now the roof began to fall in. Mike Malone became acquainted with a gabby woman at the Roosevelt Hotel and picked up some gossip that set the Intelligence Unit hot on the trail of Seymour Weiss. The tip concerned the sale of the hotel in 1936 to LSU—naturally—for use as a nurses' dormitory. A $25,000 "commission" allegedly given to Louis C. Le Sage proved to be the key. After Weiss and Le Sage had been convicted of using the mails to defraud in connection with the deal, Le Sage confessed he had given the $25,000 to Weiss but, at Weiss' command, had listed the item on his own tax returns. Weiss had reimbursed him for the taxes. As a result of Le Sage's confession, Weiss was convicted of tax fraud and sentenced to four years in prison.

Irey's men turned to Abe Shushan, the man who had beaten them in 1936. A beautiful case of larceny was developed, but it was tax-paid larceny. By now, however, the Intelligence men weren't particular. They gave the evidence to their colleagues of the Post Office Inspection Service, who quickly proved the mails had been used once again. Shushan and some of his pals were sentenced to thirty months in prison for mail fraud. It was an expensive conviction for New Orleans. Shushan, as a public official, had put his name or initials in the concrete of public projects all over the city. It cost some $30,-000 to remove them.

Last to go was ex-Governor Leche. He was indicted for failure to report and pay taxes on $31,000 he received in a kickback deal involving the purchase of 300 trucks by the state. Assistant United States Attorney General O. John Rogge prosecuted, with Special Agent Cooner sitting at his elbow. When Leche decided to testify in his own behalf, the team of Roche and Cooner cut him to pieces and forced him to admit he had made more than $1,000,000 during his three years as governor. The man who was allegedly Long's deathbed choice to run the state drew the most severe sentence of them all—ten years in prison.

The third Louisiana investigation not only cleaned up the state's political system—temporarily, at least—but also netted the Treasury $6,372,360 in additional taxes and penalties. Irey estimated that the probe cost less than $250,000.

Yet all the while the slot machines of the syndicate kept whirling. Handbooks ran openly, and the Beverly Club's casino made such good food and entertainment possible the joint became nationally known. Eventually, however, as more honest men replaced the crooks, much of the gambling moved across the Mississippi River to the little town of Gretna in Jefferson Parish. Lansky and Costello sent Dandy Phil Kastel on to Las Vegas, where Lansky's old partner, Bugsy Siegel, had developed a legal gold mine on behalf of the syndicate. New Orleans didn't become a Sunday school city exactly, but after the Intelligence Unit finished with Huey Long's machine, it was no longer a wide-open town. A hood no bigger than Carlos Marcello was capable of handling the rackets that remained. His choice was rather appropriate in that a Long lieutenant, Governor O. K. Allen, let Marcello out of prison in 1934 at the request of the mob.

Some insight into why the gamblers left New Orleans for Gretna was provided by Peter Hand, a political fixer and gambler during the Long machine's heyday. He complained that under the succeeding administrations, the police had become unreliable. As he put it: "People have lost faith in the police. Years ago they'd let you operate. Today they take your money at eleven o'clock and knock you off at one o'clock. The bookmakers got tired of that."

In Gretna there were no such worries. Beauregard Miller, the town's marshal since 1925, not only permitted wide-open gambling, but owned his own casinos as well.

The value of political influence in gambling operations was demonstrated in Massachusetts about the time Costello installed his slot machines in New Orleans.

When Prohibition ended, some bootleggers, who had worked for King Solomon of the Big Seven and later for the syndicate, closed their offices in Boston, Chelsea, and Revere and began looking about for another easy way to make a lot of fast bucks. Al Capone had demonstrated in Cicero and other cities that dogs will attract suckers as well as horses, so it was decided to legalize dog racing in the Bay State. The Cleveland Syndicate tried the same experiment in Kentucky and was so confident it opened a track near Newport without waiting for legislation to be passed. Governor A. B. "Happy" Chandler, who had a proper respect for the horse industry of the Bluegrass, closed down the illegal track after only thirteen days. The boys in Massachusetts were more cautious. They waited until State Representative Martin Hays got the law passed. When in 1934 the Bay State Greyhound Association, Inc., was formed, Hays became its legal counsel.

Four ex-bootleggers held 60 percent of the stock: Louis D. Fox, Hyman Abrams, Mario A. Ingraffia, and Arthur C. Barron. Because of the reputation of the four men, it was decided their stock should be held in the names of straws [fronts, i.e., straw men]. Some of the names suggested by the bootleggers weren't acceptable to Hays, so he substituted the names of relatives, friends, his chauffeur, and his private secretary. He concealed his own interests in the same way.

On November 30, 1935, dog racing at Wonderland Dog Track near Revere—a suburb of Boston and for many decades a stronghold of the syndicate—had become so popular a dividend of $80 per share was declared by the association. Dividend checks were drawn on the National Shawmut Bank, payable to the stockholders of record—the straws. When the Intelligence Unit began investigating, special agents found the checks were in the handwriting of Hays, who by now served as director, clerk, and attorney for the Bay State Greyhound Association. He also made sure the straws didn't cash the checks and pocket the money. Such a procedure would be dishonest. The ex-bootleggers got the dividends, but none of them saw fit to report the additional income on their 1935 returns. The same procedure was followed in 1936, when the dividends were almost four times as large. No question about it—dog racing was catching on.

The straws were required to file returns, but so low was their 1935 total income that all but two owed no tax. One of Hays' straws paid $8.47, and one of Barron's straws coughed up $48.20. The bite was larger in 1936, so Hays prepared all the returns of all the straws for that year. The combined total of taxes due was $6,147, and the real owners of the stock supplied the cash to the straws to pay the bill.

Shortly after the Intelligence Unit began its probe, all the ex-bootleggers filed amended returns for themselves and delinquent returns for some of the straws who had not filed anything. Nevertheless, neither the amended returns nor the delinquent returns reported the full amount of the dividends.

By February 26, 1937, rumors were sweeping Boston, and a bitter attack was mounted on the dog-racing industry at a legislative hearing that day. Representative James P. Donnelly started the verbal fireworks by describing racing as a "bloodsucking enterprise and legalize larceny." Lieutenant Governor Francis E. Kelly sponsored a bill to cut the track share from 11½ percent to 4 percent and to increase the state's share of the profits from 3½ percent to 11 percent. He stated: "There are two winners at the track, the operators of the track and the fat artificial rabbits the dogs chase. I have no objections if a bunch of half-starved dogs chase an electric rabbit, but I do think they are getting more than they deserve."

Leland Bickford, operator of a local news service, charged that the Revere track's backers were gangsters, and he promised to prove it. The six special agents of the Intelligence Unit who attended the hearing said nothing. Later Bickford named Ingraffia as one of the backers and called him the "vice overlord of New England." He also charged that Hays accepted $1,500 to lobby for passage of the dog-racing bill and received $10,000 when it was accomplished. He traced the rise of the bootleggers and showed their connections to Capone, to the New York mob, and to the Purple Gang of Detroit. Newspaper stories hinted that Hays would sue Bickford for libel.

It was February 5, 1940, before a federal grand jury returned indictments. Hays, who had resigned as Republican floor leader, made a desperate effort to talk the jury out of indicting him. At his request, the jurors listened to his story for five hours and then proceeded to do their duty.

The Justice Department, charged with prosecuting the cases, decided to accept a compromise. The defendants agreed to pay the full amount of taxes due, plus penalty and interest. With the exception of Hays, who agreed to plead no contest, all pleaded guilty to single counts. In return, it was agreed the remaining counts would be dropped.

Hays, Fox, Abrams, and Ingraffia were fined $2,000 each and given suspended sentences of one year in prison. Barron got off with a six months' suspended sentence and a $500 fine.

It was a slap on the wrists, but once again there was nothing Irey could do about it.

Fox eventually became a multimillionaire and the absolute boss of Revere's varied and extensive gambling joints and brothels. As a high-ranking member of the syndicate, he made investments from Las Vegas to the Virgin Islands.

Abrams, a close personal friend of Meyer Lansky's, also became an important member of the syndicate and an owner of record in Las Vegas casinos.

Ingraffia's role as Mafia boss was taken over by Raymond Patriarca of Providence, Rhode Island, and smooth relations were maintained with the syndicate for many years.

The dog-racing industry survived the scandal and flourished in a state where corruption was accepted as blandly as in New Orleans.

Ultimately, it became a key to the vast numbers racket in Boston, a simple formula involving the pari-mutuel handle providing the winning number. When dog tracks were not running, horse tracks were used. Joseph M. Linsey, another ex-bootlegger and personal friend of Lansky's, became an owner of horse and dog tracks and won a reputation in Boston newspapers as a "philanthropist" and "sportsman."

He also owned part of a Boston newspaper.

All that was for the future, however. More immediate problems of corruption claimed the Intelligence Unit's attention. In Kansas City a revenue agent attempting to probe the income of a gangster friendly to Boss Pendergast got his brains kicked out. The boys in Boston, bad as they were, didn't go to such extremes. They didn't need to.

7

THE SECOND MISSOURI COMPROMISE

THE letter was dated May 12, 1933. It was addressed to Postmaster General James J. Farley in Washington, D.C. Farley, it will be remembered, was also chairman of the Democratic Party and the man who saw no need to worry about Louisiana following the death of Huey Long. It began:

> MY DEAR JIM:
> Jerome Walsh and John Lazia will be in Washington to see you about the same matter that I had Mr. Kemper talk to you about. Now, Jim, Lazia is one of my chief lieutenants and I am more sincerely interested in his welfare than anything you might be able to do for me now or in the future. He has been in trouble with the Income Tax Department for some time. I know it was simply a case of him being jobbed because of his Democratic activities. I think that Frank Walsh spoke to the proper authorities about this. In any event, I wish you would use your utmost endeavor to bring about a settlement of this matter. I cannot make it any stronger, except to say that my interest in him is greater than anything that might come up in the future.

119

Thanking you for any and everything you can do, I remain

Sincerely, your friend
T. J. PENDERGAST

The letter didn't bring the income tax investigation of John Lazia to a halt—it just kept it from moving. The stop order came in March, three days after United States Attorney William L. Vandeventer had begun presenting the Intelligence Unit's evidence to a federal grand jury. When Boss Tom's letter was written, Vandeventer was awaiting further instructions from the United States Attorney General's office. He continued to wait.

As an illustration of the power of Pendergast, the episode serves well. The Boss controlled Missouri, even as the Kingfish had ruled Louisiana, and every racket known to man prospered and paid tribute to him. According to Elmer Irey, "Pendergast made judges, Representatives, Senators and governors," and one of his protégés, Harry S. Truman, became President of the United States.

A native of St. Joseph, Missouri, Pendergast might have become a big-league baseball player, instead of a political racketeer, had his father not considered baseball a less respectable occupation—especially for a college graduate. So young Tom went to work for his brother, Jimmy, who owned saloons in Kansas City and was a minor-league politician. Later Jimmy decided brother Tom should learn about law and order and arranged for him to become a cop in the wide-open First Ward. There Tom discovered that might makes right, and when Jimmy died in 1911, he was fully prepared to take charge of his brother's political organization.

Pendergast was thirty-nine years old when he took the reins of power from his brother. A six-footer, with large hands and great speed as a youth, he became grossly fat and—even as Bugsy Siegel had modeled himself after actor Edward G. Robinson—Tom tried to look and act like Sidney Greenstreet. He spoke in clipped tones that sounded more sinister than the words, and his eyes—despite the fat with which they were surrounded—seemed equally menacing. Here is how Federal

120

District Judge Merrill Otis pictured the boss at the height of his power:

> His throne room was a small monastic-like cubicle on the second floor of a two-story building, well removed from the center of the city. "1908 Main Street" was synonymous with power, it was the local Mecca of the faithful. To this Mecca came he who would be governor, he who would be senator, he who would be a judge, and he who was content to be only a keeper of the pound. Thither came alike great and little, craving audience and favors. They "beat a pathway" to the Boss's door, as Emerson said men would beat a pathway to the door of him who could make a better mouse trap than his neighbors (only Pendergast dealt not in mouse traps, but in ready mixed concrete, designed especially for county and city edifices and streets). Each who came, it is said, awaited, hat in hand, his turn, humbly presented his petition, listened to the mandate of Caesar, and backed away from the Presence. And those who did not actually go in person to bend the pregnant hinges of the knee, even the mightiest, telephoned respectful inquiries, as they passed through the city, asking concerning "Tom's health." The Leader's portrait adorned the walls of eminent public servants both in the capital of the commonwealth and at Washington, along with that of the Father of His Country and that of the Sage of Monticello, between these other portraits, on a somewhat higher level.

From the First Ward, Tom branched out to control the rest of Kansas City and Jackson County. By 1916 his power was such that no Democrat could be nominated for governor without his approval. In the off-year election of 1930 his organization rolled up a Democratic vote of more than 100,000 and made politicians on the national level such as Farley aware of his importance.

Taking full advantage, Pendergast consolidated his power. A Missouri Supreme Court decision removed the Kansas City Police Department from the control of the then Republican governor. In effect, the decision put the Police Department in Boss Tom's hands. Then followed what a reporter called a gift

121

from the gods—an impasse in the 1931 legislature which caused Missouri's thirteen Congressmen to be elected at large in 1932. This meant that Pendergast's approval was necessary, and the lines grew long outside 1908 Main Street.

Meanwhile, Pendergast had the rackets well in hand. During Prohibition, bootleggers and speakeasy operators paid the Boss for permission to conduct business. Gangsters were imported to see they paid their full share. Gambling was widespread and wide-open. Merchants paid from 5 to 10 percent of their profits to collectors, who dropped in every week. Those who resisted were bombed and driven out of business. Municipal contractors learned they had to cut Tom in if they were to get contracts. One, who at first refused, was warned. He reported the threat to the police and got laughed at for his trouble. A wheel came off his car one night, and a grenade exploded on the porch of his home. He decided to play ball after that, and his troubles ceased.

Despite all the money that rolled in, Tom was often short of cash. He was addicted to playing the horses, and his bets were always huge. What's more, he often lost. There was a law against horse racing in Missouri—a blue law, in Tom's opinion. He arranged for a track to be opened in Platte County, only an hour's drive by automobile from 1908 Main Street. When local citizens protested that state law was being broken, Pendergast shrugged. The citizens took the trouble to visit Circuit Judge Guy B. Park and read him the state constitution. Judge Park shrugged. That shrug made him governor.

In the August, 1932 primary, Pendergast backed Francis M. Wilson for governor and delivered 100,000 votes for him in Kansas City. In mid-campaign, however, Wilson was ungratefull enough to die. Hastily the Democrats reconvened. A Pendergast stooge nominated Judge Park as a substitute candidate. State committeemen, who had not been briefed, laughed at the suggestion. Who, they asked, was Park? Pendergast, remembering the convenient, if illegal, racetrack, told them the answer. "I think Park is a fine man," said the Boss. That was enough for the underlings. Judge Park was quickly approved, and he was elected in the Roosevelt landslide. One of his first acts was to order a four-lane superhighway built from Kansas

City to the racetrack. Obviously, he know how to thank the Boss.

Park also appointed R. Emmet O'Malley to be state superintendent of insurance, a move that was to have some interesting repercussions in a few short years.

It was in the year that Park was elected—1932—that a probe was begun into the taxes—or rather the lack of them—of John Lazia. Of Italian descent, Lazia was imported from Chicago to serve as an enforcer, even as the Jewish members of the Purple Gang first invited the Licavoli boys, Peter and Yonnie, to their city, and the Irishmen of Tammany Hall found a use for Lucky Luciano. The Mafia existed in Kansas City prior to the First World War, but there, as elsewhere, its members had been too busy killing each other to achieve any great influence.

Back in 1916, Lazia gained a measure of fame by holding up a saloon and getting sentenced to twelve years in the state penitentiary. When he got out, he went to work in Chicago until Pendergast had need of his services. Lazia had achieved a reputation of being often seen in the vicinity just before a gang killing but, when questioned, always proved he was somewhere else when the murder actually took place. With a police department as corrupt as Kansas City boasted, this wasn't too hard to do.

The preliminary probe, as often happens, was conducted by a revenue agent. Except in unusual cases, special agents of the Intelligence Unit are not called into a case until there is solid indication of possible fraud. Revenue Agent Harry D. Beach reached that stage when bank records revealed that almost $100,000 had passed through Lazia's account in 1929-30—a period when Lazia filed no income tax returns. Before writing his report, which would have resulted in the assignment of a special agent to assist and supervise, Beach decided to give the taxpayer a chance to explain. Lazia appeared for the meeting but refused to give any information.

"We shall take the proper steps," said the young agent.

Apparently Lazia decided he'd take steps too, and from his point of view, they were entirely proper. Four days after the interview two men came calling at Beach's apartment. It was Sunday, March 13, 1932, and Beach was at home. The men en-

123

tered and proceeded to beat the agent. In the words of Irey, "they kicked his brains out." Beach died shortly afterward of his injuries, his report still unwritten. Lazia, of course, was able to prove he was somewhere else when the beating occurred.

The murder of Beach brought Irey's men swarming into Kansas City, determined to complete the job begun by the dead revenue agent. If, in the process, they could also get evidence against Pendergast, so much the better. Lazia had headed Pendergast's goon squad, putting the arm on punk and honest merchant alike. Yet at first no one wanted to talk. Fear, so real as to be tasted, gripped the citizens of Kansas City—fear and a sense of hopelessness. The Boss boasted openly that his influence extended to Washington. The junior Senator from Missouri, Harry S. Truman, was—as Irey put it—"a creature of Boss Pendergast." Sure, the Intelligence Unit had made it hot for Al Capone, but President Hoover had been behind it then. Would President Roosevelt permit a valuable political ally to be embarrassed? The citizens, schooled in practical politics of the Pendergast variety, didn't think so. Why, then, stick one's neck out in an impossible cause?

The special agents refused to be discouraged. They learned that Lazia owned a piece of a greyhound racetrack in Clay County—the fad was spreading—and a piece of a gambling joint near the track called the Cuban Gardens. It had operated from September 12, 1929, until January 31, 1931. Arthur McNamee supervised the joint, and Arthur M. Slavin, a professional from Dallas, ran the casino. To prevent losses through robbery, the casino's bank was maintained in the form of cashier's checks which were accepted in lieu of cash.

Ultimately, Lazia and McNamee had an argument, and Lazia withdrew from the setup under an agreement that paid him $500 a week until his original investment was recovered. As soon as that happened, the place was raided and closed down. The lesson was pretty obvious.

The special agents discovered that the rents for the Cuban Gardens and the racetrack were paid not to Lazia, who owned the property, but to an employee of the Merchants Bank. The deeds to the property were in the names of other bank employees. When pressure was applied, the bank clerks admitted they were serving as straws for Lazia.

Early in March, 1933, the special agents had made their case. They were ready to prove Lazia had failed to report and pay taxes on income of $125,000 for the years 1929 and 1930. The evidence was given to United States Attorney Vandeventer, who just happened to be a Republican holdover. Vandeventer filed an information, a legal charge sufficient to cause the arrest of a defendant and bring him before a grand jury. Three weeks later came orders to drop the matter until further notice. On orders from Washington, the Justice Department official arranged a series of "conferences" with Lazia and his attorneys, Jerome and Frank Walsh. Such a meeting on May 10, 1933, almost ended in a fight as Vandeventer and the special agents stood firm in demanding an explanation and Lazia accused them of political persecution.

Two days later Pendergast wrote his famous letter to Farley in which he admitted "Lazia is one of my chief lieutenants." The U.S. Attorney didn't know about the letter, but in July he asked his superiors in Washington if he could proceed with the case. He was told he couldn't. This was in the period before Henry Morgenthau became Secretary of the Treasury, and Irey's hands were tied. The summer passed. The special agents used the time to dig up new evidence against Lazia. In November, 1934, when Spencer R. McCulloch disclosed the existence of the letter and its contents in a copyrighted story for the St. Louis *Post-Dispatch,* Farley said he didn't recall receiving the letter and certainly had taken no action on it.

Be that as it may, when the federal grand jury met in September, Vandeventer, in his own words, "was forced to tell the jury, when it inquired, that I was powerless to act."

The jury took advantage of an appearance in court before Judge Otis to clarify the situation. A juror rose to his feet. As the U.S. Attorney related later:

"This man [the juror] told Judge Otis that there was a matter that had not been presented to it, that it had been informed I could not present it, and he wanted to know if it could go ahead and conduct its own investigation.

"Judge Otis just looked at me. I told him frankly that I had

been directed by my superiors to refrain from prosecution until further orders, that Lazia desired an opportunity to submit
more data.

"The judge told the jury that my attitude in obeying my
superiors was proper, but he pointed out that they [the supe-
riors] are not 'your superiors,' and told them they could investigate anything they saw fit. I wired direct to Attorney-
General [Homer S.] Cummings, informed him of the situation, asked him what position I should take. He telegraphed
me to 'render every assistance possible.' I went ahead and prosecuted."

The revolt of the grand jury in Kansas City that day must
rank with the rebellion of the state grand jury in New York
that demanded, and got, Tom Dewey as special counsel. Its example was followed by a federal grand jury at Lexington, Kentucky, in 1961, which ignored the wishes of the Justice Department and, with the consent of the presiding judge, issued a
red-hot blast at vice and crime conditions in Newport and
Campbell County, Kentucky. Few grand jurors realize their
power, and even fewer care to stick their necks out to exercise
it. Legal history is usually made when they do "run away."

Washington obviously didn't intend to oppose the wishes of
the people, as represented by the grand jury. Lazia was indicted on September 16, 1933, and charged with evasion of income tax for the years 1929 and 1930 and with failure to file
an income tax return in 1929 and 1930. His correct income for
the years in question was alleged to be $58,795 and $98,121,
respectively.

The trial opened on February 5, 1934, after Lazia's attorneys
lost a number of arguments. A trial jury found him guilty on
February 28. Judge Otis sentenced Lazia to a year in the county
jail and a $2,500 fine. Light enough, but the defense was un-
satisfied. A motion for a new trial was filed on the basis that
one of the trial jurors had also been on the jury that convicted
Lazia on an armed robbery charge in 1916. At a hearing on
the motion, the juror, Albert H. Greef, said he "saw no relation between the punk kid of 1916 and John Lazia. Never was I
aware that Lazia was anyone I had seen before the day I was
called for federal jury duty."

126

In that eighteen-year interval, Lazia had changed from a "punk kid" on the North Side to that district's political leader with thinning brown hair and a nervous twitch of the facial muscles. Judge Otis believed the juror and denied the motion. The attorneys filed notice of appeal, and Lazia went free on bond.

Rumors spread along the dark streets, from joint to joint and dive to dive, that Lazia had threatened to "blow the lid off" if, in fact, he finally went to jail. He didn't do either. On July 10, 1934, at 3 A.M., he rode up to his residence, the Park Central Hotel. His chauffeur-bodyguard, Charles Carrollo, hesitated behind the wheel as Lazia stepped to the sidewalk and stood waiting for his bodyguard to accompany him inside. Suddenly two men appeared out of nowhere and opened up with automatics. Lazia died the next day. Carrollo, his bodyguard, was not hurt and immediately took over Lazia's job as Pendergast's lieutenant. Had Lazia been killed because of his threats? No one could be sure, but the men of the Intelligence Unit didn't really care. One way or another, Revenue Agent Harry Beach had been avenged.

The Lazia saga wasn't over, however. In October it was discovered that Pendergast's protégé had played a part in the infamous Kansas City Massacre of June 17, 1933. On that day, FBI special agents arrived in Kansas City with a notorious prisoner, Frank Nash, who had been seized in Owney Madden's new domain, Hot Springs, Arkansas. They were on the way to Leavenworth Prison with their man, and they got off the train to change to a car at Union Station. Two more special agents and two of Kansas City's finest were detailed to help guard against an attempted rescue. As the transfer to the car was being made, three men—one of them the famous Pretty Boy Floyd—opened up with submachine guns. The two city cops, the chief of McAlester, Oklahoma, and Special Agent Raymond Caffrey were killed instantly. Two other FBI special agents were wounded. Ironically, the mobsters also killed Nash while spraying the scene with lead. The killers escaped. Now, sixteen months after the massacre and three months after Lazia's murder, it was learned that Lazia had met with Floyd and the others on the night before the massacre. He had also

127

helped them find a physician to treat Floyd's wounded arm on the night after the mutiple killings and the following day provided an armed escort to get them out of town safely.

No wonder Farley couldn't recall receiving the letter from Pendergast when asked about it a month later. Pendergast, however, was not a bit bashful when queried by reporters. "Yes," he told them, "I wrote it. I stand by it, too. I'd do it again and I'll stand by it." To make his point clear, he added: "I don't shirk responsibility."

Neither did Irey or his new boss, Morgenthau, shirk responsibility, and when Irey reported the Lazia case might be exploited to find an opening in the defenses of the Boss, Morgenthau told him to proceed. "If half the reports about Thomas J. Pendergast are true," said the Secretary of the Treasury, "the man is a menace to society and should be in prison."

For a year Intelligence Unit special agents under the direction of Charles Berry prowled Kansas City, picking up leads and checking them out. One angle of interest was Pendergast's passion for gambling. Special Agent Rudolph H. Hartmann was told by reporter Harry T. Brundidge that the bets were tremendous. Pendergast was a special project for the reporter, and the Intelligence Unit had long before learned that information from a good newspaperman was worth its weight in indictments. Confirmation of the tip came on September 14, 1935, when a Chicago racing publication revealed the Boss had bet $600,000 in the last thirty days of the racing season in New York. What's more, said the paper, he had paid off his bets.

Irey asked his men in Chicago to check the information and soon was informed it was correct. He now reported to Morgenthau that the indictment of Pendergast was only a matter of time. Any man who could spend so much on horses just had to be evading the income tax laws unless he was frittering away an ancient family fortune. Pendergast had no ancient fortune to fritter away. He belonged to the new rich.

The source of Pendergast's gambling fund was, of course, the graft he collected routinely year in and year out, but occasionally he benefited by an extra bonanza such as the episode that became famous as the Second Missouri Compromise.

128

In 1922 the series of events that gave the Boss his opportunity began. The Missouri superintendent of insurance ordered a 10 percent reduction in fire insurance rates. Naturally, the insurance companies objected and carried their fight all the way to the United States Supreme Court, which, in 1928, upheld the superintendent. That should have ended the matter, but the insurance companies had sharp attorneys. Instead of accepting the 10 percent reduction, the companies boosted rates by more than 16 percent. This led to more litigation, of course, and the federal courts ordered that all money collected as a result of the rate increase should be impounded until the matter was settled. By May, 1935, it amounted to quite a bundle—$9,020,279. The stage was set for compromise when a special commissioner, Paul I. Barnett, was appointed to investigate and make recommendations. He recommended the insurance rates be boosted, but by how much he didn't say.

Pendergast's men in the Missouri legislature pushed through a compromise bill and presented it to Governor Park —the former judge who had been unable to comprehend that section of the state constitution which prohibited horse racing. As a matter of form, the state's attorney general, Roy McKittrick, was asked to approve the compromise's legality. McKittrick, although considered a Pendergast man, was appalled at the deal and said so. Finally, Governor Park agreed with him. After a telephone chat with the Boss, however, he changed his mind the same day and signed the bill into law.

The Second Missouri Compromise gave the insurance companies half the money in escrow—more than $4,500,000. Thirty percent, or about $2,700,000, was to pay the legal expenses of both parties. Since the state had used staff lawyers, the bulk of this slice went to the insurance companies' attorneys. The remaining 20 percent, $1,800,000, was to be distributed to the policyholders.

Even in Missouri, where people had to be shown, the deal created a stink. The legislature went through the motions of investigating and, of course, found nothing wrong. Yet some people remained unhappy, among them a new governor, Lloyd Stark, and United States Attorney Maurice M. Milligan, who had succeeded Vandeventer. Stark was a Pendergast man orig-

inally—anyone who wanted to get anywhere in Missouri politics had to be—but he proved, as Harry Truman did later,
that some politicians can put duty above personal loyalty. He
began by accompanying Milligan to Washington for a talk
with Elmer Irey.

Much of the conversation centered on Charles R. Street,
who had been named a trustee to take care of the attorney
fees. Street was already familiar to the Intelligence Unit. For
years he had practically controlled the fire insurance business
in Western states as a sort of czar. Most people assumed he
was the actual author of the compromise. Irey agreed to look
into Street's affairs. If, as was rumored, Pendergast received a
half-million-dollar payoff from the insurance companies, Street
would in all likelihood have been the payoff man. Meanwhile,
Stark and Milligan went back to Missouri to see what they could
do to harass the Boss.

An opportunity soon developed. The 1936 general election
was coming up. Pendergast wanted his state to make a good
showing, perhaps hoping to impress President Roosevelt and
by so doing ease the pressure from the Intelligence Unit. A
total of 425,000 Kansas City citizens—63 percent of the elig-
ible voters—registered for the election. A cynical reporter discovered that forty of them had been born on the same day, in
the same town, and had all come to Kansas City to live at the
same time. The suggestion that perhaps one individual had
signed the books forty times, giving the same background information but using different names, was ignored by the
authorities. On election day, Pendergast's First Ward managed
to cast 20,687 votes while having a population of only 19,923.
It was a great tribute to Lazia's successor, Charles Carrollo,
whose goon squad really got out the vote.

United States Attorney Milligan started a grand jury investigation and with help from the FBI proved, among other
things, that 18,000 of 240,000 votes examined had been altered. Pendergast fought back, allotting $100,000 as a defense
fund on behalf of the 278 election judges, precinct captains,
and clerks who were indicted. Everyone connected with the
prosecution was threatened—even ministers who preached
against evil in the specific rather than the abstract. Yet juries

convicted 63 defendants. Another 36 pleaded guilty, and 162 took the route of *nolo contendere*—no contest. Only 17 cases were nol-prossed—dropped.

It was a great victory for Milligan and for the citizens of Kansas City and Missouri. Although the Boss remained in control, it was now apparent he was not invincible. Citizens could testify against the machine and live to boast about it.

Governor Stark celebrated the victory by firing R. Emmet O'Malley as state superintendent of insurance. It was a bit like locking the stable door after the horse has escaped, but it did serve to illustrate Stark's growing independence of the political machine. Meanwhile, the Intelligence Unit discovered that Street, by means they described as various and complicated, had received $447,000 in late 1935 and early 1936 from insurance companies that had profited by the Second Missouri Compromise.

Other special agents discovered that by a strange coincidence, Boss Tom had paid off various notes totaling almost $447,000 in the same period. When the special agents put their heads together, they found that Street had withdrawn in cash the money he had received from the insurance companies, and Pendergast had paid off his notes in cash as well. Moreover, the sequence of withdrawal and payment was interesting. As surely as Street withdrew a certain sum, Pendergast within a short time would pay off a note in the amount Street had withdrawn. The conclusion was obvious. Proving it was another matter.

Street had not dealt entirely in cash, however. Checks of $10,-000 and $20,000 had been written to the credit of the City National Bank and Trust Company of Chicago. A special agent was assigned to check the records of the bank and see what had happened to the money. At first, the search proved fruitless. However, among the qualities required of special agents are listed "perseverance and imagination" and "self-confidence and reasonable aggressiveness"; the special agent possessed both. When the clerk assigned to help him was called away for a minute, the special agent flipped through a book containing carbon copies of telegrams sent by the bank. He found a telegram addressed to the First National Bank of St. Louis, advising that the Chicago bank was crediting the St. Louis bank with $10,000 and asking the St. Louis bank to pay that amount to A. L. McCormack on behalf of C. R. Street.

Greatly intrigued, the special agent persevered and ultimately found a letter covering the $20,000 transaction. Again the money went to McCormack.

This led to a probe of McCormack, a St. Louis insurance executive. He admitted receiving the money but explained it was given him by Street in return for a favor. The special agents then inquired about some $84,000 McCormack had spent in 1935 and 1936. The executive was unruffled—the money represented his life savings, he said. The special agents were also unruffled. They told McCormack that a check of his income since he earned his first dime proved that if he had spent no money for food, clothing, or rent over a sixteen-year period, he still would have had life savings of less than $55,000. McCormack shrugged.

Meanwhile, Milligan had impaneled a federal grand jury to probe the Second Missouri Compromise. McCormack was brought before it. Under oath, he swore he had lost the $10,-000 he had received from Street, one of the two checks, at the Fairmount racetrack in Illinois. Like Pendergast, he just couldn't pick a winner. Special Agent Hartmann got McCormack to admit he cashed the check on October 24, 1936, and then he dropped his bomb—the track had closed on October 10.

McCormack now faced a perjury rap and decided to sing. He described a meeting in Chicago on January 22, 1935, which he, Street, and Pendergast attended. At the session in the Palmer House, Street asked for help on behalf of the insurance company. "Make an offer," suggested the Boss. "Two hundred thousand dollars," offered Street. "Don't be silly," said Pendergast. "Half a million," said Street. "Okay," said Pendergast.

As it turned out, it wasn't okay. Two months passed, and nothing happened. Street told McCormack to offer the Boss $750,000, and this proved satisfactory. On May 9, 1935, McCormack delivered a $50,000 down payment to the Boss. Five days later the Second Missouri Compromise was ready for Governor Park's signature. McCormack continued to act as courier, bringing the loot from Chicago to Kansas City. On April 1, 1936, for example, he delivered $330,000 in one bundle. The Boss peeled off $80,000 and told McCormack to split it with Insurance Superintendent O'Malley. Six months later, after several bad days at the races, Pendergast needed cash to pay some hospital bills. Street happened to be a bit short too, and had to wait a few days. When he got the scratch together, he arranged to have the bank telegraph it to McCormack's bank in St. Louis. After all, the Boss didn't like to be kept waiting. It was this transaction which led the Intelligence Unit to McCormack.

Meanwhile, as McCormack sang, Pendergast began a war of nerves against the special agents investigating him. Telephone threats at home and office became routine. The special agents were tailed everywhere by members of Carrollo's goon squads. The right front wheel of a special agent's car suddenly flew off as he was driving to St. Louis, and the car crashed. A knife was tossed at another special agent as he questioned a gambler in a North Side joint. It narrowly missed. Another special agent was shot at as he walked down a dark street disguised, he thought, as a gambler. Even special agents in New York and Chicago were tailed and threatened by known gangsters who obviously were cooperating with the boys in Kansas City. Never had the link between crime and politics been so apparent.

In Washington, Secretary Morgenthau made sure President Roosevelt knew what was going on. Roosevelt, who loved a good detective story, found the truth even more interesting and encouraged Irey to continue. Thus, all of Pendergast's efforts to utilize his political leverage failed completely. Indeed, Irey became angry when he decided the rush to indict the Boss was premature and was unable to persuade Attorney General Frank Murphy to slow things down until the Intelligence Unit could complete other phases of its investigation. He asked for two more weeks but—according to Irey—Murphy replied: "I will not be a party to the obstruction of justice. We will indict Pendergast now."

Later Irey was to acknowledge that the premature indictment "probably saved Uncle the cost of feeding and boarding Boss Tom for a couple of extra years."

133

On April 7, 1939—Good Friday—Boss Pendergast was indicted for income tax evasion. So was O'Malley. The Boss was charged with a tax liability of $265,465 for 1935 and 1936. Irey estimated that if he had been given his additional two weeks, he could have added another half million to the total.

News of the indictment hit Missouri like an atomic bomb. The Kansas City *Star* used an eight-column headline for the first time since the United States had declared war on Germany in 1917. And immediately the Boss' empire started falling apart. Eight days after the indictment, Police Chief Otto Higgins resigned. City Manager Henry F. McElroy, who had appointed the chief five years earlier and announced he would clean up the police force, resigned a few days later. The Intelligence Unit was suddenly flooded with anonymous tips about McElroy, who went into seclusion and was reported to be trying to starve himself to death. According to Irey, the tips were fruitful. On September 14, 1939, subpoenas were issued for a grand jury investigation. Evidence in hand indicated the city manager had failed to pay taxes on at least $250,000. The day after the subpoenas were issued, McElroy died of a heart attack brought on by his prolonged fast.

State courts began investigating as well. Carrollo, Lazia's successor, got eight years; ex-Police Chief Higgins got two years; Public Works Director Matthew S. Murray got two years. Etc. etc.

Pendergast pleaded guilty to the tax evasion charge, as did O'Malley. The Boss was sentenced to fifteen months in prison and a $10,000 fine. An additional sentence of three years was suspended, and he was placed on probation for five years. O'Malley was sentenced to a year and a day and fined $5,000. He also was placed on probation for five years.

The seeming lightness of the sentences brought a storm of criticism against Judge Otis, who took the unusual step of writing a long memorandum of explanation and making it part of the court record. "Perhaps I should have yielded to passion and hatred and revenge," said the judge. "I am glad I did not yield."

The Boss was paroled after serving a year and a day. Five months before his period of probation expired, he died. News-

134

papers outlined his life and career in great detail. One quotation attributed to him seemed to sum up his outlook: "Politics isn't a part-time job. It's a business like anything else."

Meanwhile, Irey and the special agents of the Intelligence Unit had turned their attention to Atlantic City, New Jersey, where another boss had demonstrated just how profitable the business of politics could be when it is allied with organized crime. Not that any additional demonstration was really needed. Pendergast had already proved the point very nicely.

8

ON THE BOARDWALK

THE wedding was the social event of the
Atlantic City season. That it was completely unexpected did
not prevent 300 guests from crowding into the church while
3,000 well-wishers stood outside to cheer the bride and groom.
Best man was Walter G. Winnie, a leading criminal attorney.
The bride was attended by two former New York show girls.

Following the ceremony, a reception was held at the cottage
near the boardwalk where the couple had lived for six years
before deciding to get married. Champagne flowed so fast it
was sometimes difficult to distinguish between the popping of
corks and the popping of flashbulbs. Among the invited guests
were leading political figures, the elite of the sporting fraternity,
and the highest-priced prostitutes. A bittersweet flavor tinged
the affair.

Since the honeymoon had preceded the marriage, the groom
was free next day to go to Camden, New Jersey, and be sentenced to ten years in prison and a $20,000 fine. The bride, a
former chorus girl, vowed to visit her new husband in jail.
Tears flowed like the champagne at this mark of devotion. It
was August 1, 1941, and for Atlantic City an era had ended.

The luck of Enoch L. "Nucky" Johnson—the bridegroom— had run out after thirty years.

Atlantic City is located, logically enough, in Atlantic County, New Jersey, which borders the Atlantic Ocean somewhere southeast of Philadelphia. The town is on Absecon Island, a spit of land about eight miles long and one-half mile wide. During Prohibition days, the Big Seven in general and Longie Zwillman in particular landed much booze there—for reasons which will soon appear obvious.

The beaches and boardwalks of Atlantic City attracted visitors by the thousands from the crowded metropolitan areas of nearby states. They came for a touch of the sun, a breath of clean, salt air. Inevitably, the rackets followed, and just as inevitably, the racketeers soon were claiming the chicken preceded the egg. It is the old propaganda line, heard in resort areas such as Miami Beach, Hot Springs, Biloxi, Saratoga, and, most recently, Grand Bahama Island. If tomorrow some enterprising Arab discovers a wonderful oasis in the middle of the Sahara Desert whose waters cure cancer, a resort hotel complete with casino will soon be built, and within weeks the gamblers will claim credit for the flood of visitors brought in by jumbo jets.

Atlantic City during the rule of Nucky Johnson offered the numbers racket for the convenience of the waiters, maids, and assorted personnel who worked in the hotels. Casino gambling and horse parlors were available for the guests. Prostitutes were priced to oblige every economic class, with everything from the $2 whore to the $100 call girl available. From all these, Johnson took his cut. In addition, he had the usual, if less exotic, forms of graft supplied by crooked businessmen in the form of kickbacks and payoffs. Municipal employees made "political contributions" to keep their jobs.

The man who ruled over this miniature empire was a native. Of Scotch and Irish parentage, he was born in Galloway Township, Atlantic County, in 1883. His father, Smith Johnson, began as a produce farmer, but those were the days when the Irish were moving into politics, so the older Johnson quit the farm to become sheriff and, eventually, a Republican leader of the county. As such he was able to serve as sheriff four times.

Since the local law prohibited consecutive tenures, he alternated with a son, Alfred. In 1908, Nucky demanded equal rights and was permitted to become sheriff at the age of twenty-five. He had prepared himself for the post by working as a clerk in a drugstore and serving four years as undersheriff. Among the duties of the sheriff was supervision of the drawing of all petit and grand juries in the county. As the history of organized crime shows, nothing is more essential to continuing crime and corruption than controlled grand juries.

Nucky proved to be the political genius of the Johnson family and very quickly took over the county leadership of the Republican Party from his father and other rivals. Brother Alfred continued to serve as sheriff, but Nucky was now boss. He was aided, ironically, by an abortive reform effort on the part of Governor Woodrow Wilson. Reform movements that fail, or fall short of a complete sweep, often do more harm than good by creating a mood of apathy or resignation among the citizens and causing the crooks to close ranks in self-defense. In 1911, Governor Wilson—his eye on the White House—decided Atlantic County was a blot on his escutcheon and should be cleaned up. He appointed a special supreme court justice to hear cases there and ordered State Attorney General Edmund Wilson to conduct a grand jury investigation. Johnson's grand jury panel failed him, for once, and the jury indicted Johnson, a few of his allies, and his chief rival, Louis Kuehnle. The trial juries displayed a degree of discrimination. Kuehnle was convicted and sent to prison on a charge of illegally receiving county contracts, but Nucky was acquitted on charges of illegally removing registration books and election returns. Governor Wilson, having made a gesture, went on to become President, and Nucky became the undisputed Republican boss of Atlantic County.

Shortly after Nucky turned the sheriff's office back to the family, he was elected county treasurer, a title he was to keep for many years. To anyone's knowledge, he never did any work—leaving the duties of the office to underpaid underlings —but he received $6,000 a year and turned the office into his political headquarters. By 1916 he had sufficiently demonstrated his abilities to be named campaign manager for the

Republican nominee for governor, Walter E. Edge. Upon election, Edge rewarded Nucky by appointing him clerk of the State Supreme Court for a five-year term. The salary was also $6,000 a year, and Nucky saw no conflict with his county job. He accepted both salaries and let others do the work.

By 1920 he was one of a triumvirate that controlled the Republican Party in New Jersey. He shared power with David Baird, the boss of Camden County, and Morgan Lawson, who ruled the northern part of the state. In the years that followed, his approval was necessary before anyone could be appointed to a state or federal office in New Jersey. Those were the Republican years nationally, and neither President Harding, Coolidge, nor Hoover saw any point in disturbing the status quo in New Jersey. A spot of trouble did develop in 1926, when Johnson spent a fortune to elect Lawson as governor and Hamilton F. Kean as United States Senator. An investigation was officially conducted by the Senate, but no proof of corruption was reported. Johnson emerged stronger than ever.

As previously noted, bootleggers found Atlantic County a convenient spot to land shiploads of liquor from Canada, the Bahamas, and England. Nucky was in a position to promise protection from local and state authorities—such protection even including armed guards for liquor convoys which otherwise might have been hijacked by Legs Diamond or some other "outlaw." As a result, Johnson established good relations with the future leaders of the syndicate, and Atlantic City became a favorite spot for hoods who found it necessary to hide out for a while. It ranked along with Hot Springs, Arkansas, and Newport, Kentucky, as a "Little Mexico" where one was safe as soon as he crossed the county line. As a result, organized crime became so powerful in the area that not even the fall of Nucky Johnson could erase its influence. Many gangsters in New Jersey today put their roots down during Nucky's long reign.

A few figures help explain Johnson's power. Atlantic City contained more than half the population of Atlantic County and was thus able to dominate county politics. Almost half the population of Atlantic City were Negroes, who, in those days, were easily controlled. They voted as a block for Nucky's men, and in return he exploited them through the numbers racket.

When to the Negroes were added the large number of gamblers, prostitutes, and nightclub employees, plus city employees and their families, it can be seen how Johnson controlled the city. In every ward and township he maintained Enoch L. Johnson Booster Clubs to make sure everyone understood that Johnson the man, rather than Johnson the Republican leader, was boss. As with Democrats Long and Pendergast, the party label was largely meaningless on the local level —the party served the man rather than the man the party. Americans who look back wistfully on "the good old days" conveniently forget that in the brave old world they talk about, many cities and several states were controlled by virtual dictators.

So complete was Johnson's power he was able to invite the leaders of the Mafia to a convention in Atlantic City in 1929 and allow a picture to be published of him and Al Capone strolling the boardwalk. It was on Al's return from the convention that he was picked up for carrying a gun in Philadelphia and given a year's "rest" in jail while his thugs in Chicago knocked off some of the rivals who were threatening to kill the Big Fellow. Another friend was Moses L. Annenberg, boss of the bookie wire service and one of the richest men in crime. Moses and Nucky liked to make the nightclubs together with the pick of the town's chorus girls.

A big man physically, Nucky had appetites to match his size. Widowed at age thirty, he had a succession of mistresses before settling down in 1935 with Flossie Osbeck. They lived openly in a Spanish-type stucco bungalow near the boardwalk but maintained a suite in the Ritz Carlton Hotel. For Flossie's convenience, Nucky also rented an apartment in New York at 128 Central Park South. His total rent for the three places amounted to about $7,200 a year—big money in those Depression years. His taste in food ran to lobster, caviar, and three-inch steaks. Eighteeen-year-old brandy and the best champagne made his liquor bills higher than his food costs. Four 16-cylinder Cadillacs provided transportation, but he employed only two regular chauffeurs. Louis Kassel, a former wrestler, served as bodyguard and valet. Needless to say, Nucky wore only the best.

Breakfast was usually served at 4 P.M. After sleeping all day, Johnson was able to dispose of a dozen fried eggs, from four to six chops, a ham steak, six slices of buttered toast, and as many as eight cups of coffee. After so fortifying himself, he was prepared to transact business. When his lieutenants had finished reporting at about 8 P.M., it was time to get dressed and go out on the town. In the years before settling down with Flossie, he had prowled the nightclubs looking for someone to sleep with. The lucky girls—at least they considered themselves lucky to catch his fancy—were usually rewarded with furs, diamonds, or new cars. After settling down with Flossie, he spent much of his night hours in casinos—after taking the precaution to make sure the wheels were rigged in his favor. On his frequent visits to New York, he left a trail of $100 tips.

Thinking himself invincible, he made no effort to conceal either his wealth or his power. Surrounded as he was by yesmen, he seemed oblivious to the changing times. That the Republicans no longer controlled the White House or Congress worried him not a bit. Twice investigations had been made into his income, in 1928 and 1934, and each time his empire had stood firm. Although additional taxes were levied in both instances, no proof of criminal fraud could be obtained. These victories only increased his confidence. He considered himself above and beyond the law.

In 1936, however, Secretary of the Treasury Morgenthau called Elmer Irey to his office and bluntly demanded: "What goes with that fellow Nucky Johnson?"

Irey was forced to explain that Nucky always filed income tax returns and that on them he always included an item called "Other Commissions." The sums listed under that item ranged from $20,000 to $60,000. It was easy enough to prove Nucky spent more than his official salary, but even if a frightened gambler or madam admitted paying Nucky graft, his attorneys could insist the money was included in the "Commissions." To prove graft payments larger than the amount listed for commissions, it would be necessary to provoke a mass revolt of the underworld against the Boss. In reality, getting a single punk to squeal was almost impossible. Prison was preferable to Johnson's displeasure.

141

Morgenthau was not overly impressed by Irey's explanation. He stared awhile at the October leaves of tree-studded Washington and then ordered the Intelligence chief to make a complete and thorough probe of Atlantic City. He had been receiving too many complaints about Johnson, he said, and he wanted the allegations proved or disproved.

Irey, already deeply committed in Louisiana and Missouri, to say nothing of 100 other probes long and small, accepted the assignment without grumbling. Special Agent William E. Frank of the New York office was given the task of making an undercover probe. He selected Special Agent Edward A. Hill to assist. On November 5, 1936, they arrived in Atlantic City. Five years were to pass before the assignment was completed.

The special agents rented a furnished apartment and began making the rounds of the joints. Everything was wide open, and no elaborate cover story was needed. In Nucky's town it was considered bad taste to question strangers.

Special Agent Leo Marshall joined the duo. The men, dressed as cheap gamblers, floated around the small city making mental notes of everything. Bookie joints were located on the principal streets. Numbers were sold in almost every store throughout the town. Brothels were largely located in one red-light district, but girls were everywhere available. By making a few bets, by casual conversation with friendly hoods, by observing the police, the experienced men were able to estimate not only the size of the operation as far as physical numbers was concerned, but also the financial handle.

The special agents located twenty-five bookie joints and casinos. They estimated that as many as 700 persons were employed and placed the gross receipts at $8,000,000 annually. There were eight brothels, with the number of girls ranging from 100 to 300 depending on how many conventions were in town. The take was placed at $500,000. Identified were nine numbers banks, employing as many as 1,000 persons and grossing $1,500,000.

That the police knew all about the operation was apparent. When necessary, the cops would lend a hand should a sucker take umbrage at being shorn. Yet no one even assumed the cops were receiving graft. The rackets paid to operate, yes, but the money went directly to the Boss—Nucky Johnson. The police didn't complain—they owed their soft jobs to Nucky. Every member of the force had been approved by Johnson before his appointment, and every promotion required his consent. The police chief was Nucky's close friend, and the sheriff was his brother. Judges, prosecutors, clerks—all owed their jobs to the Boss. It was a closed shop tighter than any achieved by a union.

While the special agents worked undercover, Revenue Agent Walter Doxon, Jr., was assembling the income tax returns of every gambler, prostitute, or other punk whose identity had been discovered. Having established to their satisfaction the approximate incomes of these characters, the special agents needed only a glance to see the amounts reported on the returns were far short. It seemed logical that if income tax evasion charges could be made against some of the small fry, it might be possible to persuade them to talk about Johnson.

A look at city and county contracts was in order as well. During the Depression there had been little building of a civic nature. Yet the special agents picked up leads indicating the Boss got most of the garbage disposal business. Even in a depression, there is garbage to spare. Some road building had taken place in the county, and word was Johnson got his cut. Allegedly he had an interest in the construction company which got the contract for the only sizable project built from 1930 to 1936 —the $2,400,000 railroad terminal station in Atlantic City.

Early in April, 1937, Frank reported to Irey that local rackets in Atlantic City were grossing $10,000,000 a year and paying protection totaling $5,700 a week. This added up to just under $300,000 a year, and all of it, said Frank, was going to Johnson.

Even Irey was incredulous. "All of it?" he asked.

"Every dime," said Frank.

Irey chewed his dead cigar. "He's not paying taxes on that kind of money."

Frank smiled happily. "I know he isn't, Chief."

But knowledge is not proof. Gangsters, all too well aware of that important rule of law which holds a man innocent until proved guilty in a court, have even been known to convince themselves that until proved guilty of violating the law, they

143

are doing no wrong. (Such reasoning leads to the conclusion that the only real crime is in getting caught, which may help explain why many gangsters consider themselves deeply religious men who may violate "man's law" but do not violate what they call "God's law.")

Nucky Johnson, many times investigated but never found guilty of anything, learned in April, 1937, that a new probe was beginning. The news didn't bother him. He was confident the special agents would find no evidence linking him to graft. And until they did, well, he was innocent of any wrongdoing. So on with the carnival.

Aiding and abetting Nucky was the financial condition of Atlantic City. The Depression had hit hard in a tourist area. Ten of the fourteen banks operating in the town in 1929 had closed their doors, and two more were to shut down before the probe ended. Few of the gamblers, prostitutes, and political hacks had bank accounts; their cash was stashed away in "little tin boxes" and private safes. Almost all dealings were in cash, and few kept books. There was respect for order—as maintained by the Boss—but none for law.

Well aware of the problems, the small task force of six men and a secretary, Helen R. Nolan, settled down in the only office space they could find in Atlantic City—a room 10 feet by 17 feet—in the Post Office Building. Four areas were chosen for study: city and county contract graft; the prostitution racket; the numbers racket; the bookie and casino racket.

News of the investigation aroused no great interest among the citizens. Apathy and fear combined to make the community completely unresponsive. No newspaper, no honest businessman, no civic leader came forth to volunteer information. Most of them, in fact, were frightened at the thought of being interviewed. Atlantic City's cops kept a close check on the special agents, noting everywhere they went and everyone they talked to. If the Feds tried to tail Johnson, they could be sure that they, in turn, were being followed by city or county detectives. When a potential witness was served a commissioner's summons and put under oath, he lied glibly and freely. Later, when some cases came to trial, witnesses and jurors alike were

144

offered threats or bribes. Such tactics had worked for years in state courts; there seemed no reason to assume they wouldn't work in federal court as well.

If today all this sounds bizarre and outdated, very similar things happened twenty-four years later during the cleanup of Newport, Kentucky. They happened in South Florida in 1965-66 during a reform drive there, and they are happening today.

The first target of the probe were road-building contractors, of which there was only one—Morrell B. Tomlin. The contractor's father, John B. Tomlin, was an old crony of Nucky's and chairman of the Board of Freeholders' Road Committee.

Morrell Tomlin kept books, of a sort. They were so misleading the investigators decided to work from his bank accounts, which, unhappily, were in two of the closed banks. During the hot months of June and July, while citizens played on the beaches, the investigators labored in the hot basements of the banks trying to put the records in order. When assembled at last, they showed total deposits from 1920 to 1935 of $1,654,-590. Yet young Tomlin had never filed an income tax return.

Much of the profits had been passed to the father, the county freeholder. His bank accounts for the years 1930 through 1932 showed total deposits of $561,560. Unlike his son, he had filed returns, but only on nominal amounts. It seemed obvious a case could be made against father and son, but it was a possible link to Nucky the investigators were seeking. How much of the loot had he received? None, said the Tomlins, unmoved by threats of prosecution. It was decided to test their loyalty. Prosecution was recommended, and the cases were turned over to the Justice Department. The lawyers there offered the Tomlins a hearing. Father and son appeared at the hearing in worn, threadbare suits and pleaded complete poverty. They had lost everything when the banks closed, they said.

The appeal seemed to be working until the special agents presented a newspaper photograph made only a few days before. The pix showed John Tomlin attired in neat and natty evening clothes while attending a Republican Party banquet. For good measure, they presented proof that Tomlin owned more than thirty pieces of property, as well as $30,000 worth of securities.

In March, 1938, the Tomlins were indicted for tax evasion. Still they refused to talk.

Next to feel the heat was the garbage racket. Tax cases were easily made against three owners of the Charles L. Bader Company. This time a payment to Johnson couldn't be denied; the initials E. L. J. were found on the check stubs which represented bank withdrawals. However, the payments amounted only to $10,000—a sum more than covered under the "Other Commissions" item on Nucky's returns. The garbage men were also indicted in March. If more evidence was needed, the Chancery Court of New Jersey had it ready. The boys had argued over the profits once and gone to court. An accounting had been made which, among other things, made graft payments of $10,000 to Johnson in 1933 and again in 1934 part of the court record. Naturally, none of the honorable members of the court or the bar had seen fit to mention it to Internal Revenue; they all were friends of Nucky.

An investigation of the railroad terminal was more complicated and also more productive. Revenue Agent Doxon discovered that in the year the terminal was completed, 1935, the contracting company had paid a $60,000 "legal fee" to Common Pleas Judge Joseph A. Corio. The judge had cashed the company's check but had failed to deposit the money to his account. Needless to say, he was a good friend of the Boss.

An examination of Corio's returns for 1935 revealed he had reported gross revenue of only $20,800. This seemed to suggest he had handed on $40,000 of the "commission" to someone else. The judge consented to be interviewed, and he doffed his judicial robes for the session in his chambers. Reason and calm judgment were his mood as the questions began. He had spent $40,000 for business expenses and therefore had seen no need to clutter up his return by listing the money. When asked for proof of the "expenses," he lost his cool. The special agents were exceeding their authority, said the judge, and he was going "to do something" about their impudence.

This reaction only intrigued the men of the Intelligence Unit. They visited his bank and discovered it was the only one in Atlantic City to boast a recordak machine for photographing all checks deposited or withdrawn. A long look at thousands

146

of checks was necessary, but then the special agents could prove Corio not only had not spent any of the $40,000 for anything but also had deliberately made a false statement in respect to some $9,000 he had claimed as court costs and fees. The money had actually been used to pay personal expenses.

Corio suddenly lost his dignity when confronted with the facts. He wanted to settle the matter "and get it off my mind." Just name the amount he owed and he would pay it. The special agents were relentless—Corio had to tell what became of the $40,000 first. The judge just couldn't remember. The special agents wrote up the case and recommended prosecution.

Suddenly Nucky Johnson was worried. Expensive Washington attorneys were hired, and hearings in the Justice Department were obtained. An offer in compromise was made. Acting Attorney General Robert H. Jackson received an appeal. Political pressure was applied to the United States Attorney for the District of New Jersey. Everything failed. On May 10, 1938, Corio was indicted. The judge promptly had a nervous breakdown and entered a sanatorium.

Sensing an opportunity, the Intelligence Unit pressed for a Corio trial ahead of others who had been indicted. January 30, 1939, was set as the trial date. His back to the wall, Corio dropped the counsel supplied by Johnson and retained William E. Leahy of Washington. As the trial date neared, Leahy stated he had told his client to tell the truth.

The long-sought breakthrough had come at last.

The judge's statement confirmed that Nucky had used his influence to win the contract for his friends A. P. Miller, Inc. Johnson was to get three-fifths of the net profit after taxes had been paid, and Corio was to share the remainder with Miller. The plans called for the judge to receive $60,000 as a "legal fee." He was supposed to use $13,200 for taxes, leaving $46,800 to be split. Nucky got $28,000 in cash, and Miller and Corio got $9,400 each. The deal saved Miller and his corporation some $25,000 in taxes.

Instead of paying taxes on the $60,000, Corio pocketed the $13,200 as extra profit and took a chance no one would check his returns. Had he paid taxes, the scheme would have been almost foolproof. Even so, Corio's statement got him off the

147

hook as far as the tax evasion indictment was concerned. He had correctly stated his income, although it was now necessary to use different figures to total it up. Neither was there a tax evasion case against Nucky; he had reported a net loss of $56,-000 on his 1935 return. It was possible, however, to indict Johnson, Corio, Miller, and company accountant Japhet Garwood on a charge of conspiracy to evade the Miller corporation's 1935 taxes.

On March 11, 1939, the indictments were returned. They were immediately the subject of much conversation, but to the disappointment of the special agents, no one seemed greatly alarmed. The Boss had been indicted before and had beaten the rap. He would do it again.

The estimate of the situation seemed confirmed when the Justice Department dropped indictments against a trio involved in the prostitution racket. The indictments were one result of a sweeping raid by FBI special agents on the brothels of the city which came just as the Intelligence Unit began its probe and was apparently designed to steal their thunder. A lot of madams, prostitutes, and pimps were rounded up and charged with violations of the Mann Act—the law prohibiting the transportation of women across state lines for immoral purposes. Some of the women fingered Undersheriff Raymond R. Born as the dues collector and listed Nucky's chauffeur, Kassel, and a private eye named Leo Levy as the men who gave them permission to operate. When indictments against the three were dismissed shortly after Nucky's indictment, everyone nodded wisely and said, "I told you so." Some madams and pimps were still in trouble, but they had faith in Nucky, and in any case, they were expendable. As Miami madam Bessie Winkle remarked a quarter century later, there were more girls available than beds.

Special Agent Bill Frank decided to put more pressure on the women. By checking with doctors—the prostitutes were required to have weekly medical checkups—it was possible to determine the number of prostitutes. He then checked local laundry records and estimated the number of towels used each week by the brothels. Ordinarily, one towel per "John" was used, so it was possible to estimate the number of customers.

148

Since the price paid was known, and madam and prostitute split it fifty-fifty, it was easy for Frank to estimate just how much the girls had made in a given year.

The accurate information shook the madams, but all refused to talk. A number hurried down and paid back taxes. Seven who didn't were indicted for tax evasion. Still no one squealed on Nucky.

Patiently, the special agents tried the bookies. They discovered that in 1935, Nucky had pulled a fast one. Using a New York newspaper exposé of gambling as an excuse, he closed down the books for four months. Meanwhile, he made a deal with his friend Moe Annenberg, who controlled the wire service without which no bookie could operate. Sam Camarota, a Nucky stooge, was made sole agent for Nationwide News Service, as Moe's outfit was known, and he passed the word that only twenty-five "franchises" would be permitted in Atlantic City. The price would be $200 a week per franchise (a hike of from 100 to 800 percent, depending on volume), of which $40 went to Nationwide and $160 to Nucky. Each Monday, Camarota made the rounds collecting, usually tailed by a special agent, and ended at Johnson's cottage, where he left $4,000.

Some of the bookies frozen out by the coup were angry enough to talk—about other bookies. It became possible to estimate the income of most of the active ones. Polite notes inviting each to come in and talk about delinquent taxes were mailed out. The boys came in, paid up, and, like the girls, refused to incriminate Nucky. One man, quaintly known as Willie Wallpaper, admitted that he paid $140 weekly for "ice," the underworld argot for graft, but he claimed he didn't know who got it. Willie and several other gamblers were indicted on February 16, 1939, but the wall of silence remained unbroken.

The numbers racket was the final chance. It was played in Atlantic City much as it is played everywhere else except in Florida, where two-digit numbers were—and are today—used. While there were nine banks, or numbers houses, all paid the same odds, the same commissions, and used the same source for the winning number. The average player is a superstitious cat, using dream books for inspiration and patronizing one house over another for reasons peculiarly his own. In any case, he likes to feel he has a choice. Even when, as in Atlantic City, the racket is controlled by one man, it is usually divided into several operations to give an impression of competition and the sucker a "choice."

Again an accurate estimate was made of income, and the twenty-five "bankers" were questioned. All stood firm, refusing to squeal on Nucky. Fourteen were indicted for tax evasion. Still no squealers.

So far, of course, there had been many indictments, but no trials. Possibly, if some convictions were obtained, the boys and girls might lose a little of their faith in the Boss. Special Agent Frank and his team recommended a special prosecutor be appointed from outside New Jersey, as had been done in Louisiana. The job went to Joseph W. Burns, and he was effective. Trials of the small fry began, and conviction after conviction were obtained. The good citizens of Atlantic City were astonished—Nucky's boys were going to prison like ordinary crooks. It was a good beginning, and hopes were high; but the judge's wife became ill, and court recessed. Nucky sent word that paroles were near, and the citizens relaxed.

When the trials resumed, there were several more victories and one important defeat. Numbers banker Leroy Williams was acquitted. He credited the hexes his attorney put on the jury, rather than the attorney's legal ability, and neglected to pay the attorney his fee. This annoyed the attorney, Isaac Nutter, and he decided to help the Intelligence Unit with information, not hexes. His aid resulted in fourteen perjury indictments against numbers racketeers who had denied under oath the existence of a syndicate. The case looked good, but the trial ended in a hung jury. A second trial brought a verdict of acquittal. Atlantic City citizens laughed out loud. The Boss was invincible, and this proved it.

With Nutter assisting, an investigation revealed the first jury had been fixed. In the second trial no fix was necessary because one of the jurors was a bosom pal of two defense attorneys and managed to convince the jury that a decision, one way or the other, was wanted by the government. Since he insisted on acquittal, the other jurors were forced to agree.

Now the Intelligence Unit had a new weapon, and some of the

numbers men showed signs of cracking. On May 1, 1941, a new series of trials began. The last one on the list was the rather weak conspiracy case involving Corio, Miller, and Nucky. This time the jury wasn't fixed or misled, and guilty verdicts began coming faster and faster. Soon the boys began pleading guilty, hoping for a lighter sentence.

Meanwhile, a federal grand jury returned a new indictment, charging Johnson with collecting $46,000 in 1935 and $62,400 in 1936 and again in 1937. All the money had come from the numbers racket. For those years, under "Other Commissions," Nucky had listed only $23,000, $30,000, and $28,000. Ordinarily, it would have been enough, but the numbers boys had finally buckled and talked.

The trial of Johnson on the second indictment began on July 14, 1941, almost five years after Frank and Hill arrived in Atlantic City to see if the complaints received by Morgenthau had any substance. In the interim, the Intelligence Unit had secured the conviction of four contractors, twelve numbers bankers, two bookies, and a pimp for tax evasion; six numbers men, a bookie, two pimps, and two madams for perjury; and fourteen persons for jury tampering.

Nucky's attorneys fought hard. As character witnesses they produced a former governor and a former Senator. Nucky, however, left little doubt in anyone's mind when he was asked: "Do you consider the numbers game illegal?"

"Yes," said the Boss, "if you get caught."

Nucky was caught. It took the jury only five hours to consider the complicated case and find him guilty. It was then he decided to make an honest woman out of Flossie Osbeck.

It would be nice to add that Nucky's sentence to ten years in prison and a $20,000 fine convinced everyone in Atlantic City that crime doesn't pay. It would be nice—but not accurate.

Corruption is an illness of the body politic. The virus remains in the bloodstream long after the original source of the infection is removed. The Intelligence Unit put the Boss in prison and collected $1,000,000 in taxes and penalties, but the rest was up to the patient.

Nucky died in 1968 as this book was being written. The evil he did lives on in Atlantic City.

9

MOE'S LITTLE MISTAKE

On May 11, 1936, Moses L. Annenberg decided his son-in-law was becoming too greedy. Moe had nothing against greed personally. It was all right to make some extra fast bucks, but not at the risk of endangering the regular supply. In a letter to the son-in-law, Stanley Kahn, he made this point:

> We simply cannot have everything. Mussolini, when he started out to grab Ethiopia, had to very carefully consider what he might be plunging into but Mussolini had nothing to risk because Italy was on the bum and those who might have opposed his ambitions had by far and away much more to risk than Mussolini. Our position is similar to that of the English nation. We in the racing field own three-quarters of the globe and manage the balance. In other words, the few little nations that are left have to pay us tribute to continue. Now isn't that the most beautiful and most satisfactory position to be in which ought to satisfy even me?
>
> Have you ever stopped to figure our earnings and how that might be upset by a little mistake such as we are dis-

cussing? For example, we have a number of enemies with unusual ability that are eager for a chance to get even with us and upset the monopoly, who would be willing to work for almost nothing just for revenge, and who would contribute their talents more enthusiastically than our own people just for a chance to upset our apple cart?

These two paragraphs of fatherly advice reveal several things about Moe Annenberg: his fifth-grade education, his ego, and his realism. They also reveal a certain gift of prophecy. It was a "little mistake" that upset his monopoly and brought his empire tumbling. The "enemy" that took advantage of it was, however, the Intelligence Unit, which had the quaint notion that Annenberg should pay his fair share of taxes.

Moe Annenberg was for the bookies of America what Arnold Rothstein was for rum-runners and narcotics peddlers—the man who put the racket on a businesslike basis. Organized crime owes as much to Annenberg as it does to Meyer Lansky who put off-the-top skimming from casinos on a routine basis. The boast that equated Annenberg's organization with the British Empire was not an empty one.* Not only did he provide every bookie in the nation with essential data, but he also built a legitimate publishing business to protect it by using newspapers to influence elections. On October 6, 1938, United States Senator Joseph F. Guffey of Pennsylvania charged the following in a radio broadcast:

"In all the years that I have fought against the Republican misrule, it never entered my mind that the day would come when I would be obliged to attack the leadership of the Republican Party in Pennsylvania on the ground that it was allied with organized crime, that it was controlled by an associate of underworld figures, that it was degenerating into an instrument for the protection of gambling.

"Yet that is the situation now facing the Commonwealth of Pennsylvania. The once-great Republican Party today has

---

* Ironically, thirty-three years later, in 1969, Moe Annenberg's son, Walter Annenberg, was to be appointed by President Richard Nixon U.S. Ambassador to England.

sunk to the blackest of all depths, to the deepest pit of moral degradation, under the leadership of a man who is kingpin of illegal pool room gambling from coast to coast, a man who brings to the Republican Party the methods, the tactics, and the morality of the underworld.

"That man is Moses L. Annenberg.

"Moe Annenberg has a nationwide monopoly on race track wire services. His income from this source alone is conservatively estimated in excess of six million dollars a year. With his vast wealth, and with his newspaper, the Philadelphia *Inquirer* which he bought for fifteen million dollars cold cash, it was an easy matter for Moe Annenberg to seize control of the Republican organization from its aging and shattered leaders who were demoralized by defeat after defeat at the hands of New Deal candidates. He took the Grand Old Party by default.

"It was Moe Annenberg, and no one else, who handpicked Arthur James as candidate for governor. . . . This is the man who has openly boasted that after he has seized political control of Pennsylvania he will dominate the Republican National Convention in 1940 and thus name the next President of the United States. . . ."

While Senator Guffey was undoubtedly influenced by partisan political influences, it is unlikely that he overestimated Annenberg's power or ambition. Indeed, the Intelligence Unit found it was almost always necessary to underestimate the man. Elmer Irey stated bluntly "that neither he, his heirs and assigns, nor the United States Government ever knew exactly how much he was worth."

If it was difficult to tell how high Moe climbed, it was easy to determine how low he started. Annenberg was born in East Prussia in 1877. His father, Tobias Annenberg, came to Chicago in 1882 and found work as a peddler. Two years later he sent for his wife and seven children and found them a home in a tenement on South State Street. Eventually, Tobias operated a junkyard on South Dearborn Street. Moe, who was almost always hungry, quit school at the age of twelve and worked at a variety of jobs. He saved his nickels in the best Horatio Alger tradition, and like Alger's heroes, he was "rough and ready." At the age of eighteen, his talents brought him a job as a subscription solicitor for a Chicago newspaper, and he was on his way. Nine years later he was circulation manager for the Chicago *Examiner,* one of William Randolph Hearst's many newspapers.

"Yellow journalism" is in disrepute today, yet it was but a by-product of the bitter circulation wars waged by newspaper giants who today are considered respectable. The wars were literally what the name implies, at least on the street level. Reporters might compete as gentlemen for scoops and editors blast one another in high-flown language; but on the streets of America hired goons battled with iron pipes, brass knuckles, and steel knives for choice locations from which papers could be sold for three cents each. Many of the gangsters who became rich during Prohibition owed their success to the training in violence they received working for newspaper "circulators" such as Annenberg and Mickey McBride.

A lean and still-hungry young man, Annenberg proved his ability to control men and break heads. He did such a good job in Chicago he shifted in 1907 to Milwaukee, where Hearst was fighting two competitors. So well did Moe do his job it was possible for Arthur Brisbane, a top Hearst executive, to buy up the competition and create the *Wisconsin News.* Annenberg was appointed publisher and general manager.

Never a man to be content with one enterprise, Annenberg had begun the development of a newspaper and magazine distribution business during the years in Milwaukee. He branched out into real estate and other businesses and was approaching millionaire status by the time he was appointed circulation manager of all Hearst newspapers and magazines in the country. In 1920 he set up headquarters in New York, where, just to keep busy, he also served as publisher of the Hearst-owned *Daily Mirror.*

In 1922 a new opportunity presented itself. The *Daily Racing Form,* the Bible of horseplayers everywhere, was up for sale. Moe and three friends bought it, and Annenberg was at last in the field where he could make uncounted millions. A little later he got control of the *Morning Telegram,* a New York daily devoted to theatrical and sporting news. By 1926 his private empire had grown so large he was forced to quit the

Hearst organization. With the addition of the *American Racing Record,* which Moe and friends formed in Cincinnati, his control over the material used by horseplayers as guides to betting was complete. Or rather, it would be if he could get rid of his partners. This feat was achieved in an unusual way. On November 17, 1932, a federal grand jury indicted Annenberg, his son, Walter, five Annenberg corporations, and six associates, including the two he wanted to be rid of—Huey E. Murray and Joseph D. Bannon. The charge was sending obscene literature—one of Annenberg's magazines—through the mail. Murray and Bannon were greatly embarrassed by the indictment and filed suit against Annenberg. Meanwhile, four individuals and one of the corporations entered guilty pleas, were fined, and the remaining cases were dismissed. The Annenbergs, Murray, and Bannon were among those whose cases were dropped. Upshot of the affair was the withdrawal of the still-angry partners. Annenberg paid them a total of $2,250,-000, and now in fact, was boss.

Now Moe turned to another phase of the betting business —the wire service. The suckers could make their choices as self-styled experts, but the bookies needed accurate information in order to fix odds before the races and quick data on the outcome of the races. A few scattered wire services existed, the largest of which was Mont Tennes' General News Bureau in Chicago. Moe had taken the first step in 1927 by buying 48 of the 100 shares of General News. John Lynch, a Chicago gambler, decided Moe had a good thing started, so in 1929 he bought 40 shares. The remaining 10 shares were purchased by nephews of Tennes and their wives. Moe immediately began to muscle in on the other stockholders. He formed the Universal Publishing Company to print wall sheets, those huge posters listing all upcoming races which once covered the walls of all respectable bookie joints. As the races were run, clerks posted the winners and the final odds paid for the convenience of the assembled suckers. General News had previously been the chief supplier of wall sheets, and some of the stockholders resented the loss of business.

Annenberg had just begun, however. On August 27, 1934, the Nationwide News Service was incorporated in Chicago. Completely controlled by Annenberg, it was obviously designed to compete with General News, which was managed by Annenberg. Lynch and the nephews of Tennes considered this a slight conflict of interest. Their worst fears were borne out in the next two years of operations. In 1934, General News made a profit of $1,435,281—up from the previous year, but not by much—while the new Nationwide ended up $3,788 in the hole. In 1935, however, the situation reversed itself. General News lost $45,634, while Nationwide made $1,119,085. Even more amusing was the fact that the Cecelia Company, the firm used by Annenberg to hold stock in General News, claimed a loss of $580,788 for the year 1936 on the ground that its stock had become worthless because of the competition from Naionwide News.

Moe had proved he could make it, coming and going.

Lynch and associates angrily filed suit. Moe had a simple defense: He was engaged in an unlawful business, and the court had no jurisdiction in the matter. A Chicago newspaper decided the case was interesting and began to print front-page stories. This upset many people, including the Chicago Syndicate consisting of such ex-Capone lieutenants as Frank Nitti, Tony Accardo, Murray "the Camel" Humphreys, and the like. Publicity was bad for the gambling business in general. Stories about the huge profits of the wire services would inevitably cause people to wonder about the profits of the bookies who bought the service. The only question for the syndicate to decide was which individual it wanted in charge of the wire service—Lynch or Annenberg.

A postponement was secured in the suit to permit Annenberg to buy out the other stockholders. Lynch didn't want to sell at first, but abruptly he caved in and accepted the low price of $15 per share for his stock. Thus, for $750,000, Annenberg gained complete control of a company which had made an annual profit of almost $1,500,000.

Why did Lynch change his mind? An answer came later from James M. Ragen who moved from the job of vice-president of General News to become general manager of Nationwide. Ragen noted, in an affidavit in 1946, that on the day Lynch surrendered, he delivered $100,000 in cash to Nitti for services rendered. Obviously, the Chicago boys had picked Annenberg and had been well paid to persuade Lynch to take what he could get and get out.

Now Moe had his monopoly on both phases of the business of supplying bookies. Leased wires carried race results to more than 15,000 customers, who paid Moe $20,000,000 in a three-year period alone. What's more, Annenberg was in a position to make deals with friends such as Nucky Johnson in Atlantic City which increased his profits, his prestige, and his political power. Nationwide grew steadily, gobbling up the small outfits that tried to compete and opening new territories as bookie operations expanded around the country. Illegal betting became larger and larger, corrupting more and more cops, city officials, and state politicians in the process. In Louisville, Kentucky, illegal bookie joints became so many and obvious, for example, police persuaded the operators to move upstairs so passing citizens wouldn't notice them. Even so, it was possible to walk for blocks in some sections of town and hear the calling of every race at a distant track via loudspeakers in a dozen handbooks. Eventually, the widespread use of air conditioning made it necessary to close the windows, cutting off the sound. This, in turn, made it possible for police to declare the handbook a vanishing institution—and many naïve non-bettors believed them. Out of sound and sight, out of mind.

In those years it was a general custom to close all books during the local racing season, thus forcing would-be bettors to go, or send runners, to the track and feed the pari-mutuel machines. This helped the industry in two ways—the large crowds were cited as proof that people really liked to see horses run and were sincere in wanting to "improve the breed." Additionally, it increased the pari-mutuel revenue of which the state got a cut and it allowed gamblers to declare racing to be essential to a state's economy. This argument worked so well that in 1941, when the Florida Racing Commission discovered that Tropical Park near Miami was controlled by Owney "the Killer" Madden and John Patton, the notorious "Boy-Mayor" of Burnham, Illinois, and ex-lieutenant of Al Capone, it decided to suppress the information for fear of destroying the pari-mutuel system in Florida.

158

By the 1950's, however, the betting industry had grown so large the tradition of closing during the racing season was abandoned. If anything, the bookies did a larger business when the horses were running a few miles away and newspapers were carrying information about odds, long shots, and making the jockey into a folk hero. For this huge increase, Moe Annenberg deserved much of the credit.

In 1934, Moe reentered the newspaper publishing business. He bought the Miami *Tribune,* a tabloid, in bankruptcy proceedings. A couple of murders had focused attention on gambling, and a few spirited citizens were demanding that officials take action against the wide-open joints. The possibility existed that the entire town might be shut down. Annenberg used the *Tribune* to help elect three city commissioners who, he felt, would be discreet enough to transform a danger into an advantage. Over the years organized crime has learned to use reform sentiment by diverting it against independents. A few raids and suitable statements by public officials can satisfy the do-gooders and eliminate competition at the same time.

Robert R. Williams, one of the three commissioners favored by Annenberg, was selected by his colleagues to be mayor of Miami. Sure enough, the heat on gambling soon cooled. The *Tribune* had little chance against the well-established Miami *Herald,* and Annenberg had more profitable deals in mind. He suspended publication in 1937, declaring in his final editorial that he was leaving the city in "safe hands." Safe for whom?

The politicians he had helped elect were soon in trouble. The city and the Florida Power and Light Company were in litigation. Exactly what happened remains a grand jury secret, but it is apparent that a deal similar to the Second Missouri Compromise was at least discussed. In any case, two months after Annenberg suspended the *Tribune,* power company president Bryan Hanks charged he had been asked for a bribe by the mayor to settle the dispute. Mayor Williams and some of his colleagues were promptly indicted and just as promptly acquitted.

For once the citizens of Miami were unsatisfied. Anger soon crystallized into a recall movement, and in 1938 the "safe hands" in which Annenberg had left the city were voted out of office. Gamblers continued to play at politics, however, and in one weird episode tried to frame a mayor and city manager by sending two men to Newport, Kentucky, to get themselves arrested in a brothel while posing as the two officials. At intervals in years to come, syndicate-controlled newspapers flourished briefly.

In 1936, Moe made his real bid for power in the newspaper field by purchasing the ancient but honorable Philadelphia *Inquirer* for $15,000,000. Senator Guffey was quite correct in saying "cold cash" was paid for it. Annenberg arranged several bank loans, pledging as collateral the stock of several of his corporations, such as Regal Press, Nationwide News, and Triangle Publications. Investigators who later probed the deal noted "that some interesting observations might be made regarding the extent to which the payments of bank loans growing out of the purchase of the Philadelphia *Inquirer* are dependent upon the continued operation of gambling establishments throughout the United States."

The episode well illustrates the relationship of crime to legitimate business. Annenberg promptly proceeded to demonstrate the relation of crime to politics via legitimate business. In that 1938 speech, Senator Guffey charged:

"Moe Annenberg, at a time when he was known to be on terms of open intimacy with at least one member of the [New Jersey] Supreme Court, published in advance the decision of that court on the constitutionality of the grand jury bills. Such a publication, ten hours before the decisions were handed down, demonstrated a brazen contempt for the dignity of the highest court in this commonwealth."

The Senator continued: "Many think of Annenberg as a newspaper publisher, but his publishing is incidental to his traffic in gambling information, and his newspaper is nothing more or less than an instrument of political power to protect his far-flung illegal enterprises."

Perhaps it was the Senator's blast that did the trick, but in any case, Annenberg's "handpicked candidate" was defeated, and Democrat A. H. Moore became governor.

By 1936 Moe's empire had grown so large it would require

160

several pages to list his holdings. The wire-service business alone was divided into fourteen corporations controlling thirty-six branches and providing exclusive functions to all the bookies in 223 cities in the United States and Canada. The publishing business, which included good and bad newspapers and magazines, required twenty separate corporations. The wall-sheet business was divided into five corporations and partnerships too numerous to mention. To handle his magazine and newspaper distributorships, Moe set up sixteen corporations. Real estate, insurance, theaters, liquor stores, and laundries were split among fourteen corporations. To handle foreign affairs, he had seven corporations in various countries.

What's more, all these corporations locked, interlocked, and ran helter-skelter until not even Moe could be sure of their alleged function. One of their real purposes, the Intelligence Unit decided, was to make it virtually impossible to assess Moe's income or tax responsibility. Some corporations would show staggering losses because others were stealing away the business. So complete was the network that Moe could juggle profit and loss as tax advantage indicated.

No one could be sure of Annenberg's net worth, but figures filed by him when he was seeking bank credit gave some indication. In 1930 he claimed to have only $7,858,343. In 1938 he listed $19,396,308. Meanwhile, he lived in a style suitable to an emperor. Estates were maintained on Long Island, near Philadelphia, and in Florida. He had a 900-acre ranch in Wyoming which included "the second-best trout stream in the world." Moe liked fishing and pinochle. He was a good fisherman and a bad pinochle player. In fact, Moe only knew one man he could honestly and consistently beat at the game. Luckily, the fellow worked for him in Chicago. Whenever Moe's ego needed a boost, he would send the employee an urgent telegram ordering him to come to Florida, or New York, or San Francisco as quickly as possible. A few victories, and Annenberg felt better.

Another employee was also in great demand, but she was usually available. Gertrude Boze was paid $16,300 as a *Daily Racing Form* clocker, and her salary was deducted as a business expense. No one could discover any work she ever did in her official position, but there was ample evidence that Moe continually clocked her form.

It was in 1935 that the Intelligence Unit decided Moe was worth a routine check. As Irey described it, "a polite little Internal Revenue agent, hat in hand, got so rough a brushoff that he replaced his hat and strode out to inform his superiors that something was peculiar."

When special agents appeared, it was Annenberg's time to be polite. Grandly, he offered the investigators an office in which to work and promised to supply all the records they wanted. The office turned out to be an "oversize telephone booth," and the records were such that trails led here and there, doubled back, and ended eventually in some strange financial limbo. Special Agent Nels Tessem, who had cut his investigative teeth in the Capone probe, headed the inquiry. It was the kind of investigation that demanded good eyesight and endless patience. Two years passed before Tessem dug up a set of false stock certificates. Soon he began finding doctored minute books, the erasures plainly visible. A check of stockholders uncovered many straws, some of whom were astonished to learn they owned stocks and others, more hip, who admitted the only money they saw in connection with the stock was the check Moe sent them to be forwarded for taxes.

Not the least of the frustrations Tessem encountered was that records of the wire-service business—the single largest source of revenue—were kept in code. Many noncoded records essential to the investigation apparently just didn't exist. There was no longer any doubt that Moe was evading taxes on a huge scale; the problem was how to prove it to a judge and jury composed of ordinary mortals. Such proof as had been found would require a jury of financial wizards, and even then the odds would favor incomprehension.

Annenberg was well aware of the situation and took the position that his bookkeeping system had simply not kept up with his business. He was willing, he said, to pay a few million in back taxes if it would make the government happy. While conceding privately that such a settlement might become necessary, Irey ordered his men to keep digging.

Four years after the examination of Moe's records began,

Tessem got a break. Upon reporting for work at the tiny office Moe had so generously provided, he noticed there was even less space than usual. The special agent going off duty—the job required work on a twenty-four-hour basis—pointed to a pile of metal boxes which, he said, had just been brought in. Gloomily, Tessem examined the pile, wondering what new device to add confusion Moe had supplied. There were nineteen boxes, and they had been shipped from Annenberg's Long Island home. Every box was marked PRIVATE RECORDS.

A quick look inside convinced Tessem that someone had made a little mistake. He rushed out to get a subpoena with which to seize the precious boxes before the mistake was discovered and corrected. The subpoena was served in time, but Annenberg's attorney refused to honor it and ordered the boxes moved to his private office, where they were originally supposed to go. Tessem arranged to have the lawyer before a federal grand jury the next morning. By afternoon the boxes were in his hands.

Closer examination revealed why the attorney was so disturbed. The records had been intended for use in Moe's defense. They included documents explaining the private codes by Annenberg and canceled checks, cashbooks, ledgers, and letters Moe had claimed were no longer in existence. In short, they filled every hole in the government case and gave it new dimensions.

Ten hand trucks were needed to haul all the records into the grand jury room in early June. The jurors spent two months studying them and on August 11, 1939, indicted Moe ten times. He was charged with evading $3,258,809 in taxes from 1932 to 1936. With the addition of interest and penalties, the total bill came to more than $5,500,000. And that was just the beginning; more indictments followed.

Annenberg, always a realist, began to wiggle. He had one advantage. Despite all the records, it was still impossible for the Intelligence Unit to prove, or even know, just how big his income was. This made a compromise possible, relieving both Annenberg and the government of the uncertainty of a jury trial. The problem was to decide how much. It was within the power of Internal Revenue to agree on the amount of civil liability, but only the judge could determine if a jail sentence was also to be imposed. Rather than face a jury, Annenberg agreed to pay $8,000,000 over a five-year period with interest of 6 percent. The amount was the largest ever paid by an individual tax evader.

In return, the Justice Department dismissed all but one count of one indictment. Annenberg's attorneys submitted to the court a 138-page statement explaining why Moe shouldn't go to jail. Justice countered with 109 pages of reasons why he should. The district court judge noted in his decision that Annenberg's plea for leniency, coming as it did on the heels of his guilty plea, had the effect of asking the court "to transform the plea of guilty into one of not guilty except as to some items which are trivial in comparison with the large amount of evaded taxes charged in the count under consideration." In terms reminiscent of those addressed to Al Capone, the judge concluded:

> The court is without authority either to compromise or to pardon. It has a larger duty to the public. The main object of criminal punishment is to prevent further crime. To grant the plea of the defendant in this case would be to say to business men: "You may organize your affairs in a network of corporations and avoid the payment of your just taxes, and when called to account by the Government for what you really owe, nothing worse will happen to you than to be compelled to pay what you should have paid long ago."

He sentenced Annenberg to serve three years in prison. Shortly after Moe's release, he died.

The importance of Annenberg's empire to organized crime was well illustrated by what happened to the wire service he built. Shortly after Annenberg was indicted in 1939, James Ragen asked Mickey McBride of Cleveland to take charge of it. Ragen had worked for Annenberg in Chicago in 1910 during the newspaper circulation wars. Later he had moved to Cleveland as circulation manager of Mark Hanna's newspapers. In time, Ragen needed help, so he brought McBride from Chicago. Ragen went back to Chicago in 1922 to work again

164

under Annenberg. When Nationwide News Service was formed by Moe, Ragen became general manager. McBride stayed in Cleveland and developed an empire of his own. Ragen was indicted along with Annenberg in 1939. As it turned out, his guilty plea was accepted, and he was given a suspended sentence; but at the time he could not know he would be so lucky.

McBride claimed he didn't want Nationwide but was persuaded to take it. On November 15, 1939, Nationwide went out of existence. Five days later Continental Press came into being and took over the entire wire-service operation. As the Kefauver Committee commented later: "One man [Annenberg] stepped out of this complicated business and another man [McBride] took it over without any formal transfer or without the passing of a single dollar."

On paper, McBride was represented in the business by his son, a student at Notre Dame, after 1942. Ragen and his son were also partners, and Ragen ran the business. Within three years he had made the mistake of challenging the Chicago Syndicate. The boys in Chicago took advantage of Annenberg's departure and refused to pay for the wire service after he quit. Ragen decided in 1945 to make them pay. The Chicago Syndicate responded by forming Trans-American Publishing and News Service, Inc., and set out to compete with Nationwide. Ragen became so angry he squealed to the police about one of his men who deserted Continental for Trans-American. When the deserter was sent to prison for a crime committed thirty years before, the Chicago hoods gunned down Ragen on the street. He lived for a few days, squealed some more, and gave birth to a legend that Nitti and the boys slipped poison into his hospital food and thus finally finished him off.

Even with Ragen out of the way, Trans-American made little progress in ousting Continental, né Nationwide, from the handbooks of the country. Annenberg had built well, and the organization he had constructed continued to show a profit despite the competition. Finally, the National Crime Syndicate stepped in and ordered the so-called wire-service war ended.

James Ragen, Jr., sold the two-thirds he and his father owned to young Eddie McBride, who held it for his father, Mickey. Less than two weeks later, Trans-American announced it was going out of business. To save the face of the Chicago hoods, the syndicate set up the Illinois Sports News as a subsidiary of Continental, and it collected payment for the wire service from Chicago bookies.

The syndicate also found it necessary to execute Bugsy Siegel, who had sided, for reasons which will become apparent in the following chapter, with Trans-American in its dispute with Continental. Meyer Lansky defended his old partner but accepted the majority decision with his usual good grace.

Continental continued to profit until 1950, when the Kefauver Committee exposed its operations from coast to coast. So great was the heat the syndicate decided to decentralize. Bookies continued to get the data they needed, but Continental vanished.

Other parts of Annenberg's empire survived and are still making money. The old magic died with Moe, however. It was he in his youth who found the Promised Land and exploited it.

Special Agent Tessem and his chief, Elmer Irey, had reason to congratulate each other when the file on Annenberg was closed at last. The five-year probe had cost the government $1,000,000, but the investment had paid off at 8 to 1. Not even Annenberg would sneer at that, although he could blame it all on a "little mistake."

10

THE BORN LOSER

THE movie industry in Hollywood has always been fascinated by gangsters, and the hoods have returned the compliment. The Intelligence Unit found on many occasions it was difficult to separate the good guys from the bad. Even the white hat worn by Tom Mix wasn't much help.

That the National Crime Syndicate practically took over the movie industry in the 1930's has long been established. That it still exerts tremendous influence there is not so well known.

Elmer Irey became interested in Hollywood early in 1928 when a stool pigeon—to employ one of Hollywood's clichés—whispered that many movie stars were knowingly evading their income taxes. It developed that five tax "consultants" were helping the stars cheat, largely by claiming false expenses. Marjorie Berger, with seventy clients, was the biggest of these consultants. She received thirty months in prison for her activity and a $5,000 fine. Twenty-two movie stars pleaded guilty, and others offered compromises. More than $2,000,000 were collected in taxes and penalties from the stars.

Tom Mix, the cowboy hero who always got his man and rode

off into the sunset leaving a wistful girl behind, was accused of defrauding the United States out of more than $100,000, but it was the case of Marion Davies that drew most attention.

Miss Davies, whose real name was Douras, was a close friend —to put it politely—of publishing giant William Randolph Hearst, the man who gave Moe Annenberg his start during the newspaper circulation wars. When called into conference and told she owed $1,000,000, the movie star suddenly rushed from the room. A few minutes later, Irey received a call from a stenographer who reported an "apparently deranged" woman was in the ladies' room moaning about owing a million.

The Hearst press came to the lady's rescue and gave the Internal Revenue Bureau hell. No mention was made, of course, of the fact that the probe showed much of Miss Davies' money had been paid to her by Hearst-controlled corporations. Ultimately, she settled by paying $750,000. An additional $250,-000 was collected from Arthur Brisbane, editor of the Hearst newspapers.

Charlie Chaplin was forced to cough up more than $1,000,000 in the first of several battles he had over the years with the Intelligence Unit. Eventually, the sad-faced clown left the country in an unsuccessful effort to avoid paying the additional sums he owed.

The Intelligence Unit was happy enough to leave the movie stars to their filmed heroics and turn to real-life gangsters. Eventually the pursuit of gangsters led them back to Hollywood.

Two seemingly unrelated events set off one of the most difficult probes in Intelligence history. In Chicago, Tommy Maloy, business agent of the local chapter of the Motion Picture Operators Union, was machine-gunned to death, and in New York, Bugsy Siegel, erstwhile partner of Meyer Lansky, was sent to Hollywood to organize crime on the West Coast for the syndicate.

Years passed before law enforcement agencies understood what was going on. In the interval a labor union was taken over by the syndicate, and the management of the movie industry was shaken down for millions.

168

The story really begins with Willie Bioff. Willie was a pimp. Indeed, he was arrested for pimping in Chicago in 1922 and sentenced to six months in jail. Released on appeal after eight days in the pokey, he continued pimping. Someone gave him back his bail money, and everyone conveniently forgot his jail sentence. It was Chicago in the days of Torrio and Capone, remember.

A minor member of the Capone organization, Willie struggled along without working, but without getting rich either. He dabbled at this and that without conspicuous success and in 1932 tried to organize the kosher butchers of Chicago into a union. That didn't work very well either. Willie decided he was a born loser.

Life took an upturn one day when Bioff ran into another born loser, George E. Browne. George was business agent for Local 2 of the Stagehands Union, but more than half his members were out of work and the 150 with jobs had their pay cut by 20 percent. Willie tried to console George by talking of the problems of organizing kosher butchers in the middle of a depression, and the boys decided they had a lot in common. A friendship born of discouragement sprang up between the two men. Browne found a conversation with Willie was as refreshing as a bottle of imported beer—and he usually drank 100 bottles a day in his quest for comfort.

When drunk, Browne liked to imagine he was a tough guy and occasionally would make the rounds of the speakeasies waving a pistol and issuing challenges to one and all. The hoodlums thought it was very funny. That, in short, was both Browne and Bioff's complaint—no one ever took them seriously.

Out of their discussion of mutual troubles an angle developed. Browne set up a soup kitchen to feed the 250 members of the union who were unemployed. Bioff contacted some politicians and, by promising he could control the votes of the starving men, won a few contributions to the kitchen. This minor success started the wheels turning in Willie's head. He knew only a few politicians, whereas Browne knew most of the theater owners in Chicago. Why not put the arm on them? In-

169

stead of promising votes, as with the politicians, threaten a
strike by the 150 union members who were still working. The
stick instead of the carrot.

Browne was willing. The idea of acting the part of a muscleman appealed to his frustrated ego. Likely targets were John
and Barney Balaban who owned several movie houses and employed several union members. Bioff had no illusions, however, about George's tough-guy role, and it was he who visited
Barney Balaban. The approach was indirect. Willie didn't ask
for anything for himself, but if that 20 percent cut weren't
restored, there'd be a strike.

Balaban countered with an offer to contribute $150 a week
to the soup kitchen. Much encouraged, Willie shot the works:
He demanded $50,000 a year for the kitchen. After some dis-
cussion, and somewhat to Bioff's surprise, Balaban agreed to
contribute $20,000. That would pay for a lot of soup. Bioff
told the victim to write the check to "a starving lawyer friend"
so, he said, the union could write it off as a legal expense.

The lawyer took out $4,000 to recompense himself and pay
taxes, and Browne and Bioff split the rest. The soup kitchen
and the starving union members weren't overlooked, however.
After all, Browne was a union official. He bought two cases of
canned soup, costing $2.50 each, and gave them to the soup
kitchen. Then the boys went out to celebrate.

By the time they reached Nick Circella's joint, they were
competing for the role of big spender. The leaders of the Chicago Syndicate had well-developed curiosity bumps, and it so
happened that Circella was entertaining Frankie Rio. Frankie
had taken over the mob briefly when both Capone and Frank
"the Enforcer" Nitti had been "away" on income tax raps but
had surrendered it to Nitti willingly enough when he finished his sentence. Nitti appreciated this cooperative attitude, and Rio remained high in the councils of the syndicate.

Circella and Rio watched Willie and George celebrate for a
while, and Nick wondered out loud where two such punks got
so much dough. Rio suggested they inquire. The question
sobered Bioff instantly. He managed to pull his partner away
and out the door.

Browne was still sleeping off his hangover next morning when the telephone rang. Frankie Rio calling. Rio didn't waste words, ordering Browne to meet him at a street intersection in an hour. The frightened George called Willie, who bravely volunteered to accompany his friend. At the intersection of Twenty-second and Michigan, a car drove up. Rio and George Pierce, another member of the gang, were inside. "Screw," said Rio to Willie, and Willie departed. He was too worried to obey orders, however. Was his old pal, his comrade in misery, about to be taken for a ride? Up today, down tomorrow—the story of both their lives.

Meanwhile, Browne was being given a ride around the streets of Chicago. He talked fast, hoping dully that he could convince Rio his live body was of more value than his corpse. He achieved his purpose and was dropped off after two hours with the assurance he would be hearing from Rio in the future.

The summons came two days later. "You and Willie get out to Frank's house." Browne wasn't sure exactly who was meant, but Bioff had no doubts. It was Frank Nitti who wanted to see them.

Gathered in Nitti's living room was as choice a collection of hoods as one could hope to find in hell. Phil D'Andrea, technical head of the Mafia in Chicago and former Capone bodyguard; Charley "Cherry Nose" Gioe; Paul "the Waiter" Ricca; and Louis "Little New York" Compagna. There was also a stranger, a cold-eyed little man from New York whose real name was Louis Buchalter but who was more commonly called Lepke. He was a close associate of Lansky and Lucky Luciano, a member of the board of the National Crime Syndicate.

Nitti wasted few words. He announced the syndicate had decided to organize a shakedown of movie theaters all around the country. Meanwhile, the Chicago boys were going to cut themselves in for half of Browne and Bioff's profits.

There wasn't much the two punks could do about it, and Nitti proceeded with the next order of business. Browne had been defeated in 1932, when, in one of his ambitious moments, he ran for president of the International Alliance of Theatrical Stage Employees and Moving Picture Machine Operators of the

United States and Canada (IATSE). It takes ambition, indeed, to seek to be an officer of a union with a name that long. Why had he lost? asked Nitti.

George, fat and shaking, blamed his defeat on the big Eastern city locals.

Nitti glanced at the silent Lepke. "You'll run again in June," he said, "and win. The Eastern outfits will vote for you."

In June, 1934, delegates to the convention of the union with the long name met in Louisville, Kentucky, at the Brown Hotel on Broadway. George Browne could have considered the hotel's name a good omen, but he knew omens were unnecessary, considering the number of Chicago and New York hoods who were staying at the hotel as guests of the union.

John Herchenroeder, for many years city editor of the Louisville *Courier-Journal,* still remembers that 1934 convention. It puzzled him. For some reason the union members didn't seem to be interested in the usual publicity story a progressive newspaper is ready to give a national convention.

"We sent a reporter over to the hotel," said Herchenroeder, "but he couldn't get in, so we ignored the convention."

Thus, in complete privacy, the syndicate took over the union. Browne was elected without even token opposition. According to Irey, Frank Maritote of the Chicago delegation beat up a few people just to keep in practice but on the whole everything went smoothly.

The real bosses held a convention of their own back in Chicago. Again Lepke was present as the delegate from the national syndicate. Nitti ordered Browne—president Browne, that is—to put Circella on the payroll. He also advised that the syndicate would now take two-thirds of the loot.

Finding a suitable spot for Circella was no great problem. All that was required was a murder. Tom Maloy was the victim.

Maloy had been around a long time. In the days before the First World War, he drove a car for Mossy Enright—boss of the building trades union. The car was called the Gray Ghost, and it usually carried several veteran killers. When the heat began to build up on Mossy—he was murdered in 1920—Maloy became a motion-picture operator and ran a small gambling

172

joint under the stage of the movie house. He proved his toughness and ability to manage men in several legendary escapades
and soon found himself business manager of Operators Local
110 of the IATSE.

As a union official he developed several profitable angles.
Only men who agreed to kick back 10 percent of their salary
were permitted to join his union, and they, of course, got all
the high-paying jobs. If they lacked sufficient education to take
the examination for a city license, Maloy provided stand-ins to
take them. There wasn't much danger of anything going wrong,
for the licenser of motion picture operators for the city of Chicago was Tom's brother.

With the advent of talkies, it because necessary to hire
faders to make sure the recorded sound kept pace with the
lip movements of the actors. Science, however, soon made the
technique obsolete by putting the sound on the film. Nevertheless, Tom refused to let the faders be fired—unless, of
course, he was paid $1,100 per discharge. He was paid.

The threat of a strike was also used by Maloy to clip the operators from time to time. Browne and Bioff couldn't even claim
credit for the idea—although it was new to them. And of
course, if Maloy needed a gold-plated toilet costing $4,000, he
could use the union treasury for the purchase.

Maloy ruled his union ruthlessly. Opponents such as Jacob
D. Kaufman and Fred F. Oser were silenced by the simple ex-
pedient of having them murdered. Life got complicated, however, when Nitti and his boys began moving in. One effort
failed. A man thought to be Maloy was kidnapped outside
Maloy's home, but upon examination he turned out to be
George Graham, a Maloy bodyguard. The Outfit, as the Chicago boys liked to call their organization, tried to make the best
of a bad bargain. The boys called Maloy and asked if Graham's
life was worth ten grand. When Maloy replied it wasn't worth
twenty-five cents, Graham was released unharmed.

A second effort almost succeeded. The boys snatched a maid
who worked for Maloy and persuaded her to give up the keys
to the house. It was generally assumed that Maloy—learning
from the Capone case—had a lot of cash stored away inside the

173

house. However, a nosy neighbor saw the maid picked up and called the police, who broke up the robbery attempt.

Persistent was the word for the Outfit. Maloy disappeared for a time and upon his return from a "hunting trip in Canada" reported to police that some $65,000 had been taken from his house in his absence. Apparently he just didn't want to admit he had been kidnapped.

All the publicity naturally attracted the attention of the Intelligence Unit. An investigation developed evidence that Maloy had failed to report and pay taxes on income of $350,000 for the years 1929 through 1932. An indictment was returned on January 25, 1935, but by then Nitti and his pals were looking for a nice spot in which to install Nick Circella. On February 4, 1935, two days after Maloy pleaded innocent to the tax rap, he was gunned down on the streets of Chicago. A week later president Browne appointed Circella to replace the late, lamented Maloy as head of Local 110.

Shortly thereafter Clyde Osterberg was fatally shot. Clyde had annoyed Maloy by trying to form a rival union and got his skull cracked for his trouble. Maloy's successor was not so softhearted in dealing with troublemakers. Osterberg admitted before dying that he knew who shot him, but true to the code, he refused to name anyone. However, one of his bodyguards disclosed that none other than Willie Bioff had warned Osterberg he wouldn't live long unless he forgot about a rival union. Willie, it seemed, had sized up the situation pretty well.

The big shakedown could now begin. Bioff called together the operators of all Chicago movie houses and blandly informed them that in the future each would need two union projectionists in each booth at all times. After all, with just one present, the show might not go on if he dropped dead from a heart attack or something. The operators protested they couldn't afford to hire two men to do the work of one. Willie countered— they couldn't afford a strike either. After the operators had pondered this statement for a while, Bioff came up with an alternate solution. If the operators would pay $100,000, the matter would be dropped.

The operators paid.

A similar routine was performed in New York, but there

cate—which, thanks largely to Hollywood, had a great reputation for ruthlessness. The Chicago boys were the boogeymen of crime.

Details were turned over to Joe Schenck, the movie companies' representative, and he worked out a compromise under which the large companies paid $50,000 a year in tribute and the smaller ones, $25,000. But Willie was under pressure to produce immediate cash. The next day Schenck and movie executive Sidney R. Kent, arrived at Bioff's room carrying large bundles wrapped in brown paper. Each bundle contained $50,000.

One major step remained. Now that all employees of Hollywood studios were in Browne's union, a 2 percent levy on their earnings was imposed—a sort of occupational tax, you might say.

Meanwhile, the National Crime Syndicate decided to make sure Willie and his Chicago friends were playing fair. Bugsy Siegel was officially designated the syndicate's representative in charge of the West Coast. His orders were to keep an eye on Bioff and Browne, as well as to consolidate all existing rackets and develop new ones. Bugsy had always loved gangster movies and soon made a big hit with the stars and starlets of Hollywood. He encountered some difficulty from Mafia elements led by Jack Dragna, the so-called Al Capone of Los Angeles, but Bugsy had the muscle to bring Dragna into line.

An old friend from New York days helped introduce Bugsy to Hollywood society. George Raft had been something of a punk hood in his youth before becoming famous for his gangster roles on film. Sponsoring a real big-league syndicate boss such as Bugsy was a big help to his image. Many of the Chicago big shots began visiting Hollywood, enjoying the awe with which they were received. The union, of course, paid all expenses. Some of the syndicate members—the more thoughtful ones—took advantage of their power to buy into the corporations that owned the studios. It was a good investment. Abner "Longie" Zwillman, for example, helped produce several box-office smash hits. Others, who owned nightclubs with casinos attached, arranged to have top Hollywood stars appear in Newport, Cleveland, New Orleans, Miami, and Hot Springs. Nothing like a name personality, it was discovered, to bring the suckers to the casinos.

So it was that organized crime got a stranglehold on the entertainment business, where its influence, if less conspicuous, still remains strong today.

Opposition to the take-over of Hollywood came from Robert Montgomery, president of the Screen Actors Guild. He persuaded the guild to finance an investigation of Bioff. The probe discovered that Willie was a pimp. It also uncovered information to the effect that Joe Schenck gave Willie $100,000 in 1937. This wasn't quite right, but it led to a halfhearted investigation by the state legislature, which produced more publicity than facts. The publicity, however, led to the Intelligence Unit's return to Hollywood.

Alf Oftedal was assigned to probe Schenck, and Charles Emery was told to look into Bioff. It didn't take either man long to come up with enough evidence to prove their subjects had been cheating the government, but it was June, 1939, before indictments were returned. The resulting publicity disclosed that Bioff had neglected to serve the six months' sentence for pandering he received back in 1922. Chicago officials were embarrassed, and the governor of California was happy to help them extradite Willie.

While sitting in jail, Willie was visited by Cherry Nose Gioe, and in a burst of his old born-loser attitude, he suggested he might as well quit the racket. The next day Little New York Compagna came calling and warned Willie that no one resigned from the syndicate unless he wanted to do it feetfirst. Willie promptly withdrew his resignation.

Meanwhile, Schenck was being questioned by Matt Correa and Boris Kostelanetz, two determined young Assistant United States Attorneys in New York. Joe managed to straighten out the bit about the hundred grand he had allegedly given to Willie. What happened, he said, was that Willie wanted to buy a ranch like all his movie friends, but all he had was cash. A payment in cash to legitimate people might arouse undue interest and attract the tax boys, Willie reasoned, so he gave the money to good old Joe, who wrote a check for the like amount. Ironically, when Schenck's check came to the attention of Mont-

178

gomery's investigators, they suspected a payoff, and the resulting publicity did attract the Intelligence Unit.

A born loser was Willie.

Schenck was convicted of tax evasion in March, 1941. He seemed shocked to be sentenced to three years in prison, and after thinking about it for a while, he decided to squeal. He did his talking to a federal grand jury in New York with such good results that in May, 1941, Bioff, Circella, and George Browne were indicted under the federal laws forbidding interstate racketeering.

Circella pleaded guilty rather than answer questions. Bioff and Browne saw little point in doing likewise since Nick got eight years, so they tried to lie out of everything. As a result, Bioff got ten years and Browne eight. Off they went without talking—the fear of the syndicate effectively closing their lips.

The investigation, once the income tax phases were closed out, properly belonged to the FBI. However, Pearl Harbor came along in December, and, as Irey put it, "the FBI had a lot of other problems ferreting out Jap and Nazis spies." After much pulling and hauling, it was decided that Special Agent Oftedal would continue to work with the United States Attorney's office in New York. As Oftedal put it in an office memorandum dated April 7, 1942: "It is understood that I am in no sense to work under the direction of the United States Attorney for the Southern District of New York. I am, on the other hand, to cooperate with and assist him, maintaining all the time, however, my identity with the Intelligence Unit and under the immediate direction of the Head of the Unit."

The following day Irey sent letters to the various special agents in charge around the country in which he outlined a plan to "conduct simultaneous interviews of the prospective witnesses whenever and wherever such action appears possible and advisable."

A huge probe got rolling, and by June 20, 1942, Irey was able to write to the special agent in charge at Chicago a long letter in which he noted:

> The case as it now stands presents many interesting possibilities. The indications are that the principal violators

179

referred to herein were constantly alert to the requirements of the income tax law and endeavored to protect themselves against the dangers of being prosecuted for income tax violations. There is strongly emphasized in the evidence now available, however, two or more major conspiracies to violate the laws of the United States. The principal offenders that are still at large, of course, appear to be Frank Nitti, Paul Ricca and Louis Compagna.

In many ways it was a frustrating investigation. Willie, responding to Oftedal's charm, provided some information but always stopped short of fingering the top men in the syndicate. Stalemate threatened, and even Oftedal became discouraged. In a personal, handwritten letter to Irey on July 7, 1942, he told his chief:

> I have no work here for Special Agent Emery. There isn't much for me to do either unless we can somehow overcome the present stalemate. Our leads of information are nearly exhausted and we have not yet obtained direct evidence against any of the three principals, Nitti, De Lucia [Ricca] and Compagna. In fact the prospects for ever getting "the goods" on them seems extremely slim. In view of this I seriously question if we, of the Intelligence Unit, should not withdraw from the picture. The gangsters appear to have carefully complied with the requirements of the income tax law. Furthermore our unit is not equipped to tackle such a difficult and long drawn out undercover investigation.

On July 27, 1942, Oftedal sent Irey a long FBI report on the progress of the investigation. To it he added this biting memo of his own:

> The writer, Special Agent John P. Gleason of the Federal Bureau of Investigation, was never present when any of the secret informers to whom he refers . . . were interviewed. The reader would get the impression that Gleason was present, however. . . .
> The special agent carefully refrained from identifying

any representative of the Intelligence Unit by name, and only in four instances did he refer to the Unit at all.

One might easily be misled into believing that in only those four instances referred to did the Intelligence Unit have anything to do with the case. As a matter of fact, all of the information contained in the report of Agent Gleason was developed by agents of the Intelligence Unit in cooperation with Assistant United States Attorney Kostelanetz.

It may be recalled that in my report of June 26, 1942, I stated that agent Gleason was sitting in on our interviews and that he had requested copies of confidential memorandums which we had prepared. These copies were not furnished him but he was given access to them and it was largely through this access to our confidential memorandums that he was enabled to prepare the attached report.

As an ironic footnote, the author was not permitted to read Gleason's report on the grounds that it was the property of the FBI—the FBI objects to people reading its reports. This was done despite Oftedal's statement that the information in the FBI report was taken from IRS reports. How Oftedal got the report in 1942 isn't explained, but it well illustrates the sometimes intense rivalry that has existed between the FBI and the men of the Intelligence Division.

After a series of conferences in New York between Irey and his team on the one hand, and the U.S. Attorney's staff on the other, it was decided to continue on the case. Feelings were occasionally strained on both sides, owing to the complicated nature of the probe and the difficulty of coordinating the thousands of details in a dozen cities. Patience paid off, however, as the overnervous syndicate took a few too many precautions.

The body of Nick Circella's girlfriend, Estelle Carey, was found on February 2, 1943, by Chicago firemen. She had been beaten to death. The house had been set on fire in an effort to burn the body, but firemen put the blaze out quickly. Immediately the word passed on the underworld grapevine—Estelle, lonely for Nick who was in prison on the income tax rap, had been about to squeal.

One day after the murder, Mrs. George Browne received a

telephone call warning her to keep quiet and to tell her husband to do the same.

This was too much for Bioff and Browne. "Whatta you want to know?" asked Willie.

A grand jury asked the questions. One item Bioff disclosed concerned Murray Garsson, the federal employee who had blundered into the Lindbergh case. It turned out that Garsson had collected $200,000 from Joe Schenck for *not* investigating him.

The boys in Hollywood had seen too many gangster movies.

The indictment was returned on March 18, 1943. Charged with conspiracy to obtain money by the use of force, violence, or coercion from persons engaged in interstate commerce were Nitti, Compagna, D'Andrea, Ricca, Frank Maritote, Gioe, John Rosselli, Louis Kaufman, and George Pierce. The indictment against Pierce was later dropped, and Nitti also avoided trial.

On the day the indictment was returned, Nitti walked down to the railroad track in Riverside, Illinois, and waited until a train came along. In full view of the train's crew, he pulled out a gun and blew off half his head. Frank the Enforcer had done one hitch in jail because of the Intelligence Unit; he didn't intend to do another.

It was New Year's Eve when the remaining defendants heard the judge sentence them—with the exception of Kaufman—to ten years in prison and fines of $10,000 each. Kaufman got off with seven years.

Perhaps it should be noted that Lepke escaped for the very good reason that he had been sentenced to die for murder in 1941. Bugsy Siegel, who had not taken an active role in the various shakedowns, also avoided indictment. Soon, however, the syndicate itself would execute Bugsy in the home of his mistress, Virginia Hill.

In 1947 the Intelligence Unit wanted Bioff and Browne to testify in matters relating to taxes owed by Nitti's estate. A memo dated April 21 noted that the men's attorneys advised "that Bioff and Browne are in hiding and living under assumed names, as a matter of personal safety, and that under no circumstances would they advise their clients to appear in Chicago."

The attorneys were wise, for a few weeks later Chicago was shocked to learn that all their top hoods had been paroled en masse after serving one-third of their sentence. But that is another story.

Browne dropped out of sight, but Bioff reappeared in Phoenix, Arizona, in the early 1950's. He became a buddy of Gus Greenbaum, a big wheel in Las Vegas. Gus introduced him to a famous resident of Phoenix, one Barry Goldwater, and Willie the Pimp and Barry became good friends. Goldwater, who flew his own plane, chauffeured Bioff all around the Southwest. Meanwhile, Greenbaum put Willie in charge of entertainment at the Riviera in Las Vegas with the idea that because of his previous experience, Willie would be able to persuade the name stars to work for less.

On November 5, 1955—two weeks after Goldwater flew Bioff to Phoenix from Las Vegas—Willie came out of his home and started his car. The bomb under the hood blew Willie and the car all over the neighborhood.

A born loser was Willie Bioff.

11

BLACK AND BITTER

ORGANIZED crime was on the ropes, groggy and bewildered by a series of blows, when on December 7, 1941, bombs fell on Pearl Harbor. Lepke, boss of Murder, Inc., had been sentenced to die only one week before. The Chicago Syndicate was facing a probe that, as related in the last chapter, would cause Frank Nitti to kill himself and send other top leaders to prison. Lucky Luciano was already in prison with no prospects of getting out. Racketeers in other cities were feeling the heat of an aroused public opinion. Even Meyer Lansky had largely abandoned his stateside activities and was attempting to build a new gambling empire in the more friendly climate of Havana.

Abruptly, the situation changed. Public attention and the nation's energies and resources were directed against the external enemy, the international gangsters of Germany and Japan. The National Crime Syndicate was all but forgotten in the crisis. Federal agencies which had been fighting crime turned now to the pursuit of spies and saboteurs. Gangsters who had been public enemies before were suddenly wooed as potential allies. Lansky and Luciano, the two most important men in crime, were put in charge of the still highly classified Operation Underworld. Their job was to mobilize gangsters along the East Coast to protect shipping and to cooperate with the Mafia in Sicily in preparation for an American invasion.

Luciano was rewarded for his services when the war ended by being released from prison and deported to Italy, where he ruled over the international narcotics traffic until his death by heart attack in 1962. Was Lansky rewarded? No final answer is possible, but he has been strangely immune to prosecution on the federal level. Twice the Intelligence Division has recommended prosecution, and twice the Justice Department has declined. Lansky remains the only top man in the National Crime Syndicate to escape untouched. Except for a three-month stretch in jail on gambling charges in New York, his record is clean. Yet because of his brains and the troubles of his colleagues, he rules as undisputed chairman of the board. His personal wealth has been estimated at $300,000,000. If immunity was granted him, the nation has paid high for his secret services during Operation Underworld.

Not only did the war take the heat off organized crime, but it also offered the gangsters new opportunities in black-market operations. The Intelligence Unit, as part of its wartime duties, made many important cases against operators in the black market, but it now seems obvious the syndicate was able to add tremendously to its bankroll while allegedly cooperating in the fight against the Axis.

One big case involved Robert Gould of Cincinnati. A latter-day George Remus, Gould operated as a whiskey broker on a huge scale. Gangsters throughout a wide area of the Midwest bought vast amounts of liquor from him at prices far in excess of the limits fixed by the Emergency Price Control Act and resold it in syndicate-owned bars and taverns at still higher prices. The Intelligence Unit cooperated with its brother agency, the Alcohol Tax Unit, in the investigation, and Gould was indicted in 1945 on forty-eight counts. Federal District Judge Mac Swinford sentenced Gould to six years in prison and $480,000 in fines.

In his appeal Gould contended that the Emergency Price

185

Control Act was unconstitutional in that it conflicted with the Twenty-first Amendment, which, argued Gould's attorneys, left the control of the manufacture and sale of liquor to the individual states—in this case, Kentucky. This argument was rejected by the Sixth Circuit Court of Appeals, which noted:

> It is only necessary to add that if the State of Kentucky had, as contended, been invested by the Twenty-first Amendment with limitless powers over the manufacture, transportation and sale of liquors, it would have been legally impermissible for the government, in prosecuting the war, to have compelled the distilleries within its borders to convert their operations from the manufacture of distilled spirits for consumption to the manufacture of alcohol so vital to the making of munitions. The effect upon the war effort would doubtless have been grievous, if not indeed catastrophic.

Gould avoided prosecution on income tax charges by agreeing to pay $2,500,000 in a lump sun. Since Moe Annenberg had paid his larger fine in installments, Gould's payment represented the largest ever paid at one time. Yet his operation had netted $10,000,000. It was obvious Gould would have enough to live on when he got out of prison. He got out of prison quicker than expected. Parole was given him after he made a large political contribution during that era of easy virtue known as the Truman Scandals.

Another case which required years to settle centered on Hyman H. Klein, head of a group of individuals who created an international corporate maze by means of which they manipulated some $20,000,000 in liquor profits. Thirty-seven foreign corporations were utilized in the project.

The opportunity came in 1943, when the Canadian government relaxed its prohibition against the manufacture of liquor for drinking purposes. Klein went to Canada and contacted three directors of United Distillers, Ltd., one of whom was his brother, Isadore Klein. An agreement was reached under which Hyman Klein could obtain an inferior brand of liquor at $8.05 a case. On December 22, 1943, Klein organized the United

186

J. Edgar Hoover molded the FBI. A mild-mannered man with gold-rimmed glasses that gave him a scholarly appearance, Irey possessed the ability to inspire others. Under his leadership, the Intelligence Unit gained a strong *esprit de corps*. It spurned the easy headlines; its men worked slowly and patiently, using intelligence to find the small detail and imagination to exploit it when found. No target was too big, no situation too complex, no politician too powerful.

Irey was an admirer of Lincoln, and his office contained books and a small bust of the Great Emancipator. Unlike Hoover in his younger days, Irey had no liking for nightclubs. He was a trustee of St. Stephen's Lutheran Church in Washington and attended regularly. A family man, he enjoyed spending time with his children. A nephew, later to be a famous special agent, Richard Wallace, said that all kids adored "Uncle Irey."

Irey worked hard, attempting to keep an eye on scores of investigations big and small. His men knew they could depend on him for help. Often, to their official reports, they attached handwritten notes to "the Chief." They depended on him to go, if necessary, to the President for the political muscle some situations required. Yet no one, not even an Irey, can go on forever making political enemies while pursuing an ideal, however legitimate. When Roosevelt was replaced by Truman, Irey knew his time was running out. Hoover, wiser, perhaps, or more concerned with survival, had been careful to avoid stepping on political toes. Irey had gone after Huey Long, had convicted Truman's friend Tom Pendergast. Ill health gave him an excuse to retire gracefully, yet his associates believed he was making a sacrifice for the service. He knew, or thought he knew, that his usefulness was ended. Better to let a new man, a man with no responsibility for past achievements, take over and try to get along with the new President.

It is interesting to speculate what sparks might have flown had a healthy Irey tangled with a Commissioner Nunan, for example. But the truth remains that in the world of politics, as elsewhere, a man can be no braver or more honest than his boss—if he expects to keep his job.

Behind him, Irey left a tradition—to see that his silent investigators follow the money to its ultimate destination and get the man who gets the money. In 1937, Irey prepared a thick summary of the Intelligence Unit's major cases. He planned to have the summary updated at intervals; this was not done. But the volume remains as proof of past achievements and one man's vision of the future

Several years later, during the height of the so-called Truman Scandals, Columnist Marquis Childs took a long look backward and put things into perspective. He wrote:

> Somewhere along the road that is paved with good intentions the guardians of the integrity of the bureau of internal revenue got lost. . . . Something new was added with the appointment of the late Robert Hannegan of St. Louis to be commissioner of internal revenue in 1943.
>
> Hannegan was a shrewd, intensely hard-working politician. . . . What he did in the commissionership was not in any way wrong by his standards. But they were the standards of a politician and after he took over, an infiltration of politicians into collectorships and other important revenue posts was speeded up.
>
> At about the same time something else happened that also made a profound difference. A dedicated and remarkably able public servant went into semi-retirement and shortly died. [He died on July 19, 1948.] Elmer L. Irey, as head of the intelligence unit in the bureau of internal revenue, knew neither fear nor favor. Evildoers who had broken every law were finally caught up with when they failed to pay their federal income taxes.
>
> One by one some of the biggest crooks in the country went to jail after they had made a mockery of local laws. Irey defied a threatened assassination in the course of providing the evidence that convicted Al Capone. Other gangster overlords out of the dreadful era of prohibition were put away as a result of Irey's tireless efforts.
>
> Nor were politicians immune. More than any single individual, Irey was responsible for putting Missouri's boss Tom Pendergast in prison.
>
> Irey invariably had the backing of his chief, Secretary of the Treasury Henry Morgenthau, Jr. The treasury

190

does not, of course, prosecute the cases it prepares. That is the function of the department of justice. But Morgenthau did not hesitate, when he thought the justice department was delaying, to demand action.

With Morgenthau's backing, Irey supplied two things. The first was the constantly repeated example of what happens to those who cheat Uncle Sam on their tax returns. Again and again this was reflected in headlines that ended with the clanging of the prison gates.

The second and related factor this nemesis of the treasury supplied was a constant pressure that pervaded not only his own unit but the entire bureau. Irey was particularly alert to the slightest hint of wrong doing by agents or collectors. This pressure, which knew neither friend nor foe, was part of the morale of an organization that was aware of its high responsibility.

With that pressure removed, an important element in the operation of the bureau of internal revenue was missing. And it went out just at the time when it was vitally needed—in the wake of the most costly of all wars, when billions had been spent in such haste that corruption and favoritism were almost inevitable. The moral laxity that war always produces flourished in the boomtime prosperity that has been almost unbroken since 1945.

That was the moment when extra vigilance was imperative if the standards of the past were not to deteriorate. That they have deteriorated we are seeing in the shoddy business exposed by the house subcommittee.

The customary letter of commendation was not forthcoming from President Truman. Secretary of the Treasury John W. Snyder did write a thank-you note, commenting in part:

The Treasury Enforcement Agencies have compiled an enviable record and it is in very large measure a direct result of your untiring efforts, particularly your insistence on the need for close cooperation among the various Agencies.

Your record of public service, covering a period of over forty years, is one that is rarely equalled, and you have

191

every reason to be proud of it. Your departure from the Department is leaving a gap that will indeed be difficult to fill.

With Irey gone in 1946, Truman was too busy with the United Nations, the cold war, and the state of the economy to pay much attention to internal corruption. Only after the inevitable scandals spilled all over the front pages of the nation's newspapers did he act to correct the situation. The Bureau of Internal Revenue became the Internal Revenue Service; the Intelligence Unit became the Intelligence Division; an Inspection Division was created to provide internal policing. Scores of dishonest officials were fired, and some of them convicted. The final proof of a new integrity came when the Intelligence Division sent their old boss, Joe Nunan, to prison.

Before that happened, however, organized crime had a field day. It was the era of the big fix. Leaders of the Chicago Syndicate were paroled and sent home. Robert Gould was paroled and retired to a plush home in Miami Beach to enjoy his millions. It was during this period that Luciano was released by Governor Tom Dewey—who had ambitions to succeed Truman as President—released from prison where Prosecutor Dewey had put him and deported to Italy for services allegedly rendered. Meyer Lansky saw him off on the boat.

The professionals trained by Irey watched and waited as the National Crime Syndicate took advantage of every opportunity even as individual gangsters had done during the Harding era. Case after case went out the window. Permits, long denied, were granted to gangsters to operate legitimate liquor companies. Under the leadership of Lansky and his old partner, Bugsy Siegel, Las Vegas was developed from a small desert town into a national gambling center with the syndicate in full control. Regional gambler centers, strictly illegal, flourished as never before at Newport, Hot Springs, Biloxi, Cicero, Youngstown, Miami Beach, Broward County, and elsewhere. The syndicate moved to control the developing television industry, invested in oil wells and gold mines, made deals with corrupt union officials and alliances with such businessmen as Harry Bennett of the Ford Motor Company. Such men as

192

George Remus, "King of the Bootleggers" (1927).

Al Capone being escorted to his trial.

NOTORIOUS PROHIBITION FIGURES

Moe Dalitz, charter member of the Cleveland Syndicate.

Meyer Lansky. As a young man he was known as "Johnny Eggs."

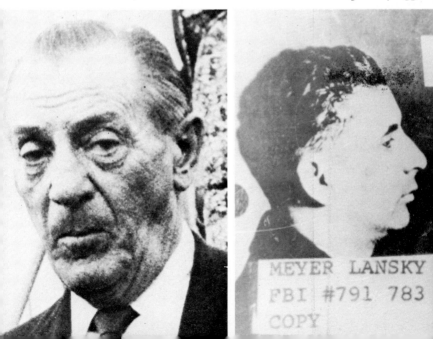

MEYER LANSKY
FBI #791 783
COPY

Deputy marshals, with portion of records impounded by the court in Moe Annenberg case.

Bolita policy equipment (Miami).

Lincoln Park in downtown Louisville, Kentucky, site of highly profitable real estate venture for Abner "Longie" Zwillman, labeled "Al
Capone of New Jersey."

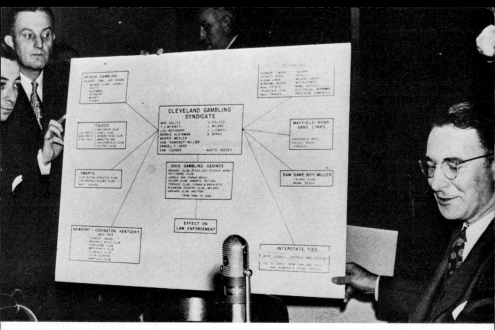

The Cleveland gambling syndicate network, as shown by the late Senator Estes Kefauver in Cleveland hearings.

Wearing badge and gun, Flo Bratten, secretary to Vice President Alben Barkley, is sworn in as deputy sheriff of Campbell County—whose principal city is the notorious Newport, Kentucky.

(Left) Police break into the Hi-De-Ho Club, Newport, Kentucky, "night-club" run by city marshal.

(Right) Frank "Screw" Andrews, ex-numbers king of Newport, swings at Cincinnati *Post* and *Times-Star* reporter Bryon Schumaker during investigation of reform Sheriff George Ratterman.

(Left) "Big Ruth" Jarvis, of Hi-De-Ho Club.

(Right) Tito Carinci, manager of Newport gambling casino, the Tropicana Club, flanked by strippers from the club at the 1961 Ratterman trial. April Flowers, left, and Rita Desmond, right, later admitted that much of their testimony in case was untrue.

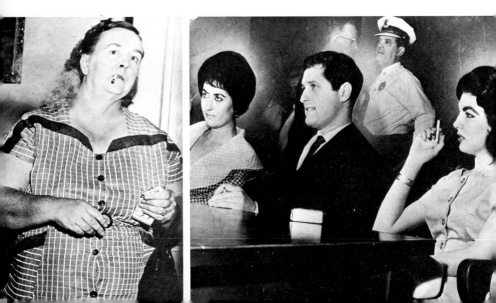

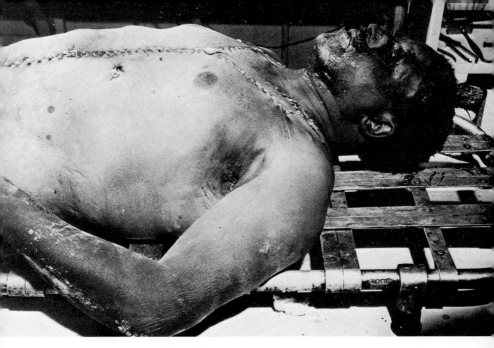

Newport numbers king Melvin Clark after autopsy.

A youthful A. B. "Happy" Chandler poses moments after taking the oath of office for his first term as governor of Kentucky in December, 1935. Chandler later proclaimed the "right of the people of Newport to have it dirty" if they liked it that way.

New York gangster Joey Rao *(left)* and "Trigger Mike" Coppola, East Harlem numbers king, with Mike, Jr., in 1952.

Edward Levinson *(foreground)*, associate of Bobby Baker, indicted for income tax evasion related to "skimming" operations in Las Vegas casino. Photo was taken by Los Angeles police with hidden camera.

Longie Zwillman made millions in real estate deals—Zwillman bought and sold a square block in the heart of downtown Louisville in one of that city's most profitable land deals in history.

From being down for the count in 1941, the National Crime Syndicate recovered to the point where it threatened to take over the nation by 1950. Then came Senator Estes Kefauver and his Special Committee to Investigate Organized Crime in Interstate Commerce. In a series of hearings in 1950-51, Kefauver revealed the shocking truth about the syndicate and its relation to business and to politics. Senator John Williams of Delaware laid bare the corruption in government agencies, and a subcommittee of the House Ways and Means Committee headed by Representative Cecil R. King followed up with hearings. The nightmare ended for the vast majority of honest men in the house that Irey built. They resumed their duties in full knowledge however, that organized crime was by now far more powerful than it had ever been before.

Almost the first order of business was former boss Joe Nunan.

Nunan was born in 1897 in Brooklyn and went to school there. Having entered Fordham University in 1914, he interrupted his college career in 1917 to go with the Fordham Ambulance Corps to France, where he rose from private to second lieutenant. Discharged in 1919, he returned to college and received his law degree in 1922. He married a Brooklyn girl that following year and became the father of four children.

Politics attracted Nunan, and as will be remembered, New York politics in those days were controlled by Tammany Hall. In 1929 he was elected to the New York State Assembly and in 1930 to the State Senate, where he remained until 1940. He lost his job when Wendell Wilkie carried Queens County for the Republicans in his unsuccessful effort to stop Roosevelt after two terms. As a reward for loyal service, Nunan was appointed Collector of Internal Revenue for the First District of New York. On March 1, 1944, he became Commissioner of Internal Revenue. During all this period he had been a member of the law firm of Tolbert, Ewen and Patterson.

Upon his resignation as commissioner on June 30, 1947, he returned to the private practice of law. In addition to the New York firm, he helped organize a Washington, D.C., firm known as Wenchal, Tannenbaum and Nunan. Obviously, he expected his service in Washington to attract clients. It did.

On February 2, 1951, the King Subcommittee to "investigate the administration of Internal Revenue laws," was set up. Shortly thereafter ex-Commissioner Nunan filed amended joint returns for himself and his wife for the calendar years 1949 and 1950. Special agents of the Intelligence Unit were assigned to work with the King Subcommittee and, in October, 1951, were ordered to do a special examination of Nunan.

It soon developed that Nunan had no checkbooks or canceled checks for the years prior to 1951. Neither had he any personal books or records to substantiate the date on his income tax returns. The investigators were told he retained no accountants or attorneys to assist him. Schedules and details clearly required by printed instructions on the returns had been omitted. Nor did the ex-commissioner claim any special knowledge as a tax expert despite his experience. In fact, he admitted it was only "the chance of politics" that made him a federal official in the first place.

When the special agents pointed to his lack of records and asked for a net worth statement, Nunan declined to give it. Undiscouraged, the investigators plowed ahead and soon discovered that many items of income had been omitted from his returns for the years 1946 through 1950. They ranged in size from $200 to $900, but in 1946 alone they totaled $11,720. Nunan also had a habit of paying in cash. When he bought some stock in 1946, he handed the broker 160 hundred-dollar bills and 14 fifty-dollar bills for a total of $16,700. Later another cash payment of $11,252 was made the same year.

Cash deposits and expenditures for the four years totaled $98,092. For the five years, 1945-50, the special agents unearthed $160,000 of deposits and expenditures in excess of Nunan's reported net income. During the period one dress shop was paid $29,500, of which $12,014, was paid in cash.

Nunan had an answer to all questions. Aware that the ledger sheets of his bank for the years prior to 1937 had been destroyed, he said he had $170,000 in his bank account in March, 1933. Fearful the bank might fail, as so many were doing, he began withdrawing large sums from the bank and putting it—

as so many of his colleagues in New York were doing—in the proverbial little tin box, which he kept on a shelf in the bedroom of his home. Shades of Tammany Hall!

Most of the money really belonged to his wife, he explained, and she had a key to the box. Aware that records showed he rented a $10 safe-deposit box at a bank on July 1, 1935, Nunan said that he shifted the cash from the box at home to the box at the bank and kept it there until the end of 1944. Then, having apparently decided the banks were solvent after all, he began returning the cash in piecemeal deposits to his bank account. Thus the money which the government considered income over the years 1946 through 1950 really was just the $170,000 he had started with back in 1933.

One difficulty with this explanation was the fact the story kept changing every time he was questioned by the special agents, the United States Attorney, and the grand jury. Thus the amount he had left in his checking account, despite his fears the bank might close, varied from $10,000 to $25,000.

Mrs. Nunan did her best to confirm her husband's stories. She explained she had inherited a large sum from a rich uncle —another variation of the Tammany Hall tales heard by Judge Seabury—and an additional amount from her father. All these funds were turned over to her husband, she said, prior to 1932.

The special agents checked out the story in great detail and were ultimately able to prove to a jury's satisfaction that there had been no $170,000 fund to begin with. In fact, Nunan had operated on a slim income in those early days. Almost all his money had been made after he became a federal employee by "the chance of politics," and a lot of it had come after he returned to private law practice. Take the case of Brown & Bigelow, for example.

Some six months after Nunan ceased to be commissioner, the advertising firm of Brown & Bigelow decided it wanted to market some securities. The stockholder's meeting was set for December 6, 1947, and it was necessary to secure a closing agreement from the Bureau of Internal Revenue before the meeting. Company attorneys went to Washington to arrange it but were told there were so many similar applications ahead of theirs that such prompt action was impossible. The attorneys then retained the ex-commissioner, who made a few telephone calls and secured the closing agreement. For his services, Nunan was to be paid $25,000. Instead of cash, he asked for stock which the company had bought at $9.50 a share. As nearly as it could be figured on that basis, Nunan got 2,630 shares valued at $24,985. A bill in that amount was made out by Nunan, and the stock was sent to Nunan on January 2, 1948.

Interestingly enough, however, Nunan's bill was not on the letterhead of either of Nunan's law firms but, instead, bore a personal topping. The stock was not sent to Nunan at his law firm but to his private address. The law firm's bookkeeper had no knowledge of the matter. It was definitely established that the stock became Nunan's personal property. Brown & Bigelow manufactured remembrance advertising—pens, calendars, etc.

In 1950, Anheuser-Busch, Inc., was about to complete a $30,-000,000 brewery in Newark and anticipated some trouble over "permits and things of that sort." Nunan was put on a retainer of $500 a month, none of which reached his law firms. Nor was it reflected on his 1950 income tax return. Nunan explained that he was not hired to perform legal services but to "try to get Anheuser-Busch beer into certain places in New York."

When called to testify before the King Subcommittee, Nunan took the Fifth Amendment when asked about a liquor permit granted the Gotham Liquor Company in 1946, while he was commissioner. His reluctance to talk about it is understandable in view of the record.

Keyman in Gotham was Louis I. Pokrass, a former bootlegger. After Repeal, he joined with Lansky, Costello, and Joe Adonis in an alleged legal liquor business called Capitol Wine and Spirits. Gangsters can seldom resist the opportunity to operate a legitimate business in illegal fashion, and Pokrass was no exception. An investigation resulted in 1942, and Pokrass was able to settle by paying $100,000. However, Capitol's basic permits were revoked. Assets of the company were sold, and the funds received were invested in Bugsy Siegel's Flamingo Club in Las Vegas, which was then under construction. Although it was syndicate money, Pokrass became a vice-president, taking orders from Lansky, who was the largest syndicate shareholder other than Bugsy.

Meanwhile, Pokrass tried repeatedly to get back into the liquor business. The appointment of Nunan as commissioner gave him a new opportunity, and he formed Gotham. Despite all past rejections, his latest application was given routine treatment—and rejection was recommended. However, Carroll Mealey, Deputy Commissioner of Internal Revenue and boss of the Alcohol Tax Unit, got orders from Nunan to approve Pokrass' application, and it was approved. Mealey was rewarded by Pokrass with a mink coat, a new car, and later— after Pokrass entered the television business with Lansky and Costello—two $1,000 checks for "legal expenses."

About the same time, Nunan also arranged for Joseph Reinfeld to get a liquor application approved for Somerset Liquor Company. Reinfeld had headed the Reinfeld Syndicate during the great days of the Big Seven in partnership with the Bronfman brothers of Canada and Longie Zwillman, the "Al Capone of New Jersey." Much of the liquor brought to Rum Row off the East Coast was transported there by the Reinfeld Syndicate.

Nunan, who admitted he met Costello prior to 1946 at meetings in bars and later at a party Costello gave at the Copacabana for the Salvation Army, also admitted he was retained by Reinfeld upon leaving federal service. His retainer, he said, was $7,500 a year. In return, he appeared "once or twice in the Bureau for Mr. Reinfeld."

The ex-commissioner admitted, when asked, that he ordered the Intelligence Unit not to cooperate in the investigation of an Internal Revenue employee in Chicago by a federal grand jury. When the frustrated grand jury failed to indict the man, Nunan arranged for his promotion to a higher position.

Nunan was not the only man to meddle with Internal Revenue personnel. His deputy commissioner continued the practice after Nunan left the department. A problem developed in Louisville, where Howard B. Taylor was district supervisor. According to sworn testimony, the powerful liquor industry of Kentucky wanted Taylor transferred "because he required them to comply strictly with all regulations."

Political pressure was applied to move Taylor to New Orleans and to transfer Fred C. Farrell from New Orleans to Louisville. On February 10, 1949, Mrs. Flo Bratten, confidential secretary of Vice President Alben Barkley—formerly a Senator from Kentucky—called Mealey and told him:*

"A very distinguished group of personal friends of the Vice President and mine want to call on you tomorrow. The junior and senior Senators from the State of Kentucky, Chapman and Withers, and the best Congressman of all, Carl Perkins. Now what time tomorrow?"

Mealey set up the meeting for 9:30 A.M. Five days later he talked to Farrell in Louisville.

"Congratulations on your new job," he said.

"Got in this morning," replied Farrell. "Furniture got held up in a flood. I called to let you know I'm here and see if there are any more instructions."

"No, there aren't, except this. I told Barkley's people that they should agree on one man to direct things down there. They said they would and as soon as I know I'll get in touch with you."

"I wish you would," said Farrell. "We'd certainly be glad to have that."

On the same day, February, 15, 1949, Mealey called Mrs. Bratten in Barkley's office and reported:

"I talked to those Senators and Congressmen and because of the fact that Farrell was going in there today, I told them to get in touch with you folks. If you people would pick one man down there Farrell should check with all the time, I will so instruct him, but I would like it to be one certain person."

Mrs. Bratten replied: "Well, the Vice President is out of town."

"Well, whenever you can," said Mealey, "but I think he should say to Farrell to see this guy. Don't you think so?"

"Yes, that is right. How about McTigue getting that appointment?"

"That is fine," said Mealey.

* This and following transcripts of telephone conversations were introduced in evidence before the House of Representatives Subcommittee on Administration of Internal Revenue Laws, holding hearings into the Truman Scandals.

This exchange not only discloses the state of affairs to which the Bureau of Internal Revenue had sunk, but also proves once again the relation of politics to big business. If Mrs. Bratten seemed to be exercising unusual authority for a confidential secretary, her actions were consistent with later developments. Eventually, she caused the Vice President considerable embarrassment.

On December 2, 1952, Nunan was indicted on five counts of tax evasion. He was charged with evading $91,086 in the years 1945-50. Eighteen months later his trial began. Mrs. Nunan testified about the "rich uncle" and identified him as former Tammany leader Charles F. Murphy. Other witnesses included big-time gambler Frank Erickson, who testified he had lost $1,800 to Nunan at odds of 9 to 1. Nunan in winning proved he was an expert politician—he bet Truman would beat Dewey in 1948. Still another witness was a former Truman pal, James P. Finnegan, who was serving a jail sentence for misconduct in office during his tenure as tax collector at St. Louis.

It took a jury three hours and five minutes to convict Nunan on all five counts. Judge Walter Bruchhausen told the jurors their verdict was justified, and on August 3, 1954, he sentenced the ex-commissioner to five years in prison and a $15,000 fine. In passing sentence, the judge said Nunan's conduct "cannot be condoned."

Ironically, in the period between conviction and sentencing, Mrs. Nunan inherited $166,000 from a cousin.

On May 4, 1954, Mealey was indicted on four counts of tax evasion. He had resigned as deputy commissioner on October 5, 1951, listing ill health as the reason. Apparently it was a valid excuse. The trial was postponed repeatedly because of Mealey's health. His attorneys sought to have the charges dismissed, but it was not until 1963, when another Democrat was in the White House, that this was done. Even then, action was taken only after evidence was submitted that Mealey was near death. Shortly after the case was nol-prossed, he did die.

Of all the cases to grow out of the so-called Truman Scandals, perhaps the one attracting the most interest involved Daniel A. Bolich, former Assistant Commissioner of Internal Revenue, and influence peddler Henry W. Grunewald. The activities of Grunewald were first exposed by the King Subcommittee, which heard testimony that Senator Owen Brewster passed on $5,000 of Grunewald's money to then Senate candidate Richard M. Nixon to aid his political campaign. Another $5,000 went to Senator Milton Young. Both Senators admitted they received the money but said they didn't know it came from Grunewald.

Bolich was special agent in charge of the New York office of Intelligence when in the fall of 1948 he was promoted to assistant commissioner. He moved to Washington and lived in a hotel suite. Grunewald paid the rent.

Two instances of bribery to fix tax cases were involved in the 1954 indictment of Bolich and Grunewald. One concerned Pattullo Modes, a New York dress manufacturing company. From 1942 to 1946 the company defrauded the government of taxes on more than $300,000. The second fix was for the benefit of Gotham Beef Company of New York, which had failed to report income on sales of meat above ceiling prices. The sales amounted to around $100,000.

Intelligence Unit men were closing in on both companies, and by coincidence the law firm of Schopick & Davis was retained by both. The attorneys decided some "real help" was needed, and to get it, they turned to Bolich's friend Grunewald. He could help, he said, but it would cost Pattullo Modes $100,000 and Gotham Beef $60,000. This was agreeable, and the money was placed in safe-deposit boxes with safeguards that it would not be delivered to Grunewald until official notice of "no criminal prosecution" was received. Grunewald, whose code name was Captain Henry, arranged for Bolich to kill the cases, and the money was released.

On March 28, 1955, Bolich, Grunewald, and New York attorney Max Halperin were convicted. Each was fined heavily and sentenced to five years in prison. On appeal, the Supreme Court ordered a new trial on the grounds that the trial judge failed properly to distinguish in his charge to the jury between "concealment in order to achieve the central purpose of the conspiracy and concealment to cover up an already executed crime."

Grunewald died on September 25, 1958, as defense at-

200

torneys fought a delaying action. Bolich and Halperin were acquitted the following year, when the case was tried for the second time. By then the Intelligence Division was worrying about Bernard Goldfine and his "gifts" to Republican officials. Nixon, whose career had been aided by Grunewald's money, was Vice President.

12

WITHOUT CONFESSION

ON August 4, 1941, a businessman in North Cohocton, New York, picked up a popular magazine and became indignant. The article that aroused his anger concerned an attractive young lady called Virginia Hill. She was described as "Broadway's biggest spender—with a mysterious, limitless fund of cash."

Pictures accompanied the story—pictures of Virginia doing the rumba in her bare feet, of champagne parties in New York nightclubs, of her wardrobe of 100 gowns and 50 pairs of shoes.

The businessman sent a copy of the article to the Bureau of Internal Revenue. His covering letter noted that "such performances are the most effective recruiting service I can think of for the ranks of the Communists and Socialists." He also mentioned that recently a prominent citizen of Atlantic City had been sent to the penitentiary after "an investigation sprouting from suspicion as to why he was cutting up so much easy money in New York nightclubs."

Elmer Irey, who knew all about Nucky Johnson's gay mode of life, was sufficiently impressed to send the article to the special agent in charge of the New York office with the suggestion that "when convenient, one of your agents make inquiries concerning the filing of returns by this individual in the New York area."

This is the first official notice taken by the Intelligence Unit of the woman whose mysterious role in organized crime has never been fully explained. Years passed before the special agents began trying to answer some of the questions about her. First the war came to delay a probe and was followed by the corrupt years when the Intelligence Unit was handcuffed. It was only after Virginia shocked the Kafauver Committee by blandly attributing her wealth to the fact that she was "the world's best lay" that a probe began.

Virginia used more than twenty aliases in her career, but she was born Onie Virginia Hill on August 20, 1916, in Lipscomb, Alabama, near the steel city of Bessemer. The oldest of nine children, she was possessed of both beauty and what special agents called "exceptional intelligence." Both were to be needed to make her into an international playgirl who lived like a princess in the resorts of three continents.

Her father was a marble polisher and horse trader by profession and a habitual drunkard by choice. He deserted his family when Virginia was fourteen, leaving her to support her mother, three sisters, and five brothers. Three years later Virginia left home to ply the only trade that paid her well. She visited the Chicago World's Fair, which was featuring A Century of Progress and prostitutes from around the nation. It was there she was "discovered" by Joe Epstein, who became her lover, her friend, and her financier in that order.

Epstein was head of a large bookmaking combine known as Stern & Horwick which maintained offices at 10 North Clark Street and 720 North Wabash Avenue in Chicago. Others in the outfit included Edward Stern, Julius Horwick, Jack Terman, and James Mondi. In Capone's heyday, Mondi was a big shot, but he lost power when Scarface Al went to prison. Epstein was an accountant and apparently taught Virginia much about money and how to use it.

In her testimony before the Kefauver Committee, Virginia explained her relationship to Epstein: "I got to know him, and we became friends, and good friends, and then he told me that I should take care of my money, and then I told him when I have it, I always spend it, so he says, well, he'll hold it for me; try, you know, to keep me from spending all, you know; that I had to think about tomorrow and all that stuff."

Epstein began using Virginia as a courier, delivering cash to winners and picking up the loot gathered around the country by syndicate collectors. In the process she met most of the nation's top gangsters: Costello, Adonis, Lansky, Kastel, Zwillman, Joe Fischetti, Moe Sedway, and Bugsy Siegel. Some people she swore she never met—Luciano, for one, and Mickey Cohen for another. Siegel borrowed Mickey's car once, she said, and let her use it. Someone stole the car from her, but that was as close as she came to Cohen.

Apparently in the syndicate there was a certain willingness to share a good thing and no ill feelings if the good thing moved on. Thus Adonis had Virginia as his mistress before she met Siegel, but he surrendered her to Bugsy without regret. It was in this period that she began to be mentioned in gossip columns and society pages. The New York *Journal-American* reported on March 8, 1939, that she had suffered a fractured skull and scalp lacerations in the crash of a light plane. She was described as an "actress." In December, 1940, the same paper had her as a "23 year old Georgia oil heiress" who was returning to New York from a visit to her mother in Chicago. In 1941 she was still an "oil heiress" who had won her fight to be divorced from her third husband, Carlos Gonzales, a rumba dancer.

The divorce was granted in January. By June 20, 1941, the *Journal-American* reported she would soon announce her engagement to Major Riddle, "trucking tycoon and former fiancé." Riddle (the first name is Major) later became a gambling figure of some note in Las Vegas and the author of *The Weekend Gambler's Handbook,* but he never married Virginia.

By August 4, 1941, the same newspaper was calling Virginia a "much photographed Manhattan glamor girl," and noting she had more fur coats than any woman in the country. On November 4, 1941, however, the newspaper was reporting that Virginia had gone West to Hollywood, where she was being called "the feminine Diamond Jim Brady." The story noted that her money "is wired to her and she loses no time in putting it into circulation." Movie mogul Sam Goldwyn, the story continued, was planning to add a scene to his current movie, *Ball of Fire,* in which Virginia would play herself in the role of hostess.

The *Journal-American* continued to play up Virginia's antics. On December 13, 1941, it reported she "spends $7,500 a night" and explains her wealth by saying, "I married money." Eight days later, however, the paper said Virginia was joining the Red Cross in Chicago and calling off all parties "for the duration" of the war. A week later came the startling news that Virginia "bopped a press agent in the Havana Madrid." Six months later she was reported to have leased Falcon's Lair, the former home of Rudolph Valentino in Hollywood.

And so on.

Virginia met Siegel in 1943 on one of Bugsy's periodic visits to New York to report on his stewardship of the West Coast. For the next five years, she listed Los Angeles as her residence although her travels and big spending continued unabated. When the war ended, the syndicate decided the temper of the times called for expansion in the gambling field. This was Lansky's province, generally speaking, but as Western boss, Siegel would have a part. Three major projects in different parts of the country were launched in 1945.

In Broward County, Florida, north of Miami, the Colonial Inn, next door to Gulfstream Park, became a plush casino. Lansky's eight partners included Frank Erickson and Joe Adonis. In the corrupt atmosphere cultivated by Sheriff Walter Clark, expansion soon followed, and in short order the racetrack was virtually surrounded by casinos of "rug" quality.

Conditions in and around New Orleans were still attractive to the syndicate, especially in Jefferson Parish. The plush Beverly Club opened on the outskirts of town. Costello and Kastel, who had put slots in New Orleans back in the days of Huey Long, were the principal partners of Lansky in this venture.

In Las Vegas, Siegel, Lansky, and eight other partners purchased the El Cortes Hotel. The joint, while profitable enough, didn't measure up to either Lansky's or Bugsy's vision. In 1946 the hotel was sold, and the money was invested in the Nevada Projects Corporation, which was set up to operate the fabulous Flamingo, already under construction. The Flamingo was Bugsy's dream, the first of many casino-hotels to be built outside Las Vegas on what was to become known as the Strip. Its construction came at a time when materials were still scarce and the only reliable source was the black market. The syndicate had plenty of connections there, and Siegel was able to get what he needed. Nevertheless, his eagerness to see his dream become reality caused him to lose his cool, and expenses mounted to what were then considered astronomical figures.

Siegel was the largest stockholder in Nevada Projects, holding 195 of the 1,000 shares. Third largest stockholder was W. R. Wilkerson, publisher of the Hollywood *Reporter*. Wilkerson, along with G. Harry Rothberg, had been Siegel's sole partners when the Flamingo was begun. He sold his interest in April, 1947, to the corporation. Rothberg, who had 95 shares, was the former owner of the Regents Wine and Liquor Distributors of New York, which handled black-market liquor shipments for the syndicate. His brother, Sam Rothberg, was the second largest stockholder with 150 shares. Sam was former vice-president of the American Distilling Company, Inc., which had produced some of that black-market liquor at its Pekin, Illinois, plant. Lansky had 100 shares, as did Louis I. Pokrass, head of the Gotham Liquor Company and buddy of Internal Revenue Commissioner Joe Nunan. Hyman Abrams, that old ex-bootlegger and longtime friend of Lansky from Boston, held 22½ shares. The rest was in the names of attorneys, a dentist, and a minor hood known as Allan Smiley.

Virginia was on hand on December 26, 1946, when Bugsy opened the casino for action. The hotel was still incomplete, but the impatient Siegel could wait no longer. Everything went wrong. Bad weather grounded the planes Bugsy had chartered to bring Hollywood to Nevada. The casino actually lost money. Two days later Siegel closed everything down and tried to console himself with Virginia, who was living with him in the hotel penthouse

One woman was not enough for the handsome Siegel. Virginia, usually as tolerant as the hoods she slept with, couldn't abide one of them. Wendy Barrie, an actress of some reputation, was a problem. Apparently she thought she actually loved Bugsy and two years earlier had gone so far as to announce her engagement to him. Amused, Siegel kept her on the string. Her presence at the Flamingo annoyed Virginia, and the girl from Alabama believed in direct action. One night she socked it to Wendy, a punch the steelworkers of Bessemer would have admired. Allegedly Bugsy was shocked at such unladylike conduct and said so. Virginia promptly took a handful of sleeping pills—the first of several attempts at suicide—but the now-remorseful Siegel got her to the hospital in time.

Meanwhile, the so-called wire-service war was going on. Various writers of near fiction have claimed Siegel broke with the National Crime Syndicate and tried to keep control of the western end of the rival Trans-American Publishing and News Service long after Ragen had been shot and Mickey McBride had taken over Continental. Siegel, remembering the value the Chicago boys had been to him through their control of Hollywood, did help Trans-American in violation of syndicate wishes. However, the Flamingo occupied all his attention. He neglected the assorted rackets he had so carefully developed to give full time to his dream. The board of directors of the syndicate decided Bugsy would have to die, but at Lansky's suggestion he was allowed to live long enough to get the Flamingo off and running. After all, Lansky had a lot of money invested, as did other members of the syndicate, and they knew Bugsy would succeed if anyone could.

Siegel could not have been ignorant of the situation. He allegedly flew to Havana, where Lucky Luciano, in violation of his parole, had secretly established himself, and appealed. Presumably he hoped that if the Flamingo proved to be a resounding success, he might be pardoned. However, Bugsy was a member of the board, and while lesser figures in crime can sometimes be forgiven, an effort by a board member to be independent threatens the very existence of syndicate unity. As a charter member, Bugsy had to know this.

Virginia found him hard to live with during this period. After one bitter quarrel, Bugsy suggested she go down to Miami Beach and buy herself a house there. He gave her approximately $50,000, she said when questioned by special agents in 1951, and she used $20,000 as a down payment on a plush house on Sunset Island No. 1. It was a nice place, but, again according to Virginia, the pollen from the tropical flowers that surrounded it aggravated her hay fever, and she spent little time there. In Beverly Hills, California, she rented a home at 810 Linden Drive.

Meanwhile, the Flamingo reopened on March 27, 1947, and soon was making money. In May the casino cleared more than $300,000, and Bugsy was happy. There seemed a chance the syndicate might decide he was worth more to it alive than dead.

The day after the Flamingo reopened, a passport was issued to Onie Virginia Hill. Virginia's signature was witnessed by Dr. Margaret J. Chung, a mystery woman in her own right. Virginia asked permission to visit Italy—to which Luciano had reluctantly returned—England, France, Norway, Spain, Portugal, Greece, Holland, and Switzerland. A letter accompanying the application stated: "The purpose of this trip to Europe is to make arrangements for importation of wines and liquors and to sign necessary papers for the establishment of this agency of the Compague Commerciale des Vines et Spiritsneus [sic] of 4 Rue de Castiglione in Paris, France."

Was there another motive?

Mrs. Betty Cromwell, a close friend of Virginia's, told special agents later, that Virginia once revealed in a candid moment that "Bugsy quietly divorced his wife and married me in Mexico City. When Bugsy was killed, I never disclosed we were married because I wanted his children to get his money."

Other underworld sources have stated that Siegel planned to join Virginia in Europe just as soon as the Flamingo paid off enough to satisfy the syndicate and replenish his personal bankroll.

On June 10, 1947, Virginia flew out of Los Angeles alone. She spent two days in Chicago with her old friend Joe Epstein, and he accompanied her by plane to New York. A few days were spent at the Hampshire House, and on June 16 she arrived in Paris by air. A young Frenchman met her at the airport and escorted her to various night spots such as Maxim's. She used the alias Mrs. Nunn.

Four days after her arrival in Paris, Siegel was sitting on the sofa in the living room of Virginia's rented house on Linden Drive in Beverly Hills. Allan Smiley, a junior stockholder in the Flamingo, was at the other end of the sofa. Outside the window a syndicate executioner aimed a .30-caliber Army carbine. Siegel, sitting under a lamp in front of the undraped window, was a perfect target. The killer fired nine times, taking no chances. Two bullets hit Bugsy in the face. His right eye was found some distance away on the tiled floor. Two other slugs hit him in the chest. Five shots went wild, one of them putting a hole through a painting of a nude holding a wine glass. Smiley, whose real name was Smihoff, was unhurt. Had he been there simply to finger Bugsy for an imported killer who might be unfamiliar with his target? Recorded telephone conversations later indicated Smiley was very unhappy with the syndicate because promises made for services rendered had not been fully kept.

Twenty minutes after Bugsy was killed, the syndicate took over the Flamingo. Mickey Cohen, a protégé of the Cleveland Division, replaced Bugsy as Western boss, much to the disgust of Jack Dragna of the Mafia.

Siegel's attorney, Joe Ross, another minor stockholder in the Flamingo, gave special agents this list of Bugsy's known assets:

1. In commercial account at Union Bank, $3,137.75.
2. An insurance refund check, $108.53.
3. One thousand shares of American Power and Light Company stock. It had been pledged as collateral on a bank loan which had an unpaid balance of $7,375, plus interest. The loan was made in January, 1947.
4. Two hundred and twenty shares of stock in Nevada Projects Corporation with par value of $250 per share.
5. Promissory note dated August 6, 1946, from Nevada Projects for $113,750. This was a loan to the company and not part of Siegel's investment.
6. Another promissory note from Nevada Projects for $25,000. It was dated February 6, 1947.

209

7. One 1946 Chrysler convertible coupe.

8. Five hundred shares of Thickol stock, no value listed.

9. Interest in a bookmaking concession at Frontier Turf Club, Las Vegas, worth $5,853.89.

10. Interest in a bookmaking concession at Golden Nugget Turf Club, Las Vegas, worth $32,313.46.

The attorney said he knew of two safe-deposit boxes in Siegel's name but doubted they contained much of value. He also said Siegel owed about $8,000 on his 1946 income tax returns.

In one of the safe-deposit boxes was found ten $100,000 bearer bonds of the Republic of Bolivia. The bonds had been defaulted and were estimated to be worth only $62,500. Total value of Siegel's estate was said to be "in excess of $600,000." Bugsy had come a long way since the days when he and Lansky guarded booze shipments against the "outlaws" led by Legs Diamond. Lansky, however, still had a lot farther to go.

When the news of Siegel's death reached Chicago, Epstein called Virginia at the Westminster Hotel in Paris, where she was staying in a suite. Virginia had been living it up with her twenty-one-year-old escort, a member of "one of the finest families in France." Upon getting the news, she went into seclusion at the hotel until July 2. Not even the young man could comfort her. Finally, however, he was able to persuade her to take a trip. A limousine with chauffeur was rented, and Virginia, the young man, and his mother piled in and rode to the French Riviera. Upon arriving at Monte Carlo, Virginia sent the car back to Paris with its driver. The bill was 100,000 francs, or $633, for the two-day trip.

Virginia checked in at the Old Beach Club Hotel but remained moody and depressed. On July 9 she took an overdose of sleeping pills and was rushed to the Hôpital de Monaco. She was there only twenty-four hours. Upon release, Virginia moved to La Réserve, an expensive hotel at Beaulieu with a nurse in constant attendance. The young Frenchman and his mother went back to Paris, where on July 23 Virginia returned, to stay this time at a suite in the Ritz Hotel.

Still moody over Bugsy's death, the fugitive from Alabama tried again to join the man she said she had married. On July 26 she took another dose of pills and was hurried to the Amer-

ican Hospital in a suburb of Paris. She stayed there until August
7. An officer of the American consulate arranged for her to fly
back to the States, and she went immediately to her home on
Sunset Island, Miami Beach.

Conditions were not the best in Miami Beach. This time it
was the local citizens instead of the pollen that bothered her.
Despite newspaper stories describing her as "an Alabama heiress," the neighbors assumed her money came from the late
Bugsy—and they didn't want to be near her.

Since Al Capone found a home on Palm Island in Biscayne
Bay, Miami Beach has been a magnet for gangsters. Thousands
settled in the area. Some were big shots like Robert Gould,
Joe Massei, Al Polizzi, Bill Dwyer, Tony Ricci, Joe Adonis,
Lefty Clarke, and Trigger Mike Coppola. Others were younger
men on the make. Just up the road in Hollywood, Florida,
lived Bugsy's old partner, Meyer Lansky, who bossed a casino complex and invested heavily in Miami Beach real estate.
It didn't take rumor long to circulate that Virgina was "hot,"
and the good citizens felt uneasy to have her around.

At the insistence of Miami Beach police, Ed Bishop was hired
to guard Virginia. Bishop, a private eye, later was to play a
curious role in South Florida events. Rumor had it that Virginia in a moment of frankness gave him useful information.

Charles "Chick" Hill, Virginia's brother who had been traveling off and on with her since he was seven, left California,
where he and his wife had been living in his sister's rented
house on Linden Drive, and appeared in Miami Beach. Police
reports indicated that $100,000 in jewelry disappeared from
that house after Bugsy was killed, and it was assumed that
Chick and his wife, Jerri Mason, took it to Virgina. Some
months later, at Big Sky Lodge, Montana, Virginia gave her
landlady, Mrs. Edith Brissey, "certain jewelry." The bill of
sale noted the gift was "in payment for the hospitality and
comfort given me during very trying times when everything
seemed hopeless."

Shortly after Chick arrived on Miami Beach, neighbors were
talking about a curious incident involving Chick and a suitcase
full of money. A local attorney, who admittedly was among
those attempting, as he put it, "to force Miss Hill to move her

residence elsewhere," later passed the story on to special agents. It seems the roaches were big and many, so it was decided to call in an exterminator. When the roaches were dead, Chick opened a suitcase full of cash and extracted a single $100 bill with which he paid the exterminator. The incident caused neighbors to whisper that Virginia had all of the late Bugsy's cash and the syndicate would soon try to collect it. Nervousness increased.

Less than two weeks after arriving on the Gold Coast, the brokenhearted woman tried once more to kill herself. On August 22, she was taken to St. Francis Hospital, where she remained in a coma for sixty-seven hours. No one who knew the facts could doubt that this was a deadly serious effort at suicide, but Virginia learned that prices for failure were higher in Miami Beach than in Europe. The doctor's bill: a cool $3,-500.

Chick Hill had driven to Miami Beach in a Cadillac convertible which Siegel had bought for Virginia after she had purchased the house on Sunset Island. Allegedly it had been purchased from Sunset Motors, Inc., of Sunset Boulevard in Lansky's town of Hollywood, Florida, but investigators could find no record of the company and no such street in Hollywood. They did locate a Sunrise Boulevard some 10 miles to the north in Fort Lauderdale, however. It was in this car on September 3, that Virginia left Miami Beach.

Before leaving, she arranged with attorney Alexander S. Gordon to sell the house, which was valued at $50,000. She also arranged with Gordon to ship to Joe Epstein at the St. Clair Hotel, in Chicago, her vacuum cleaner, an antique chest, a carton of spices, and a box of books. Everything else except what she could carry in the car was left behind. Unfortunately for the curiosity of historians, no list of titles in the box of books was retained by the attorney.

Gordon was given $500 in cash and $300 in money orders to be used as expenses. It was not until March 15, 1948, that the attorney took care of the doctor bill.

The house was sold in March, 1948, the purchasers assuming an $18,042 balance on a first mortgage. Attorney Gordon sent Virginia, then in Mexico City, a cashier's check for $21,-

ooo. Apparently the house had depreciated in value as a result of her brief use of it.

Virginia and her brother drove up to the Grand Hotel at Point Clear, Alabama, but made no effort to revisit the old home town of Lipscomb. The next stop was the wild and wide-open gambling town of Biloxi, Mississippi, on the Gulf of Mexico. Epstein joined the party there, and they drove on by way of the Grand Canyon to Salt Lake City to Big Sky Lodge at Swan Lake, Montana. Chick Hill and his wife, who had joined the party, left Virginia there and drove the Cadillac to their home in Pensacola, Florida. Epstein took Virginia on several fishing trips before returning to Chicago. One of the jaunts into the hills cost $800.

In 1951 special agents attempting to reconstruct Virginia's movements and expenditures* encountered a first-class mystery at Swan Lake. Information was obtained that Lewis Leach, Jr., piloted a seaplane to the lake on several occasions while Virginia was staying at the lodge nearby. Reportedly, he delivered a number of packages to her. For many years, Virginia had been suspected of carrying not only cash but narcotics around the country, and she was on intimate terms with many of the big men in the racket. The agents wondered what was in those packages.

When it was discovered that after moving on in November to Spokane, Washington, where Epstein supplied a new wardrobe, Virginia went to Phoenix, Arizona, the suspicions grew stronger. A check of the Siegel file revealed a friend, Charles Ward, had a ranch near Phoenix and was a convicted narcotics peddler. Ward was sentenced in 1921 to ten years at Leavenworth Prison. Thereupon occurred one of those stranger-than-fiction stories. In prison, Ward became friendly with Herbert H. Bigelow, of Brown & Bigelow, who was serving a short stretch for income tax evasion. When they got out, Bigelow hired Ward as his manager, and upon his death "under alleged peculiar circumstances" in 1933, Ward inherited Bigelow's fortune of $2,500,000. He became president of Brown and Bige-

---

*Four thousand francs a day for her suite at Westminster Hotel in Paris; 10,000 francs a day for the suite at the Ritz; $136 for her stay at American Hospital; $366.12 for the hospital in Miami Beach, etc.

low—the firm, it will be remembered, which retained ex-Commissioner Nunan in 1947 to make some telephone calls. In 1936, Ward tried to get control of the company and found himself short. He borrowed $100,000 from Siegel and repaid it the next year, when he was unable to get the stock at a price he wanted to pay

The investigation was inconclusive, however, although Virginia's move from Phoenix to Mexico did nothing to dispel the suspicion. It was from Mexico that Ward had smuggled narcotics.

If Virginia was attending to business for the syndicate in Phoenix, her heart was still with Bugsy. On December 12, 1947, she was found unconscious in her room after another overdose of sleeping pills. She was taken to the Good Samaritan Hospital in Phoenix and registered as Mrs. Norma Hall. Eight days later she was released and resumed her travels. Chick brought her car, and she drove on toward Laredo, Texas. Just short of the border, she stopped long enough to call Epstein in Chicago after midnight and crossed into Mexico on December 23. Her next stop was Mexico City, where she was to remain for eighteen months.

In Mexico, Virginia began to recover from her grief. She maintained an apartment in Mexico City but spent much time at Acapulco and at San José de Purua, where she was known as Onie Brown. Chick shed his wife, who didn't like Mexico, and joined his sister. In 1949 he married Virginia's good friend Susan Cora, a former Mexican actress, and they opened a flower shop in the Hotel del Prado.

It was at this time that Virginia met Mrs. Cromwell, an American divorcée living in Mexico on her alimony. Virginia was in the company of Chato Juárez, son of the then Mexican Minister of Finance. Mrs. Cromwell described how angry Virginia became when a Mexican scandal sheet claimed she owned a huge yacht docked at Acapulco, was a friend of Luciano's, and assisted him in smuggling dope into the United States. She considered a libel suit against the paper, Mrs. Cromwell said, but was dissuaded by friends who said Mexico had lax libel laws. Hardly an unbiased observer, Mrs. Cromwell admitted that Virginia's "main preoccupation was self-enjoyment."

She liked to give lavish parties but also enjoyed fishing and water skiing. She paid for everything in cash and maintained no checking account. As for Epstein, she quoted Virginia as saying Joe once told her: "I brought you up."

Just a paternal interest, apparently.

A constant long-distance companion, said Mrs. Cromwell, was the same Dr. Chung who had helped Virginia get her passport. Special agents became very interested in "Ma" Chung and upon investigation found another mystery. Or perhaps it was but one phase of the overall puzzle.

Dr. Chung proved to be a highly regarded San Francisco specialist in woman's diseases. During the war years she established a procedure whereby some 1,500 airmen and submariners became known as the Bastard Sons of Mom Chung. Each was given a small jade Buddha, a card, and a number with which to identify themselves to one another. Although her office was in Chinatown, her prices were too high for Chinese patients. She had plenty of money and employed a white chauffeur to drive her Cadillac.

Nevertheless, an amazing number of people suspected there was more to Dr. Chung than met the eye. As with Virginia, all kinds of allegations found their way into official files—but no proof. No doubt exists, however, that she was very close to the girl from Alabama over a period of several years.

Special agents questioned Dr. Chung on October 10, 1951, about two cashier's checks she had received from Virginia. She couldn't remember what the $100 check was for but said the $3,000 check was intended to be used for plane tickets and other expenses when Virginia went to Europe before Bugsy's death. She had planned to accompany Virginia, she said, and they had also planned to ship a 1941 Cadillac to Spain, where—according to Virginia—it could be resold for as much as $20,000. For some reason, Dr. Chung continued, Virginia left without her or the car. Later, with Virginia's permission, she bought a new stove costing $1,200, which she used to entertain 150 servicemen each weekend. The balance she still owed Virginia, she said.

The interview didn't help very much.

Another good friend in Mexico was an aide to the President

of that country. He had some sort of business relationship with Epstein and, according to Virginia, was involved in the rackets. He followed her to Chicago in 1949, proposed marriage, and gave her $15,000 to splurge at Sun Valley, Idaho. It was a Christmas present, she said. A highly ironic one.

Virginia left Mexico in June, 1949, and lived in Chicago for the balance of the year. The Sun Valley expedition came early in 1950. She spent $11,500 during a six-week spree that became the subject of a column by Drew Pearson. Mrs. Cromwell came up at Virginia's expense and stayed two weeks. And Virginia fell in love once more. The aide to the Mexican President surely must have felt cheated.

Hans Hauser, an Austrian ski instructor at Sun Valley, was engaged to actress Ann Sothern, but he forgot all about her when he met the "Underworld Glamour Girl," as Pearson called her. The whirlwind courtship featured a visit to the ski races at Aspen, Colorado. Marriage followed at Elko, Nevada, on February 24.

There was no honeymoon as such. Virginia flew to Chicago to tell Epstein about her new love. Hans went back to Sun Valley and was fired because of the publicity given the marriage. The unemployed foreigner joined his new wife at the Ambassador-East Hotel in Chicago. All the publicity had attracted the interest of the United States Immigration and Naturalization Service, which began wondering about Hauser's status. Hans retained an attorney in Spokane, Washington, and departed there by train for an interview. The train was met some 25 miles outside Spokane by unidentified "friends," who carried the not-so-happy bridegroom the rest of the way by car. Special agents later learned that Hauser was carrying $15,000 in a sock. He turned the money over to a friend, James Crick, Jr., who acted as his agent in paying the attorney and buying a Cadillac convertible.

Virginia joined her husband in Spokane. After a few weeks she went to New Orleans, where she was house guest at the Roosevelt Hotel of Dandy Phil Kastel, that old associate of Costello and Lansky's. Ultimately Hauser joined her, and they flew over to Cuba, where she registered at the Sans Souci as Mrs. Onie V. Reid. Most of the summer was spent at Bar Harbor, Maine. Virginia was pregnant by now, and when the baby was about due, she followed the example of hoods such as Trigger Mike Coppola and Lansky who use the hospitals of the Boston area when they need medical attention because they provide excellent medical care and, perhaps as important, arrangements for privacy. Her son, Peter, was born at St. Elizabeth Hospital, Brighton, Massachusetts, on November 20, 1950.

Virginia checked into the hospital as Mrs. Oma Herman. Dr. William J. McDonald, chief of the obstetric department at the hospital, was in attendance and issued a birth certificate in the name of Peter Herman. Thereupon, four or five days after the birth, the mother confided that she was really "the notorious Virginia Hill Hauser," and the doctor had to change the birth certificate. His bill was only $275, which seems to prove it is cheaper to give birth than attempt suicide.

After a month in New York, the Hausers returned to Spokane in late January, 1951. On March 15, Virginia enlivened the proceedings of the Kefauver Committee, although the record shows she was less frank in the public hearing than when the Senators talked to her in an executive session. Nevertheless, she attracted almost as much attention as Costello. Among those interested was the Intelligence Unit. Almost ten years had passed since Elmer Irey ordered his men to make inquiries "when convenient." Irey was dead now, but Special Agent Clifford M. Rice took up the complex case with an energy Irey would have approved of. Scores of other special agents from Boston to Spokane assisted, and the probe spread to Mexico and France.

The heat began to build. On July 4, 1951, Hans and Peter Hauser boarded a plane in San Francisco and departed for Chile. Virginia dropped from sight, and a nationwide search began for her. Reporters learned she was en route by air to El Paso, Texas. Other reporters found her there on the morning of July 6. She was none too happy to be found.

Meanwhile, Bill Frank, the special agent who had counted the towels in Atlantic City and was now in charge of the Seattle office, issued a jeopardy assessment against Virginia—a device used when it is feared a taxpayer may try to dispose of property to avoid paying an overdue tax bill. Virginia flew back to Spo-

kane next day to find a sign on her door: SEIZED FOR THE AC-
COUNT OF THE UNITED STATES.

"Well," she said, "at least they watered the lawn."

Her good humor soon faded. After consulting an attorney,
she told reporters: "They never served me notice. They can't
put a lien on the house until they do. They're the Gestapo.
Talk about the German Gestapo, the federal Gestapo, that's all
they are." Somewhat sadly she added, "I've done nothing
wrong. I can't understand why everyone keeps hounding me."

A month later the house and its contents went on sale at
public auction. Eager buyers bought everything from the
garbage cans on the back porch to mink coats. The personal
property realized about $15,000, and an equal amount was ob-
tained from Virginia's equity in the house. Virginia left Spokane immediately thereafter and, after considerable travel, arrived in Mexico City on November 1. From there she flew to
Santiago, Chile, to join her husband and son. The family wandered around South America until May, 1952, and then flew to
Europe. Eventually they settled near Salzburg, Austria, in the
Alps. The skiing was good.

On June 23, 1954, a federal grand jury in Los Angeles indicted Virginia on charges that she had evaded $80,180 in
taxes. Special Agent Rice knew what her defense would be if
the case ever came to trial. In several interviews before leaving the country, she declared once again that she had received
"gifts" from men which she didn't consider taxable. All the
money she didn't spend, she said, she turned over to Epstein,
who doled it out to her when needed. He also handled all her
income tax affairs, she added.

The investigation uncovered ample evidence that Epstein
did send a steady flow of cash to Virginia over a period of many
years. Chick Hill recounted one episode in Mexico when the
postman delivered an envelope which was supposed to contain $5,000 in currency. All it had in it was a thin scarf. Vir-
ginia complained to postal authorities who arrested the letter
carrier and recovered half the money. According to Chick, Epstein also sent canned goods to Virginia when she visited Europe.

In 1956, Virginia, through an unnamed intermediary, offered to return to the United States and surrender if advised in advance of the amount of bond that would be required and given assurance of a speedy trial. The Justice Department, which had responsibility for prosecuting, curtly replied that it had "a policy of not entering into any agreements with fugitives." She officially became a fugitive on October 12, 1956, two days after her offer was rejected. "Wanted" posters went up on post office bulletin boards across the country. The poster described Mrs. Hauser as "White; female; age 39; height 5' 4"; 130 lbs.; complexion fair; hair auburn; eyes gray." It also said she was "formerly a paramour and associate of gangsters and racketeers."

On April 9, 1957, Virginia called Edward E. Keller, Jr., American vice-consul in Bern, Switzerland, and again volunteered to return home if by doing so she could end "the persecution and notoriety." She assured Keller she no longer had contact with gangsters. Exactly eleven days later, an undercover agent for the Bureau of Narcotics saw—or said he saw—Virginia dining with her old lover Joe Adonis, in Rome's plush Colony Restaurant. Adonis had been deported to Italy several years earlier.

In June, 1958, Special Agent Rice received information that Virginia wanted to return home in order to be free of Hauser, who had not been able to obtain United States citizenship. Other reports indicated she was running short of cash and might be willing to plead guilty to the charge if promised a light sentence. No deals were made, however, and Virginia remained in Europe.

On February 9, 1965, a routine notice of tax deficiency was sent to Virginia. She sent it back, accompanied by a note to Commissioner Sheldon S. Cohen:

DEAR MR. COHEN:
   I dont see how I could owe the tax department anything as for those years I was living on money I took from Joe Epstein of Chicago. It was money that he had given me years before and I had given back to him to keep for me so if you still think I owe this money why dont you send this bill to him when I last saw him in Japan in 1962 he

219

told me he still had around a hundred thousand dollars
of mine as for me I have no money.

Yours truly,
VIRGINIA HAUSER

Epstein said he had not sent Virginia any money since Christmas, 1963. Virginia was angry, he explained, because he had
tried to persuade her to return and face the music. He claimed
he had not replied to her last letter five months before in
which she said she was considering writing her autobiography.

Apparently Virginia was playing her last card.

On April 20, 1965, Virginia tried to kill herself once more.
The sleeping pills failed again. She told doctors at the pro-
vincial hospital near Salzburg that Epstein had threatened to
cut off her flow of cash unless she returned to America.

Peter Hauser, now fifteen years old and in training to become a waiter, sent this message to Chick Hill in December,
1965: "We are probably coming back to the States now. . . .
We were in Vienna in the USA Embassy, and are waiting for a
note from there. Will contact you again later. Merry Christmas."

A worldwide alert was sounded. It was assumed that if
Virginia did return, she would be traveling incognito. Over the
years she had been spotted in Hong Kong, Japan, and Cuba,
to say nothing of Rome and Paris. She might try to enter the
country from any direction. Hauser was no problem—she had
left him.

Nothing more was heard. And on March 22, 1966, she went to
some woods near the village of Koppl. Using water from an icy
stream, she swallowed twenty-eight sleeping pills. This time
there was no one to find her, to rush her to a hospital, to pump
out her stomach. Two days passed before her body was discovered.

With her died the answers to many mysteries. As the official
death certificate put it: "Onie Virginia Hauser née Hill, without confession."

13

SOME LIKE IT DIRTY

ORGANIZED crime has long been acutely conscious of the dangers of publicity. Al Capone provided an object lesson very early. Scarface, whose hero was Mussolini, enjoyed the spotlight and lived to regret it. The smart boys, however, had better instincts. They learned to use the clowns of crime to draw attention away from their own activities. The Mafia, with its internal intrigues and primitive reactions, was a perfect front for such men as Meyer Lansky and continues to be one today. Occasionally, the very size of an operation makes complete concealment impossible, but it's seldom indeed that the public gets more than a glimpse of the semi-invisible men who actually rule the National Crime Syndicate. The possibility exists, of course, that there are some leaders who have achieved complete anonymity and may not be recognized for years—if ever.

The Kefauver Committee in the two years it functioned turned up a wealth of information about the relation of crime to politics. It exposed conditions in a score of cities and embarrassed police chiefs, sheriffs, mayors, governors, and even ambassadors. Local revolts against corruption broke out all around the country in the wake of the hearings. Legislation was passed by Congress requiring gamblers to purchase federal wagering-tax stamps, to make monthly reports of all wagers accepted, and to pay a 10 percent tax on the same. The measure was admittedly designed to force gamblers out of business, rather than provide additional revenue. It is perhaps significant that such an approach was used at a time when the Bureau of Internal Revenue was racked by scandal and in the process of being reorganized. Why, in view of the reputation of the FBI, was not the task of eliminating illegal gambling given to J. Edgar Hoover's men? Perhaps they were too busy fighting the Communist menace, as, in 1942, they had been too busy chasing Nazi spies to tackle the syndicate.

Nevertheless, the greatest contribution of the Kefauver Committee was the publicity given individual gangsters. The fallout continued long after the committee's files had been buried to remain for fifty years in the National Archives. The troubles of Virginia Hill were not unique. In the next few years many of the top hoods exposed by Kefauver were put into prison by the Intelligence Division, and others were so harassed their usefulness to organized crime was destroyed. A partial list gives impressive proof:

Buster Wortman, boss of East St. Louis; Peter Licavoli, veteran gangster of Detroit and Tucson; Mickey Cohen, successor to Siegel on the West Coast; Santos Trafficante, Mafia boss of Tampa; Albert Anastasia, former Lord High Executioner of Murder, Inc.; Moe Dalitz, charter member of the Cleveland Syndicate; Longie Zwillman, so-called Al Capone of New Jersey; Frank Erickson, king of the gamblers; Frank Costello, partner of Lansky; and so on. Other Treasury agencies nabbed such men as Vito Genovese. Joe Adonis was deported. The list goes on.

Some of these cases will be discussed in later chapters, but several books would be required to do justice to the record compiled by the Intelligence Division in the post-Kefauver years. More books would be needed to tell the story of the corrupt officials whose control of an area made regional gambling centers possible. Take Broward County, Florida, for example.

A sprawling county just north of Miami, Broward occupies

the central portion of the Gold Coast between Dade and Palm Beach counties. It stretches from the Atlantic on the east to the silent reaches of the Everglades on the west. Only the strip along the coast is thickly populated, with much of the rest devoted to ranches, farms worked by migrants, and swamps where alligator poachers make neat profits. Fort Lauderdale, which calls itself the Venice of America, is the largest city, but there are scores of others. Law enforcement is fragmented. Only the sheriff and the grand jury have countywide jurisdiction.

Prior to the Kefauver Committee hearings in 1950, Walter R. Clark had been sheriff of Broward County for eighteen years. In that period the syndicate led by Meyer Lansky established itself, put down roots, and gained political control.

Clark was a butcher by trade before running for sheriff in 1932. His brother, Robert L. Clark, who served as his chief deputy, was a Fort Lauderdale fireman. The Clarks were Florida natives, a distinction that becomes more rare with the years as thousands upon thousands flee the snows of yesteryear for a chance to die in the sunshine. Many of the new arrivals have fought their battles for civic virtue in other cities, other times, and have little interest and even less knowledge of local conditions. This difference worked greatly to the advantage of Sheriff Clark, as was well illustrated by the following exchange between Clark and the Kefauver Committee's chief counsel, Rudolph Halley:

MR. CLARK. I was elected on the liberal ticket, and the people want it and they enjoy it.

MR. HALLEY. What do you mean by the "liberal ticket"? Did it say on the ballot you were going to allow gambling to go on?

MR. CLARK. The people know I am more or less liberal-minded.

MR. HALLEY. How do they know it? Do you advertise that you don't enforce the law?

MR. CLARK. I don't do that.

MR. HALLEY. Did you ever take before the people the issue whether you should allow gambling to be open or closed?

MR. CLARK. The newspapers more or less carried it as an issue.

MR. HALLEY. And you were elected anyhow?

MR. CLARK. Yes, sir.

The use by Clark of the word "liberal" was ironic but not unique. From Newport to Hot Springs to Beaumont, the word has been employed to mean, basically, a liberal interpretation of antivice laws, and that, in turn, means a policy of nonenforcement. In reality, such corrupt officials and their supporters, are ultraconservatives when described in conventional political terms.*

Broward County voted heavily for George Wallace in 1968. The John Birch Society is very powerful there.

When Walter Clark took office in January, 1933, the biggest gambling operation in the county was the Plantation Club on Hallandale Beach Boulevard just north of the Dade-Broward county line. It ran openly, drawing many of its customers from Miami. Local men were in charge. Shortly after the National Crime Syndicate was formed in 1934, Meyer Lansky explored South Florida—part of his assigned territory—and decided Broward County offered an excellent opportunity for development. The Plantation Club was taken over by the syndicate and made the center of a growing complex of handbooks and casinos. Lansky, however, found it convenient, because of the "big heat" in New York, to remove himself to Cuba. He cultivated Fulgencio Batista, the country's dictator, and began building a new empire there. His plans were interrupted by World War II, however, and by the subsequent ouster—for six years —of Batista. In the interim, he began developing his Broward interests. Sheriff Clark had given proof of his ability to keep things stable.

In 1942, Governor Spessard Holland felt obliged to notice that things were pretty wide open in Clark's domain. Utilizing the power available to a Florida governor, he ordered the sheriff to close down specific gambling joints, including the Plan-

---

* A working alliance between the National Crime Syndicate and the right wing in America has been a very real, if unpublicized, fact of life for decades. It became very apparent when the civil rights movement became militant. Yet it is an alliance few care to talk about.

tation Club. When Clark ignored the order, Holland suspended him from office.

Special agents of the Intelligence Unit later reported that Clark bought his job back. Under Florida law, the State Senate must act on suspended officials. If the decision upholds the governor's findings, the official is out for good. If not, he is returned to office with full back pay for the period he was under suspension.

A year passed before the Senate got around to acting on the Clark case. Meanwhile, the suspended sheriff gave $25,000 to an influential senator from Palm Beach County to assure a Senate vote in his favor. To get so much cash quickly, he borrowed $15,000 from a newspaper publisher. How much the senator kept for himself and how much he passed out to his colleagues are unknown, but the Senate found Clark innocent and restored him to office in 1943. He was reelected the following year without difficulty and again in 1948.

Clark and his brother, meanwhile, had gone into business for themselves. The Broward Amusement Company was formed to operate slot machines, jukeboxes, and the like. The one-armed bandits were everywhere—filling stations, grocery stores, and, of course, gambling joints. They were strictly illegal, but their operating headquarters nonetheless was the sheriff's office in the courthouse.

A second source of cash was the numbers racket. Traditionally, two variations were played. One, known as Cuba was based on the drawing every Saturday in Havana for the Cuban national lottery. The last two digits of the winning number in Havana was the winning number in Broward County. Winners were paid at 60 to 1. The same odds applied to bolita, a game played with 100 numbered balls. Daily drawings were held at several locations, with one of the players plucking the ball with the winning number from a sack.

In his testimony before the Kefauver Committee, Sheriff Clark said, "Bolita is a game that niggers play." Nevertheless, the dimes and quarters added up to thousands of dollars yearly, as Dutch Schultz and Trigger Mike Coppola had discovered in New York.

The monopoly on slot machines and numbers held by the

Clark brothers represented a working agreement with the syndicate which concentrated on casinos and handbooks. Jake Lansky, Meyer's brother and longtime lieutenant, was a frequent visitor to the sheriff's office. Jake was in charge of Broward to all intents and purposes. Meyer, with his responsibility as a member of the board, had too much going in New Orleans, New York, and Las Vegas to give personal attention to operating details. Much later, after the casinos closed and slots were confiscated, the numbers racket assumed greater importance to the syndicate. It was taken over and put on a businesslike basis in both Dade and Broward counties. In Clark's day, however, it was his personal franchise.

In return, the syndicate was allowed complete freedom to operate its casinos and handbooks on a lavish scale. Such joints as the Colonial Inn, the Club Boheme, and the Club Green Acres compared favorably with the Beverly Club in New Orleans and the Beverly Hills Club near Newport, Kentucky. Top name stars from Hollywood provided the entertainment, and a fleet of Cadillacs was maintained to carry the suckers from the plush hotels along the Gold Coast.

Clark cooperated in many ways. Guards, assigned to protect the armored cars used to carry cash to and from the casinos, were made deputy sheriffs. Other deputies served as bouncers at the clubs—and sometimes as bill collectors. Top hoods such as Vincent Alo, better known as Jimmy Blue Eyes—Joe Adonis, Tony Ricci, Lefty Clarke and, of course, Meyer and Jake Lansky, bought or built houses in Broward County. Phil "the Stick" Kovolick, who along with Lepke and others had posed for a picture with Bugsy Siegel before the Bug went West, moved to Broward, where he served as Lansky's bodyguard. Scores of other gangsters big and small found sanctuary in Clark's kingdom, safe in the knowledge that Sheriff Clark was in Jake Lansky's pocket.

Officials of various Broward cities were also in Lansky's control. The Kefauver Committee heard testimony from frustrated reformers on how budding revolts were nipped before they could flower. Lee A. Wentworth of Hollywood told how he was offered a choice of a "silver dollar or a silver bullet" when he attempted to get injunctions against gambling joints. The offer, he said, came from Jake Lansky, who was accompanied by Joseph Varon, local attorney for the Lanskys.

As late as 1947, police in Hollywood tried to protect fugitives. When New York police asked the local cops to pick up Andy Sheridan, who was wanted for murder, Hollywood's finest took the problem to Jimmy Blue Eyes, Lansky's Mafia aide. Jimmy told them to "forget it." The New York cops persisted, however, and threatened to expose the Broward situation. Reluctantly, the local cops finally went looking for the man who had been openly sunning himself at Lansky's pool for weeks. Sheridan, a little overconfident, ignored a timely tip and was caught at the airport. He went back to New York, was convicted, and sent to the electric chair. The Hollywood boys said he had only himself to blame.

The sheriff, however, with countywide powers, was the most important official. In addition to his own rackets, he could expect regular payoffs and political contributions. His brother, Chief Deputy Clark, told Revenue Agent Irving Fish in 1947 that graft presented a peculiar problem. If one reported it on his tax returns, said the deputy, the FBI could get him. If one didn't report it, the Intelligence Unit would get him.

Nonetheless, Sheriff Clark admitted to Kefauver that Jake Lansky "and the boys in the south end," where the casinos were located, raised money for his campaigns. He didn't know how much; he left such routine details to others.

The Intelligence Unit had been interested in Sheriff Clark long before Kefauver came to town. Ironically enough, the first tax probe of the sheriff was made at his request. In 1940 the sheriff became alarmed at reports the FBI was probing him on behalf of the IRS—a strange rumor reflecting the public's inability to distinguish between the two federal agencies. Thanks to the Intelligence Unit's policy, under Irey, of silent investigators, as well as the FBI's public relations program under Hoover, many people, including the sheriff, automatically assumed the FBI was the investigative arm of the federal government. Clark asked Special Agent J. J. Brown for a conference and, on February 22, formally requested in writing that his affairs be investigated.

Nothing much was turned up in the months that followed.

227

As far as the special agents could determine, Clark had little income and practically no tax liability. Special Agents Nels Tessem and J. L. Dasher obtained a sworn statement from the sheriff that his income was confined to his salary and the profits of a small farm. Efforts to get gangsters to admit they paid protection to the sheriff were fruitless; as in the case of Nucky Johnson, no one wanted to talk. It soon became apparent that Clark wouldn't have asked for the probe if he hadn't been sure all the rat holes were covered.

Following Lansky's decision to enlarge Broward operations in 1945, Clark began his personal expansion. The Broward Amusement Company was organized, and in its first year Clark reported $12,910 as his share of the profits. Bolita sales of $252,735 were also listed for 1945. By 1947 he was reporting gross sales of $780,000. Business was booming, and apparently the Clark boys had decided there was nothing to fear from the FBI after all.

In 1948 the Intelligence men began a new probe of the sheriff. It was interrupted by the Kefauver hearings, which confirmed much the investigators had learned and made the information public. Governor Fuller Warren was presented with a problem: Should he buy Clark's argument that he was giving the people what they wanted, or should he suspend the sheriff?

Warren had made his feelings clear shortly after taking office in 1949. In a statement issued in January, he began: "I am liberal minded. I believe in local self-government, and particularly in local law enforcement. I am not a reformer, but I have an inescapable obligation to protect the revenue of Florida's state government. Unlawful bookmaking on horse and dog racing is depriving the State of millions of dollars of racing taxes. . . ."

It will be remembered that only a few years before the State Racing Commission had decided to say nothing about mob ownership of Tropical Park for fear that confidence in the parimutuel system would be damaged. Florida had fallen into the same trap as Nevada—by basing state revenue to a large extent on gambling, it was necessary to tolerate the crooks who controlled it. In 1967, Lansky used the same device with the new government of the Bahamas.

A second statement issued a few days after the first was even more revealing. The governor began: "I am reluctant to intervene in local law enforcement. I believe deeply in the right of the people to have the kind of local law enforcement they choose by election of sheriffs and constables. My reading of history convinces me that human rights have suffered far more than they have benefited by remote control of local law enforcement."

Thus concisely did Governor Warren present the case for fragmented law enforcement, without which Capone could not have found safety in Cicero outside Chicago, Kastel could not have operated the Beverly Club outside New Orleans, and Lansky could not have built his Broward empire.

Yet despite his philosophy, the Kefauver heat was too great for Governor Warren to withstand. He was forced to suspend both Sheriff Jimmy Sullivan in Dade County and Sheriff Clark in Broward. Sullivan managed to get reinstated, only to resign quickly, but Clark's luck had run out. Not only was he not reinstated, but also the Intelligence Unit was ready to indict him for failure to pay $24,259 in additional taxes for the years 1945 through 1947.

(In view of Clark's known wealth, the amount charged to him seemed small enough. In reality, the size of the evasion has little bearing on a case of this type. The key is proof of fraud, of deliberate evasion on the part of the taxpayer. Special agents must be able to prove a specific amount. They were sure, for example, that Capone evaded far greater sums than he was charged with doing, but—as in the case of Clark —they were restricted to the facts they could document. Since the penalty is the same, regardless of the figure, it made little difference to the actual case, but as a matter of motivation, the special agents work harder to get a big crook than a small one. Top gangsters are usually very careful to conceal a million-dollar deal but tend to get careless when small amounts are concerned. Much of the Intelligence Division's success has been due to attention to the small detail. As will be shown

229

later, the conviction of Frank Costello started with a check for $5.10.)

The sheriff suddenly became ill and died. His brother, Robert, tried to carry on the dynasty. Charging that Walter had been unjustly harassed, Robert offered himself as a candidate in his place. He was soundly beaten at the polls in 1952. Apparently even the voters of Broward, once given some facts, wanted the laws enforced.

In the post-Kefauver era the casinos became floating crap games. Lansky abandoned Broward—although maintaining his home and influence there—to rebuild his empire in Havana, where Batista was once more in power. The open handbooks retreated to the back rooms; the numbers racket remained, growing larger all the time until it attracted the syndicate, but it was largely confined to the poorer neighborhoods and could easily be ignored by the average citizen.

A strange political combination evolved in Broward—an alliance of Republicans and Democrats. The sheriff's office was usually held by a Republican who was protected by Democratic officeholders. Repeated efforts by reformers to remove the sheriff were frustrated by the Democrats. The syndicate take-over of the numbers racket was able to proceed smoothly, and graft once more became a source of revenue for elected officials. The good citizens of Broward were assured that reformers were simply Communist agents attempting to destroy faith in local law enforcement. The citizens found this easier to believe than the idea that some of their local officials were taking orders from a crime syndicate. The lessons of the Kefauver hearings were forgotten.

A pioneer in the numbers racket was Howard G. Pinder. More than anyone else he built it up in Dade and Broward counties to the point where it became attractive to the syndicate.

Pinder and his partner, H. C. Williamson, came to the Intelligence Division's notice as a result of a venture into real estate and the construction business. A great demand for housing existed in South Florida after World War II. Pinder and Williamson bought a lot of land and started building apartment houses. They subcontracted much of the work, and soon the rumor started that they were crazy. They paid their bills in coins, instead of currency or by check.

A plumber reported that he was paid off with a nail keg full of dimes and quarters. He and his wife, he said, sat up all night counting the coins and putting them in rolls to take to the bank. Another subcontractor reported that when he called at Pinder's office for his money, he was given a washtub full of coins. He had to call a truck in to haul it away. Someone else confided that Pinder was so tight that on one occasion he tore an expensive shirt to pieces while trying to recover a quarter that had rolled under a stove. While he boasted of his wealth, he bought a washing machine on the installment plan.

It soon became apparent that Pinder was operating a huge and growing numbers business. Investigators found that it was called the Pinson House, *Pin* for Pinder and *son* for Williamson. An attempt to get Pinder under the new wagering-tax law passed as a result of the Kefauver investigations was impractical. When the law was passed, scores of gamblers, who obviously feared the Intelligence Division more than local law enforcement, bought the $50 tax stamp and made the monthly report of gross wagers accepted that the law required. Thus there was no violation of federal law. Numbers were illegal under state law, of course, but despite the fact that all such violators had listed their business addresses with the IRS, neither the police nor the sheriff's office were apparently aware the information was available to them. The situation changed, however, when Florida passed a law making possession of wagering-tax stamps prima-facie evidence of gambling. Everyone turned in his stamps and, after some hesitation, continued with his business. When the undermanned Intelligence Division was unable to make quick cases, the gamblers decided the Feds were overrated. Shortly thereafter the state law was declared unconstitutional. This took the heat off the local police agencies, and the gamblers decided they were home free. Very few bought new stamps.

At the time Pinder was being considered, he had a stamp. It was decided to fall back on the old-fashioned methods and get him on tax evasion. Special Agent John McRae was given the job, assisted by Special Agent Wilbert C. Kleppick.

Shortly after the investigation began, Pinder's wife was murdered. Intelligence men, who heard rumors she was about to talk, wondered how the murderer got through a fenced yard in which a large German shepherd roamed free. The dog—or so went the theory—must have known the murderer, for he didn't bark. Yet as far as local law enforcement was concerned, the case went into the books as another of many unsolved murders.

Pinder was indicted on June 23, 1952, on charges of evading $195,000 in taxes. It was three years before the case went to trial. In the interval, Pinder let his wagering-tax stamp expire.

The jury was out for eight days, and the case ended in a mistrial. Investigation revealed that the first vote was eleven to one for conviction. The sole holdout was a man who said he was getting his instructions from God. The special agents had a notion that a less lofty master was involved. In any event, the inspired juror was able to outlast his colleagues and make necessary a new trial.

When the second trial began, McRae let the jurors get word that special agents would be on their tail everywhere they went. In reality, there weren't enough men for the job, but the bluff worked. Pinder was found guilty and sentenced to three years in prison. It developed later that four jurors, all county employees, favored acquittal. The foreman, however, had a wife expecting a baby, and he wanted out. After two days of deliberation, he arranged a compromise to find the defendant guilty on one count only. Another compromise was also arranged. The judge reduced Pinder's sentence to one year on the grounds that his health was bad.

Nine months later Pinder was released. The numbers racket had continued unchecked while he was "away." The special agents were not entirely happy, and upon discovering Pinder had no wagering-tax stamp, they decided to try that avenue. It was one of the first probes made of its kind in Florida and in many ways was something of an experiment. The special agents lacked both experience and equipment, but they had something that compensated—imagination.

It took quite awhile to locate the countinghouse—the central spot where all bets are brought and the few winners

in and out of traffic, off and on the expressways. His trackers on the ground were able to stay completely out of sight while Hilker kept them informed from the plane on the direction and street Pinder was traveling. Confident at last that he was unobserved, Pinder headed for his new countinghouse in a suburban area.

McCall, a full block in front of Pinder, crossed a main intersection. Suddenly it occurred to him that he might be too far ahead. Suppose Pinder turned at the intersection. He might get away before the special agent could turn around. Acting on impulse, McCall cut sharply into the driveway of a modest home. Over his radio came Hilker's voice: "He's continuing up the street. Now he's turning into a driveway. There's a Chevrolet parked in the driveway. It looks like Harry's car. Hell, it is Harry's car."

McCall glanced around. Parked behind him, blocking the exit, was the man he had been trailing. The special agent thought fast. If Pinder glanced into the Chevrolet, the radio and other equipment would give the show away. What to do?

There was only one thing to do. McCall hastily opened his door and sauntered back to Pinder.

"I'm leaving," he said. "How about letting me out?"

"Sure thing," said the numbers racketeer. He backed out into the street. McCall went back to his car, put it into reverse, and with a wave of thanks drove slowly away. After getting out of sight, he wiped his face.

There were some anxious days in store for McCall and his colleagues. Did Pinder suspect anything? They knew it had become common practice for numbers operators to rent a room from a respectable family for use as a countinghouse when needed. Thus it was possible that Pinder would assume the man in the driveway had been visiting the owners. If so, he might not even ask questions. On the other hand . . .

The special agents found an empty house across the street and rented it. A week went by. Agents were in the house on Saturday waiting to see if Pinder would show up. He didn't show. Everyone, including McCall, was now convinced they had been "burned" the week before. Kleppick insisted they try once more. He pointed out that such a cagey customer as

Pinder might have two or more countinghouses to avoid using the same one on consecutive weeks.

The stakeout was resumed the following Saturday. It was 4 P.M. before Pinder showed up. The special agents raced downtown to get a search warrant and get back before Pinder could add up all the bets. They were successful—and Pinder's first question was: "How did you find me?"

Discreet questioning brought knowledge that Pinder had not suspected McCall. The idea that a special agent should get to his countinghouse ahead of him was too fantastic even to consider. McCall and McRae, both of whom were soon to be promoted to supervisor, suddenly felt much better.

This time no chances were taken with a judge and jury. The court was petitioned to declare Pinder in violation of his probation. He went back to prison to serve the five years imposed after the first raid. When he was released, he bought a huge ranch near Lake Okeechobee and turned his business over to a friend, Charles Robertson. In years to come, Robertson became powerful enough to make and unmake sheriffs and to hold out almost alone against the syndicate, which under the leadership of Fat Hymie Martin gradually got control of the numbers racket along the Gold Coast. When the sheriff began taking orders from Martin instead of Robertson, the angry "independent" told all to a special writer for the Miami *Herald*. The resulting uproar caused the voters in 1966 to change the office of sheriff from an elective to an appointive basis in Dade County and helped bring the defeat at the polls of the incumbent Broward County sheriff. The changes came none too soon, for the Supreme Court in 1967 knocked most of the teeth out of the wagering-tax law on the grounds that it forced gamblers to incriminate themselves. Once again the only enemy the local operators had to worry about was local law enforcement.

Jaffe, meanwhile, continued to pioneer in the use of planes. Assigned in 1962 to get photographs of the waterfront home on Key Biscayne of Murray "the Camel" Humphreys for the Chicago office, the special agent scored a unique first. He took pictures of the house from a car on the street and from the deck of a Coast Guard patrol boat at the rear. Then he asked to be flown over the house at an altitude of 100 feet. When the pictures were processed, it was discovered that the Camel's pretty young wife was posed prettily beside the pool in the back patio.

Imagination, say the special agents of the Miami office, often pays unexpected dividends.

14

THE CEMETERY CLUE

DREW Pearson, America's modern muck-
raker, devoted part of his October 18, 1951, broadcast to a discussion of Frank Costello's testimony to the Kefauver Committee a few days earlier. Pearson concluded by urging "that a
special tax squad be appointed" to investigate Costello.

Two days later the special agent in charge of the New York
office of the Intelligence Division, J. R. Baradel, wrote a memo
to his boss, W. H. Woolf, the man who had succeeded Elmer
Irey. Baradel's memo concluded with these words: "The suggestion of Pearson that a special squad be formed to investigate
Costello is somewhat belated inasmuch as one has been in
existence for three years, but it serves to demonstrate the squad
is not out after headlines."

A check of the record proves Baradel was right. Back in 1947
this memo was written on the official stationery of the Commissioner of Internal Revenue:

TO: Under Secretary Wiggins
FROM: Commissioner Schoeneman
               In re: Frank J. Costello

In order that you may have an idea as to what is being done in connection with the present income tax investigation of the above-named taxpayer, there is attached a report by Special Agent S. Whitman Cordes, dated August 21, 1947.

Investigations concerning this taxpayer are being conducted in other divisions, including Dallas Division, Atlanta Division and San Francisco Division. These inquiries are being made specifically with respect to the Louisiana Mint Company of New Orleans, Louisiana; gambling operations at Green Acres and the Colonial Inn, Broward County, Florida. Investigation is also being made at Las Vegas, Nevada, to determine what connection existed between the gambling activities of Frank Costello and Benjamin Siegel, there being indications that Costello is involved to a certain extent in connection with the $5,000,000 Flamingo Club at Las Vegas.

Attachment

Some inkling of the problems involved in the early phases of the probe is given by a letter marked "Personal" from Chief Woolf to the then special agent in charge in New York. Woolf reported the Undersecretary of the Treasury returned the Cordes report with a handwritten note: "Good going! Let's put on all the heat possible."

The special agent in charge in New York to whom this encouraging information was given was Daniel A. Bolich—the man later to be indicted with influence peddler Henry Grunewald. It seems safe to suggest that he was not particularly interested in putting the heat to the powerful Costello.

The investigation of Costello in 1947 began with a February 27 report by Special Agent Howard J. Werner on conditions in Las Vegas. Werner wrote:

Perhaps the investigation which will prove most interesting and profitable concerns the latest addition to amusement centers of Las Vegas which opened on December 26, 1946, under the name of "The Flamingo." This monstrous establishment covers acres of ground and consists of a hotel, restaurant, cocktail lounge, gambling casino, shopping center, swimming pool, outdoor café, and a nightclub and dining room that seats in excess of 700 persons.

The Flamingo is owned and operated by a syndicate using the name, "Nevada Projects Corporation," and is incorporated in the State of Nevada. The central figure behind the corporation is the notorious Benjamin "Bugsy" Siegel, who is having a private penthouse erected on the top of the hotel building. The Flamingo is advertised and broadcast as having cost $5,000,000. Actually, information received from one of the contractors, is that the cost was in excess of $6,000,000, most of which was derived from black market operations during the war.

The theory that the funds originated in the black market is fostered by the fact that the backers wanted the structure erected in the desert in approximately eight months, despite the scarcity of various materials, fixtures and labor. To achieve this, plasterers and electricians were paid as high as $40 per day; common laborers often received in excess of $100 per week; fabulous prices were paid in the Los Angeles market for commodities that could not be purchased elsewhere because of the national shortage; and no expense was spared to provide the finest quality obtainable in every phase of construction.

Opening night at The Flamingo, which cost $15 per person for admission, including dinner, featured Xavier Cugat and his orchestra and Jimmie Durante. The show is reputed to have cost $35,000 per week. . . .

In September, 1946, Siegel made a trip to New York to obtain additional funds for construction of the resort. It is not known how much he obtained, but it is believed he entrusted $500,000 to Louis Pokrass—one of Frank Costello's henchmen—and his wife, Lena Pokrass. In any event, a personal certified check, drawn by Louis and Lena Pokrass on a New York bank in the amount of $250,000, was deposited shortly thereafter in the commercial account of the general contractor for the Flamingo at the Bank of Nevada, Las Vegas.

Another deposit to the contractor's account was made on the same day in the amount of $100,000. When Siegel returned from his trip to New York, he is said to have carried $1,100,000 with him to Las Vegas. He has a safe built into the floor of his inner office at the Flamingo.

Benny Siegel's partners in New York are said to be: Frank Costello, leader of the Union Sicilio (spelling uncertain) and notorious gangster of the east coast; Joseph A. Doto, alias Joe Adonis; and Meyer Lansky, well-known gambler in New York, Florida and Chicago.

Siegel, Costello, Adonis and Lansky are said to own the Colonial Inn and the Greenacres in Hollywood, Broward County, Florida, and control all gambling activities in most of the state of Florida. The foursome allegedly had an income in excess of $10,000,000, in Broward County in 1946.

Werner continued to discuss various persons associated with Siegel. He concluded the report with this intriguing remark:

In the midst of all this scheming and tax evasion are the local city and county commissioners who hold the authority as to whom shall be issued liquor, café and gambling licenses, as well as issuing permits for construction and remodeling. Graft and bribery are rampant in Las Vegas, yet the income tax returns of the commissioners, the sheriff and the constables reflect that during the past four years they reported for taxation only the salary received from Clark County for their appointed or elected position.

Meanwhile, Special Agent Cordes in New York was probing Alliance Distributors, Inc., which had sole distribution rights in the United States to peddle certain brands of scotch. He discovered that Irving Haim purchased stock in the English firm supplying the whiskey to Alliance at a cost of $325,000. The money was put up in 1937 by a William Helis, an oil operator in New Orleans. Haim gave Helis a note for $225,000, and Phil Kastel, that old partner of Arnold Rothstein and Costello's, signed notes for the rest. Costello's name appeared as endorser on Kastel's notes.

Also discovered was the fact that on an application to lease an apartment at 115 Central Park West in 1937, Costello listed his occupation as "general salesmanager for Alliance Distributors, Inc." The minutes of a liquor company associated with Alliance revealed that on May 5, 1938, at the suggestion of Haim, Costello was appointed a personal agent of the com-

241

pany to promote the scotch brands. He was to receive £5,000 (about $25,000) annually, plus a commission of 5 shillings (about $1) per case in excess of 50,000 cases shipped to the United States.

Word came next from New Orleans, where the Louisiana Mint Company was under investigation. On December 4, 1947, Special Agent D. B. Holt reported that Costello's activities in the state began in July, 1935, when he made a deal with Huey Long to operate 986 slot machines in New Orleans under the name of the Bayou Novelty Company. The slots were closed for two weeks when Long was shot, but Costello made a "new deal" with New Orleans Mayor Robert S. Maestri and Governor Richard W. Leche.

Holt noted that in 1937 he and Special Agent E. D. Matheny secured an indictment charging Costello, Kastel, and four others with conspiracy to evade the income taxes owed by Kastel. The resulting trial, to no one's surprise, ended in a verdict of innocent for everyone. Bayou reopened as the Pelican Novelty Company, which featured pinball machines equipped with an automatic payoff device. Meanwhile, Costello got the state courts to rule that slot machines that paid off in mints with each play were legal. The Louisiana Mint Company was organized in 1942 and continued in operation until 1946. In fact, noted Holt, "only last week, November 25, 1947, the New Orleans police raided the company's warehouse and seized approximately 1,000 of the machines valued at $200,000."

Partners in Louisana Mint were Costello, Kastel, Jake Lansky, Peter Hand, and Fred Rickerfor. Costello's monthly profits ranged from as high as $12,375 to as low as $4,500. Meanwhile, Mrs. Loretta Costello, Frank's wife, was picking up an average of $2,000 a month as Kastel's partner in the Crescent Music Company, a jukebox outfit organized in September, 1944. And in December, 1945, the Beverly Club opened in Jefferson Parish, outside New Orleans.

Holt noted in conclusion that Costello had five brothers-in-law "down here to protect his interests."

From Florida came discouraging news. Jake Lansky was interviewed on September 25, 1947, and "stated he would testify under oath that Costello has not now, nor did he ever have any investments in Colonial Inn or Greenacres." Lansky quoted Costello as saying, "I want no part of anything in Florida—too many headaches. I have headaches enough."

On January 28, 1948, Special Agent Cordes prepared a status report on the Costello probe. Thirty-eight pages were required to list all the angles under investigation. Cordes noted that:

> at the outset a conclusion was reached that a successful income tax case would require direct testimony of payments to Costello which constituted unreported income to him, rather than to rely on a showing of unwarranted increases in net worth. For one reason, there is no practical starting point at which Costello's net worth can be even approximated, and, in addition, the assumption is valid that his present holdings are so well concealed as to be beyond the reach of the Treasury Department. . . . Attention was therefore given principally to indications of evasion of income tax on the part of persons reputed to be affiliated with Costello and the entities controlled by them.

At the stage reached this far, Cordes could list only four "entities" in which Costello had an admitted interest: 79 Wall Street Corporation (real estate); Louisiana Mint Company (slot machines); Crescent Music Company (jukeboxes); and Beverly Club (casino gambling). Thirteen other entities in which Costello allegedly had an interest through nominees were named. In three of these, Meyer Lansky had an established interest. It now seems apparent that the Intelligence Unit was making the same mistake many have made before and since by attempting to make Costello the king of crime. It is perhaps human nature for writers or investigators to want to believe their subject—be he Capone, Lepke, Giancana or Costello—is truly the Big Fellow and gives orders to everyone else. Such a mental attitude automatically reduced Lansky to the role of nominee of Costello. One can understand the desire to simplify organized crime by giving it a single boss, but had Cordes been able to assume that Costello was only a member of the board, along with Lansky, Zwillman, Siegel, Adonis, and the rest, he could have spared himself much trouble. Yet for years, New York writers had been proclaiming Costello Prime Minister of the underworld, much as years before Chicago writers had given Capone a larger-than-life reputation. The special agent can hardly be blamed for his approach under the circumstances.

The investigation proceeded, and if it achieved little in building a case against Costello, it uncovered some fascinating information about organized crime.

Special Agent George C. Vilas reported on February 20, 1948, from Miami. He noted that in the past six months, land parcels in the area were purchased for a sum in excess of $4,500,-000. All were paid for in $1,000 bills, delivered to the escrow agent by Dr. Anselmo S. Alliegro. It developed that Dr. Alliegro was a Miami resident but a Cuban citizen. The land became the property of the Ansan Corporation. George J. Baya, secretary of the mysterious outfit and a Miami attorney, told Vilas he had no idea who the stockholders were. The president, he added, was Elena Santerio y García.

Vilas also reported he had received information that when Lucky Luciano was deported, Meyer Lansky and Frank Costello boarded the ship at Ellis Island to say good-bye. Costello allegedly carried suitcases containing around $2,000,000—Lucky's share of gambling profits amassed while he was in prison. When Lucky violated his parole and came secretly to Cuba, according to the information, he employed Cuban Senator Santerio, the father of Elena Santerio y García. This raised the possibility that the president of Ansan was only reinvesting Luciano's money in the Miami area—money that had been given him by Lansky and Costello. Much of the money she had invested was in new bills in numerical sequence.

From Las Vegas came information about Morris Rosen, who held twenty-two and a half shares of stock in the Flamingo. Rosen was identified as "a front man for Meyer Lansky and acts as a nominee for Lansky and the syndicate in some of their enterprises. Rosen travels to Las Vegas about every six weeks to 'audit' the records of the present operations of the Flamingo. Leading members of the gambling syndicate are reported to be vacationing in Hot Springs, Arkansas, at the present time."

From Hot Springs on February 16, 1948, came a report on conditions in Owney "the Killer" Madden's adopted town. Hot Springs was enjoying one of its periodic attacks of virtue under a reform mayor, and the casinos were temporarily closed. Despite syndicate propaganda that it was gambling that kept the town alive, people continued to come to the hot springs to bathe their aching bones. The report noted:

> Frank Costello makes regular semi-annual visits to Hot Springs. There is no doubt but that he is closely associated with Owen Madden, of Hot Springs, in large scale gambling operations. Owen Madden is the alleged owner of the Southern Club, an exclusive gambling house in Hot Springs, and is believed to have considerable stock in the Cotton Club in New York City. [The report was about twenty years behind the times as far as the Cotton Club was concerned.] Costello visited Hot Springs in March–April, 1947, and in October–November, 1947, and always stays at the Jack Tar Court where he occupies a three-apartment cottage. Madden has reserved this cottage for Costello, tentatively, for March 15, 1948. Costello is usually accompanied to, or is met at, Hot Springs by several other persons who occupy this cottage with him but do not register. Costello and Madden are frequently seen together in Hot Springs.

From Miami Beach came information on the S & G Syndicate, which controlled bookmaking on the beach. The syndicate collected $180 a week, from hundreds of handbook concessions, to be paid for protection. A Miami Beach city councilman, Bill Burbridge, was listed as "payoff man." He paid off each week in Suite 710 in the Cromwell Hotel.

The suite consisted of six rooms and a telephone switchboard operated by eight girls. The betting "runs to a million dollars daily. No books are kept and the money is transferred to other states. Special messengers accompanied by armed guards transfer the money by plane." High-stake card games were also a feature of Suite 710. "In the 1947 season, Ray Ryan, Evansville, Indiana, lost $600,000 in Suite 710. At the end of the season, Ben Cohen brings fifty to one hundred men to court to answer to the names of men arrested during the season and who forfeited their bail. Thus they get 'refunds' of the bail that was forfeited."

None of this was helpful in building a case on Costello, but the Intelligence Unit was to remember Ben Cohen.

Special Agent Holt in New Orleans reported on April 11, 1948, on an interview with Phil Kastel and Eugene McGee. A name from the past was McGee. In the 1920's he had been law partner of "the Great Mouthpiece," William J. Fallon, and had helped defend such men as Arnold Rothstein. Now McGee was in New Orleans working for the Beverly Club. He disclosed a new partner had been added, Carlos Marcello. Back in Huey Long's day, Marcello had been released from prison by political influence. According to Kastel, "it was necessary to take Marcello into the partnership because of his close association with the law enforcement officers of that parish. He said that he personally received $45,000 from Marcello, part of which was by check. Marcello was not interviewed because of a pending investigation of his income tax liability by this office." Carlos owned 15 percent of the casino.

A rumor that Costello had invested heavily in oil royalties was denied by Kastel and McGee. They said, however, that they had invested $20,000, but Costello had not been interested.

On May 12, 1948, Special Agent Paul F. Snyder reported from Boston that he had questioned Hyman Abrams—the old bootlegger and dog-track pioneer—about his investment in the Flamingo Club. Abrams explained he went to Las Vegas in 1946 because "My girl went out there to get a divorce." He decided to go along, he said, and took Morris Rosen with him. Upon arriving, he invested more than $100,000 in the belief "that people will always gamble and at the Flamingo they were to be offered a chance to satisfy their inclinations."

Abrams was well able to afford the investment, the special agent said. The dog track outside Boston paid dividends of $85,000 yearly from 1944 to 1947. In 1944 alone, Abrams paid $77,000 in income taxes on a net income of $198,000. Since 1939, according to Abrams, he had made between $300,000 and $400,000, after taxes.

246

And Abrams, as a possible front for Costello, was written off. Obviously, he was a big man in his own right. At any rate, he was closer to Lansky than to Costello.

Intelligence Chief Woolf added a bit of information to the Owney Madden file on May 21, 1948. He reported that a check of records disclosed Madden was investigated for income tax evasion in 1933. "Additional taxes and penalties, in the amount of $73,553, were recommended. There was no recommendation for prosecution." Possibly the special agents in 1933 could find no evidence of fraud on which to base a recommendation. It is equally possible, however, that policy determined the decision. The probe covered the years 1924 to 1931, but it was made about the time Madden was "assisting" Charles Lindbergh investigate the kidnapping of his son. Since the Intelligence Unit was also helping at the time, the coincidence raises the possibility that at Lindbergh's request the policymakers passed the word that Owney was to be rewarded for his civic gesture. Years later, when the author examined the file, he detected a certain embarrassment over Madden's unofficial association with Intelligence on the part of officials. It seems obvious that Owney was used at the insistence of Lindbergh—a man of tremendous influence—but whether Madden escaped prosecution because of it may never be known. In any case, Irey and his men refused to let Capone out of prison to help Lindbergh, but Madden was already on the scene when they arrived.

The wide-ranging probe continued to produce considerable information on organized crime, but as months passed, little evidence was developed pertaining to Costello's finances. Typical was a report passed on in December, 1949, by Special Agent Werner to the effect that Allan Smiley—the man on the couch when Bugsy Siegel was blasted—had steered a wealthy woman rancher into the Beverly Club, where she lost "a small fortune." Allegedly, Smiley then steered her to "Moe Davis" in Chicago, who "took" her for $106,000. Werner noted that "Moe Davis" was an alias of Moe Dalitz, head of the Cleveland Syndicate and friend of Lansky's.

Shortly before that memo was written, Costello on November 26, 1949, achieved the ambition of many politicians—he made the cover of *Time,* the weekly newsmagazine. It was recognition, but not the kind a top gangster enjoys.

Time traced Costello's rise from the slums of New York's 108th Street, to which he had been brought in 1895 from Italy at the age of four. His one prison sentence in 1915 for illegal possession of a pistol was described. The magazine went on to tell of Frank's climb to wealth during rum-running days and credited him with calling the famous peace conference attended by Capone in Atlantic City in 1929. His friendship with Rothstein and Jimmy Hines was covered, and his business relationships with Kastel were explored. The "deal" with Huey Long and with Britain's scotch whisky dealers was reviewed. And the famous episode in 1943 when District Attorney Frank Hogan tapped Costello's phone was repeated. Hogan's men tuned in just in time to hear Thomas Aurelio thank Costello for getting him nominated to the New York Supreme Court and pledge his "undying" loyalty. The article concluded: "The U.S., which had drunk Frank Costello's whiskey, played his slot machines and looked the other way when his money was slipped to public officials, didn't think he was a very pleasant fellow. It never would."

During 1950 and the early part of 1951 the Intelligence Unit's probe took a back seat to the Kefauver hearings. When Costello testified in New York, fascinated millions watched on television. Perhaps the dramatic climax came on March 15, 1951. Virginia Hill stepped off the witness stand, and an angry Costello took her place. It was the fifth time he had been grilled, and he was getting desperate. Abruptly he addressed Rudolph Halley, the committee's counsel:

"Mr. Halley, am I a defendant in this courtroom?"

"No," said Halley.

"Am I under arrest?"

"No," repeated Halley.

"Then I'm walking out," said Costello.

A brief wrangle followed. Chairman Kefauver intervened to ask: "Do you refuse to follow the direction of the Chair?"

"Absolutely," said Costello.

"Then," said the soft-spoken Senator from Tennessee, "I think it only fair to tell you that under those circumstances—

I have just consulted with Senator Tobey—we will have to ask for your arrest by the United States Senate to bring you in to testify, and we will also have to ask for a contempt proceeding against you."

Costello walked out anyway—and the underworld held its breath. He came back the next day, however, and on four other occasions. But Kefauver was as good as his word. The "Prime Minister" was held in contempt by the Senate. On April 8, 1952, a federal district court in New York sentenced him to eighteen months in prison and a $5,000 fine. While he was "away," the long tax probe finally came to a successful conclusion.

On April 4, 1952, Frank W. Lohn, who had just succeeded Woolf as Intelligence Division boss, wrote a long memorandum to the new Commissioner of Internal Revenue, John B. Dunlap. He noted that early in 1948 a special squad under the direction of Special Agent Cordes was set up in New York to investigate racketeers with "emphasis being placed on Frank Costello." He added that while fifty agents were now engaged in the rackets investigation, they had been unable to devote "all of their time to Costello and his henchmen." Dunlap said he planned to detail "an outstanding special agent" to review the facts in hand and make recommendations.

Two specal agents were assigned: Richard L. O'Hanlon and Edward A. Hill. In their report dated May 6, 1952, the special agents made a number of recommendations involving six racketeers: Costello, Adonis, Salvatore Moretti, Tom Luchese, Zwillman, and Joe Profaci. The most important suggestion as regards Costello was that the "net worth approach" be tried. It had been discarded originally in favor of an investigation of Costello's associates in the belief Costello was the supreme boss of crime. Now he would be treated as just another mobster.

Five special agents signed the final report on Costello which was submitted February 9, 1953. They included: Edward P. Dolan, Peter F. Geissler, Wilfred T. Leach, John F. McElligott, and John R. Murphy.

Almost four pages were devoted to Thelma Martin, identified as the "girlfriend" of Costello's for twenty years. She was elusive; agents calling at her apartment at 1056 Fifth Avenue never found her in. Letters requesting an interview were not returned, but Thelma didn't show either. It was learned that an unidentified woman visited the apartment at intervals and picked up Thelma's mail. Since September, 1952, she had paid her rent monthly with postal money orders purchased in various post offices around New York. A brother, Jack Meyers, was located, and he said Thelma was in Mexico City.

The special agents commented: "From the foregoing, it appears that Thelma Martin does not desire to be interviewed."

Other people did talk. That Costello was a "frequent visitor" to Thelma's apartment was established. Telephone records of her unlisted number showed frequent calls by Costello from her apartment. One such call went to Art Samish, the California lobbyist who once boasted he controlled the legislature. Records at the Jack Tar Motel in Hot Springs showed that twice a year Thelma was in residence for two weeks or more at the same time Costello was there. The couple never arrived or departed together. The agents even discovered that on May 19 and May 27, 1948, Costello sent two dozen roses to Thelma.

The young lady was unemployed and filed no income tax returns. Yet her rent was $4,500 annually; in 1949 she paid $4,500 in cash for a Cadillac; she deposited between $500 and $700 monthly in cash in her bank account; she wore expensive clothes and always paid for them in cash; she employed a maid for $200 a week.

Efforts to find Thelma's alleged husband, Jack Martin, failed. The special agents concluded that "it is doubtful if there is such an individual." They also concluded that Costello "is keeping her [Thelma] to the extent of at least $15,000 annually."

The special agents wondered what Mrs. Costello was doing with her free time. They began examining microfilm records of New York banks. Costello seldom wrote a check, but perhaps Mrs. Costello was more careless. A check for $5.10, signed by Loretta B. Costello, was found. Special Agent Murphy was not a man to overlook details. He trailed the check to a bank on Long Island, where he discovered the $5.10 had been paid to a plant nursery which specialized in supplying flowers for cemeteries. The nursery identified the cemetery as St. Michael's, and the cemetery superintendent revealed he had sold the Costellos a lot for $4,888. The money had been paid in cash.

Feeling rewarded for his trouble, Murphy decided to take a look at the lot. He found it occupied by a marble mausoleum —apparently Costello intended to rest in the same kind of comfort he enjoyed in life. The contractor who had built the mausoleum said it had cost $18,615 and had been paid for in four installments—each time in cash.

The $5.10 had grown to $23,508.10, as a result of Murphy's digging. Furthermore, he knew the circumstances surrounding the construction of the monument to Costello's ego would help prove willful fraud when the case came to trial.

Other checks signed by Mrs. Costello were traced. It soon became apparent that Frank's wife had been determined to keep up with Frank's mistress in the realm of expensive clothing at least. At one shop alone the bill for one year was $4,900.

In totaling up Costello's assets and liabilities, the special agents found the ghost of Arnold Rothstein. As a result of legal action brought in 1943 by the administrator of Rothstein's estate, Costello had been forced to pay $5,000 he owed to the long-dead gambler. They also discovered that Costello purchased several lots in Hollywood, Florida, in 1948, and still others in 1950. He had planned to build a home there near Lansky, but the Kefauver heat killed the idea.

The special agents concluded their final report by recommending:

> that criminal prosecution be instituted against Frank Costello in violation of Section 145(b) of the Internal Revenue Code for attempting to defeat and evade his personal income taxes for the years 1946 to 1950, inclusive. . . . The total additional taxes for the years involved, namely 1941 to 1950, inclusive, amount to $384,824.67, and the total penalties for the same period amount to $201,442.05, making a grand total of $586,266.72.

On March 11, 1953—one month and two days after the final report was submitted—Costello was indicted on four counts of tax evasion. The arraignment was on April 23, and Costello had to be brought from federal prison at Milan, Michigan, where he was serving his sentence for contempt of Congress. Trial was delayed until he completed the sentence. It began on April 5, 1954, and ended on May 13. He was found not guilty on one count and guilty on three counts. Judge John F. X. McGohey sentenced him to five years in prison and $30,000 in fines, plus court costs of $4,111. To prove its case, the government called 165 witnesses and introduced 365 exhibits. Costello presented only one witness, an accountant who had prepared elaborate charts purporting to show that the government's evidence really proved Costello owed no additional taxes. Revenue agent Albert Sohn listened carefully to the hours of technical testimony. At a luncheon break before the start of cross-examination, he pinpointed the weaknesses in the accountant's figures and—in the words of Chief Assistant United States Attorney Lloyd F. MacMahon—made it possible "to destroy the testimony of this witness on cross-examination."

United States Attorney J. Edward Lumbard singled out Agents Leach, Sohn and Murphy for special praise. He wrote to the Commissioner of Internal Revenue, T. Coleman Andrews: "Your Department has every reason to take great pride in all of the men who worked on this case. The three mentioned above particularly deserve full recognition for the outstanding performance of their duties."

Costello continued to fight gamely to stay out of prison. His motion for bail pending appeal was twice denied, and he was taken into custody. On June 19, 1954, however, he was released on order of Supreme Court Justice Robert Jackson pending a determination by the Supreme Court of the constitutionality of the net worth approach to tax evaders. On April 5, 1955, the court of appeals upheld Costello's conviction for 1948 and 1949 and reversed the conviction for 1947. This had the result of reducing the fine imposed by $10,000, but since he had been given three concurrent sentences of five years each, it did nothing to reduce the time he was to spend in prison. On March 5, 1956, the Supreme Court upheld the conviction and in doing so established the principle that an indictment may be based entirely on hearsay evidence. On May 14, 1956, Costello surrendered and went back to prison.

He wasn't finished, however, as Inspector Owen Burke Yung discovered. On November 9, 1956, Yung received a visit from Costello's new attorney, Edward Bennett Williams. According to a memo prepared by Yung:

> Mr. Williams stated that he was Mr. Frank Costello's attorney; that he had represented him in denaturalization proceedings in New York last year; that because he, Williams, had been able to show that wire-tap evidence had been used by the Bureau of Immigration and Naturalization, . . . the case against Costello had been dismissed. He stated that during his investigation for Costello on the denaturalization case, he had obtained certain evidence that wire-taps had also been used in connection with Costello's income tax investigation. . . .

According to the inspector, Williams concluded by saying "that if I felt I could not disclose I had tapped Costello's wires for the Internal Revenue Service, I need not answer him and he 'would understand.' "

Yung said he had no connection with the Costello case and had no knowledge of any wiretaps. Williams advised him, he added, "that he was going to make a motion for a new trial in the near future."

Again Costello was released from prison pending the outcome of the motion for a new trial. While free, his troubles were compounded. Apparently, the syndicate retained its faith in Costello and had continued to cut him in on operations. However, a serious dispute developed between Albert Anastasia, the old Lord High Executioner of Murder, Inc., and Meyer Lansky. Anastasia wanted permission to muscle in on Lansky's new gambling empire in Havana. When Costello and other members of the board decided at a meeting in New York in March, 1957, in favor of Lansky, Anastasia was furious. He accused Costello of disloyalty to the Mafia. On May 2, 1957, a gunman bounced a slug off Costello's head as he walked into the lobby of 115 Central Park West. Frank wasn't seriously hurt but was taken to a hospital. Detectives searched his clothes and found a scrap of paper on which were written some interesting figures: "Gross casino wins as of 4-26-57—$651,284.

Investigation proved the figures matched the first day's play at Las Vegas' newest casino—the Tropicana. It had just been opened by Costello's old lieutenant, Phil Kastel. A probe into hidden interests in Las Vegas casinos now began.

A new meeting was called. Trigger Mike Coppola was forced to interrupt a vacation in Las Vegas and fly to New York. The syndicate decided Anastasia had to go, and on October 25, 1957, he was blasted in the same hotel where Rothstein had died almost three decades earlier.

Meanwhile, a hearing was held on Costello's motion for a new trial. That old tapper, now retired, former Special Agent William Mellin, recalled bugging three telephones in New Orleans during the period of the Second Louisiana Purchase. One of them was in the rooms used by Kastel and Costello in the Roosevelt Hotel. However, attorney Williams was unable to prove that any evidence relative to the income tax case of Costello was secured. New York police admitted they also had bugged Costello's phones, but only after getting court permission. Nothing they heard was used by the Intelligence Division.

On December 16, 1957, Costello's motion was denied. On May 20, 1958, the court of appeals affirmed the denial. Once more Costello returned to prison to serve the remainder of the five-year sentence imposed four years before.

The run of bad luck continued. While he was still in prison, a new effort to strip him of citizenship was successful. In applying for naturalization in 1925, Costello had listed his occupation as "real estate." The district court held that this was "willful misrepresentation and fraud" since Costello's true occupation was bootlegging. On February 21, 1961, the Supreme Court affirmed the decision. When in June, 1961, the gangster was released from prison, Attorney General Robert F. Kennedy ordered him to register as an alien.

In the last analysis, publicity destroyed Costello as a syndicate boss. It was a lesson the mob accepted. Publicity brings heat, attracts Senate committees and ambitious prosecutors.

The real leaders of crime stay in the background and let Mafia figureheads such as Costello and Sam "Mooney" Giancana get the headlines and the investigations. Contrast the careers of Costello and Meyer Lansky. They began together and even worked together in New York, Miami Beach, New Orleans, Las Vegas, and Havana. Yet today, when in the midst of the greatest uproar over crime in history, Lansky—if he is mentioned at all—is identified only as a tool of such men as the late Vito Genovese or Gerald Catena. Lansky admittedly has the money, the brains, and the muscle, but he has avoided the limelight, lived quietly, and has served only three months in jail in his life. He remains the one major gangster the Intelligence Division—to say nothing of the FBI—has been unable to beat.

Lansky's wealth is officially estimated to be in excess of $300,-000,000. Costello, on the other hand, was picked up by New York police three years ago on—of all things—vagrancy. Today, when everyone talks about the Mafia, the real leaders of crime have become almost invisible. Only the Intelligence Division, which concentrates on the money flow, poses any threat to them.

15

DEEP IN THE HEART

Two men who were to become targets of the Intelligence Division were involved when Lyndon B. Johnson took the first step in 1948 that brought him so suddenly to the White House in 1963; George Parr, affectionately known as the Duke of Duval, and Jack "Big Fix" Halfen. Texas in those days was syndicate-controlled. As one drove east toward Louisiana, where Carlos Marcello had been made into "the Big Little Man" by Frank Costello and Meyer Lansky, conditions became completely wide open. Houston resembled a frontier town, its oil wealth adding a sheen of sophistication that was lacking in Beaumont, a few miles to the east. On the Gulf Coast were Port Arthur and Galveston, where, amid mean and dirty surroundings, millions were made from illegal gambling and prostitution.

Congressman Lyndon Johnson decided in 1948 that he was ready to move up. He wanted to become Senator, but there was one problem: Governor Coke Stevenson had similar ambitions. The primary election saw Stevenson trounce Johnson by some 73,000 votes. It was a good victory, but not good enough to avoid a runoff election.

256

The syndicate had a choice to make—Johnson or Stevenson. Regardless of other factors, one fact stood out. According to Big Fix Halfen, it was decisive. If the syndicate went with Johnson, the governor would be annoyed. Win or lose, Stevenson would still be governor for six months. As governor, he commanded the famous Texas Rangers. To annoy him was to risk turning loose the rangers on the gambling joints and brothels. Obviously, Stevenson was the man to support.

Johnson knew Texas politics, however, and he turned to the Duke of Duval for help.

The Parr family had ruled Duval County for two generations. Located in that jagged strip of land between Mexico and the Gulf in South Texas, Duval and a number of neighboring counties are largely populated by Mexican-Americans. The dynasty was founded by Archie Parr, who came into the area around 1900, won the loyalty—or at least the obedience—of the peons, and became rich in land and cattle while doing so. His son, George, carried on the tradition and improved on it. An army of some 200 "special deputy sheriffs" kept law and order respected and at election time made sure that citizens voted for the man the Duke had decided to support. This ability to turn out a bloc vote in a wide area of South Texas made Parr a power in state politics. All candidates came hat in hand to Duval County and agreed to whatever terms the boss demanded.

On the day of the runoff election, Johnson received 99.1 percent of the vote in Duval and did almost as well in the seventeen surrounding counties, where Parr's influence was strong. Yet it appeared that even this was not enough. When the final returns were in, Stevenson seemed to be the victor. Almost 1,000,000 votes had been cast, and the governor emerged with 112 more votes than the Congressman.

Six days after the election the folks in Jim Wells County— one of those dominated by Parr—got to rummaging around in Box 13, and, lo and behold, they found 203 uncounted votes. Not too surprising, 201 of the votes were for Johnson and only 2 for Stevenson. This gave LBJ two things—a plurality of 87 votes and the nickname Landslide Lyndon. The governor charged fraud, but before anyone could get around to checking Box 13, someone carelessly burned the ballots it contained. Johnson went off to the Senate and, eventually, to the White House.

Halfen, meanwhile, was also profiting by the 1948 election. Up in Houston, people were wondering if incumbent Sheriff Neal Polk would seek reelection. A constable, M. L. Woolley, wanted to run if he didn't. Halfen, who was a friend of both men, offered to "bet" Woolley $17,500 that Sheriff Polk wouldn't run. Woolley agreed, and a contract was drawn up. The money was given to Bill Williams, a restaurant owner, to hold. Sure enough, Polk decided to quit politics. Williams turned the bet money over to Halfen, and shortly thereafter Big Fix and Sheriff Polk took off together for a hunting trip to Alaska.

Halfen was born of respectable parents in Kansas City, Missouri, in 1913. He got bored in his teens and joined a passing carnival show. The show seemed to be a good place to pass counterfeit half-dollars, but someone caught on. Halfen was arrested, given a lecture, and released. He put his carnival experience to good use, touring Texas with the wife of Pretty Boy Floyd and a homemade film about the bank robber. Arriving in Houston, the young man saw possibilities in the wide-open city. All the rackets needed, he decided, was an organizer. Assorted racketeers were at the mercy of the politicians so long as they were competing with one another, but once organized, they would be able to dictate to the political bosses. This sound argument was accepted by the hoods, and by the late 1930's Halfin was ruling as the Big Fix. He established working relations with Marcello, who supplied Houston bookmakers with a racing wire service. Through Marcello, the Big Fix was able to meet the top men in the syndicate. Pinball machines— known in Texas as marble tables because the balls were the size of children's marbles—blossomed all over Houston. As gambling devices they were second only to slots, yet they had an innocent appearance and could be classified as games of skill for amusement purposes.

All was going well with Halfen, who assumed quite naturally that LBJ was just another politician who understood the rules of the game. Johnson, however, had ambitions to be more than the junior Senator from Texas. With the help of the Duke of Duval, he had beaten the mob once but narrowly. In the future he would need more muscle. To get it he arranged for his secretary, Charles Herring, to be appointed U.S. Attorney for the Western District of Texas. Such was Johnson's ability to "reason together" that he persuaded the Eisenhower administration to leave the Democrat in the key post. Shortly thereafter, the Intelligence Division completed a probe of Halfen, and Herring submitted its evidence to a grand jury.

Some Johnson critics have maintained that Herring was only repaying Halfen for the injury done his former boss in the 1948 election and, at the same time, making it clear to the mob that Senator Johnson now had more muscle than even the Texas Rangers. Offsetting this is the fact that Halfen was a tax evader. In securing his indictment, both U.S. Attorney Herring and the Intelligence Division were doing their simple duty. As with Pendergast and Nucky Johnson, the Big Fix was immune to punishment on local and state levels. It cannot be denied, however, that as long as there are more gangsters than the Intelligence Division can cope with, someone must make a decision on which ones will be investigated. On a higher level, politics may enter into the decision, but the men of the Intelligence Division need not, and should not, know anything about it. Crime plays ball with politicians in both parties, often at the same time. The Intelligence Division simply takes the gangsters as it finds them.

The trial of Halfen began on June 21, 1954, in Austin. Key witness was ex-pinball machine operator Thomas Jefferson Vondy. He told of collecting $5 weekly for every pinball machine in every joint, plus $1 per month per machine in "dues." The money, he said, was turned over to Halfen, who used part of it to buy protection from police chiefs, sheriffs, and constables. Between March and June, 1948, Vondy added, he turned over $16,650 to Halfen.

Ten other ex-operators confirmed part of the story. They told of putting money in an envelope each week and dropping it on Vondy's desk. What he did with it, they said they didn't know. They did know, however, that they got the protection they paid for.

259

Evidence was introduced to show that protection money in Houston alone totaled $50,000 a week. The Intelligence men privately estimated it was at least twice that amount. They had reason to know. A witness who prepared Halfen's 1947 tax returns was Revenue Agent E. C. Werner. At the time he worked for Halfen he was a private accountant.

The trial provided information on a very unusual venture known as Great Southern Airways, which, among other things, flew Texas suckers to the casinos run by Owney "the Killer" Madden in Hot Springs, Arkansas. Halfen testified that a partner in the airline was Congressman Albert Thomas. When the United States decided to sell surplus warplanes at bargain prices, Thomas and Halfen arranged to buy ten C-46 planes for $8,600 each. They thought they had a bargain but soon discovered other C-46's available at $1,000 each. Halfen testified Great Southern decided to back out of the deal and let the government reclaim the planes. In reality, only a $2,600 down payment had been made on one plane. The United States Attorney in 1948 was Brian Odum, and he obtained a deficiency judgment against Great Southern.

Halfen wrote out a cashier's check for $2,500 and sent it to Odum as an offer to compromise. Odum returned it. Big Fix then sent the check to Congressman Thomas with the suggestion he fix things up with Attorney General Tom Clark. According to some sources, Clark's memo on the subject was "mislaid" in the Justice Department. In any event, the compromise was not accepted, and the check was ultimately applied to the amount still owed by Great Southern. The plane was seized as well. Clark later became an Associate Justice of the Supreme Court, and his son, Ramsey Clark, was made Attorney General after LBJ became President.

Halfen, testifying in his own defense, said he had a contract with the Coin Machine Operators Association which paid him about $50,000 a year. His duties, he explained, were "to place the coin machine business in a better light so it would be accepted by the public" and to help defeat "certain legislation which was then being considered to abolish certain types of coin machines."

As for the government's contention that he owed $40,000

260

in back taxes for the years 1947 and 1948, Halfen insisted he had reported all his cash receipts. However, all his records were in possession of a now-dead tax expert, and he didn't know what had become of them.

In summing up the case for the government, Herring called Halfen "a payoff man of astronomical proportions." The jury required only fifty-five minutes to find Halfen guilty. Reporters noted that the Big Fix showed no emotion when the verdict was read. U.S. District Judge Ben H. Rice, Jr., an almost legendary figure because his integrity was unquestioned, sentenced Halfen to four years in prison and a $15,000 fine. Halfen took off for Peru while appealing the case but returned to serve every day of his sentence.

Many politicians had bad dreams in Texas over the next four years as investigators, writers, and federal officials sought to persuade the Big Fix to tell all he knew. He was taken from prison at one point and moved around Texas for two weeks while pressure was applied to make him talk. If he squealed, it never became part of a public record. When he had served his time, the Big Fix left Texas to become a gunrunner in Latin America. Bad check charges sent him back to prison in 1961. Still the belief that he had damaging information about LBJ kept interest in him alive until the question became moot with Johnson's 1968 decision to retire from politics.

In the period when Halfen was being roped and branded by the Intelligence Division, a revolt began against LBJ's 1948 benefactor, the Duke of Duval. A Freedom Party was organized to woo away the Mexican-Americans who for so long had been ruled by the Parrs. Governor Allan Shivers broke with Parr, and State Attorney General John Ben Shepperd began a series of investigations.

In a Texas factional fight, rash is he who assumes that any party to a cause, pro or con, is not motivated by political interests. Nevertheless, Shepperd was determined to break Parr's power. Aiding him in Duval County was Jacob S. Floyd, an old attorney known to the Mexican-Americans as *El Víbora Seca* —the Dry Snake. In the 1952 primary election the Freedom Party polled some 1,200 votes in Duval—an astounding break with the past.

The Benavides School District in Duval became a target.
Evidence was uncovered that a lot of nonexistent people had
received large sums from the school district. J. L. MacDonald,
an oil-company employee who had been warned to leave the
county by a Spanish-speaking voice on the telephone, persuaded Diego Heras to talk. Heras, a county employee, produced a large number of canceled checks from county files and
swore the money obtained from them had ended up in Parr's
possession. MacDonald took the evidence to Austin, where he
conferred with Shepperd. Then he went on to Washington
for a chat with the Intelligence Division.

State investigators and special agents swarmed into Duval
and began digging. A lot of records disappeared mysteriously,
but enough remained to prove widespread graft, kickbacks,
and embezzlement of public funds. The Duke had ruled like a
king, taking what he wanted and ruthlessly crushing those who
got in his way.

He continued to fight in the old way as troubles mounted,
and the old methods boomeranged. When a group of Freedom Party workers held a night meeting at the home of Man-
uel Marroquin, Parr tried to spy on the meeting. Marroquin
protested. The Duke of Duval allegedly cursed him soundly
and waved a pistol. In the past that would have been sufficient,
but times had changed. The Mexican-American, emboldened
by the presence of federal agents in the community, signed a
warrant for Parr's arrest. Rangers were sent to pick him up.
They located him at the courthouse in Jim Wells County. His
nephew, Duval Sheriff Archer Parr, was with him.

When the rangers tried to arrest the Duke, Sheriff Parr accused Ranger Joe Bridge of not acting as a good ranger should.
Bridge responded by slapping the sheriff in the face. Ranger
Captain Alfred Allee grabbed the sheriff's pistol. Thereupon
the Duke of Duval entered the fray by grabbing Captain Allee, who reacted by hitting Parr in the head with his pistol
butt. It was a day for law and order in South Texas, and it
ended with the rangers locking up the hitherto-untouchable
boss.

Mexican-Americans were very impressed. Never before had
anyone laid a hand on George Parr. Apparently realizing

262

his prestige was damaged, Parr managed to have the two rangers indicted on charges of assault to commit murder. He also sought an injunction to prevent the rangers from molesting him. A three-judge panel denied the injunction after a hearing in which many witnesses described Parr's ruthless actions of the past. In the eyes of many humble citizens of Duval County, Parr was no longer God.

The Intelligence Division knew Parr from old. In 1931 it had nabbed him for failure to file tax returns in 1928 and 1929. Parr had pleaded guilty in that case and escaped with a $5,000 fine and two years' probation. President Truman pardoned him later, restoring his full civil rights.

Special Agents W. H. Ninedorf and Edward W. Henley spearheaded the new probe. With Duval County in a state of revolt the problem of obtaining evidence was greatly simplified. On November 15, 1954, a three-count indictment was returned in the Corpus Christi division of the Southern District of Texas. Parr was charged with evading $85,654 in taxes by filing false returns in 1949, 1950, and 1951. Two weeks later the IRS struck again—tax liens totaling $1,171,567 for the years 1945 and 1947 were filed against Parr and his former wife.

Now began a long legal battle. Parr's attorneys petitioned the federal district court to move the trial to Laredo on the grounds that he couldn't get a fair trial at home because of "local prejudice." The government's claim that it would be under "a severe handicap" if forced to try the case in Laredo was disregarded.

The government attorneys promptly secured a new indictment at Austin, where Parr's income tax returns had been filed. The next day, May 4, 1955, they moved to dismiss the original indictment in Corpus Christi. Parr's attorneys objected, and when the indictment was dismissed, they appealed. The court of appeals upheld the dismissal, and the legal question was carried to the Supreme Court. One of Parr's attorneys who argued the case before the Supreme Court was later to sit on that body as an Associate Justice. Abe Fortas, a close friend of LBJ's, was also to make history when his nomination by President Johnson to be Chief Justice was blocked in the U.S. Senate and finally withdrawn in 1968. He resigned from the Supreme Court in May, 1969, after a new scandal, becoming the first Associate Justice in history to quit under pressure. Fortas was equally unsuccessful in 1956; the Supreme Court ruled the lower court was correct in dismissing the Corpus Christi indictment.

It was a Pyrrhic victory for the government, however. The vote was close—five to four—and even the majority held that if Parr were tried and convicted on the second indictment, he would have proper grounds for appeal. The minority made it plain that in such an eventuality, they would consider the conviction invalid.

Meanwhile, the investigation into the school district graft had resulted in Parr's being indicted for mail fraud. United States Attorney Malcolm Wilkey took a long look at the situation. Faced with what almost seemed a certain reversal if Parr was convicted at Austin on the income tax case, Wilkey decided to let the tax case wait and try Parr on the mail fraud charges.

All the evidence collected in the two investigations was used in the trial, which began in July, 1957. In twenty counts, Parr was charged with defrauding the school district of more than $200,000. On July 17 he was convicted along with ten co-defendants. Two weeks later Federal Judge Joe M. Ingraham sentenced Parr to ten years in prison and a $20,000 fine. The other defendants drew lesser sentences.

Parr showed no emotion as the stiff sentence was imposed. His attorney, Percy Foreman, commented: "This was only the first round. We have nine rounds still to go."

It proved to be a realistic appraisal of the situation. Once again Parr's attorneys appeared before the Supreme Court, and this time their victory was complete. The conviction was reversed, and no new trial was ordered. The mail fraud charges were dead.

In the period while legal arguments were being made about the site of Parr's trial, the Duke of Duval ran for sheriff. With the help of 950 absentee ballots, he won by 2,808 to 2,092 votes. But the costs of his legal battles were grinding him down. Prior to the trial for mail fraud, he filed a petition of bankruptcy.

U.S. Attorney Wilkey was helpless to proceed with the income tax case, hopeless as it looked, while the mail fraud conviction was making its way up the chain of appeal. Under the Justice Department's dual prosecution policy, a defendant cannot be prosecuted on additional charges if he has been convicted and sentenced on substantially the same set of facts in another case. By putting all his eggs in one basket, Wilkey, in effect, agreed not to follow through on the income tax case until the mail fraud was settled. By the time this happened Parr's accountant, the chief witness against him, had died. In addition, the Supreme Court had ruled in *James v. United States,* reversing a criminal conviction for willfully failing to report income derived from embezzlement. The court held the embezzler had a right to rely on a 1946 case that had declared embezzled funds to be nontaxable. It seemed obvious that Parr would plead the same defense and would probably be upheld on appeal.

Years had passed, and with it had gone much of the interest in George Parr and his South Texas empire. With the odds seemingly insurmountable, the Department of Justice gave permission to dismiss the income tax case. In April, 1963—almost nine years after the indictment was returned—the case was dropped in open court.

Seven months later John F. Kennedy was murdered on the streets of Dallas, Texas, and Lyndon B. Johnson—the man Parr helped win a Senate seat—became President of the United States.

Meanwhile, back over on the eastern part of the Texas ranch, folks were talking about Galveston's former head wrangler, Fred M. Ford. The federal vigilantes were after him too.

From the time Jean Lafitte founded Galveston in 1817, the Gulf City had enjoyed a notorious reputation. Its Post Office Street was famous among sailors for the number and quality of its brothels. Gambling joints were equally wide open. Vice had become a way of life.

Ford was born in Galveston in 1900. He dropped out of school in 1913 to become a delivery boy. The job made him familiar with his city. In 1925 he became a policeman at a salary of $120 a month. It was almost public policy in those days that cops supplement their salary with the "fringe benefits" gamblers and madams were so eager to supply. By 1940 Ford had advanced to police chief.

World War II brought many more sailors and other servicemen to Galveston, and the booming industrial complex of nearby Houston added to the take. Ford took full advantage of the prosperity. Jealous rivals, who figured he had been head steer long enough, managed to butt him aside in 1947. The ex-chief promptly opened a gambling joint of his own, the Club Southerner.

In 1949, Special Agent Matthew P. Harris, assisted by Revenue Agent Joseph Wanderscheid, began a probe of Ford's tax returns. They got a big break when they visited Mrs. Margaret Lera on Post Office Street. The beautiful dark-haired madam was cautious at first, but Wanderscheid displayed the strange charm that eleven years later was to win the confidence of the newly divorced wife of Trigger Mike Coppola. In short order, he persuaded Mrs. Lera to talk. The madam told of paying $100 monthly to Chief Ford for permission to operate two brothels. What's more, she agreed to testify in open court.

Harris and Wanderscheid dug up other evidence which proved Ford had spent $48,857 more than his income in the years 1945 through 1947. In fact, during those three years, he spent $10,758 more than he had made in salary during the twenty-two years he had been on the police force.

The case was wrapped up and sent to Washington with a recommendation for criminal prosecution.* Months passed, and

* While there was a special reason for delay in Ford's case, recommendations for criminal prosecution are no simple matter. The average citizen has many safeguards to protect him when he comes under the scrutiny of the IRS. A revenue agent—from the Audit Division—usually takes the first look at his returns and makes a preliminary investigation. If he finds evidence of fraud, of deliberate evasion, a special agent from the Intelligence Division is put in charge. He works with the revenue agent in preparing a case. If, in his opinion, the evidence of fraud is sufficient to stand a court test, he makes a recommendation for prosecution in his final report. The recommendation is then reviewed by his immediate superior, by the district chief, by the regional chief. If all concur, it is sent to the national office and reviewed once more. The case may be sent back for additional work to strengthen it, or it may be killed. If prospects still look good, it is sent to the Justice Department with recommendations for prosecution. The process begins again. Justice attorneys, who must prosecute, take

then years. It appeared the Ford case was one of many that were destined to die on the vine. The Kefauver Committee hearings, however, so shocked the public that a new racketeer drive was launched late in 1951. Someone remembered the Ford case, all wrapped up and ready to go. Wanderscheid, by now an acting special agent, said many people were amazed at the speed with which an indictment was secured against Ford early in 1952.

"They didn't see how we could build a case so fast," said Wanderscheid.

The trial began almost a year later before District Judge Ben H. Rice, Jr. Lyndon Johnson's old secretary, U.S. Attorney Charles Herring, was prosecutor and all too aware that it had been twenty-five years since a jury in Travis County had returned a guilty verdict in an income tax case.

A series of merchants were the first witnesses. They testified on expenditures made by Ford. J. M. Levy admitted that as a customer, Ford started small. His first purchase in 1946 was a $25 poker table. The next year, however, he bought $3,342 worth of merchandise. An auto dealer testified that six weeks after Ford was fired as chief, he paid $2,082 in currency for a new car. And so it went.

The madam, still faithful to the promise she made to Wanderscheid more than three years before, testified that she ran two brothels and in 1943 left $100 at Ford's office. Starting in 1945, she said, she made regular payments "to the police department" of $100 a month. Mrs. Lera didn't say, however, that she knew Ford got the money, but she did say the payments stopped when he left office. In 1949, she added, the ex-chief

a long look. Once again, they can send it back for more work, or they can kill it. If the case survives, however, it is sent back to the district where it began and turned over to the local U.S. Attorney. He can object, and if his objections are well founded, he can kill the case. If he doesn't object, the case then goes before a federal grand jury, which, in effect, reviews it once more. If an indictment is returned, the case is scheduled for trial. Once again, a jury of laymen decides if the evidence is sufficient. If the verdict is "guilty," the defendant can, and usually does, appeal. Ultimately, the case may go to the Supreme Court.

Because there are so many checkpoints along the way, a special agent knows he must have a good case before he makes that first recommendation for prosecution. The taxpayer is given the benefit of most doubts. Consequently only those facts which are solidly backed by evidence are used. As a result, a Clark, a Capone, a Costello, may have actually cheated on $1,000,000, but be indicted and convicted only on $10,000.

asked for her support in his unsuccessful bid for the office of police commissioner.

Another witness was a tall, handsome woman who identified herself as Ford's former girlfriend. Her testimony that Ford took her to gambling joints and nightclubs where the drinks were free because he was chief was stricken from the record by Judge Rice.

Special Agent Harris testified that Ford denied taking payoffs but did admit to accepting a suit of clothes from a gambling joint. Harris' partner put it a little differently. On cross-examination he was asked if Ford didn't deny he took payoffs from prostitutes.

Wanderscheid took his time before replying. "I wouldn't say he denied it," said the agent slowly. "He just wouldn't admit it."

Laughter rippled across the courtroom. Defense attorney Douglas McGregor, a former U.S. Attorney, turned on his heel. "That's all," he snapped.

Ford's lawyers offered only three witnesses in defense. All testified about Ford's good character, but the value of their opinions was qualified when one of them commented: "Sure, I heard some things, but they were not out of the ordinary. You hear that every man who has been police chief is supposed to take graft."

In Galveston, that was probably the truth.

In summing up for the defense, McGregor called Ford "a patriot" because he had purchased $11,000 worth of war bonds. "I feel constrained to believe the assistant U.S. district attorney has forgotten Pearl Harbor," thundered the lawyer.

Herring replied: "It doesn't seem patriotic to me for a person to buy war bonds with the money he should have used to pay taxes and then cash in the bonds."

Apparently the jury agreed with Herring. It required only nineteen minutes to convict Ford on all counts. Special Agent Harris noted in passing that the people of Galveston thought the income tax probe "was a joke" when it began. When the verdict was given, however, tears replaced laughter among Ford's friends in the courtroom. Nine days later Judge Rice sentenced the ex-chief to four years in prison. He was freed on $5,000 bond pending appeal.

The cynics chuckled when, one year and two days later, the Fifth Circuit Court of Appeals reversed the guilty verdict and ordered a new trial. The principal error assigned concerned the testimony of Mrs. Lera. The appeals court held the judge erred in overruling a defense motion to strike her testimony on the grounds that she had not actually connected the defendant with the payoffs she said she had made "to the police department."

Wanderscheid was given the job of overcoming the doubts of the madam prior to the new trial. The woman was skeptical, but while refusing to pledge full cooperation, she gave him leads to much new information. In the process, the special agent became acquainted with many of the prostitutes in the eastern part of Texas and later used them in other cases. Mrs. Lera wanted Ford convicted, he discovered, because the payoff system was bleeding her of profits. Practically anyone with an official connection—including city truck drivers—felt free to stop by and demand a payoff in either cash or services. Other madams felt the same way, but none was willing to dare the wrath of the Establishment.

When the second trial began in June, 1955, the prosecution was handled by Fred Ugast, an Assistant U.S. Attorney General from Washington. A small man physically, Ugast was considered one of the best trial lawyers in the Justice Department. Seven years later he would again work with Wanderscheid in the Trigger Mike Coppola case.

One government witness called was Galveston Mayor Roy Clough. While waiting to testify, the mayor declared himself in favor of what he called "decent prostitution" and predicted it was in Galveston to stay. "I'm in favor of an open town," said the mayor, "but a clean town." On the witness stand the perspiring mayor said Ford had a "bad reputation" while chief.

Once more Harris and Wanderscheid established the facts of Ford's reported income and his much larger expenditures. Once again they had to depend on a single madam to testify he received payoffs. Mrs. Lera, wearing a chic black dress and a small white hat, was cautious in answering Ugast's questions. Once again she failed to establish her payoffs went directly to Ford.

Wanderscheid watched and listened, wondering how he could persuade the woman to be as frank in court as she had been in private conversation. He recalled his first meeting six years before. At that time Mrs. Lera had kept him and Harris waiting for fifteen minutes while a cute girl in a nightgown chatted away in the public parlor. When at last Mrs. Lera appeared to invite her guests into the private parlor, the girl whispered: "When you get through, we'll have a party—for free."

The special agent never saw the young girl again. Later, he had heard that she retired after being badly beaten in a mysterious episode. Mrs. Lera had refused to talk about it. Could the incident be related to her reluctance to tell all? It was worth exploring.

Defense attorney McGregor saved Wanderscheid the trouble. He cross-examined the madam roughly, questioning her about her own tax troubles, which had been settled out of court. Implied in the questions was the suggestion she had saved her neck by turning government witness against Ford. The woman became annoyed. Reporters noted that "her temper rose."

The cross-examination ended with the noon recess. Mrs. Lera went straight to Ugast.

"Put me back on the stand," she said angrily. "I'm ready to tell everything."

On redirect examination Mrs. Lera told of asking Ford "if the detectives had been delivering what I had been sending him, and he said, 'Yes.' "

What had she been sending? "Money," said the still-angry madam, and she named the men she said she used to deliver it. Wanderscheid and Harris relaxed.

The jury took its time on the second trial, deliberating for four hours and forty minutes before finding Ford guilty on all counts. Once more Judge Rice sentenced him to four years in prison. On April 19, 1956, the Fifth Circuit Court of Appeals upheld the verdict. It noted that Mrs. Lera's question to Ford was enough to meet the objections raised at the first trial. Ford's attorneys also argued on appeal that evidence given the grand jury was not based on firsthand knowledge. In rejecting this contention, the court cited the Supreme Court's decision in the Frank Costello case. In that decision the High Court had ruled: "An indictment returned by a legally constituted and unbiased grand jury . . . if valid on its face, is enough to call for trial of the charge on the merits. The Fifth Amendment requires nothing more."

Ford went to prison. Before departing, he happened to meet Wanderscheid.

"I don't blame you," said the ex-chief. "It's all my fault. I brought my troubles on myself."

The two men shook hands.

Such victories were important but they did little to clean up Texas. Scandal after scandal shook the state in the 1950's. On the state level there were land scandals, insurance scandals, oil scandals. In Beaumont, Port Arthur, and Galveston, prostitution and gambling were wide open and acknowledged to be so by men elected or appointed to enforce the law. The newspapers of Texas, with a few courageous exceptions, were blind to conditions. Typical was the experience of Allan Wegemer, a reporter for the Beaumont *Journal*.

In 1955, Wegemer wrote a series of articles about gambling and prostitution in Beaumont. As a result, he was called before one of those trained grand juries so familiar to any reporter who challenges organized crime in an area where crime has political control. The jury treated him with hostility and issued a report describing his allegations "as a reporter's pipe dream."

The newspaper fired the troublemaker. He found a new job in San Antonio. In 1961 the General Investigating Committee of the legislature held a series of hearings in Beaumont on the heels of coordinated raids its probers had inspired. Wegemer was called as a witness. He told of visiting sixteen brothels in Port Arthur and Beaumont and of his experience with the grand jury. Within an hour after testifying, he was fired by the San Antonio newspaper. He was "too controversial." This decision was made despite a report issued before Wegemer testified by the investigating committee: "From evidence obtained from the raids conducted by undercover agents working with the

Committee, it is apparent that vice operations here [in Beaumont] are the oldest, largest and most thoroughly organized in the State."

Later that year Attorney General Robert F. Kennedy was to speak of "the rape of Beaumont by organized crime." With help from Kennedy's "coordinated war on crime," the local citizens finally overthrew the corrupt political machine that had made vice possible. In that bitter struggle, the Intelligence Division played a major role.

16

A MAN CALLED ABE

THERE was much interest in Louisville, Kentucky, in 1946 when the United States announced it would receive sealed bids from prospective purchasers of Lincoln Park.

Originally the park had been the site of the Post Office. The old building had been torn down in 1935, when a huge new structure was erected on Broadway. The vacant lot occupied a square block in the heart of the business district. Pending a decision on its disposal, the lot was converted into a park.

When the bids were opened, the winner proved to be a group headed by Jules Endler of Newark, New Jersey, with a high bid of $1,803,013. A syndicate of Louisville businessmen was second with a bid of $1,735,000. Some agitation arose aimed at blocking the sale to the unknowns, but it died when Endler arrived in town. Sandy Wood, a *Courier-Journal* reporter, was much impressed. He wrote: "Endler, looking more like a Hollywood movie star than a man with a dream to put into brick and stone, came to Louisville yesterday."

The reporter noted that Endler recently financed two movies and that he resembled actor Ronald Colman in appearance.

Any remaining fears were quieted when Endler held a press conference and announced plans to construct a four-story de-

273

partment emporium, a 3,500-seat theater, and a restaurant "of national repute" on the property. An artist's conception of the project was published, and intellectuals were reminded of Louisville's reputation as the Athens of the West.

At intervals over the next four years, announcement was made to the effect that work would begin in the immediate future. Meanwhile, Lincoln Park remained Lincoln Park. On April 23, 1950, the news broke that Endler had sold two-thirds of the site "for more than the total cost of the land" and expected to make a net profit of "considerably more than $800,000" when he sold the rest of it. Regrets over the lost "dream" of five years before were tempered by admiration of the businessman.

One-third of the park was sold by Endler to a dime-store chain. The other corner went to a rival dime-store chain. And in 1951 the middle section was sold to a department-store chain which catered to low-income customers.

So much for the theater and the restaurant of national repute. The dime stores did feature lunch counters, however.

It was not until July 11, 1951, that the people of Louisville learned who the romantic-looking Endler represented. On that day a somewhat anxious Endler admitted to the Kefauver Committee that he had been the nominee of Abner "Longie" Zwillman.

Two years later the *Courier-Journal* described the Lincoln Park deal as "one of the most profitable real estate speculations in Louisville history." For Zwillman, profitable deals were standard procedure. Those movies Endler had boasted about in 1946 were also Zwillman-financed. The husky six-footer had even played a leading role in one of Hollywood's most sensational off-camera romances. Jean Harlow, the sexy "Blonde Bombshell" of the thirties, fell in love with Zwillman when he visited the movie capital during the syndicate take-over of the industry. Zwillman was moved deeply enough by Jean's tragic death to attend her funeral and got almost as much attention from the public as Clark Gable.

It was on June 30, 1947—while Louisville was still waiting for Endler's dream to materialize—that Special Agent Edwin A. Baldwin, of the Intelligence Unit's New York office, wrote a memorandum. At the top of the page he listed "Abner Zwill-man, alias Abe Zwillman, etc.; Joseph Doto, alias Joe Adonis, etc.; and William Moretti, alias Willie Moore, etc.," all of New Jersey.

Zwillman, he noted, "an ex-bootlegger, is the most important racketeer in New Jersey, and through his lieutenants controls all the slot machines and cigarette vending machines in New Jersey. He exercises control over the gambling racket in northern New Jersey and concessions for gambling activities are obtained through him. Zwillman is also reported to be providing political protection for fellow racketeers, and to be also interested in labor union rackets."

Adonis was identified as "an overlord of the Brooklyn underworld." Moretti was said to be "a close associate of the other two" and a "leading Bergen County (New Jersey) racketeer." He could have added information supplied by the famous Abe "Kid Twist" Reles, the canary of Murder, Inc. Reles testified in 1939 that two years earlier he had been called to testify before a grand jury investigating the disappearance of Louis "Lepke" Buchalter.

According to Reles, he was about to grasp the knob of the door to the grand jury room when two men slipped up beside him for a friendly chat. They advised him, he said, to swear to the jury not only that did he not know where the dread Lepke was hiding, but also that he didn't even know the man.

Reles said he took the warning seriously and went in and perjured himself "up to the ears." The warning came from men he feared—Willie Moretti and Longie Zwillman. The health and happiness of Lepke in that period when he hid while almost all witnesses against him were being murdered was Zwillman's primary responsibility. And it was Longie who finally persuaded Lepke to surrender to J. Edgar Hoover.

That Reles was justified in taking the 1937 warning seriously was demonstrated convincingly on November 12, 1941. He had talked at length about Murder, Inc., and was scheduled to talk some more when suddenly he died under circumstances that have never been explained. He plunged to his death through a window on the sixth floor of the Half Moon Hotel in Coney Island. Armed guards and steel doors protected him, yet the syndicate's long arm sent him sprawling to the sidewalk. Revenge was obtained and a warning given to other potential stool pigeons. Zwillman and Moretti, to say nothing of Albert Anastasia, were suspected, but the probe got absolutely nowhere.

Baldwin, aware that Zwillman had been considered one of the judges who approved the executions which Murder, Inc., carried out with such efficiency, concluded his memorandum by recommending that *F* cases be jacketed for each of the three men and that their cases be assigned the New York office for investigation. *F* was the routine designation for fraud cases. When a new antiracketeering drive began in 1951, the letter *R* (for racketeer) was used.

Baldwin's recommendation was stamped approved by his immediate superior, Special Agent in Charge Daniel A. Bolich, and sent to Washington, where the probe was okayed. Little progress was made, however, until Bolich was given his new job as Assistant Commissioner of Internal Revenue in 1948.

The special agents assigned to dig into Zwillman's affairs had the benefit of an earlier probe by Special Agent Walter Fowler in 1937. Fowler had checked the years from 1929 to 1936, the period when Zwillman as a member of the Big Seven and a partner in the Reinfeld Syndicate had made millions in smuggled booze. Nevertheless, he had concealed his wealth so well it was impossible to prove its existence. The probe showed he maintained no records and avoided openly dealing with banks and brokerage houses. Fowler recommended that Zwillman not be told the search was fruitless and the case be reopened at a later date. As a result, it was possible to get written consent from Zwillman extending the statute of limitations on subsequent years up to 1943. Zwillman was also officially notified that since the probe was not closed, he must keep adequate books and records. This was done, and from the records submitted it was possible to determine that as of December 31, 1946, Zwillman and his wife had a declared financial net worth of $623,672.60.

This was important—a net worth case must have a starting point if any increase is to be measurable.

Inasmuch as Zwillman had filed tax returns listing rather modest incomes, it was clear a huge civil assessment could be made on those years for which criminal prosecution was barred by the statute of limitations. Zwillman's attorneys notified the Intelligence Unit that their client would pay $106,000 if, in return, the investigation would be closed as of December 31, 1946. Upon studying the matter, however, it was decided that more money would be gained if reportable income were taxed in the years an increase in net worth was discovered.

Special Agent Alexander A. Kuszynski on December 29, 1947, reported the investigation would continue but no criminal prosecution would be recommended because the greatest increase would probably fall in the Prohibition years for which the statutes of limitations had expired.

This, in itself, represented a victory for Zwillman. Anti-racketeering sentiment was at a low ebb in the postwar period. The businessmen types then running the show were satisfied to pry a few hundred thousand out of a man who had made millions in illegal business.

Zwillman was born in Newark, New Jersey, in 1904, the second of seven children. Reuben Zwillman, his father, died while Longie was still a youth. In fact, Zwillman didn't know his own name for years. Special Agent Baldwin checked the taxpayer's first tax returns and noticed he had signed his name Abraham. He asked Zwillman why he changed to Abner. The gangster said he grew up being called Abe and it was not until he was a man that his mother mentioned his real name was Abner. His birth certificate confirmed her statement.

Longie attended public schools in Newark. His father's death made it necessary for him to quit school and work at any job he could find. Eventually, he became a huckster. With the organization of liquor smuggling on a huge scale, Longie found his place. He was hired by the Reinfeld Syndicate as a truck driver, assigned to haul liquor from unloading zones along the East Coast. So ruthless was Zwillman that no hijacker dared bother him. Quickly he was promoted and proved he had executive ability, as well as muscle. Soon he became a full partner in the combine and was in charge of transportation by road and rail from Boston south.

The Reinfeld Syndicate was divided into two parts: The Canadian end was headed by the four Bronfman brothers. Samuel, Abraham, Harry, and Allen. They began as owners of small hotels and ended as the richest men in Canada and head of Distillers-Seagram, Ltd. It was the Bronfmans' duty to buy Canadian booze and ship it around the East Coast to Rum Rows of Boston and New York. The so-called High Seas Operation was legal; it was not until the liquor was taken inside the legal limit by boats shuttling back and forth between the mother ship and the shore that the law was violated.

Joseph Reinfeld, a native of Poland, was ten years old when he arrived in this country in 1909. He was first arrested in Newark in 1918 and fined $5. In 1925 he was charged with murder in Newark. Allegedly he killed Prohibition Agent Louis Lafara, in what police discreetly called "a dispute over money matters." The murder took place on the eve of a trial resulting from the seizure of the rum ship *Harrishof*. Agent Lafara seized it at a Newark pier with 800 cases of contraband liquor on board. Reinfeld was never indicted in the murder, and the charge was dropped. His only federal conviction was in 1920, when he pleaded guilty to a charge of transporting ten barrels of liquor from Newark to New York. He was fined $200.

The Reinfeld Syndicate maintained a sales office in Newark. A customer desiring to buy liquor would visit the office, deposit his money, and receive a receipt entitling him to a specific amount of whiskey. He would then take a boat out to the ship and collect his cargo. Zwillman, who owned 50 percent of the syndicate, made several trips to Canada to buy liquor from the Bronfmans.

It was an immensely profitable operation, and it was followed in 1933 with another almost as liquid. The partners in the Reinfeld Syndicate organized a legitimate company, Browne Vintners. Zwillman and a partner, Joseph "Doc" Stacher, held a large block of the stock. The company made money; but in 1939 it fell under the scrutiny of District Attorney Tom Dewey, and the boys decided to get out. The Schenley liquor empire was interested and discussions were held with Zwillman, but in December, 1940, Browne Vintners was sold to Seagram's. The price: $7,500,000. And now the boys got into a dispute which eventually made much of their dealings a matter of court record.

278

As a result of the sale, Browne Vintners had to pay income taxes. The sum of $900,000 of the purchase price was placed in escrow, of which $574,000 was earmarked for taxes and the rest for liquidation expenses. Reinfeld had several meetings with Zwillman and Stacher before a compromise was reached. On May 11, 1943, he paid Zwillman and Stacher an additional $385,000. Another dissatisfied partner, James Rutkin, got $250,000.

Zwillman, meanwhile, had established a dual reputation as a killer and as a successful businessman. He was constantly questioned about various murders, but he served only a six-month sentence in 1930 for assault with intent to kill. In 1939 he was again sentenced to six months for contempt of court when he refused to give a federal judge information about his associates in rum-running days. The sentence was overturned on appeal, however.

In 1933, Zwillman made news by offering a $50,000 reward for the capture of the kidnappers of Charles A. Lindbergh, Jr. An official report noted dryly that his motive was apparently the fact that "police were blocking the highways in the hunt for the kidnappers and incidentally seizing trucks loaded with contraband liquor."

Zwillman played an important role in the formation of the National Crime Syndicate and sat as a member of the board of directors. A friend of Luciano and Lansky, he had a piece of all syndicate investments. Following the murder of Dutch Schultz, he was designated by the FBI as "Public Enemy Number 1 of New Jersey."

The Public Service Tobacco Company, Inc., of Hillside, New Jersey, became a typical syndicate business. The firm was founded by two rum-runners, William and Albert Lillian. When the brothers refused to cooperate with the Big Seven, Al was murdered in 1933. William refused to surrender the tobacco company, however, and was given a severe beating by unknown persons. He then turned over his interests to Zwillman, Stacher, and Gerald Catena. Another partner was Michael Lascari, a foster brother of Lucky Luciano's. A second company, Manhattan Cigarettes, was the vehicle used by Zwillman to get control of much of the coin machine business. Later Trigger Mike Coppola became a partner in the company.

The Federal Automatic Company, Inc., of Hillside, was created to rent washing and drying machines to laundries. It brought Zwillman as much as $16,701 profit in one year. The E. & S. Trading Company of Newark dealt in scrap metals and brought annual profits as high as $91,247. The Harb Kegtap System, Inc., was set up in 1936 to manufacture beer-dispensing equipment and was one of the few enterprises involving Zwillman that lost money; it was liquidated in 1938. Other companies included GMC Trucks Sales, Inc.; Greater GMC Parts & Service Co., Inc.; the S A & S Trading Company, Inc.; and United States Yeast Corporation.

Meanwhile, Zwillman was living like a king in the Waldorf-Astoria and enjoying the syndicate's conquest of Hollywood. What was later described as a romance developed between the gangster and actress Jean Harlow. When Bugsy Siegel arrived in town, Longie introduced the Bug to the Bombshell.

In 1949 Special Agent Hugh E. Kifer explored that glittering period of make-believe. Special Agent Cangialosi asked him to check reports that a Dr. Benjamin Blank lent $10,000 to Longie shortly after Jean Harlow's death. Interviewed in Beverly Hills, Dr. Blank said he was introduced to Zwillman by Siegel in the early 1930's. When Longie came West to attend the funeral, he said, he treated the gangster at his hotel for an undisclosed illness. He denied making a loan to Zwillman but said he did lend $20,000 to Siegel "to cover up for some stock." Some of that money could have been passed on to Longie, he concluded.

The probe spread to Florida, where it was suspected that Jack Friedlander represented Zwillman in the S & G Syndicate in Miami Beach. Friedlander formerly had been a lottery operator in Newark, moving to Florida in 1939. A number of cancelled checks bearing the endorsement of "S & G Service" were seized in an Essex County, New Jersey, gambling raid. Immediately Friedlander was suspected. Investigation proved, however, that Friedlander was a member of the Little Syndicate in Miami, and not the tightly controlled bookmaking operation across Biscayne Bay in Miami Beach.

Special Agent Cangialosi was not too proud to seek help from

280

the FBI in his probe of Zwillman. Recalling the "public enemy" label given by the G-men, he asked Intelligence Chief Woolf to obtain permission to review the FBI files. Almost two months were required for the request to move through channels, but on October 13, 1948, Assistant Attorney General Theron L. Caudle wrote to Woolf. According to Caudle, he had obtained the following memorandum from FBI Director J. Edgar Hoover:

> Please be advised that a search of the records of this Bureau fails to reflect that Zwillman has ever been the subject of an investigation conducted by the Federal Bureau of Investigation. It is noted, however, that Zwillman's name appears in the file entitled "United States Yeast Corporation; Interference by Violence with Interstate Commerce" and in the matter entitled "Fur Dressing Investigation; Louis Buchalter, with aliases; Antitrust; Harboring; Conspiracy." Your attention is invited to the fact that the information concerning Zwillman which appears in the above files was obtained through collateral inquiry incident to another investigation.

Another dead end. It would appear that Hoover, while ready to make headlines by calling Zwillman a public enemy, had not bothered to investigate him. The incident confirms that the FBI, although busy building an image, selected its targets carefully and wasted little energy in attacking the leaders of organized crime. In fairness, however, it should be added that until Attorney General Robert F. Kennedy sponsored new laws in 1961, the FBI had very limited jurisdiction in areas where organized crime was active. The Intelligence Division, free to follow the flow of money whatever its source, was the syndicate's only foe until Kennedy pushed Hoover into the fight.

Special Agent Cangialosi was ordered to active duty in the Army in 1951. Special Agent Eugene F. Coyle took charge of the case and in a status report on March 15, 1951, noted some bad news. Tentative findings for the years 1942-46, he said, reflecting additional taxes of $535,874, "were nullified by a recent disclosure that the bulk of the net worth cases were accounted for by substantial income received by Zwillman on which the tax had been paid by nominees."

Among these nominees was Jules Endler, who had fronted for Longie in the Louisville real estate deal.

Coyle also noted: "Difficulties are reluctant and evasive witnesses (fear of Zwillman), lack of records and the fact that, to a large extent, his transactions are in currency."

In October, 1951, attention centered on a Western Union money order dated February 17, 1946, in the amount of $6,000. The money order, payable to Zwillman, was addressed to the gangster in care of the Hollywood Beach Hotel, Hollywood, Florida. It was purchased by Richard H. Nolan, an associate of imprisoned labor racketeer Joseph Fay.

When questioned, Nolan said he sent the money to Zwillman at Fay's request. Allegedly it was in payment of a debt. The money order bore the endorsement of both Zwillman and Jake Lansky, Meyer's brother and local lieutenant. Special Agent Edward M. Cohen interviewed Jake at his Hollywood home and received the usual bland replies. Lansky acknowledged his signature but said he didn't remember the incident. He assumed he "may have run into Zwillman or someone else in the bank and endorsed it" to facilitate his getting the cash. He was sure it couldn't represent gambling losses since Zwillman never gambled very much. He was equally sure that neither he nor Meyer had ever had any business dealings with Zwillman.

Another joke.

By June, 1952, the Intelligence Division was ready to move against Zwillman despite his protests to the Kefauver Committee in March, 1951, that he was much overrated. Senator Charles W. Tobey of New Hampshire asked him if it was true he was known as the Al Capone of New Jersey.

Longie laughed and answered: "That is a myth that has been developing, Mr. Senator, for a good many years, and during the time when I should have had sense enough to stop it, or get up and get out of the state, I did not have sense enough. . . . It blossomed and bloomed until here today I am here, and in my opinion I don't belong here today, but I am here. . . . Those rumors go around. They accuse me of owning places. I walk into a restaurant and I own the restaurant. I walk into a hotel and I own the hotel. I take a shine twice and I own the bootblack, too."

"Well," said Senator Tobey, "those are the penalties of greatness."

Zwillman stepped down from the stand and winked at the next witness, Morris Kleinman. Years before Kleinman in Cleveland and Zwillman in New York had exchanged liquor in times of temporary shortages. Kleinman had been convicted years before of income tax evasion, had served his time and emerged bigger than ever as part of a nationwide gambling syndicate. Longie's troubles had been delayed, but they were beginning to catch up with him.

On June 11, 1952, Intelligence Chief Frank Lohn approved a jeopardy assessment of $518,483 for the years 1933 to 1946 against Zwillman. Transfer assessments against his wife and children—to whom Longie had transferred considerable stock —were also made. The action brought a letter from Morris Shilensky, one of Zwillman's attorneys. Shilensky commented:

> Although Mr. Zwillman's tax matter has been pending in the Department for a great many years and has been under active examination for the last six or seven years, a jeopardy assessment for about three-quarters of a million dollars was filed against the taxpayer without any warning or notice to us or our clients. The Collector immediately made levies against Mr. Zwillman's property and also that of his wife and children. . . .
>
> The real answer as to why the taxpayer has been treated in this unusual manner may be that his name has been placed on a so-called "racket" list, at least, so the newspapers report. Apparently while Mr. Zwillman's name remains on this list for special treatment no subordinate officer of the Bureau will treat Mr. Zwillman as he has the right to be treated, namely, as any other citizen and taxpayer. We think everyone will agree that if there is such a list and Mr. Zwillman's name does not belong on it, he has been and is being treated unfairly.

The point raised by the attorney is one debated today in the Internal Revenue Service. Some high officials insist the Intelligence Division should not be asked to serve as a law enforcement arm when its proper function is simply to make sure the public is aware that even crooks have to pay their taxes. This approach frowns upon "racketeer drives" per se, while acknowledging that many gangsters who violate the law to make money will not hesitate to violate it again to keep as much as possible of the loot. Other officers argue that the Intelligence Division has the most sweeping jurisdiction of any federal agency inasmuch as the object of organized crime is to make money. They maintain this power to check gangster's income is the ultimate weapon of society against crime, and unless it is used, the entire system may fall apart.

This debate, which sometimes sees one side in the saddle and then the other, explains the stop-and-go nature of the Intelligence Division's battle against the syndicate since Elmer Irey retired. Theory, as much as politics, sometimes determines policy.

Zwillman's former partner in the Reinfeld Syndicate, James "Nig" Rutkin, was interviewed on March 12, 1953, at the Hudson County Jail. He had been sent to prison for income tax evasion, and he maintained to the special agents talking to him that his investigation was instigated by Joseph Reinfeld. According to the ex-bootlegger, Reinfeld arranged to give former Commissioner Joe Nunan an affidavit that purported to show Rutkin had received much additional money from Reinfeld. The purpose of the plot, said Reinfeld, was to kill a new civil suit he had brought against Reinfeld in connection with the vast profits made during rum-running days. He had earlier been warned, he said, that if he didn't drop the suit, he would be indicted for tax evasion by Nunan. Nunan still had influence, he added.

It will be remembered that Nunan went to work for Reinfeld when he left the federal service.

Special Agent Cangialosi, back from the Army, submitted his final report on January 7, 1953. On June 14, 1953, a federal grand jury shocked everyone by returning no bill in the Zwillman case. The special agent was asked to submit a report explaining why no indictment had been returned. He was both bitter and blunt, listing eight reasons. They follow:

1. Disjointed discussions and conferences held by Department of Justice representatives.

2. Inexperience of Department of Justice attorney making initial partial presentation of case to the federal grand jury.

3. Failure to cover all evidence bearing on Zwillman's willful intent to evade payment of his income taxes.

4. Failure to develop and emphasize the unidentified income of $30,000 reported by Zwillman in 1946 as from "Other Sources."

5. Failure to cover Zwillman's record of unfavorable income tax history during the earlier years.

6. Failure to cover Zwillman's police and criminal records, as well as stress his unfavorable reputation and character.

7. Failure to consult with Enforcement Division (IRS) attorney as well as failure to follow his "Suggested Theory of Prosecution."

8. Failure to see to it that the grand jurors heard testimony of Jules Endler, a very significant witness.

Special Agent Cangialosi noted that another unfortunate development was that the case was presented to a new federal grand jury instead of a "so-called 'Rackets' Federal Grand Jury which for eighteen months had been hearing testimony on the entire New Jersey crime picture." The special agent well knew that grand juries must be educated before the lay members can begin to understand and appreciate the complexities of organized crime. This fact is the big reason why state grand juries are generally ineffective, although composed in the main of honest and sincere citizens. A corrupt state attorney needs only to keep jurors uninformed in order to maintain the status quo as far as organized crime is concerned, and unless information and direction are supplied by a grand juror, there is little possibility a community can be aroused to the enemy within.

Cangialosi, in evaluating the failure of the grand jury, gave no weight to Rutkin's charge made a few weeks earlier that Joe Nunan was "still a powerful figure in government" with the ability to stop any probe. He said a supplemental investigation into the no bill was "not warranted" but added he had no alternative but to recommend a representation of the case to another grand jury. He suggested that the jury selected to hear the new presentation "be called into session under such circumstances as will enable and permit all grand jurors to benefit from the full representation of the case."

A key bit of evidence in the case of Zwillman involved the Tanforan Racetrack at San Bruno, California. The original tip came from Gene Bowles, a reporter for the San Francisco *Chronicle*. The Tanforan property was taken over by the United States at the outbreak of World War II and used as a detention center for Japanese-Americans. After the war it was sold to a group headed by Guy Standifer, described as a gold mine industrialist. Bowles charged the real owner was Joe Reinfeld.

Investigation revealed that considerable influence was used to speed construction of a racetrack on the property. Major General Harry E. Vaughn, the military aide of President Truman, intervened in 1948 to expedite the construction permit. Housing Expediter Tighe E. Woods testified that General Vaughn told him haste was needed because "something" was before the California Racing Commission that could cause Tanforan to lose its franchise if construction were long delayed. Other testimony disclosed that two major stockholders were Eugene Mori, president of the Garden State Racetrack in Camden, New Jersey, and William G. Helis of New Orleans. Years before, Helis had been described as "the richest Greek in the world" by Elmer Irey—this was before the man who in 1968 married Jackie Kennedy made his pile. According to Irey, Helis got rich during the reign of Huey Long's puppet, Robert Maestri, who served as Louisiana's commissioner of conservation before becoming the nonelected mayor of New Orleans. As commissioner, Maestri permitted Helis "to operate his oil leases without restriction," Irey wrote, and Maestri as one of the stockholders in Helis' company made a cool $1,157,161.

Jules Endler, the man who charmed Louisville, admitted to Intelligence agents that Zwillman had an interest in the Tanforan track in the name of a nominee. Yet Endler was one of two witnesses not subpoenaed before the grand jury that

286

returned the no bill. Cangialosi wanted him to testify before the next one.

The wheels began to turn once more. It was late March, 1954, before the new grand jury at Newark—the previous one had sat at Trenton—began hearing witnesses. Presumably time was given for the jurors to learn the facts of life about organized crime. On May 27, 1954, Longie was indicted on charges of evading $46,000 in taxes for the years 1947 and 1948. Newspaper stories disclosed that only a short time before, Zwillman had announced plans to contribute $250,000 for a slum clearance project.

Almost two years passed before the case came to trial, and six weeks were required to present the pros and cons. A jury of six men and six women debated for twenty-six hours before informing Federal Judge Reynier J. Wortendyke that it could not reach a verdict. Once again, Longie appeared to have won by default. It was March 1, 1956.

Determinedly, the Intelligence Division began a probe into allegations that three jurors had been bribed to hang the case. Indictments were returned in late 1958 against Sam Katz, one of Longie's bodyguards, and Peter La Placa, a former bodyguard of Willie Moretti's.

The Moretti brothers, Willie and Solly, had played important roles in the New Jersey underworld since Prohibition. Willie had contributed the classic statement to the Kefauver Committee: "Jeez, everything is a racket today." The committee questioned both Moretti brothers about an alleged meeting in August, 1950, in which the brothers offered to give bribes of $2,500 to anyone connected with the numbers racket to get out of town to avoid testifying. Among those said to be attending the meeting was Peter La Placa.

Not enough witnesses left town, and Solly Moretti was indicted and convicted on gambling charges. Willie blamed a Mafia colleague, Vito Genovese, for his brother's troubles and decided to squeal. For some reason his appearance before a state grand jury was delayed. Six days before he was scheduled to appear, four men gunned Willie down on October 4, 1951, in a Cliffside, New Jersey, restaurant. In his pockets were found some $1,850 in cash and an October 14, 1950, clipping which quoted New Jersey's governor as saying he hoped no witnesses would be shot in the gambling probe.

On May 6, 1952, Solly Moretti died mysteriously in Trenton State Prison. No autopsy was performed, despite underworld reports that he had been killed by a blow on the head.

The deaths of the Moretti brothers left La Placa unemployed, but by 1958 it had become obvious that even Longie Zwillman could offer no snug harbor. The jury fix had failed, and a new trial on tax evasion was soon to be held. Eleven years had passed since Special Agent Baldwin listed Zwillman, Adonis and Moretti as *F* cases. Adonis had gone to jail with Solly Moretti and upon his release was deported to Italy. Only Zwillman remained, and time was running out for him. In addition to the bribery charges confronting his lieutenants and the unfinished tax case that had inspired the bribes, there was new trouble. Senator John L. McClellan, assisted by his young legal counsel, Robert F. Kennedy, was probing the vending machine racket. Longie had been under subpoena for almost a year, and he knew the investigation was approaching the hearing stage.

Rumors swept the underworld that Longie was about to buckle. The strain of fighting off the persistent special agents of the Intelligence Division for so many years, plus his new troubles, had brought him to the brink of surrender. He was confident a deal could be arranged. It would cost a lot in back taxes and perhaps some time in prison, but it seemed the only way out. If, to save his own skin, it would be necessary to sacrifice some of his colleagues, well, there was precedent for it in the recent history of New Jersey.

Zwillman, it must be remembered, while cooperating with the Mafia, was a member of the board of the National Crime Syndicate. In 1958 he had been called to Las Vegas to help his old colleagues of the Cleveland Syndicate lease the huge Stardust Hotel and Casino. The 1,300-room hotel was the dream of Tony Cornero Stralla, but he died of a heart attack before it was completed. Jake "the Barber" Factor of Chicago fame took it over and finished the job. Morris Kleinman, Moe Dalitz, and Sam Tucker—who had built the Desert Inn—were interested in adding the Stardust to their empire. Zwillman, as a man who bossed the Mafia in New Jersey, was helpful in arranging the details. Also assisting was his old partner, Joseph "Doc" Stacher, of Reinfeld Syndicate days. The deal was easily arranged.

Yet the Mafia members in New Jersey were worried as they considered the possibility that Zwillman might break and talk. Gerald Catena, a good friend of Meyer Lansky's, had reason to believe that with Longie out of the way he might move into the vacant seat on the board of directors. Lansky owed him something for solving the problem of Albert Anastasia, the former Lord High Executioner of Murder, Inc., who had been knocked off in 1957, when he tried to muscle in on Lansky's gambling empire in Havana.

On the morning of February 27, 1959, the body of Longie Zwillman was found in a storage closet in the basement game room of his twenty-room house in West Orange, New Jersey. Nearby was a bottle of bourbon and a glass. He had been strangled by an electric-light extension cord, some 44 feet long.

Police called it a suicide.

The theory seemed bizarre. To have killed himself, Zwillman would have had to tie one end of the cord around his neck, throw the other end over an exposed beam in the closet, and slump downward while holding the loose end in his hand until he suffocated.

Murder was not within the jurisdiction of the Intelligence Division, and the men who closed the case on Zwillman had no choice officially but to accept the police verdict. What they thought unofficially was quite another matter. They believe today that Longie was executed.

In any case, "the Al Capone of New Jersey" was dead.

Shortly thereafter, Longie's ex-bodyguard, Sam Katz, pleaded guilty to the charge of bribing a juror in Zwillman's 1956 tax evasion case. He was given six years in prison. La Placa waited until his trial was under way to change his plea to guilty. He got eight years.

As an epilogue, consider the case of Doc Stacher. On July 23, 1963, Zwillman's old partner was indicted on two counts of evading income taxes. Robert K. Lund, later to be Assistant Chief of the Intelligence Division, headed an investigation that lasted for years and reached from Newark to Los Angeles and from Eau Claire, Wisconsin, to Miami Beach. The probe uncovered Stacher's secret interests as a partner of Lansky in several Las Vegas casinos.

A year of legal argument followed before Stacher changed his plea to guilty and filed an affidavit giving his "word of honor" that, if permitted, he would leave the United States for Israel and never return. The Russian-born Stacher had been denaturalized in 1956 on the grounds that he concealed his long police record when he applied for citizenship in 1930.

On July 31, 1964, Doc was fined $10,000, and given a suspended five-year prison sentence on condition he keep his promise to go to Israel. The sentence ranked with the parole given Lucky Luciano in reward for his service during Operation Underworld in World War II. Exactly why the sixty-two-year-old Stacher deserved a break, no one explained.

It had taken many years, but in one way or another, the Intelligence Division had rid the country of two of its most clever gangsters.

17

SPECIAL PROJECT NO. 4

SOME may wonder why in a history of the Intelligence Division's never-ending battle against organized crime, a textile tycoon would be given more space than such notorious gangsters as Mickey Cohen, Albert Anastasia, or Tony Accardo. The answer is simple—Bernard Goldfine was an organized crime all by himself.

More investigators were assigned to probe Goldfine's intricate affairs than worked on Capone, Torrio and Costello combined. In the best gangster tradition, Goldfine considered himself above the law. He bought protection on every level of government up to, and including, the White House, and he made the vicuña coat as famous as the mink coats of the Truman era. The resulting scandal tarnished the image of the Eisenhower administration and contributed to the defeat of Richard Nixon in his first bid for the Presidency.

An organized crime was Goldfine, but there were also allegations that he was not an isolated, independent operator. Not all the allegations were investigated, and not all questions were answered. High-ranking politicians of both political parties were involved. The case was officially classified as "sensitive." The Intelligence Division was ordered to probe Gold-fine's income, and it did just that. Some of the information developed along the way was intriguing, but it pointed toward areas in which the Intelligence men had no jurisdiction.

Among the allegations that found their way into official files were these:

1. "Dr. Harry Sagansky is reported to be a bookmaker in Boston and it is alleged that he has cashed large checks for Goldfine. It is reported further that Goldfine has approximately 26,000 shares of stock in the Las Vegas Jockey Club."

2. "It was alleged that a well-known newspaperman from Boston is the bagman for Goldfine and that City of Boston officials are paid well for any favors done in behalf of Goldfine or his companies."

3. "Goldfine is alleged to have purchased two treasurer's checks in the amount of $2,500 each, to the order of United Jewish Appeal. Joseph Linsey, head of the appeal, is an associate of Goldfine."

Taking the allegations one by one, it can be noted that Doc Sagansky, as he is known in Boston, was identified as "chief of the New England gambling rackets" in Kefauver Committee testimony in 1950. He was still operating in Boston in 1968.

As for the "well-known newspaperman in Boston" who allegedly served as bagman, it can be said that Joe Linsey, a former bootlegger in the days of the Big Seven and a personal friend of Meyer Lansky's, was revealed in 1967 to be a part owner of the Boston Herald-Traveler Corporation. He, as noted in allegation three, also served as head of the United Jewish Appeal and as a fund raiser for Brandeis University. Among those he persuaded to contribute was Meyer Lansky.

Both Linsey and Goldfine were known to Boston newspaper readers as "noted philanthropists." A corrupt city is Boston, and a corrupt state is Massachusetts. Descendants of the original "Yankee" stock have been overwhelmed by waves of Irish, Jewish, Italian, and Greek immigrants. Ethnically, the melting pot failed to work, and today each group occupies its own section of the city. There is even a well-developed Chinatown. With the exception of some publicized blood feuds which have littered the streets with bodies of dead punks, the leaders of various criminal groups have worked well together. Territories and rackets are defined, and joint ventures are always welcome. Boston gangsters have been permitted to invest surplus cash in projects from Las Vegas to the Virgin Islands. The relations between Boston and Miami Beach are unusually close, thanks largely to Lansky, who grew up in Boston and still has many associates there.

All the details of all of Goldfine's operations in and around Boston may never be known, but no doubt exists that he contributed greatly to the amoral climate which made life easy for organized crime in all its aspects.

Bernard Benjamin Goldfine was born in Russia, on October 15, 1889. A new persecution of the Jews was just getting under way, and thousands upon thousands began a mass movement to the promising land beyond the ocean. They had lived for decades an uncertain existence, at times buying their lives and property by bribing Russian officials. It was even necessary for the Goldfines to bribe border guards to escape from Russia. A youth of fourteen at the time, young Goldfine had every opportunity to learn the power of money.

With his family he landed in New York on February 11, 1904. Boston was their objective, as it had been for the parents of Meyer Lansky and Moe Dalitz. They found a home in that section known then and now as East Boston, a slum area where many Jewish immigrants settled. Records at the Immigration and Naturalization Service office in Boston show that Bernard became a citizen by virtue of his father's naturalization on November 20, 1911.

The father, Samuel Goldfine, became a junk dealer in a city dominated by Irish cops and Irish politicians. The Jew occupied much the same position as regards the Irish in Boston as he had with the Russian people. Similar methods were needed to survive. Bernard attended high school for one year before quitting to work at a variety of jobs, ranging from messenger to shoeshine boy.

Indication that the Goldfines were quick to learn the ways of their new country came when Bernard and his older brother, Morris, were indicted in federal court in 1909 on a charge of conspiring to conceal assets in a bankruptcy case.

Bernard pleaded guilty; but the case was not prosecuted for reasons unknown, and the charges were dropped. The incident was enough to instill confidence—and, perhaps, the first touch of arrogance.

Enough assets were concealed in the bankruptcy case to permit Bernard to enter the woolen business the following year. With a partner, Gordon Wayness, he formed the Strathmore Woolen Company and was on his way to becoming a textile tycoon. Eventually he was to control five large woolen mills and to convince many easily convinced politicians that without him the woolen industry would follow the cotton mills to the South.

Prosperity arrived with World War I. The Allies, and later the United States, needed millions of uniforms in a hurry. Goldfine's mills supplied their share, and Goldfine became wealthy in the process. In 1917, he married Charlotte J. Goldblatt and bought his bride a big house at 72 Beacon Street in the Chestnut Hill section. Goldfine was moving up in the world, and he wanted the world to know it.

Wealthy when Prohibition came along, Goldfine avoided the pitfalls and opportunities of the booze business. However, he enjoyed the gay social life of that frantic period and was known as a gay blade in the speakeasies and nightclubs of Greater Boston. A heavy tipper in public, he enjoyed being seen in the company of important people, to whom he gave expensive presents. Some compulsion, born perhaps of ghetto life, made him seek reassurance in the easily purchased friendships of public officials. His employees grumbled, however, that he was a stern taskmaster and a veritable Scrooge toward the people who worked for him.

In the late twenties and early thirties he cultivated Republican friends, seemingly able to discover in some of them the potential for advancement that would make them men of power in the future. A county prosecutor in New Hampshire would later become United States Senator Norris Cotton. A state legislator named Sherman Adams would later be governor of New Hampshire and, still later, the man who bore the unofficial title of Assistant President of the United States. Still another young man on the rise was Maine's commissioner of finance, Frederick Payne, who would someday be governor.

Another cultivated friend was James Michael Curley, the legendary Irish boss of Boston, who also served as governor of Massachusetts. Curley was a Democrat, but Goldfine wanted friends on both sides of the political fence. In years to come, almost everyone of political significance in New England found it difficult to refuse the generous Goldfine's gifts, and many of them managed to return favor for favor. He numbered among his friends such men as Senator Styles Bridges, House Majority Leader John W. McCormack, a former Secretary of Labor Maurice J. Tobin, and Governors Foster Furcolo and Paul A. Dever. The latter became Goldfine's attorney— or one of them—when he completed his term in office.

How then did a man with so many friends in high places on both sides of the political fence come so suddenly and completely to ignominy? From dinner at the White House to bankruptcy and prison? From philanthropist to buffoon?

Legend has it that the fall of Bernard Goldfine began on April 16, 1958, when the Boston *Globe* carried a story containing some charges by John Fox, ex-publisher of the defunct Boston *Post*.

Fox, now dead, was another self-made man who came out of "drab poverty" in the Irish section of South Boston to be known briefly as a moneyman. "Appearing out of nowhere," as *Fortune* magazine described it, Fox got control of New England Gas & Electric Company in 1947. By 1952 he was publisher of the *Post*. He used the newspaper as a weapon for personal profit—common enough in Boston journalism—and, according to sworn testimony, was able to blackjack Governor Dever into arranging a $150,000 loan from Goldfine. Dever endorsed the note. More loans followed until the total was $400,000. In return, the *Post* supported Dever in the 1952 election. A clearer case of selling editorial influence has seldom been recorded.

The *Post* folded four years after Fox took control. The bitter ex-publisher later testified in a Congressional hearing about the death of his newspaper. He commented: "I was forced to the conclusion, which has subsequently been confirmed, that extremely powerful forces high in the Federal

Government of the United States had been brought to bear through departments and agencies of the Federal Government, and that these forces were not unconnected with the Boston Herald-Traveler Corporation and Bernard Goldfine."

The Herald-Traveler Corporation was engaged at the time in a continuing battle for television channel five—WHDH-TV. Competition was intense, and all sides were utilizing every iota of influence available. The channel was tentatively awarded to the *Herald-Traveler,* and charges of foul play were being investigated by the House Subcommittee on Legislative Oversight—a fancy name meaning high-level graft. Investigators were in Boston April 16 when the Boston *Globe,* a rival of the *Herald-Traveler,* carried a rather sensational story about a hearing in a civil suit against Goldfine.

George Heddendorf, a college instructor, had invested in Goldfine's East Boston Company—a real estate firm that once owned much of East Boston. In 1952, feeling he wasn't getting the money his investment warranted, he asked to look at the company's books. When Goldfine brushed him off, the stubborn Heddendorf filed suit. The case dragged on for four years. Goldfine's attorneys refused an offer to settle for $75,-000. So the college instructor filed a new suit in federal court in which he charged Goldfine with mismanagement. Other minority stockholders joined the suit. Attorney for one of them was Fox—the bitter ex-publisher. The case came up in 1958 before Federal Judge Charles E. Wyzanski, Jr., one of the most respected jurists on the federal bench. On April 15 the angry Fox blew the whistle on Bernard Goldfine.

The charges were sensational. Goldfine, said Fox, had "tapped the till" of the Boston Port Development Company, a subsidiary of East Boston, to the tune of $6,788,819. He also charged that the Eastern Racing Association bought 12 acres of land near its Suffolk Downs Racetrack in East Boston from Goldfine's company and paid for it with a note for $500,000 and 5,000 shares of stock in the association. The note was paid off later, Fox continued. The stock was split at thirty-five to one and became worth $2,050,000. Company books showed no accounting for it, Fox said.

Here should be noted an interesting coincidence—principal

owner of the Eastern Racing Association was ex-bootlegger Joe Linsey. And it was in the name of the association that Linsey bought shares of the Herald-Traveler Corporation. As previously mentioned, Linsey was usually referred to as a "philanthropist" by the Boston press.

It should also be noted that Fox's charges were never proved, but the allegations—sensational as they were—got little attention after Fox's next comment.

"I asked Mr. Goldfine," he said, "how it was possible for him to keep on embezzling, which he admitted he was doing. . . . He told me that as long as he had Sherman Adams in his pocket, he could do it."

This bombshell as reported next day attracted the interest of the investigators from Washington. The probe of the television station was dropped temporarily. For Adams was President Eisenhower's most influential assistant. The press called him the Assistant President. He had a reputation for toughness and honesty. In 1952 he had flayed the Democrats with the scandals of the Truman era and had promised an end to influence peddling. To suggest he was in anyone's pocket was to suggest the incredible.

Frank McLaughlin, counsel for the investigating committee, went to see John Fox a few minutes after reading the story. On the same day he picked up a copy of the stockholder's suit. Before leaving Boston, he discovered that Goldfine had paid hotel bills for Adams and his family on twenty-one separate occasions. The bills totaled $3,096.56. Obviously, there was some fire beneath Fox's smoke.

Newspaper reporters dug up additional facts: Goldfine had given Adams a vicuña coat worth $700 and had lent him an Oriental rug worth $2,400. President Eisenhower, speaking through his press secretary, expressed confidence that the allegations were false. Less than a week later Adams admitted they were true.

Now Goldfine was on the spot—as far as the investigating committee and the public were concerned. As far as the Intelligence Division was concerned, he had been under investigation since April 18. On that date the special agent in charge of the FBI in New York sent a letter to the Intelligence Division's office in the same city. The letter reported that checks totaling $1,250 were issued in 1956 to Philip Kramer, vice-president of the International Ladies Garment Workers Union, by the Strathmore Woolen Company. The company charged the money to "Sales Promotion and Travel," "although Bernard Goldfine, treasurer of Strathmore, advised that the checks were issued as donations to Histadrut, for which Kramer is the Boston, Massachusetts, representative."

Exactly why the FBI passed the buck to the Intelligence Division is not clear—but Goldfine was a hot potato at that moment.

New York sent the letter to Boston, and on April 24 an unnumbered case was set up and assigned to a special agent. By April 30 it was discovered that Strathmore Woolen had failed to file a corporate tax return for 1956. On June 5 the case was reassigned to Special Agent Joseph F. Bishop. A case number was assigned on June 13. Revenue Agent Jeremiah Cronin was ordered to join Bishop in the probe three days later.

Special Agent Bishop, meanwhile, visited the offices of the United States Attorney in New York in quest of Strathmore books and records. A federal grand jury had subpoenaed them in connection with a labor racketeering probe. The agent learned they had been "lent" to the law firm of Dewey, Ballentine, Bushby, Palmer, and Wood. The firm, which was representing Strathmore, was headed by Thomas E. Dewey, the former Assistant United States Attorney who had convicted Waxey Gordon and Jose Miro a quarter century before.

On June 23, 1958, the regional commissioner for Intelligence, D. W. Bacon, held a conference of all officials involved in the probe. It was decided to form a special group of special and revenue agents to devote full time to Goldfine's empire, the complexity of which was already apparent. Following the meeting, Bacon issued a "personal and confidential" memorandum notifying all concerned "that the investigation involving Bernard Goldfine and the various corporations with which he is connected will henceforth be referred to as Special Project No. 4."

The probe was on in earnest. Evidence was already in hand to prove how sensitive the case might be. The first special agent assigned, on April 24, had been suspended on June 5, the day the case was reassigned to Bishop. He was officially charged with insubordination, but the Inspection Service had discovered something worse—he had fixed one case and accepted favors from taxpayers in others. As quickly as civil service procedure permitted, the special agent was fired. Some months later Strathmore Woolen paid the bill to have the ex-agent's house repainted.

The Intelligence Division held its collective nose and began probing the cesspool.

The House Subcommittee on Legislative Oversight had already given the country an insight into the uses Goldfine had made of his friends in high places. A series of hearings began in June, 1958, and was climaxed on August 13, when the House of Representatives cited Goldfine for contempt of Congress.

One episode uncovered by the hearings proved typical, rather than unique. Beginning in 1951, the Federal Trade Commission received a number of complaints that Goldfine's companies were mislabeling their products. Cloth that was supposed to contain 90 percent wool and 10 percent vicuña actually had 10 percent nylon in its content. The FTC moved slowly enough—it was December, 1953, before formal action was taken. Goldfine's firms were ordered to provide a list of customers who had received the mislabeled material and to state if the customers had been informed of the mislabeling.

Goldfine, it was discovered, took the letter to "Assistant President" Sherman Adams who promptly got on the telephone to FTC Chairman Edward F. Howery. As a result, Goldfine received a memorandum outlining details of the complaints and supplying the names of the complainants. Goldfine wrote a letter to the FTC in which he promised to be a good boy in the future. Adams, after spending a weekend at Goldfine's expense at the Waldorf-Astoria in New York, checked to make sure the FTC was happy. Apparently it was satisfied, although Goldfine had still not complied with the rules.

Goldfine's customers were not happy, however, and in the next eighteen months they complained repeatedly that Goldfine was still mislabeling his products. An FTC examiner recommended that criminal charges be filed. Goldfine again went to Adams for help, and on April 14, 1955, the "Assistant President" arranged for Goldfine to meet with Howery. Apparently all went well, and Goldfine called the White House from the FTC offices to report so to Adams. The recommendation for criminal prosecution was overruled, and the charges against Goldfine were dropped.

In 1956, Goldfine asked Adams to help him out of trouble with the Securities and Exchange Commission, which had brought contempt charges against Goldfine in federal court in Boston for failure to file annual statements in connection with the East Boston Company. The case was pending before Judge Wyzanski, and Goldfine tried in vain to influence the judge. Three days before a series of hearings in the case began, Goldfine attended a charity benefit in which Mrs. Wyzanski was interested. Goldfine donated $1,000 "in honor of Mrs. Wyzanski." From the bench, the judge discussed the "unprecedented and rather disagreeable incident" and refused to disqualify himself in the case.

Appeals to Senators Payne and Cotton were also made in the SEC matter. Payne admitted Goldfine gave him a vicuña coat, paid $674 in hotel bills for him, and "lent" him $3,500 to buy a house in Washington. The Intelligence Division discovered that Cotton's law firm was paid $40,819 by Goldfine's companies during the years 1952 through 1957 and that they paid $12,000 to Cotton in the same period for "professional services" and "travel expenses."

Adams was able to achieve more than the Senators. The criminal contempt charge was dropped, and Goldfine paid a $3,000 fine for his company. Cheap enough.

Goldfine testified before the subcommittee on July 11, 1958, and seemed to enjoy relating details of his gifts to Adams, Payne, and a few others. Apparently he thought they were so far above the law that by associating himself with them he would also be immune. Where questions concerned details of his business, however, he refused to answer on the grounds that they were not relevant to the investigation. As quickly as legislative and legal procedures could be followed, Goldfine was indicted for contempt.

Shortly thereafter Senator Payne was defeated for reelection by shocked Maine voters. It was obvious that with the midterm elections approaching, Adams' continued presence in the White House at Eisenhower's elbow would hurt the Republican Party. The "Assistant President" went on national television to announce his resignation on September 22. He blamed "a campaign of vilification," instead of Goldfine, for his decision. Nevertheless, the portly textile tycoon suddenly found himself politically naked. But he continued fighting. His hopes for beating the contempt indictment were based on a bizarre incident on July 7.

In the early hours of that morning, reporters were called to Goldfine's Washington hotel and shown a microphone near the door. It proved to be connected to a recording machine in an adjoining suite. Reporters found syndicated columnist Jack Anderson and Baron Shacklette, chief investigator for the subcommittee, in the room with the recorder. Subsequent investigation revealed that the pair had been listening in on Goldfine during the weekend of June 29-30. The chief investigator was promptly fired after admitting he had acted independently of the committee.

When the contempt case came into court in 1959, Goldfine's attorneys asked that the matter be dismissed on the grounds that the unanswered questions "were framed from information illegally gained" by electronic eavesdropping. The motion was denied when the government said it could prove the questions were based on information obtained a month prior to the bugging incident. Despite the denial, the episode proved valuable to Goldfine, who abruptly withdrew his not-guilty plea and threw himself on the mercy of Judge James W. Morris. The judge called the bugging affair a "mitigating circumstance" and suspended the sentence of a year in jail and a $1,000 fine on the condition that Goldfine answer the questions if given a new opportunity.

The news was not all good, however. On the same day, a three-month jail sentence imposed in Boston for contempt of court was upheld on appeal. The case grew out of Goldfine's refusal to turn over certain records to the Intelligence Division.

Goldfine's new troubles began on July 21, 1958, when special agents served administrative subpoenas on representatives of five of Goldfine's companies: Lebanon Mills Corporation; Lebandale Mills, Inc.; George Mabbett & Sons Company; Strathmore Woolen Company, and Northfield Mills, Inc. A large quantity of records was produced but, with the consent of the Intelligence men, were merely made available at Goldfine's offices in Boston. After some weeks of checking the mountain of paper, the special agents became convinced that certain key documents had not been included. On November 5 a formal demand was made for the records. A month later Judge Wyzanski issued a court order plainly describing the missing records and demanding they be produced and delivered to the IRS by noon, December 8. Approximately 1,300 pounds of records were delivered by that date, but not the ones most desired. On December 10 the government filed petitions for criminal contempt judgments against Goldfine and his secretary, Mildred Paperman. A hearing was scheduled before Judge Wyzanski for December 16. When it ended three days later, the judge found both parties guilty. On the day before Christmas he sentenced Goldfine to three months in jail and Miss Paperman to ten days, but he released both on bond pending appeal. Eighteen months passed before the Supreme Court refused to consider the case, and by then Goldfine was in still deeper trouble.

On August 7, 1958, three attorneys representing Goldfine met with Intelligence Division officials in Boston. John J. Deneen, assistant regional commissioner for Intelligence, was blunt. He informed the attorneys that a recommendation for criminal action against their client had been made. Edward D. Hassen, one of the three attorneys, protested.

"Does it seem fair in view of everything that's happened to go and bring this man in on a criminal charge at this time without even giving him notice of any kind?" he asked. "There is definitely a lot of so-called rush on the part of certain people to kick a man when he is down. It seems to me that that is what is being done here. Apparently there is somebody here who feels they want to kick Goldfine."

That someone didn't want to kick Goldfine became apparent. The Intelligence Division recommended in the summer of 1958 that Goldfine be immediately prosecuted for willfully failing to file timely income tax returns for himself and certain of his corporations. Someone in the Department of Justice disagreed on the grounds that such action would jeopardize the prosecution of felony charges of tax evasion against Goldfine. The debate continued for almost a year. In June, 1959, top officials of the IRS tried once more to prod Attorney General William P. Rogers into taking the desired action. In a long memorandum to Assistant Treasury Secretary Fred. C. Scribner, Jr., Acting Commissioner of Internal Revenue Charles I. Fox renewed his request that the Attorney General be asked to implement the long-pending recommendations. Fox also reviewed the tax evasion investigation:

> It is expected that investigation of the substantive cases against Bernard Goldfine, Miss Mildred Paperman, and the four key entities controlled by Goldfine, will be completed about October 1, 1959. As you know we have encountered considerable resistance regarding the production of corporate books and papers. . . . In spite of missing records our agents are of the opinion they will be able to support felony recommendations against Mr. Goldfine, Miss Paperman and the four named corporations for some of the years, if not all of them, by the October 1 date.
>
> The agents' findings, in substance, indicate that Goldfine flagrantly misused corporate funds for his personal benefit. He caused very substantial personal expenditures to be charged to various corporate expense accounts. He made very extensive purchases of gifts to members of his family, personal friends and friends in political life. He cashed checks which were charged on corporate books as travel expenses, sales promotion, or some other expense account and apparently converted the funds to his own use. He caused apparently fictitious commission expenses as well as fictitious loans to himself to be set up on corporate books. Insofar as Miss Paperman is concerned, our agents' findings

303

tentatively reflect a net worth and expenditure picture far in excess of her reported income. She reported an aggregate of approximately $16,000 over the years 1952 through 1957, whereas it appears that her combined bank deposits and expenditures during this period exceeded $100,000.

The affairs of Mr. Goldfine, individually, and his four key corporations are so intertwined as to make each case dependent upon completion of the others. Also the full tax picture on Goldfine individually is contingent on the results of the investigations of the key corporations. I might add that, in addition to the key corporations, there are roughly about 60 other related individuals and entities involved in the over-all investigation, many of which have already been completed with results of no particular significance. Some of the others will probably result in prosecution recommendations. As you know, this investigation has been actively pursued since June 1958, and some 45 agents have been assigned to it, virtually all during this period.

In view of the foregoing, I am inclined to agree with Chief Counsel that the Government's best interest would not be prejudiced if criminal proceedings were instigated on the failure to file cases prior to the completion of the pending felony investigations.*

Attorney General Rogers would not be moved, however, and the work on the tax evasion case continued. On March 11, 1960, Goldfine was indicted on charges of evading $450,961 in personal income taxes and $340,784 in corporate income taxes. Miss Paperman was hit with a charge of evading $25,589 in personal taxes. It was disclosed that Goldfine had filed no personal income tax returns for 1956 and 1957.

Back during the Congressional hearings of 1958, Representative John Moss reminded Goldfine that "you are subject to the same laws as the rest of us." Goldfine replied, "That remains to be seen." Now, almost two years later, the proof was becoming visible. It became even more apparent four

---

* Another memo disclosed that the probe as of the end of the fiscal year 1959 had cost $62,381.84. Another $9,000, it was estimated, would be needed to complete the probe.

months later, when, his appeals exhausted, Goldfine was ordered to serve the ninety-day sentence for contempt imposed by Judge Wyzanski in December, 1958.

Goldfine still had his illusions—he asked permission to speak to the judge "in private." Wyzanski refused flatly. Goldfine conferred with his attorneys and then asked the judge for "two weeks to straighten out my financial affairs." Again the request was denied. He was ordered to the U.S. Correctional Institution in Danbury, Connecticut, immediately. The short, balding man, now sixty-nine years old, shook hands with the black-dressed Miss Paperman, and made a final request of the federal marshals who would take him to prison. No handcuffs, he asked, while being led from the courthouse. The request was denied. He was linked with another prisoner, a former bank official who had been convicted of embezzling $35,000, and taken away.

The three-month sentence was up on October 2, 1960. Goldfine was returned from Danbury to Boston to stand trial on the tax evasion charge. It began—or was supposed to begin —the next day. Attorney Edward Bennett Williams interrupted the selection of a jury to insist his client was too ill. Judge George C. Sweeney at first denied Williams' motions to delay the trial until Goldfine could be examined by doctors but changed his mind and appointed three psychiatrists to test the defendant. On October 12 they testified that Goldfine was suffering from a manic-depressive psychosis of long standing. One quoted Goldfine as saying, "I'm a political football. The Democrats are trying to do me in. I'd be better off dead. What is there to live for?"

As the judge declared Goldfine mentally incompetent to stand trial and committed him to a mental institution, Miss Paperman watched silently from the rear of the room. She was scheduled to be tried in eleven days. When her turn came, she pleaded guilty. The judge fined her $12,500 and suspended a four-month jail sentence. She was put on probation for two years.

For many cases, that might have been the end, but not for Goldfine. Politics had nothing to do with it. The scope of corruption centering on the arrogant Goldfine had sickened all investigators who had probed the matter. And many questions remained unanswered.

In February a new examination was given Goldfine, and he was adjudged capable of handling business affairs. March 15, 1961, was set as the new trial date. Ten days before the day arrived, Miss Paperman flew to Washington and turned over a list of persons who, over the years, had allegedly accepted some $600,000 in gifts from Goldfine. Named were thirty high-ranking politicians, businessmen, and federal agents. Federal agents rushed to Boston and began checking stores to confirm gifts purchased by a man who bought friendship.

News of the blond girl Friday's disclosures made headlines, although no names were mentioned. The possibility of even bigger scandals to come upset both Democrat and Republican politicians. Miss Paperman's decision had a tinge of maliciousness about it—the more so when it was learned she released the list only after appealing in vain to some of the people involved to aid her troubled boss.

All the publicity caused a two-month delay in the trial. On May 15, 1961, Goldfine pleaded guilty. Miss Paperman, twenty-three years his junior, also pleaded guilty to a new indictment charging her with evading $340,000 in corporate income taxes.

On June 5—three weeks later—Goldfine and his secretary declined an opportunity to speak, and Judge Sweeney passed sentence. Goldfine was given a year and a day in prison and fined $110,000. Miss Paperman received a suspended sentence of indeterminate length and was placed on probation for three years.

Two conditions of probation were imposed by the judge—and new shivers went down the backs of assorted politicians. Both were ordered to pay all taxes, penalties, and interest due the government, and for Goldfine alone that totaled an estimated $6,000,000. The second condition required them to disclose "all information of whatever character" concerning some $600,000 in cash Goldfine had withdrawn from his companies.

This was the slush fund, the money allegedly spent to bribe politicians and public officials.

Miss Paperman's famous list was of itself insufficient since she had no personal knowledge that the individuals named actually received the gifts assigned to them. Confirmation from either Goldfine or the recipient was necessary. In making disclosure a condition of probation, the judge was telling Goldfine, in effect, to talk or spend an additional eighteen months in prison—a term that was otherwise suspended.

The Attorney General of the United States or such representative bodies as grand or petit juries were designated by the judge to receive the information from Goldfine. Meanwhile, it was back to Danbury for the prisoner.

Slowly the rumors died; the fears subsided. If Goldfine talked, nothing was done about it. He was released from prison in ill health after serving seven and one-half months. He turned over all his property, including the house on Beacon Street, to the government to satisfy the tax debt, which had grown to $11,000,000. One more court appearance provided a tragic epilogue. He asked Judge Sweeney to order the court-appointed receivers to pay him $200 a month for living expenses.

"All the money I have in the world is in my pocket," he said.

When asked how much he had in his pocket, the broken old man pulled out a small roll of bills and counted them.

"I have thirty-three dollars," he said.

The judge granted his request for living expenses. In 1967 he died of a heart attack. He was seventy-six years old.

18

AN ATTACK OF VIRTUE

THAT crime and corruption are universal human failings deriving inspiration from no one political party or ethnic group, was illustrated in Kentucky as well as in Boston and Texas. To put the Bluegrass State into perspective, it is necessary to go backward in time to, if not the point of beginning, the first page of the current chapter.

When considering conditions in northern Kentucky, across the Ohio River from Cincinnati, one could start with George Remus, king of the bootleggers, who corrupted law enforcement in the area on a massive scale. Or one might leap forward to 1940 when the Cleveland Syndicate broke out of Ohio and captured the Beverly Hills Club near Newport. Instead, we will begin with Flo Umberhocker.

In 1919, Flo left her home in Louisville to take a job in Washington, D.C. In 1925 she became secretary to Representative Alben Barkley of Paducah, Kentucky. It was the start of a long association. Flo was with Barkley in 1926 when he moved to the Senate. She was still with him in 1937 when he became Majority Leader, and she was at his side in 1948 when he was elected Vice President of the United States. Along the way she had married Frank P. Bratten, a Maryland real estate broker. Perhaps significantly, she met him at Laurel Racetrack.

Donie Carmack, a Louisville *Courier-Journal* reporter, did a feature story on Flo in 1944. She wrote in part:

> Flo's lively, Southern manner dispenses immediately with all formality toward her. To Washington and the thousands of Kentuckians she knows by name, she is simply Flo. . . . As secretary to the Senate majority leader she is one of the top five or six Washington secretaries and a personage in her own right. . . . The secretary handles a great deal of the Senator's business on her own and receives a dozen or so letters every day directed to her personal attention.

Perhaps it was her love of horse racing that made her acquainted with the gamblers of northern Kentucky, but whatever the reason, Flo began to make frequent visits to the area. Senator Barkley might head for Paducah when he visited the bluegrass roots, but Flo stopped at Newport. Her favorite host and hostess were Mr. and Mrs. Albert Masterson.

Red Masterson, as he was known, was the unofficial police chief of Newport—the "Enforcer." A gambler and a killer, he once boasted that he got his "first square meal in a Newport whorehouse." Yet the confidential secretary of one of the nation's most popular and powerful men found him charming.

Flo's visits to Kentucky each May for the Kentucky Derby became the occasion of an annual party attended by the elite of Newport's gangsters and politicians. At such an event in 1946, Flo was made an honorary deputy sheriff of Campbell County—whose principal city was Newport. The oath was administered by Circuit Judge Ray L. Murphy, as Sheriff James Lang looked on. Flo was presented with a gold badge, a pearl-handled revolver, a cartridge-filled gunbelt, and a holster.

The party was officially sponsored by two brewery executives and Henry W. Jenisch, regional manager of the Reconstruction Finance Corporation.

At a similar party in 1947, Flo received a silver service. In 1948 she officially became a resident of Campbell County by purchasing the country home of Indiana's famous artist, Henry Farney. The mansion was on a hill overlooking the Ohio River and the syndicate-owned River Downs Racetrack. Mrs. Bratten persuaded the State Highway Department to build a private road to her new home. Some of her neighbors who were unable to get the public road in the area repaired were annoyed.

How did Flo return all the kindnesses showered on her by the gangsters of Newport? The answer came in 1951, when she was accused of having "peddled the influence of the Vice President's office" to help her friends obtain loans from—what else?—the Reconstruction Finance Corporation.

The old and honorable RFC, created by the Republicans back in the twenties to help businessmen, had been a natural target for the crooks who came to power under Harry Truman after World War II. It served the purpose later provided by the pension funds of the Teamsters Union—supplying cash to gangsters who didn't want to gamble with their own funds. RFC loans built luxury hotels in Miami Beach and casinos in Las Vegas and financed projects in Cleveland for Masterson's partner, Charles "Chuck" Polizzi. In Boston, Bernard Goldfine secured a $12,000,000 RFC loan to build a parking lot under Boston Commons by utilizing political influence on both local, state, and national levels. Only the scandals developing around Flo Bratten prevented the project from being built.

Accused with Flo was Charles E. Shaver, general counsel of the Small Business Administration. He had traveled on the Barkley plane during the campaign tours of 1948, when Barkley helped Truman score his amazing victory over Thomas E. Dewey. Among those taking political advantage of the situation was Senator Richard Nixon, the man scheduled to succeed Barkley as Vice President.

A Senate investigating committee reported that Shaver and Mrs. Bratten "operated as a team" and dealt with RFC applications from all over the country. Mrs. Bratten, it must be remembered, spoke for Barkley when dealing with government agencies, although most apologists for the affable "Veep" were ready to assume he knew little details of her activity.

Despite the fact that Nixon noted "irreconcilable conflicts" in the statements made by Flo and Shaver, Barkley's confidential secretary was "absolved" of any criminal act. Shaver was indicted, pleaded guilty, and was given a two-year suspended jail term and a $1,000 fine.

Flo was not even fired by Barkley, but he relegated her to a side office. Her influence gone, she quickly discovered that even her gold badge would buy nothing in Campbell County. The gangsters back home considered her too hot, and Red Masterson stopped meeting her plane when she flew in from Washington. Soon she sold her mansion and moved to Pennsylvania. The big house overlooking the river became Campbell Lodge, a Catholic boys' home.

With the victory of Eisenhower-Nixon in 1952 after a campaign in which honesty in government was a big issue, Barkley retired to Paducah. Still the beloved Veep to Kentuckians, he was able to make a comeback and win election to the Senate. Rumors spread, however, that his income taxes were under investigation. Columnist Drew Pearson charged the probe was inspired by top Republicans.

That Republicans did attempt to use the Intelligence Division as a political weapon was pretty well confirmed in 1958, when GOP candidates were instructed by the national committee to call attention to the fact that no Republican had been indicted or prosecuted by the Eisenhower administration —only Democrats. A possible exception was Bernard Goldfine, but since he had never bothered to register or vote, no one could be sure.

Traditionally, however, the Intelligence Division's duty is to investigate income tax evaders, whatever their political loyalties might be. Until the time when the division is given enough money and manpower to investigate *every* suspected tax evader, charges of political motive are sure to arise. In probing Barkley, just as in probing Nucky Johnson, they were only doing their duty.

Barkley *was* under investigation in 1956. Indeed, his case was nearing the indictment stage when the Veep was stricken while telling an audience of college students that he would "rather be a servant in the house of the Lord than sit in the seats of the Mighty." In his pocket at the time was $9,000 in cash and $2,000 in checks. When his will was probated in 1960, it was disclosed that his widow had paid the government $343,-444 in back taxes. His estate, before the tax bill was paid, was valued at $632,801. Yet, according to a newspaper story, his friends had considered him to be a poor man financially. Only his unexpected death prevented a scandal.

A. B. "Happy" Chandler, twice governor of Kentucky and political rival of Barkley, put it this way: "Barkley was not a lily of the valley or a bright and shining star."

Chandler was the man who proclaimed the "right of the people of Newport to have it dirty" if they liked it that way.

Some citizens who didn't want it dirty took advantage of Kefauver Committee revelations about syndicate gambling operations in Newport in 1950-51 and launched a reform movement. Despite considerable publicity, little was achieved. By 1953 the syndicate had extended its control over both the rackets and the politics of the area and seemed more invincible than ever.

The Kefauver heat did hurt several individuals, however, and the wagering-tax law that followed caused such nationally known gamblers as Gil "the Brain" Beckley to desert the Glenn Hotel in Newport for new bases in Canada. Among those joining him there was Edward W. Curd of Lexington, Kentucky, a victim of the fallout from the Costello probe.

On April 30, 1951, Special Agent Peter F. Geissler, a member of the "Get Costello Squad" in New York, noted that Costello in his testimony before Kefauver said he won $26,000 in 1950 by betting on football games with Curd in Lexington. Geissler suggested that Curd be interviewed about it.

Special Agent William W. Hummel—later to be chief of the Intelligence Division's Kentucky office—drew the assignment. Curd gave him a copy of a $26,800 check issued by Curd, using the name of Charles Duffield, Jr., to Costello. Curd was interviewed in the offices of his attorney, John Y. Brown, a perennial candidate for governor of Kentucky on the Republican ticket.

Hummel immediately began an investigation of Curd's income tax returns. His investigation disclosed that Curd was born in Cave City, Kentucky, in 1904, but moved at an early age to Lexington, in the heart of the horse-breeding country. Gambling, as Curd later put it, was a way of life in the area, and no disgrace was attached to professionals who accepted bets from leading citizens over mint juleps. He drifted to northern Kentucky and became associated with James Brink, an ex-bootlegger who operated the plush Lookout House. On June 13, 1936, Curd, Brink, and Louis "Sleepout Louie" Levinson were indicted but beat the rap without great difficulty. Levinson was the brother of Ed Levinson, a nationally known gambler who left Sleepout in charge of the Flamingo Club in Newport while he became a power in Miami Beach, Las Vegas, and the Caribbean. In the process he also became business partner of a man called Bobby Baker.

Curd returned to Lexington and opened up a handbook in the Mayfield Bar. He prospered, bought a horse farm, and a winter home on Star Island in Miami Beach. Known to the gambling world as Scotty he was famous for his ability to estimate how an injury to a football player would affect the point spread of a game. Most bets were based on the point spread rather than the outcome, so this was considered a useful talent by other professionals.

Costello's loose lip created heat for Curd, and by July, 1952, he knew an indictment was near. He sold the horse farm for $400,000 and fled to Canada shortly before a federal grand jury acted on Hummel's evidence and returned a six-count indictment for tax evasion.

In Canada, Curd teamed up with Beckley and continued to accept bets from old customers in the United States. He operated primarily in Montreal and Windsor but maintained apartments in a number of cities.

The twice-divorced Curd fell in love with Pauline Desmarchais, and when the Royal Mounted Police raided his bookmaking establishment in the Prince Edward Hotel in Windsor, he took Pauline and her sister, Susan, with him and fled to the Caribbean. After island-hopping for most of 1957, he disappeared for an entire year, only to reappear in Canada to surrender to United States officials at Detroit. Two days later, on

313

December 10, 1958, he pleaded guilty to the income tax charges and was sentenced to six concurrent year-and-a-day terms in prison. He was also assessed almost $400,000 in back taxes.

Released from prison in September, 1959, he went to his home in Biscayne Bay. There, in occasional talks with reporters, he alternated between berating Special Agent Hummel and moaning about the good old days in the bluegrass. He established himself in Nassau, meanwhile, by creating the L & W Realty Company. Paul A. Desmarchais, father of Pauline, was president, and Pauline was listed as secretary.

So it was that when events in Newport in 1961 caused a flood of gamblers to flee to the Caribbean in search of new opportunities, Curd was there to welcome them. In 1967 he bought a huge new mansion next door to the official residence of the governor of the Bahamas on top of the hill overlooking Paradise Island, where a huge new casino complex had bloomed. Manager of the casino was Eddie Cellini, who had formerly worked at the Glenn Hotel in Newport.

The trouble in Newport started in 1957 with a group of ministers and church laymen. Some years before, that silver-tongued orator Alben Barkley noted in a speech that much of Kentucky's prosperity depended on the liquor and horse-racing industries. "An attack of virtue could ruin us," said the Veep. Just such an attack of virtue was what the ministers had in mind.

Their campaign developed so slowly that the syndicate took little notice until 1960, when, to everyone's surprise, a special grand jury revolted and indicted Sheriff Norbert Roll for failure to act against wide-open gambling and vice. With Judge Ray L. Murphy—the man who had made Flo Bratten an honorary deputy—on the bench, and veteran Commonwealth's Attorney William Wise prosecuting, no one was surprised when the sheriff was acquitted. Enough citizens became angry, however, to swell the ranks of the reformers. By May, 1961, the movement was strong enough to field a candidate for sheriff —ex-professional football quarterback George Ratterman.

Then followed a typical syndicate ploy. Ratterman received word that Tito Carinci, operator of a casino-nightclub in downtown Newport, wanted to quit the rackets. He needed advice. Would Ratterman meet with him? The candidate, feeling the opportunity to get information was too good to pass up, agreed. What followed made history.

At the meeting in a plush Cincinnati hotel, Ratterman was given a mild dose of knockout drops. Groggy and confused, but still on his feet, he was taken by Carinci across the river to Newport and upstairs to a bedroom above Tito's nightclub in the Glenn. Another loaded drink put him out cold. He collapsed on the bed. A stripper was stationed on the bed with him, and cooperative police, who had been waiting for the call, came in and arrested Ratterman on prostitution charges. His trousers were removed, and he was taken to the police station wrapped in a bedsheet.

The frame, a routine practice in Newport, fooled few. Even some "liberal" citizens became angry, and the attack of virtue became more severe. In a sensational police court trial, Ratterman proved he was framed, and the charges against him were dismissed. Robert F. Kennedy, who had recently become Attorney General of the United States and launched a "coordinated war on crime," took advantage of the incident to order a full-scale probe of Newport. Civil rights came under the jurisdiction of the FBI so the brunt of the Ratterman probe fell on that agency. Special Agent Frank Staab was put in charge. The investigation centered around the youthful Carinci and a veteran Newport attorney, Charles E. Lester, who twenty-one years earlier had helped the syndicate get a foothold in Campbell County.

Under orders from Kennedy, the Intelligence Division began investigating the tax returns of gambler and official alike. Eventually, during the long hot summer that followed, most gambling places closed as part of a campaign to convince the voter that vice was essential to the community's economy. The one major exception was the numbers racket, which operated throughout the Greater Cincinnati area from headquarters in the Sportsman's Club in Newport. In charge was Frank Andriola, known locally as Screw Andrews, but the banker was the boss of the East Harlem racket, Trigger Mike Coppola. Mike had married an area girl, the widow of a syndicate gambler, and lived in semiretirement on Miami Beach. Couriers brought his cut from Newport and from Harlem, where the racket organized years before by Jose Miro was more profitable than ever.

Andrews was well qualified to work for the notorious Trigger Mike. His record totaled forty-six arrests, beginning in 1923, when he was one of a group of youths who killed an innocent bystander while playing with a gun. A bootlegger in the days of George Remus, he served time for interstate theft in 1937 and for gambling in 1945. In 1955 he was charged with the murder of a numbers competitor, Melvin Clark, and successfully pleaded self-defense. Another term in federal prison came in 1956, when he attempted to evade the federal occupational tax on illegal slot machines.

Despite his record, or perhaps because of it, Andrews was on good terms with the politicians of Newport and Campbell County. His Sportsman's Club was a block from the police station, and he operated as openly as did the six brothels which were even closer to the comedians who wore uniforms. On one occasion when an officer, for reasons no one understood, attempted to arrest Screw, the husky Andrews beat the man up, tore off most of his clothes, and kicked him into the street. His fellow cops considered it quite funny.

Banked by Coppola, Andrews was able to eliminate competition and consolidate the vast racket under his control. Some competitors were killed, others bombed, and still others arrested by cooperative police. By early 1959 the cold-eyed Screw was in complete command. He sold his nightclub and some adjoining property to the Newport Housing Authority as part of an urban renewal program for a huge sum, then rented the building back while waiting for a new club to be constructed on the banks of the Ohio. So confident had Screw become that he reopened his business in the summer of 1961 when everyone else closed on syndicate orders as part of the effort to brainwash the voters into believing that reform was bad for the economy.

It was a mistake.

The Intelligence Division, eager to make a contribution to the cleanup of Newport, made Andrews a priority target.

Early in June—a month after Ratterman's arrest—an undercover agent was assigned to visit the Sportsman's Club. The dangerous job was assigned to Special Agent Hilton Owens, and he executed it perfectly. One important bit of information concerned the night number, so called. Screw sold numbers tickets five days a week based on a number obtained from the share and bond dollar volume of the New York and American stock exchanges, but he also conducted a nightly drawing at the Sportsman's Club which was similar to a bolita operation. He paid taxes on the day number but insisted that since bettors were present when the night number was drawn, he was conducting an on-premise gambling operation, which, like casino gambling, was exempt from the wagering tax. Owens, in his undercover role, killed that argument when he discovered that only a small fraction of the bettors were present to see the number drawn.

The special agent reported that as soon as the winning number was selected, announcements were mimeographed, and runners and writers present carried them to their stations throughout the Greater Cincinnati area. A battery of telephones began ringing as hundreds of absent bettors called in to learn the winning number. Later it was discovered that the drawing was rigged. A machine was used to push numbered Ping-pong balls upward on a stream of air until six tumbled free and rolled into a chute. The device looked honest, but examination proved preselected balls were stored in a hidden compartment and released at will by the operator of the machine. The numbers on the balls were, of course, selected in advance to make the winning number the one which had received the least play from the suckers. The payoff odds were 600 to 1, but the few winners were usually shills, who returned the winnings to the house.

Raid preparations were elaborate. Wall charts were prepared showing the layout of the interior, and the premises were divided into areas and assigned to individual agents. The raiding force consisted of thirty-five special agents, many brought in from other regions. It was equipped with seven cars, high-powered flashlights, heavy sledgehammers, a wrecking bar, handcuffs, a fire extinguisher, and a variety of bags,

317

boxes, envelopes, tags, string, and tape for securing the evidence. Each raider was armed.

At 9:30 P.M. the party was assembled and briefed. It was August 22, 1961. A convention of Shriners, 10,000 strong, was meeting in Cincinnati, and many of the delegates had found their way to the Sportsman's Club—the only gambling joint still running in stricken Newport. Zero hour was set at 11:30 P.M., the usual time for the drawing—or blowing—of the night number. Owens, the undercover man, was told to get inside the club and to be waiting near the door. In the event the sledgehammers failed, it was his job to open it.

At exactly the designated moment, the first car drove up to the entrance of the club. Owens watched as a lookout rushed in shouting, "Raid." As expected, the hammers failed to dent the steel door, but Owens opened it quickly. Three special agents sprinted to the rest room area and found several men, including Andrews' nephew, attempting to flush numbers tickets down the toilets. Other agents poured in and took their assigned stations. A second raiding party of five men hit the nearby Corner Liquor Store, also owned by Andrews, which had been used as an alternate headquarters in the past. Doors there were unlocked, and no difficulty was encountered.

The Shriners, who had received more excitement than they bargained for, were screened and released. Several numbers writers tried to sneak out with them, but Owens, who knew them all, prevented the exodus. Teams of agents armed with prepared questionnaires began interviewing the twenty-five employees and writers who remained. On the basis of their answers, six were arrested. Andrews was not on the premises, however.

A systematic search followed. Several hidden rooms were found, one containing a dozen telephones which were ringing softly and continuously as suckers called in to learn the winning number. Every call was additional evidence the night number did not constitute on-premise gambling. Entry to another hidden room was gained when a special agent found two nailheads in the rear of a closet and a piece of wire with exposed ends. He placed the tips of the wire on the nailheads, completing a circuit which activated a small motor. The wall

318

slid back, revealing a room literally filled with numbers records. Behind another wall were found thirteen slot machines, so mounted as to swing out ready for action at a second's notice.

Three safes were found, but apparently only Screw had the combination. It was the next morning before two locksmiths could be located, and it took them several hours to open the safes. One contained $1,500 and betting records. The contents were seized. The second held $23,000, but no records. That money was not seized in the absence of proof it was connected with the gambling. The third, and hardest to open, yielded a rich harvest: guns, betting records, and $55,000. Its contents were confiscated. Also seized were seventeen adding machines —the indispensable tool of the numbers racket—a typewriter, a duplicator, and a vast amount of numbers tickets, tapes, and financial records. Special Agent Joe Fischer, the raid leader, was well satisfied when fifteen hours after the raid began, he quit the building.

The hard work had just begun, however. Six special agents toiled for weeks sorting and tabulating the seized records. Other agents began an inspection of recordak film at the West Side Bank in Newport. A major break came when it was discovered that many of the club's checks bore coded notations. When the code was broken, a list of some 200 writers for the racket was compiled. A special grand jury was convened in Cincinnati—where most of the writers lived and worked— and twelve teams of agents began interviewing the suspects. Each team was equipped with blank grand jury subpoenas, and as testimony was extracted, the suspect's name was written in and the subpoena served. Approximately fifty-three talkative witnesses appeared before the grand jury.

Some two weeks after the grand jury recessed, the Corner Liquor Store went up in flames—one of several mysterious fires of the period. The next day special agents searched the burned-out building and found huge bundles of numbers tickets piled in heaps. Some were charred but proved useful as evidence in the trial that followed.

A new grand jury was called at Covington, Kentucky, across the Licking River from Newport, and the evidence gathered in Cincinnati was presented, along with the material seized in

319

Newport. In December, 1961, a thirty-five-count indictment was returned against Screw Andrews and seven associates, including two nephews.

The big raid on the Sportsman's Club contributed to the heat in Newport and made that river city take on the aspect of a ghost town. FBI Special Agent Staab looked down deserted York Street one day and said the scene reminded him of a Western movie after the gold supply had been exhausted and the miners had moved on.

"At any minute I expect to see a tumbleweed come rolling down the street," he commented.

Staab's probe of the Ratterman frame was complete, the big break coming when the stripper who had been assigned to pose almost nude with the unconscious Ratterman reversed her story and admitted the truth. The *Courier-Journal* in Louisville, which from the first had aided the reformers in their long campaign, broke the story. A few days later, on the eve of the election, a federal grand jury in Lexington indicted Carinci; his partner, Marty Buccieri; attorney Lester, and three Newport cops for conspiring to violate and violating Ratterman's civil rights. The jury also declared that "the foul odors of bribery and corruption cover Campbell County officialdom like a pall."

Ratterman won election by a landslide margin, and gamblers, prostitutes, and dope peddlers began leaving town in droves. Las Vegas and Miami Beach attracted most of them. Among those leaving was Gil Beckley, who had ended his exile in Canada years before and returned his betting operation to the Glenn Hotel—the spot where Ratterman had been put to bed with the stripper. Beckley went to Surfside, just north of Miami Beach, where he set up shop in the Blair House—a Teamster-financed pad where many gangsters lived. Carinci, under indictment, couldn't leave immediately but joined him later.

Meanwhile, the Intelligence Division's probe of the background of Newport gamblers confirmed that ultimate control of the operation rested in the hands of syndicate bosses in other states. Most of the huge profits had gone to the absent operators. Beckley, a most knowledgeable man, estimated the total

320

Newport gambling handle as "at least $100 million a year." How much other rackets brought in, there was no way to estimate. Yet local operators, as well as the crooked officials, had been satisfied with financial crumbs. They wore diamond rings, drove new cars, dressed in expensive suits, and carried themselves arrogantly—but the big money went to the syndicate. In the eyes of the local population, they were big shots, who could, and did, get away with murder. In terms of the real bosses, however, they were cheap punks and quite expendable.

The Intelligence Division was able to make a case, however, against ex-Sheriff Norbert Roll, the man who had been so easily acquitted the year before in state court.

Roll, fifty-two, was a typical political hack of the area. A Newport native, he was a high school graduate and the father of seven children. For twelve years before becoming sheriff in 1958, he served as master commissioner of Campbell Circuit Court under Judge Murphy. He also kept books for a Newport bar that openly violated state liquor laws, as did almost every other joint in Newport. For the years 1956 through 1959 his income ranged from $6,522 to $12,072—small enough when you consider he had the power for two of those years to close casinos making millions.

His troubles stemmed not from the size of his income but from the fact he had not bothered to file income tax returns for the years in question. Like many officials in Newport, he considered himself above the law. Governor Bert Combs, under pressure from the reformers, ousted him from office in 1961, and in 1962 the Intelligence Division sent him to prison for a year. Roll complained he was being persecuted.

Shortly after Ratterman took office in 1962, he teamed up with the Intelligence Division in a joint venture. On the day assigned, sheriff's deputies raided every handbook still operating in Campbell County whose operator had purchased the required federal wagering-tax stamp. At the same time, special agents of Intelligence hit every bookie who had not bought the stamps. At day's end, it was impossible to get a bet down in a county where until a few hours before there had been hundreds of handbooks.

The trial of Carinci, Lester, and the rest began in June, 1962. It was largely an FBI show, but Special Agent Vincent Brennan of Intelligence supplied vital testimony by proving the arrest of Ratterman was preplanned.

Brennan swore he visited Lester's office prior to the arrest and heard the attorney deliver an obscene attack on the reform candidate. While in the office, the special agent saw some anti-Ratterman campaign literature that listed the as yet unfiled charges against him.

Despite the evidence, which, if complex, was overpowering, the trial ended in a hung jury. A new date was set, and the trial of Screw Andrews began. The same two attorneys from Kennedy's Organized Crime Section of the Justice Department, William Lynch and Ronald Goldfarb, who had presented the Ratterman evidence, now turned to the equally complex numbers case. Some of the defense attorneys were the same as well. This time, however, the results were different. The trial lasted a month. The government established that Andrews had reported for tax purposes only one-seventh of his total wagering business and owed $387,555 in excise taxes. The jury found all the defendants guilty.

On July 31, 1962, Judge Mac Swinford sentenced Andrews and his seven colleagues to five years and $10,000 fines. Ultimately, when appeals had failed, all went to prison.

Another year passed before the defendants in the plot to frame Ratterman were again brought to trial. More than two years had gone by since the reform candidate's arrest, and public indignation had cooled considerably. However, the reformers planned to field candidates to run that fall against Judge Murphy and Commonwealth's Attorney Wise. Both men had held office since shortly after the Cleveland Syndicate invaded Kentucky in 1940. Thus the trial took on new importance.

In many respects, the courtroom drama was a replay of the 1962 trial, but it had a different ending. In a confused verdict, the jury found attorney Lester and casino boss Buccieri guilty of conspiring to frame Ratterman, but it acquitted Carinci and the three Newport cops who arrested him. Lester and Buccieri were sentenced to a year in prison, but were released on bond pending appeal. Ultimately, the Sixth Circuit Court of Appeals upheld the conviction and noted in passing that the evidence was sufficient to convict "all of the defendants on all of the charges."

Carinci, somewhat exhilarated by his acquittal, announced he was a candidate for mayor of Newport on the Wheel of Fortune ticket. Much to the disgust of Murphy and Wise, he endorsed those officials and perhaps by doing so contributed to their defeat by the reformers. No longer popular in Newport, the muscular young gambler joined his old friend Beckley at Surfside, Florida.

The Intelligence Division was not pleased to see Carinci escape punishment. Under the direction of William Hummel, now chief of the Kentucky district, a new probe began. Special Agents Frank S. Coots and Ralph Winkler were in charge, assisted by Revenue Agent Robert L. Thomas. Gambling operations in Newport's Glenn Hotel was the target. A Newport institution, the hotel had been operated by Carinci, Buccieri, and associates from 1957 to 1961, when it closed following Ratterman's arrest there. The building burned in 1962 in another of the mysterious fires that followed the cleanup of the town.

As casinos went, the one at the Glenn was small by Newport standards. It was also among the most notorious—a "bust-out operation" which featured a dice game known as razzle-dazzle. The game involved the use of multiple dice and a doubling of each successive bet, with the player promised a payoff of ten times his last bet if he could achieve a certain number of points. Many players lost large sums trying, but no one ever won the game. The joint made a profit of $1,302,685 from 1958 through 1960. Suckers who lost their cash wrote checks totaling more than $1,000,000 during the period, and collectors such as Eddie Cellini visited the homes of any who, on second thought, stopped payment on the checks.

Bank records were used to trace the checks, and some 6,000 persons were contacted by letter or in person to verify details. It was February 24, 1965, before eight men were indicted on charges of evading $176,424 in corporate income taxes. In addition to Carinci and Buccieri, the defendants included

Breck Lutes, Jack Eviston, Abe Maius, Louis and Daniel Del Grosso, and Eddie Cellini.

Lutes was a convicted murderer, who had served eighteen years in Ohio before being released on parole after acting as Governor Frank Lausche's chauffeur. Eviston had been chief clerk in the Campbell County Clerk's office before entering the slot machine business. Maius had the most impressive arrest record as a former member of the Detroit Purple Gang—larcency, armed robbery, narcotics, murder—but he had served time only for violation of internal revenue liquor laws. In 1935 he was arrested with Peter Licavoli and Joe Bommarito, two top Mafia leaders, on charges of extortion by pistol. The charges were changed to disorderly conduct; the trio paid $100 fines and went free.

Cellini was the brother of Dino Cellini, a lieutenant of Meyer Lansky. Before coming to Newport, he worked at the Riviera in Havana as casino boss and was kicked out in 1959, along with Lansky and the rest, when Fidel Castro ousted Batista. Following the cleanup of Newport, he went to Haiti where the local dictator, "Papa Doc" Duvalier, was trying to revive a gambling casino. Ultimately, Cellini became boss of the plush casino that opened on Paradise Island in Nassau Harbor in 1967. Among the invited guests in attendance was Richard Nixon.

The Del Grossos were ex-carnival workers whose skill with the dice was needed to make razzle-dazzle sizzle.

Charges against everyone but Carinci and Maius were dropped by United States Attorney Bill Rivers before the trial. Subpoenaed to testify were 617 suckers who had written checks to cover their losses. After only 7 had testified, the defense stipulated the remainder would say they had written their checks to cover gambling losses at the Glenn.

The trial at Louisville ended with verdicts of guilty. In an unusual move, Judge Henry Brooks refused to delay imposing sentence. Carinci and Maius were each given three years in prison and fines of $15,000. Tito's luck had run out at last. When Maius' attorney asked for a stay of execution to permit his client to remove personal effects from his hotel room, the judge refused once more. The defendant, he said, knew he

324

was guilty when the trial started and should have been prepared to begin his sentence.

Justice had been a long time in catching up with the two men, but it was stern and unrelenting when it did.

Shortly before the Louisville trial began, Carinci was arrested in Miami Beach by special agents of the Intelligence Division and charged with placing interstate bets for Beckley. In August, 1966, he was brought from federal prison at Terre Haute, Indiana, to stand trial on the new charge. He changed his plea to guilty and was given a suspended sentence of two years and a $10,000 fine. The judge put the no longer smiling Tito on probation for two years and ruled the probation period would begin when he was released from prison.

No parole was granted Carinci. He served his full term and was permitted to go to Miami in 1968 to await the end of the probation period as a used-car salesman for Florida State Senator Dick Fincher. Few doubted that when he was free of supervision, his bust-out talents would be employed in the new gambling empire Lansky had built in the Caribbean.

Meanwhile, back in Newport, the FBI rounded up a few remaining gamblers on charges of traveling in interstate commerce to play bingo. Among those nabbed in 1968 was Red "the Enforcer" Masterson, that old host of Barkley's confidential secretary, Flo Bratten.

19

BEYOND BISCAYNE

A̲FTER a month of surveillance, the raid
on the apartment at 1330 Fifteenth Street, Miami Beach, was
scheduled for February 3, 1956. With one exception, everything went according to plan. A large bookmaking operation,
allegedly part of an international syndicate, was found, and
eight persons were arrested.

Special Agent Edward C. Hilker provided the principal excitement. His assignment was to prevent betting slips and
other evidence from being flushed down the toilet. As the other
raiders prepared to enter from the front door, Hilker—dressed
as a house painter—climbed a stepladder outside the bathroom
window. To his dismay, he found the window closed and
locked. From the noise inside he knew his colleagues had
gained entrance. Speed was essential, so the special agent broke
the glass with the butt of his gun. Reaching inside to unlock
the window, he cut his hand. Ignoring the blood, he clambered
through the window in time to achieve his objective.

As events proved, he had achieved more than he knew. A
frightened neighbor, alarmed by the crash of glass and the sight
of a man crawling through the window, telephoned Miami

Beach police. Within two minutes a squad car arrived. Upon being informed by the raid leader, Special Agent John McRae, of the situation, the police departed without entering the apartment or seeing the prisoners. Five minutes later the telephone rang in the apartment. Special Agent Wilbert C. Kleppick, assuming that a bettor might be calling, answered it.

"This is Ben Cohen," said a businesslike voice. "Have you arrested my clients?"

"I don't know," replied Kleppick. "We haven't had time to find out if they are your clients."

They were.

The episode well illustrates the power of attorney Benjamin Cohen, who for a quarter of a century made and unmade police chiefs in Miami Beach, defended top gangsters, aided Jimmy Hoffa in dispensing Teamster funds, and sought desperately to be recognized as a patron of the arts and a pillar of society.

For organized crime he was more of a pillow.

There is a curious parallel between Ben Cohen of Miami Beach and Charles Lester of Newport. Both men began their public careers as alleged reformers. In early 1930 Lester jolted Newport by securing injunctions against brothels lining South-gate Alley. Under a unique fee system then in effect, Lester received $1,300 for this service to the community. Later it was learned he had helped the madams relocate on Chestnut Street at double the rents. Judge A. M. Caldwell, in a written opinion, charged Lester with conspiring "to violate the very injunction he, as attorney, had sought and secured." Lester was disbarred, appealed, won a new trial, was found guilty for the second time, and was reinstated on the grounds that he had been punished enough.

Ben Cohen was not disbarred until much later in life, but in 1939 he offered himself to the voters of Miami Beach as a reformer. As a candidate for the City Commission, he submitted a platform which included a pledge to work for the appointment of "a city prosecutor to exclude organized criminals from our midst."

He lost.

At the time Cohen was proposing to "exclude organized criminals," his brother, Sam, was operating an illegal gambling house. Sam had an interesting record as a bootlegger and gambler who, despite repeated arrests, always escaped with a fine or a suspended sentence. In 1937 he pleaded guilty to tax evasion and once again was lucky—a six-month prison sentence was suspended, and he was fined $1,000.

Little became known about the early life of Ben and Sam Cohen. Apparently they hailed from New York. Ben played fullback for Duquesne University. In 1925, his senior year, the team lost all its games and scored only nine points during the season. Brains, not brawn, were obviously Ben's chief asset, yet, years later, he had enough confidence to threaten to toss Miami Beach City Councilman Melvin Richards out of an eighth-floor window at City Hall. Richards had called Cohen a liar.

Sam Cohen was first arrested in Florida on bootlegging charges in 1926. Ben was admitted to the Florida bar two years later. It was not until the investigation of Frank Costello began in 1947 that Ben came to the attention of the Intelligence Unit. Reports of a huge bookmaking operation on Miami Beach aroused the natural suspicion that Costello might be involved. Investigation disclosed no evidence that Frank was a member of the S & G Syndicate, as the Miami Beach combine was known, but it did reveal that Samuel P. Cohen was a partner and Ben Cohen was legal counsel.

On July 1, 1949, the special agent in charge of the Miami office wrote a memo to his chief in Washington. He listed the five bosses of the S & G and added:

> The above named individuals are partners in the oper-
> ation of a gambling enterprise at Miami Beach, Florida,
> under the name of S & G Service. It is probably the largest
> off-the-track gambling syndicate in the South.
>
> The extraordinary ramifications of this gambling com-
> bine are being made the subject of extensive investigation
> in connection with the tax drive involving gamblers and
> racketeers in the Miami area. It is, accordingly, recom-
> mended that separate case jackets be issued, charging al-
> leged evasion of income taxes for the years 1945, 1946, and
> 1947 by the individuals named next below, all of whom
> reside at Miami Beach, Florida.

Samuel P. Cohen, Charles Friedman, Jules Levitt, Edward G. Rosenbaum, Harold Salvey.

During the investigation into Sam Cohen, it was discovered that Sam leased property north of Miami Beach in 1946 on which was located the soon-to-be famous casino the Island Club, a joint operation of the Cleveland and Eastern syndicates. In conjunction with gambler Abe Brown, he ran Gray's Inn, a summer resort near Jackson, New Hampshire, in 1945 and 1946. He joined with four others to form the S & G Syndicate in 1944 after competing individually for leases on handbook locations.

The S & G quickly got a lock on almost all handbook operations in the plush hotels of Miami Beach. Syndicate gamblers from all over the country bought "concessions" from the S & G, which, in turn, provided protection from both police and unapproved competition. Sometimes the eager gamblers were forced to bid for a choice location.

Sam Cohen told investigators that he was the "outside man" for the local syndicate. Several times a day he called the central office, but most of the time he was "out on a goodwill tour—meeting different people at different hotels, taking them in and buying them a drink, maybe going out to the track. Something like that."

One-third of Sam's profits went automatically to brother Ben. Yet in an Intelligence interview with Ben and Sam on June 27, 1949, Ben "was zealous in trying to make the distinction that he was not a partner of S & G, but that he was a partner of his brother, Samuel. In the joint conversation Ben Cohen professed to be 'greatly humiliated' at the local newspaper references to him as attorney or 'mouthpiece' for S & G Service."

The report noted that Sam Cohen "dresses fashionably, is well-groomed, and is conspicuous about Miami Beach. He drives a Cadillac and appears to live on a lavish scale."

When the final report on the S & G was compiled, the huge volume of illegal business was apparent. The report noted:

Gross betting transactions handled by the S & G Service during the three years were nearly forty-two million dollars. Prizes paid to winning bettors and expenses—the nature of which were not clearly discernible—in excess of thirty-eight million dollars, were claimed as deductions and recorded in memorandum records before accounting for the net profit. The evidence has disclosed that the original basic returns of the betting activity and expenses claimed in computing the net win or loss for each bookmaker each day were destroyed. Mr. [Sam] Cohen has stated that his brother, Ben Cohen, as attorney for the S & G, advised the destruction of those records, contending that their possession would in itself be evidence of an illegal activity if it should fall into the hands of local law-enforcement officers.

Based on Sam Cohen's share of the S & G profits, it was estimated for civil purposes that he still owed taxes on $240,853, even after giving Ben one-third, for the years 1945 through 1947.

The S & G soon developed double trouble. The Chicago Syndicate, a group of hungry—and clumsy hoods—decided it deserved a piece of the action in South Florida. After all, Al Capone discovered the place. Tough as the boys from Chi believed themselves to be, they had no desire to challenge Lansky for control of the plush casinos in Dade and Broward counties. With allies in Cleveland, Minneapolis, and Detroit, Lansky was too strong. The S & G Syndicate, however, was another matter. Apparently it was a local independent group.

To get the leverage needed, the Chicago hoods joined with local kingmakers and helped elect Fuller Warren governor of Florida in 1948. Then, cashing in on the political debt, they arranged to send "special investigators" from the governor's office to lead raids against the handbooks of the S & G. The businessmen of Collins Avenue were quick to recognize the realities and accepted Chicago mobster Harry Russell (real name Weinstein) as a full-fledged partner. The raids ceased as quickly as they began. The episode became famous as the Affair of the Russell Muscle.

The muscling-in process was ill timed, however. Kefauver Committee investigators got wind of it, and eventually every-

one concerned—except Governor Warren—was questioned
by the racket busters. Warren, as did Governor Tom Dewey of
New York, declined an invitation to appear before the committee. As previously noted, however, he did suspend Dade
Sheriff Jimmy Sullivan.

The S & G broke up under the hot glare of publicity, and
even Lansky was forced to close his casinos. Gambling remained
a big business in South Florida; it just became less obvious.
And for those who longed for the good old days, there was always Las Vegas.

A number of the boys got an okay from Meyer Lansky and
decided to build their own hotel-casino in the land of legalized
gambling. Sam Cohen was one of the promoters, but because
of his record, it was impossible for him to be listed as an owner
of record. Ben, however, was spotless, and as counsel for the
corporation he could look after Sam's affairs.

The $10,000,000 eleven-story Riviera was built on the sands
of Nevada—and later amid the palm trees of Havana—by the
Miami Group. How much money Sam put into it may never
become public knowledge, but it must have been considerable.
The proof is in the fact that shortly after the casino opened in
March, 1955, Ben Cohen was retained to represent the Riviera
Hotel Corporation for twenty-five years at a monthly retainer
of $3,125. Total value of the agreement to Cohen was $937,-
500. The canny Cohen, well aware that Las Vegas figures sometimes die violently and unexpectedly, inserted a clause which
provided that in the event of his death or incapacity, his family
would receive $18,750 a year.

"Foresight" Ben called it. "Insurance" might have been the
better word.

As it happened, it was Sam who should have been taking
precautions. He died on May 4, 1955, his income tax troubles
dating back to the S & G still unresolved.

Other troubles developed. The Riviera wasn't doing too
well. Someone remembered Gus Greenbaum, a legendary
character with a Chicago background who had taken over the
Flamingo after Bugsy Siegel's sudden death and made a $4,000,-
000 profit the first year. Recently he had retired to Phoenix,

Arizona, where Senator Barry Goldwater was a good friend. Perhaps he could be persuaded to take over the Riviera and put it in the black.

Gus wasn't interested at first, but he changed his mind when his sister-in-law was smothered in her bed in Phoenix after reporting being threatened to police. Yet he didn't want to work for the Miami Group.

As in the case of many Las Vegas hotels, the financial arrangements behind the Riviera were complicated. The land had originally been owned by a Los Angeles group which included Groucho Marx. It leased the land to the Gensbro Corporation, which was owned by Morry M. Mason, head of the Taylor Construction Company, and a couple of brothers named Gensburg from Los Angeles. Gensbro, in turn, subleased the land to the Riviera Hotel Corporation, which, at that time, included the Miami Group and the Taylor Construction Company. Taylor built the hotel, using funds put up by the Miami Group. Now, when Greenbaum would have it no other way, the Riviera Hotel Corporation leased its holdings to a new organization, Hotel Riviera, Inc., which was formed by Greenbaum.

Cohen received his monthly retainer through July, 1955, but then the payments stopped. However, it was February 28, 1958, before he got around to doing anything about it. On that day he filed suit, asking for some $95,000 he said was overdue, plus "such other sums that may become due" at the rate of $3,125 per month, plus interest at 7 percent. Several things had happened in the interim.

When Greenbaum returned to Las Vegas, he took along an old friend who had settled in Phoenix and been accepted as a "labor expert" by Senator Goldwater. The friend was none other than Willie Bioff, the ex-pimp and born loser of the movie-extortion case. His "song" to the Intelligence Unit had sent the top hoods of Chicago to prison—briefly, as it turned out—but Greenbaum put Willie in charge of entertainment at the Riviera nonetheless. As has already been related, Willie didn't last long. Shortly after Senator Goldwater flew him back to Phoenix for a vacation, Bioff's car went bang on November 4, 1955, and Willie went with it.

Gus hung around a bit longer. On December 3, 1958, the maid in Greenbaum's Phoenix home found him on the bed with his head almost cut from his body. Some 50 feet away in the den was the body of Mrs. Greenbaum. She had been hit in the head before someone had slit her throat with a butcher knife from the Greenbaum kitchen. Senator Goldwater attended the funeral and heard Rabbi Albert L. Plotkin declare that "the lives of good people need no eulogy." It was the type of sentiment Ben Cohen might have uttered.

The murders were never solved. Naturally. But with the Greenbaums and Bioff gone, Ben pressed his suit. The corporation empowered its secretary, Harvey L. Silbert, to settle the matter out of court if possible. Silbert was also a partner in the Gensbro Hotel Corporation and was ready to have that solvent group guarantee any settlement. Agreement was reached, and on October 31, 1959, the following entry was made in the records of the Riviera Hotel Corporation:

(Debit) Legal	$80,000.00
(Credit) Notes Payable:	
Ben Cohen	$70,000.00
Allie Harris	$ 8,000.00
M. Mason	$ 2,000.00

To record settlement of fee dispute with Ben Cohen for $80,000 and his assignment of $10,000 thereof.

Fat Allie Harris was a New York and Miami Beach bookmaker closely associated with one of Cohen's favorite clients, Trigger Mike Coppola. His son married the daughter of promoter Lou Chesler, who within a year would begin planning a new hotel-casino on Grand Bahama Island as a front man for Meyer Lansky. When the project reached the construction stage, Mason's Taylor Construction Company would get the job.

While no final answer is possible, the Riviera episode begins to make sense when the role of Lansky in both Miami Beach and Las Vegas is considered. At about the time the Riviera was begun, Lansky was exposed as a secret owner of the

Thunderbird. Earlier he had invested in Siegel's Flamingo, and, with Costello, he had a piece of Phil Kastel's Tropicana. As a moneyman on Miami Beach, it is highly unlikely a Miami Group would invest in Las Vegas without his consent, cooperation, and silent participation. Greenbaum's attitude would have annoyed Lansky, the more so since Gus' chief muscleman, Dave Berman, was widely believed to have been the executioner of Lansky's old partner, Bugsy Siegel. Dave died of cancer before Greenbaum's throat was cut.

Lansky, for all his brains, was still a dangerous man to cheat or even to ignore.

Ben Cohen, meanwhile, had found a new source of revenue. The Teamsters Union had many millions in its various pension funds. Under the control of Jimmy Hoffa, the Teamsters filled the gap left by the death of the Reconstruction Finance Corporation. The interest rates were higher, but if you knew the right people, the money was more quickly available.

Cohen was one of the right people.

Hoffa had taken over as Teamster president on October 4, 1957, following the indictment of Dave Beck on four counts of tax evasion and five counts of conspiring to falsify tax returns. Special Agent Claude J. Watson headed the probe. At the same time Chief Counsel Robert F. Kennedy of the Select Committee on Improper Activities in the Labor or Management Field— better known as the McClellan Committee—supervised a crack crew of investigators and exposed Beck's fantastic financial manipulations. Many of his investigators, such as Walter Sheridan, went with him when, upon becoming Attorney General, Kennedy followed up the investigation of Beck with a probe of Hoffa. Many Americans, unaccustomed to witnessing such a persistent pursuit of justice, accepted Hoffa's claim of persecution and "personal vendetta."

Hoffa was a friend of long standing of Moe Dalitz, a charter member of the Cleveland Syndicate who had cooperated with Lansky in the days of the Big Seven. Joe Massei, a Mafia figure from Detroit, had been a power in Miami Beach for years. With such common friendships, it was logical that Cohen and Hoffa should do business with each other.

The minute book of the Central States Pension Fund of the

Teamsters Union shows that on March 13, 1959, Ben Cohen appeared before the board of trustees in Chicago with an application for a $2,000,000 loan to the "4925 Corporation." The board voted unanimously to approve the loan for a fifteen-year period at 6 percent interest. Hoffa presided and asked Cohen for his telephone number.

According to the minute book, Cohen and Rabbi S. Gross met with the trustees on February 8, 1961, at the Eden Roc Hotel on Miami Beach. Cohen said the Hebrew Academy had purchased land for $200,000 from the City of Miami Beach for the purpose of building a million-dollar school. Needed was a $500,000 loan. Cohen said the forty directors of the academy would sign personally for the loan. Hoffa suggested the loan be for fifteen years at 6½ percent interest. Later, the academy named a wing of the new building for Cohen.

The minute book shows other appearances on behalf of other loans by Cohen. On March 30, 1962, for example, he told the trustees that he might be unable to accept a loan for the Driftwood Inn, Huntington Beach, California, because of an unsatisfactory appraisal report. The trustees were agreeable and asked if he cared to substitute another loan. Ben, always ready, tossed in a request from the La Mesa Bowl, La Mesa, California, for $1,100,000. The trustees okayed it.

Between appearances before the pension fund trustees and annual trips to Europe, Cohen stayed busy keeping Miami Beach politicians under control and replacing police chiefs as needed. A Dade County grand jury caused some headaches in 1957 by bypassing State Attorney Richard Gerstein and hiring a special counsel to investigate conditions on Miami Beach. Cooperative deputies in the sheriff's office tapped Cohen's telephone and overheard some fascinating conversations. Eventually, however, Gerstein regained control of the jury, some sealed indictments were squashed, and Cohen sailed for Europe in full confidence the status quo would continue.

There was also time to defend such important clients as Charles Brudner and Trigger Mike Coppola.

Brudner was a partner of Frank Ritter, alias Reed, and Morris Schmertzler, better known as Max Courtney. The trio were veteran bookies who operated all over the country from headquarters in New York. Following the passage of the wagering-tax law as a result of the Kefauver heat, they transferred to Canada, where they cooperated with Ed Curd and Gil Beckley. When the scare died, the boys moved back to the States. They were closely connected with Lansky and operated for a time in Havana during Meyer's sojourn there.

It was late in 1954 when Special Agent John McRae learned of a huge bookmaking operation allegedly located in Palm Court—the Little Italy section of Miami Beach dominated by Joe Massei. The Miami *Herald*'s star reporter, Wilson McGee, got the same information. The source in both instances was Ed Bishop, the private eye who guarded Virginia Hill following the murder of Bugsy Siegel. McRae arranged with managing editor George Beebe to hold up the story pending an investigation. McRae's supervisor was Richard Wallace, nephew of the late Elmer Irey, and Wallace was a close friend of the editor.

The special agent had made one visit to Palm Court for a look around when the bookies suddenly moved out. Bishop supplied their new phone number, and the new location was soon found on Fifteenth Street.

Wagering-tax enforcement was still a relatively new field, especially in the Miami area. Both experience and equipment were in short supply. Cameras were borrowed from the Miami *Herald*, and a photographer to use it was obtained from the Alcohol and Tobacco Tax Division, which had plenty of experience in chasing moonshiners. A panel truck to conceal the photographer was borrowed from an automobile dealer. Radio equipment and field glasses were also borrowed, along with other needed items, from the Army and Coast Guard.

The new location was in a congested area, and at the height of the winter season there were no vacant apartments available from which the handbook could be observed. Surveillance had to be made from vehicles parked on the street. From noon until 6 P.M. each weekday, the suspected apartment was watched. It was occupied, the special agents learned, by Mr. and Mrs. Sam A. Kobrin. Sam, a resident alien with a long record ranging from worthless checks to robbery, had been ejected as a bookie from Hialeah in 1951.

Each afternoon a number of men dropped in on the Kobrins. Three were identified as Brudner, Herman Stark, and Irving Rich. Stark was a former associate of gambler Frank Erickson and was known to be connected with the Brudner-Courtney-Ritter combine. He had the distinction of being ejected by both Hialeah and Tropical Park racetracks. Rich had a long record as both a bookie and a casino gambler and also was unwelcome at most racetracks.

Other visitors were later identified as Louis Selikoff, Bernard Katz, Abe Schwartz, and Hymie Siegel. All four had records as gamblers and previous associations with the combine. Siegel was a relative of Bugsy. No one seemed to know if he was a brother or cousin, but it was confirmed he had worked with Bugsy at the Flamingo. It was also alleged that following the Bug's death, Hymie emptied the contents of a floor safe in the penthouse where Virginia Hill had demonstrated her talents as the world's best lay.

All in all, it was a distinguished group of punks the special agents were watching. Records from the telephone company confirmed that bookmakers in all parts of the country were in daily contact with the boys on Fifteenth Street.

During the month of surveillance, a new and obviously heavy door was carried into the apartment house and installed at Kobrin's apartment. The boys were taking precautions, and the special agents began to wonder how they would get inside before the evidence was destroyed. The solution came when they noted that about 5 P.M. each day Schwartz arrived with bookie records. The apartment building lobby contained a stairway leading to the second floor. On the day of the raid, two special agents sneaked into the building and hid in the space under the stairs. Special Agent Hilker was waiting with a stepladder to enter through the bathroom window. Seven other special agents were stationed nearby, ready to join the raiders within seconds. It was February 3, 1956.

Promptly at 5 P.M., Schwartz came walking up from his apartment on Alton Road. He entered the lobby, gave a code knock on the heavy door of Apartment 1. The door opened. Special Agent McRae led the charge from under the stairs and got to the door before it could be closed. A search warrant, secured only thirty minutes before, was read even as Hilker broke the glass in the bathroom window.

All those arrested were charged with engaging in wagering without having purchased a tax stamp. The apartment contained three telephones, an adding machine, a pencil sharpener, racing forms, bet slips, rundown sheets, and $4,862 in cash. Katz brought in $3,000 more almost two hours after the raid. He drove up, parked, and attempted to peep in the window. Special agents, who had been expecting him, grabbed him as he turned to leave. In addition to the thirty $100 bills he was carrying, they found eighty-seven bet tickets written that day at Hialeah. The agents concluded that he was the "comeback money"* man for the group.

Following Ben Cohen's call, McRae ordered the prisoners taken downtown for booking. Kobrin brought out a box of expensive cigars. Each of his colleagues took a handful. As the Intelligence men snapped on handcuffs, one of the prisoners asked why it was being done. "We're not criminals," he said.

The seized records disclosed that in three months of operation the bookies had accepted $2,135,640 in bets and evaded excise taxes of $213,564. The addition of fraud and delinquency penalties brought the total bill to $481,109.

No evidence was found to tie the Miami Beach handbook into the larger Brudner-Courtney-Ritter combination, but it was learned that on Monday following the Friday afternoon raid, a safe-deposit box at the First National Bank of Miami Beach was cleaned out. The box had been rented in the name of Ritter and Schwartz.

During the period between the raid and the submission of the final report on August 9, 1956, Ben Cohen was a frequent visitor to the office of United States Attorney James L. Guilmartin. He submitted a brief attacking the validity of the search warrant used in the raid and tried to convince Guilmartin that certain of the defendants were merely visitors in the apartment.

The visits continued after the final report was submitted.

---

* Comeback money is used to shorten the odds when a bookie finds himself with too many bets on one horse. He sends a man to the track to feed some of the bets into the pari-mutuel machines, thus driving down the official odds and making the payoff to the winners smaller.

On May 10, 1957, Guilmartin advised the Intelligence Division that he was ready to present the several cases to a grand jury on May 14. Cohen again consulted with the U.S. Attorney and apparently persuaded him to change his mind. According to information received, Cohen was willing to plead six of his clients guilty to misdemeanor charges—not having a wagering-tax stamp—if no felony charges of evasion were filed and the charges against Siegel and Selikoff were dropped.

On May 24, the U.S. Attorney bypassed the grand jury and filed an information against Brudner, Rich, Schwartz, Stark, Katz, and Kobrin. Cohen entered not guilty pleas for Kobrin, Stark, and Katz. Brudner was fined $2,500; Rich and Schwartz got off with $2,000 fines. Kobrin—apparently the object of another deal—suddenly changed his plea to guilty and was given six months in prison. The charges against Katz and Stark were dropped, allegedly because the other defendants were ready to swear they were only "on-lookers."

It was March 31, 1966, before the civil case was settled. On that day Judge David W. Dyer ordered Mr. and Mrs. Kobrin, Rich, and Stark to pay $356,788, plus accrued interest and costs. The judge found specifically that Stark *was* accepting bets.

Cohen's luck began to change shortly after the Brudner case. Back in 1950, Special Agents Edward M. Cohen and S. Lawrence Schroll, assisted by Revenue Agent Watson A. Weatherup, recommended that additional taxes of $213,622.15 be assessed against Cohen, largely on the basis of his one-third share of Sam's profits from the S & G Syndicate. Cohen fought desperately to deny the debt, but by 1958 the best he could do was settle on a compromise of $90,000. Shortly thereafter he was up to his neck in the marital and tax troubles of his favorite client, Trigger Mike Coppola.

The two were interrelated. Mike had married Ann Drahmann, widow of Charley Drahmann who had worked for the Cleveland Syndicate's Lookout House near Covington, Kentucky. Some mutual friends such as Screw Andrews, Sleepout Louie Levinson and Gil "the Brain" Beckley introduced Mike to the widow in New York. The numbers boss of Harlem fell in love with her dark beauty. Marriage followed, and Ann was taken to Coppola's mansion in Miami Beach. The marriage was stormy. Mike alternately beat Ann, helped perform abortions on her, and gave her money, jewels, and huge wads of cash.

In February, 1960, the marriage broke up. Cohen represented Mike in arranging a divorce settlement. But Ann wanted revenge, as well as freedom. By a coincidence, Revenue Agent Joe Wanderschied—the man who as an acting special agent persuaded a madam in Texas to blow the whistle on ex-Police Chief Ford—strolled up and began asking about Mike's finances. Considerable time was required before Joe won Ann's confidence, but he succeeded. Special Agent Richard Jaffe was assigned to the case, and with Ann's help, Mike was indicted on income tax evasion charges.

Pending trial, Ann visited Europe. Cohen went over to see her and, according to the angry woman, offered some persuasive arguments on why she should stay in Europe and not return to testify against his client. Ann told him to go to hell.

The reform drive in Newport coincided with the investigation of Coppola and negated an effort by Cohen to prove that most of Mike's cash really belonged to his ex-wife's first husband. With the heat on in Newport, none of Mike's friends there dared to stick their neck out for him. Special Agent Earl De Voto helped Jaffe obtain negative statements from such hoods as Levinson and Screw Andrews.

Ann returned to the United States and was waiting in the wings to tell her stories of syndicate couriers who regularly brought hundreds of thousands of dollars to Mike at Miami Beach, when the trial began. To her disappointment, Mike's attorneys—Cohen and Jacob Kossman— suddenly changed Mike's plea to guilty. He was sentenced to a year in prison and a $40,000 fine. Ann, robbed of revenge and the victim of the same kind of treatment Virginia Hill experienced after Siegel's death, killed herself in Rome six months later.

It was 1962—and Cohen's taxes were again under investigation. In fact, two months and five days after Coppola's conviction, Watson Weatherup, now a special agent, submitted his final report in the new Cohen case. Revenue Agent Thomas J. Gallagher, Jr., cooperated with Weatherup in the joint probe.

Principal item of interest centered on a commission Cohen received for arranging a Teamster loan, in the amount of $2,350,000, to Samuel Eig, a real estate developer in Silver Springs, Maryland. The transaction began in 1959 when Edward Rosenbaum, a former member of the S & G Syndicate, ran into a friend, Charles Tobin. Rosenbaum said he had a source for mortgage money but was unable to find borrowers. Apparently Cohen was trying to drum up customers. Tobin said he knew of someone in Maryland who might be interested and suggested a meeting with Cohen. Later Cohen met with Eig, who agreed the brokerage commission for Ben would be 6 percent. He also suggested they put it in writing, but Cohen declined.

The loan was easily arranged, and on February 25, 1960, Cohen sent a courier to collect the first installment of the brokerage fee. He carried this letter addressed to Eig:

> The bearer of this letter, Mr. Howard Morris, is a very dear friend of mine and you have seen him in my office on many occasions. I am taking the responsibility that you give him the package that you have for me and that it will be delivered to me. You are also authorized to turn over the check you have made payable to me. This letter will suffice as a receipt. Any courtesies you may extend to Mr. Morris will be appreciated by me, as he is my dearest friend.
>
> Most sincerely,
> BEN COHEN

Morris refused to give Eig a receipt for the $11,000 check he picked up or for the "package." Eig, however, was a cautious man. He called in two associates and had them witness the transaction. As soon as Morris left, Eig wrote a note on Cohen's letter:

> 2/26/60. Note: package referred to above contained $30,000 in cash, the amount of which was verified in my presence by the recipient, Mr. Howard Morris.

On March 8, Morris returned to Silver Spring and picked up the second installment—$30,000 in cash. The third payment of $5,000 was paid by check.

Cohen had been angry enough when he heard about the

"delegation" Eig called in to watch the money change hands, but he hit the ceiling when informed that Eig's book would reflect the cash transactions. At a meeting in Miami Beach in 1961, he told Eig that "the normal method is to cash checks in small amounts and accumulate the cash in a safe-deposit box." He had assumed, he said, that Eig had enough intelligence to know how to handle it.

Eig, who also became angry, refused to sign a backdated agreement for tax purposes which would have stated that the total $76,000 brokerage fee was cut up by Rosenbaum with $15,000, Tobin with $25,000, and Cohen with $35,000. Instead, he drew up a substitute contract that stated the commission would be 6 percent and that the broker could act in concert with others if he desired. This was intended to give Cohen an out, but he flew into a rage because it was not specific enough. Eventually, he signed it, however. On his tax returns, he reported that $10,000 of the brokerage fee went to Tobin and $30,000 to Rosenbaum.

Once again it was the old S & G that spoiled the plan. Special Agent Weatherup discovered that in 1960, at the time Rosenbaum allegedly received the $30,000, he still owed $35,000 in taxes assessed in 1951 against his S & G profits. He made no payment on the tax debt, nor was he able to reduce his medical bill, which totaled $3,750.

On July 25, 1963, Cohen was indicted on two counts of tax evasion; the government charged he neglected to report $150, 261 in the two-year period 1960-61. Trial was delayed until January, 1965. It was held without a jury before Judge Charles B. Fulton, who found Cohen guilty on one count, that involving the transaction with Eig. He was sentenced to eighteen months in prison.

Cohen appealed. Almost two years passed as the case was reviewed. Cohen continued to practice law. The federal court in Miami took notice and issued a rule prohibiting any lawyer convicted of a felony from representing a client. This forced Cohen to withdraw as attorney for Gil Beckley, who had been arrested on interstate gambling charges by the FBI. Ultimately, Beckley was given ten years, but by then Cohen was already in prison.

On November 30, 1966, his appeals exhausted, Cohen stood before Judge Fulton and begged for mercy. Couldn't the prison sentence be mitigated? The judge refused. Cohen began to sob.

"Why? Why?" he cried. "Can this be a dream? Your honor, give me mercy."

"Your sentence devastated me," said Judge Fulton softly, "but I can't believe now that I should change my mind. I just couldn't live with myself if I did anything different from what I have done."

James Horgan, Cohen's law partner, added his plea. "The fight has gone out," he said. "The light has gone out. We're here for mercy."

Still sobbing, Cohen—the once-cocky boss of Miami Beach —was led from the room to serve his sentence.

Eight months later Special Agent Weatherup died quietly. His colleagues blamed his death on the tremendous pressure he had been subjected to both before and after the conviction of Ben Cohen.

"It killed him," said a colleague. "He died in line of duty."

When Lansky's new casino on Grand Bahama opened early in 1964, the men in charge were Brudner, Courtney, and Ritter. Assisting them were several of the bookies who had been arrested on Miami Beach in 1956. Stark, for example, served as courier, bringing the cash from the casino to Miami Beach.

United States Attorney Robert Morgenthau presented Intelligence Division evidence to a federal grand jury in New York and secured new indictments against the elderly bookies. The Bahamas government refused to deport them. A long struggle followed which was largely responsible for the overthrow of the ruling political party. Ultimately, the trio fled to Israel—after "selling" their sucker list to the casino for $2,100,000. Eventually, however, they returned to New York and surrendered.

The Kennedy heat had closed the nation's illegal casinos, but Lansky had a new empire just 90 miles from Florida. The view beyond Biscayne Bay was more appealing than ever.

20

A PASSION FOR PRIVACY

IN April, 1960, the Intelligence Division launched what it called "another drive against major racketeers." Early in 1961, following the inauguration of President John F. Kennedy and the appointment of his brother Robert to be Attorney General, the drive became part of a larger effort—a "Coordinated War on Crime."

Taking full advantage of the political muscle available to the trusted brother of the President, Robert Kennedy was able to compel all federal law enforcement agencies to cooperate with one another. An Organized Crime and Racketeering Section was created in the Justice Department, and into it flowed information from the FBI and from Treasury. All too aware that many United States Attorneys get their jobs through political patronage, Kennedy recruited bright young lawyers and assigned them to work OCD—Organized Crime Drive—cases. Sometimes, as with United States Attorney William Scent in Louisville, the U.S. Attorneys cooperated gladly. When they didn't, the brash young men from Washington simply ignored them. They presented evidence directly to federal grand juries and prosecuted the cases that resulted. Squawks of local politicians were politely received and filed away.

The Intelligence Division was happy to cooperate in the coordinated effort. Again and again it proved its value.

Frank "Buster" Wortman, rackets boss of East St. Louis, was indicted for income tax evasion in 1960 and convicted in 1962. His attorney was Morris Shenker, a man who would be heard from again. In his closing argument, Shenker referred to special agents of Intelligence as "our enemies."

Mickey Cohen, the man who succeeded Bugsy Siegel as syndicate boss in the West, was convicted for the second time. In 1951, Mickey received a five-year sentence for tax evasion. He served four years. In 1961 he was sentenced to fifteen years and a $30,000 fine. Judge George H. Boldt declared: "If there be decadence in society, as sometimes charged, Mickey Cohen is an excellent specimen of it. The obstructions and impeding weight of the collective Mickey Cohens in our national community conceivably could tip the balance of our doom."

Abe Minker, numbers boss of Reading, Pennsylvania, was convicted on charges of wagering-tax evasion in 1961. He was sentenced to four years in prison and a $35,000 fine. Key to the case was gambling records torn up by Minker and dumped in trash cans. Special agents secured the trash and, in what the court termed "a masterpiece of patient and persistent effort," put the pieces together "and achieved a well-nigh perfect reconstruction of the original."

Joseph "Newsboy" Moriarity, numbers boss of Jersey City, New Jersey, was convicted on gambling charges in 1960 and again in 1962. While he was in prison, two carpenters assigned to wreck an old garage found $2,400,000 in the trunk of a car abandoned in that garage. A few days later in another nearby garage two paper sacks containing $168,675 were discovered. All evidence pointed to Newsboy as the owner. Back in 1946 the Intelligence Unit had located fifty bank accounts in Moriarity's name and sent him to prison. Apparently, Newsboy then decided to store his loot in garages. When his money was found, he filed an amended tax return, which listed $5,500 as earnings from his newspaper distributorship and $2,400,000 as "other income." He asked for a refund of $212,000, agreeing to let the government keep the cash it had seized. The refund request was denied.

John Dioguardi, also known as Johnny Dio, was convicted in 1960 for income tax evasion and sentenced to four years in prison and a $5,000 fine. Earlier Dio had been indicted for the acid blinding of columnist Victor Riesel, but the case was dropped when witnesses developed what the judge called "underworld lockjaw."

Benjamin Dranow, one of those fortunate fellows who could arrange Teamsters Union pension loans with Jimmy Hoffa, was indicted in 1961 on three counts of income tax evasion. He was convicted in 1962 and sentenced to seven years in prison and a $10,000 fine. Special agents Samuel P. Doonan and Richard W. Petterssen and Internal Revenue Agent Ivan L. Anderson received special letters of commendation from Kennedy for their work on the case. Before sentence was passed, Dranow made a short statement: "I am not ashamed of my friendship with Hoffa," he said. In 1968, from his jail cell, Dranow filed a $12,000,000 suit against the Kennedy family in which he charged that he was a victim of a conspiracy by the "sons, sons-in-law, agents and press agents" of Mr. and Mrs. Joseph Kennedy. The case was quickly tossed out of court. Concurrent with the sentence for tax evasion, Dranow was also serving a sentence for mail fraud in connection with Teamster loans.

Another weeping tax evader proved to be that tough guy of the movies and friend of Bugsy Siegel, George Raft. Only Raft cried with relief on September 28, 1965, when a federal judge declined to send him to prison for income tax evasion. The judge fined the actor $2,500.

The Intelligence Division investigated Raft as part of the Organized Crime Drive and recommended prosecution for the years 1958 through 1963, with the exception of 1962, when George got a refund. The grand jury indicted Raft on six counts. A point at issue in the probe was $50,000, allegedly paid Raft by Ralph Lowe for shares in the Capri, a Havana casino.

Raft said he purchased the shares for Lowe, a Texas oilman who didn't want to be publicly identified with the casino. He insisted Lowe's check was endorsed by him and turned over to Benjamin Berkowitz, the treasurer of the Capri. Berkowitz, it will be remembered, was the accountant who shot himself through the heart—according to police—after Special Agent Jaffe discovered a mysterious safe deposit box in Miami.

Investigators discovered that after Lowe's check was turned over to Berkowitz, two cashier's checks were drawn to the account of Berkowitz's Stewart Investment Corporation in the amount of $25,000 each. They were made payable to Raft and were in turn sold to a Cuban, Alberto Alejo, for Cuban pesos. Alejo said the cashier's checks were purchased for his father-in-law, Nicholas Sierra, as a means of getting funds into the United States after Castro took over Cuba. Sierra's endorsement appeared on the checks.

Confidential information complicated the matter even more. Intelligence got word that "Raft had taken a Texas oilman for $50,000, in connection with purchasing some points in the Casino de Capri. Raft had to give Charles 'the Blade' Tourine $40,000, and split the remaining $10,000, with another unidentified person." Tourine was suspected as being the real boss of the Capri.

After Cuba, Raft fronted for Lansky in London's Colony Club until the British deported him as "undesirable."

Many other cases were made against racketeers, big and little, but the Intelligence Division sought to maintain a "balanced program" of investigation. In doing so, they helped prove that under President Kennedy, at least, a crooked Democrat would be probed as quickly as a crooked Republican.

Raymond C. Deering, former treasurer of the Democratic Committee of New York State and a prominent banker, pleaded guilty to income tax evasion on May 2, 1963. The sixty-one-year-old defendant was fined $18,000 and placed on probation for one year.

On April 5, 1963, the former mayor of Harry Truman's hometown of Independence, Missouri, was indicted on five counts of tax evasion. A protégé of Tom Pendergast's, William H. Sermon became boss of the Eastern Jackson County Democratic Club upon the death of his brother, Roger, who had served as mayor of Independence for twenty-five years. In 1958,

William became mayor, resigning on October 9, 1961, because of illness.

The illness kept him out of prison in 1964, when he was fined $40,000 and put on probation for one year. A condition of probation required that he pay more than $400,000 in back taxes and penalties.

But racketeers and the officials who protected them were the primary targets of the Coordinated War on Crime. Kennedy's attack on Newport, Kentucky, has already been described. Beaumont, Texas, soon followed. There, as in Newport, a citizens' revolt was helped by timely indictments of officials and gamblers. Late in 1961, racket-ridden Gary, Indiana, a Democratic stronghold, was invaded. Metro M. Holovachka was indicted on three counts of tax evasion. The former prosecutor of Lake County managed to get the first indictments squashed, but he was reindicted on January 12, 1962. On February 20, 1962, he was found guilty, fined $10,000, and sentenced to three years in prison.

On the day following Holovachka's conviction, the mayor of Gary, the sheriff of Lake County, and five former members of the Hammond, Indiana, City Council, were revealed to be under secret indictment on tax evasion charges. Mayor George Chacharis, who as a supporter of John Kennedy had hoped to be named Ambassador to Greece, resigned as mayor on December 12, 1962, and entered a plea of guilty. The trial was in its third week, and a mountain of evidence linking the mayor to payoffs and kickbacks had been introduced. Charges of conspiring with Chacharis to conceal $226,000 in graft were dismissed against the other defendants following the mayor's guilty plea. The ex-mayor was sentenced to three years in prison and a $10,000 fine.

The Organized Crime Drive was in high gear and rolling when on November 22, 1963, President Kennedy was murdered on the streets of Dallas, Texas. Abruptly, as Jimmy Hoffa put it, Robert Kennedy was "just another lawyer." The muscle he had used so well was gone.

The death of President Kennedy signaled a counterattack by the forces of reaction. The opening gun was fired by famed defense attorney Edward Bennett Williams, who just happened to be defending Bobby Baker before a Senate subcommittee probing the ex-secretary to the Senate majority's affairs. Williams read a letter into the record in which he charged that Ed Levinson's telephone in his Las Vegas casino had been bugged. Levinson was the brother of Newport's Sleepout Louie and had put a long career of illegal gambling in Newport and Miami Beach behind him to operate the Fremont in Las Vegas and become a business partner of Baker in assorted deals.

Pretending to assume the listening device was placed in Levinson's phone to record Ed's conversations with Baker, Attorney Williams called the incident "an unlawful violation of Mr. Baker's right to privacy." In reality, the casinos of Las Vegas had been a major target of Kennedy's OCD. Goal was to identify the secret owners of casinos and stop the practice of skimming off un-taxpaid funds which for years couriers had carried to Lansky and other members of the National Crime Syndicate. The FBI—thrust into action when Kennedy sponsored new laws forbidding interstate travel or communication in aid of racketeering—bugged many telephones in Las Vegas. The device found in Levinson's phone was just one of them.

Williams dropped this hint: "Perhaps the committee would have an interest in learning how widespread the practice of eavesdropping by the agencies of the executive branch on officers, employees, and former officers and employees of the legislative branch might be."

The blast by Williams was made on February 19, 1964. The committee didn't accept the challenge he offered, however, and by March Hoffa had been convicted in Chattanooga on a jury-rigging charge. He was free on bail and desperately seeking something on which to base an appeal. Kennedy's campaign to get Hoffa, led by Walter Sheridan, had paid off at last, but the Teamsters president was far from beaten.

Sidney Zagri, a top Hoffa aide, began a campaign to get an investigation under way into the handling of Hoffa's case by the Justice Department. He lobbied in vain to get the 1964 Democratic Convention to make such a probe part of its platform, but he did succeed in getting the Republicans to do so. Fearing, with some justice, that Senator Barry Goldwater might not carry the country in November, Zagri managed to get a resolution calling for a probe before the House Judiciary Committee. Chairman Emanuel Celler spilled the beans, however, on September 7, 1964, by revealing the resolution was "word for word" similar to the plank offered the Democratic National Convention by Hoffa's man.

In addition to Hoffa, the resolution wanted an inquiry into the treatment afforded former Major General Edwin A. Walker who had been arrested during riots at the University of Mississippi in 1962. The charges were later dropped. Roy M. Cohn, former chief aide to the witch-hunting Senator Joe McCarthy, was suggested as another victim of the Justice Department under Kennedy. Cohn had been indicted for perjury in connection with some stock dealings he had with members of the Cleveland Syndicate at the Desert Inn in Las Vegas. In July, 1964, he was acquitted.*

Zagri, a determined fellow, had other strings to his bow. Even before Celler refused to cooperate, he approached Senator Ed Long of Missouri. An old political crony of the Teamster aide, Senator Long was chairman of the Subcommittee on Administrative Practice and Procedure of the Senate Judiciary Committee. He owed his appointment to the parent committee to Bobby Baker, who told the Democratic steering committee that the two Senators in line for the seat didn't want it when as a matter of fact, they did. In 1963, Long was appointed to head the subcommittee by Chairman James Eastland—the right-wing Senator from Mississippi.

Senator Long was receptive to Zagri's ideas. After all, his old friend, Morris Shenker—the man who defended Buster Wortman and called Intelligence special agents "our enemies" —was Hoffa's chief counsel. Long had a special relationship with Shenker of a personal nature, but that fact was not public knowledge at the time.

In preparation for the battle to come, Long selected Bernard Fensterwald, Jr., to be chief counsel of the subcommittee. Fensterwald was young, tough, and bitter. He learned the ropes under Senator Estes Kefauver during a probe of the drug in-

---

* Roy Cohn has since been twice indicted by a federal grand jury in New York on criminal charges stemming from his association with the Fifth Avenue Coach Company.

dustry in 1961-62. Like that other famous committee counsel Roy Cohn, Fensterwald came from a wealthy family and was rather independent. Kefauver, who could be stiff-necked as well, fired him. Banking on the fact that his mother had contributed $5,000 to the Kennedy campaign, Fensterwald tried to land another government job. He blamed Robert Kennedy for his failure and became an outspoken critic of the Organized Crime Drive pushed by Robert.

When Hoffa went on trial in Tennessee early in 1964, Fensterwald was an interested observer. Close at hand was Cohn, as bitter as McCarthy after his censure. Fensterwald used Cohn's office as his own, and Cohn was one of the first witnesses called by Long's subcommittee. Cohn and Long were also old friends and had visited each other in New York and Missouri. In his testimony before the subcommittee, Cohn blasted the IRS for watching his mail.

Long moved slowly, however. First, he arranged for his son-in-law to get a $12,500-a-year job in one of Cohn's four banks. The lucky employee averaged one day a month at the bank, got a $5,000 raise, and became chairman of the board. Meanwhile, Long's Tower Loan Company back in Missouri was able to get seven unsecured loans from Cohn's banks.

In the fall of 1964, Long sent a questionnaire to all government agencies, including the IRS. The questions concerned any possible "invasions of privacy" by the agencies. Meanwhile, he began to hold hearings. The Food and Drug Administration and the Post Office Department were the first targets. It developed that postal authorities had installed peepholes in certain rest rooms after discovering a few employees had been opening letters containing money and flushing the evidence down the toilet. Long decided the peepholes were truly invasions of privacy and implied they were intended primarily for Peeping Toms.

The Internal Revenue Service was slow in replying to the questionnaire because it required much time to get the information wanted from the field. Following the scandals of the Truman era, the IRS had been decentralized under a reorganization program designed to take power from the hands of a few men in Washington. Investigations had disclosed that when power was concentrated at the top, it was easy to kill cases, make deals, and in general let politics and personal profit determine policy. The men in the field were helpless to protest. Under the reorganization program, regional offices were set up around the country. The regions were in turn divided into districts. Strict orders were issued to see that all cases passed up the lines of command, being reviewed at each step along the way. Regional and district officers were given more authority, subject always to review. A special agent, if he had the nerve, had the right to appeal decisions of his superiors. No longer could an investigation disappear into a limbo of silence. Often, of course, the complicated bureaucracy slowed down the progress of individual cases and made it difficult to mount a sustained offensive. When Kennedy's War on Coordinated Crime began, some district officers used the authority delegated to them to permit special agents to employ electronic devices against top gangsters—even as the FBI was doing on a more massive scale. The situation varied from district to district, and Washington had little information in its files. Much time was required to find the answers Long wanted: how many telephone bugs, how many one-way mirrors in conference rooms, how many "pen registers" to record the telephone numbers dialed from a gangster's phone.

Long accused the IRS of dragging its feet. He was impatient to zero in on the Intelligence Division—the chief foe of organized crime. Meanwhile, the word spread along the syndicate grapevine, and suddenly gangsters began complaining loudly that their indictment or conviction was based on the illegal use of wiretaps or bugs.

One such was Anthony M. Grosso, numbers racketeer of Pittsburgh, Pennsylvania, who in March, 1964, was sentenced to nine years in prison and fines totaling $191,000. He appealed. Desperately seeking something to strengthen his case —an ironic development as later events proved—he agreed to testify before Senator Long's subcommittee in hearings that started on July 13, 1965.

Long began with this statement: "Today we start a new phase of our hearings on wiretap and eavesdropping activities by Federal agencies. For the next several weeks, we will take testimony relating to techniques used by the Internal Revenue Service, both on the taxpaying public and on their own employees."

The real fight was starting. Grosso, however, was handled with kid gloves. The record shows:

> MR. FENSTERWALD. Mr. Grosso, do you have any reason to believe that during the investigation before your indictment, or after your indictment, any of your phones were tapped?
> MR. GROSSO. Yes, sir.
> MR. FENSTERWALD. What would lead you to this conclusion?
> MR. GROSSO. Well, I was told by the assistant superintendent of police, Lawrence J. Maloney, and by the Mount Lebanon police where I live.
> MR. FENSTERWALD. That your phones were tapped?
> MR. GROSSO. That they were tapped.

After establishing that Grosso had perjured himself in his own trial, Fensterwald asked a curious question: "Could you tell me, Mr. Grosso, from your own information whether gamblers generally make use of electronic devices similar to those used by law enforcement agencies?"

"No, sir, they don't use it," said Grosso.

The indirect approach continued to be used as the chief counsel got the gambler to deny "any connection with what is generally known as the syndicate or the Mafia or the Cosa Nostra." Grosso said the numbers racket in his town had been a local affair. Fensterwald then made his point by asking: "Could you tell me as a result of recent convictions whether it has made it possible for outside elements to move into Pittsburgh?"

"Yes, sir," said Grosso piously.

"And these are the people that had been kept out in the past?"

"I would say they were," said Grosso.

The implication of this exchange was that the OCD had opened Pittsburgh's doors to the syndicate by convicting local talent. By so implying, Fensterwald was attempting to appeal to local prejudice and at the same time hold the Organized

Crime Drive up to ridicule. Exactly why a local gangster is less dangerous than one from another city, he didn't bother to explain. In any case, the syndicate had been in Pittsburgh long before Tony Grosso was indicted.

Grosso was destined to make history, however. When at last his appeal reached the Supreme Court—along with one by James Marchetti of Bridgeport, Connecticut—his conviction was reversed and thrown out. What's more, the court ruled that the wagering-tax laws under which so many gamblers had been convicted since November 1, 1951, was unconstitutional. The law as written violated the Fifth Amendment's guarantee against self-incrimination, the court by a seven to one vote ruled. Only Chief Justice Earl Warren dissented.

The decision handed down on January 29, 1968, was a tremendous victory for organized crime. The boys from coast to coast owed a vote of thanks to Tony Grosso—even if he was just a local operator. Unfortunately, it didn't do much for Jimmy Hoffa. Long and Fensterwald had kept digging, however.

Commissioner of Internal Revenue Sheldon S. Cohen attempted to cooperate with Senator Long. He appeared before the subcommittee in July to report orders had gone out to stop all electronic eavesdropping and dismantle any and all one-way mirrors. He supplied the Senator with a few more cases of bugged racketeers and promised a complete report would be furnished when all the information came in from the districts.

Cohen later acted to restore to headquarters some of the controls taken away by the reorganization of 1951. Recognizing some validity to Long's charges that top officials were still responsible for the acts of men in the field—whether they knew of them or not—he shuffled the command of the Intelligence Division. H. Alan Long, the director, was replaced by William Kolar, a former FBI special agent, who since 1960 had served as director of the Internal Security Division of the IRS. Robert K. Lund, chief of Intelligence in Los Angeles, was made assistant director of Intelligence, replacing Robert Manzi.

Had reform in the IRS been Senator Long's goal, he could have claimed a great victory and rested from his labors. Instead, he pushed ahead with charges that progressively became wilder and wilder. Commissioner Cohen no longer had any illusions about Long, and as morale in Intelligence began to slip, he stopped making concessions. The situation seemed perfectly clear one day when he dropped in on the Senator. After a chat, he started to leave. In the outer office was Morris Shenker, who, earlier in the day, had appeared in court for Hoffa.

"Everyone turned red," recalled Cohen later, "but someone introduced Shenker. Apparently he had come straight to Long to report on the court action."

Long, meanwhile, had turned to Boston where the Intelligence Division was investigating Bernard G. McGarry. Boston newspapers referred to McGarry as "a Milton businessman," but his police record listed thirteen arrests, beginning in 1928 and ranging from larceny to suspicion of murder. Back in 1959 the Intelligence Division received information that McGarry and Abe Sarkis controlled bookmaking in the Roxbury and South End sections of Boston. A probe resulted in a raid that was publicized in a sensational television documentary called *Biography of a Bookie Joint*. Among those arrested were Leo Swartz, a business partner of McGarry's, and John Galvin, McGarry's uncle. Later McGarry became a coin machine operator, and so powerful was he that his AAA vending machines were even installed throughout the North End of Boston, an area dominated by Mafia figures who had their own coin machine companies.

Long called as witnesses McGarry's attorney, Lawrence F. O'Donnell; McGarry's accountant, Donald R. Lord; and Jack Harris, a former revenue agent. Harris had been fired and was under indictment at the time, a fact that didn't bother Long but made it difficult for IRS officials—who didn't want to prejudice his impending trial—to put Harris' charges into perspective.

The three witnesses painted a sorry picture of IRS persecution of "businessman" McGarry and also claimed to have been persecuted themselves. Later, the *Reader's Digest* in one of several bitter attacks on the IRS, published their accounts of personal persecution—or at least it did for Lord and O'Donnell. Harris, who had been convicted by then, wasn't mentioned.

An incident about which there was great indignation concerned a wiretap on the telephone of Gil "the Brain" Beckley in Miami Beach. One of his many callers proved to be businessman McGarry who wanted to arrange to lay off some bets with Gil. The information was not communicated to the Intelligence Division in Boston or used in the probe of McGarry, according to sworn testimony.

Assistant United States Attorney Edward "Ted" Harrington, a youthful veteran of the Organized Crime Drive, presented the case against McGarry, who was charged with evading $40,425 for the years 1959 through 1961. On April 7, 1967, Boston newspaper readers gaped in astonishment. The front page carried two stories of tax evaders being sentenced: Bobby Baker received a one-year sentence; "Milton businessman" Bernard McGarry was sentenced to five years and a $30,-000 fine. Was McGarry so much worse than Baker?

The First Circuit Court of Appeals on December 27, 1967, upheld the conviction of McGarry and noted in conclusion: "This was a vigorously contested twenty-one day trial, preceded and accompanied by many oral and written motions. We think the rights of the appellant were zealously urged and fairly protected."

Well before the McGarry case went to trial, the Fensterwald-Long show, produced by Cohn and directed in part by Shenker, had gone on the road. On October 18, 1965, it put on a performance in Kansas City, Missouri. Joseph Rosapepe, director of IRS information, appeared in town prior to the hearing and provided the news media with background information. This enraged the Senator, who called Rosapepe as a witness and questioned him about his contacts with the journalism fraternity.

> SENATOR LONG. Didn't you tell them that you felt the information you would be able to give them would be more accurate than what would be developed in this committee?
> MR. ROSAPEPE. No, sir.
> SENATOR LONG. You did not tell that to anyone now?
> MR. ROSAPEPE. Not more accurate, no, sir. More com-

plete, if it did not come out and they wanted to know anything.

SENATOR LONG. In other words, you were sort of a "scootsquawk" for the Internal Revenue, going around after this committee.

MR. ROSAPEPE. No, sir, that is not my job.

SENATOR LONG. Did it ever dawn on you that you might be interfering with the activity of the committee of the United States Senate?

Later in the same hearings, Special Agent Charles D. Lindsay mentioned the conviction of William Sermon, former mayor of Independence and a political ally of Long's. The Senator expressed disgust—not with Sermon, but with the IRS for prosecuting him.

"Here is a man who was mayor of a city in this state," said Long, "a prominent businessman in this city, a man who lived in this city, as far as I know, all his life, a reputable citizen until you found some questions about his income tax."

Meanwhile, Hoffa was getting closer to prison all the time. In March, 1964, he had been sentenced to eight years in prison for jury tampering. In August, 1964, he received an additional five years for conspiring to defraud the union pension fund. Convicted along with him was Benjamin Dranow, already in prison for tax evasion. They were charged with defrauding the pension fund of $25,000,000 and diverting $1,700,000 to their own uses. Many of the loans from the fund had gone to top men in organized crime.

Out on bond while a team of attorneys led by Shenker appealed his case, Hoffa got a roaring reception in July, 1966, at the national convention of the Teamsters Union on Miami Beach. What's more, they defiantly reelected him to a five-year term as president. A guest speaker at the convention was Senator Long. He described Hoffa as "your dynamic and fighting president" and said he was "always delighted and thrilled" to see him "in action." For good measure he touched on the evils of wiretapping and warned they could lead to a police state in America.

For the speech, the union paid Long between $500 and $1,000—he couldn't remember the exact amount.

On December 12, 1966, the U.S. Supreme Court upheld Hoffa's conviction for jury rigging. On January 26, 1967, Shenker and six other attorneys charged the evidence in the case was "tainted" by wiretapping. Back in Washington, Fensterwald began a series of interviews with past and present officials of the Justice Department in a desperate effort to find some evidence to back up Shenker's charge of wiretapping. Many of the questions concerned possible links between the IRS and the Detroit Police Department. Nothing was found, and on February 27, 1967, the Supreme Court denied Shenker's motion. The next day Shenker tried again—filing a motion in federal court in Chattanooga, where the jury-tampering trial had taken place, charging wiretaps were used. The judge set May 8, 1967, for a hearing. On April 4, Senator Long opened a new series of hearings in Washington with most of the witnesses coming from Detroit.

Newspaper reporters finally smelled a rat. On April 3 they asked Fensterwald if the hearings were designed to help Hoffa. The counsel denied it but admitted it was difficult to investigate wiretapping without running into some reference to Hoffa. Long took the further step of reading a denial into the record of the hearings.

William Bufalino, another of Hoffa's attorneys, sat through the hearings and was seen following Long into the Senator's office during a recess. Back in 1965, Bufalino filed suit in federal court in Detroit against the telephone company in which he charged that his conversations with Hoffa were picked up. Now, following the Long hearings in Washington, he went back to Detroit and asked the court to take judicial notice of testimony given at those Washington hearings. The judge declared he was not going to conduct a Senate hearing on wiretapping. A week later he tossed Bufalino's suit out of court.

Meanwhile, the journalistic grapevine was buzzing about a possible Shenker-Long relationship. On May 26, 1967, Bill Lambert, an associate editor of *Life* magazine* and presently a member of the crack investigative task force, exposed Long's

* Which has since broken stories on Ohio Governor James Rhodes and Associate Justice of the Supreme Court Abe Fortas.

connections with attorney Shenker and bluntly charged that Long had misused the power of his subcommittee in the unsuccessful effort to keep Hoffa out of prison. He noted that Long's hearings had "blunted" the Organized Crime Drive by discrediting the IRS. And finally he revealed that Long had received $48,000 from Shenker—Hoffa's chief counsel.

Long denied everything and accused the IRS of "leaking" the information about the $48,000, to Lambert.* Just as promptly both Lambert and Commissioner Cohen denied Long's accusation.

The Senate Ethics Committee, which had reluctantly looked into accusations against Senator Thomas Dodd, took up *Life*'s charges and "found no facts" to substantiate them. It did, however, make public the names of five clients attorney Shenker "shared" with attorney Long and for which Long was paid not $48,000, but $160,000.

"I'm vindicated," said Long, but *Life* didn't agree. The November 10, 1967, issue of the magazine carried a new article by Lambert. He charged that four of the five clients had mob connections in Las Vegas and elsewhere, and the fifth—a woman Long had claimed as his client—was Shenker's client according to Shenker's affidavit. He had filed suit after the woman's death in 1962, claiming she owed him $90,000 in legal fees.

Ironically, one of the "clients" held a $50,000 interest in Caesar's Palace, a new Las Vegas casino which had been built with a $10,500,000 loan from the Teamsters. Another "client" was a part owner of the Dunes Hotel in Las Vegas. It, too, had been financed with Teamster funds. The casinos of Las Vegas had been one of the chief targets of the Organized Crime Drive that Long and Fensterwald tried so hard to discredit, and the IRS had been the most effective tool used in the campaign.

As the Senator protested in vain, the Senate Ethics Committee decided to reopen its probe. Before the results were released, however, the Senator from Missouri was defeated in a 1968 primary battle—and the question became moot. As a

---

* Actually, the "leak" did not originate from the IRS but from the Organized Crime and Racketeering Section of the Department of Justice.

lame-duck Senator, there was just time enough to make an official junket abroad, so the great investigation into invasions of privacy withered away and died.

The men of the Intelligence Division, who had been smeared by Long in newspaper interviews and magazine stories, felt it was poetic justice that the Senator should be brought low by an enterprising writer. With some amusement they repeated a quote attributed to Long when the primary returns showed he was beaten: "That's life."

Yet the damage to the Organized Crime Drive was great. Morale in both Intelligence and Justice had been badly hurt, and the end was not yet in view. Cases against Las Vegas gamblers Moe Dalitz and Ed Levinson would soon go down the drain.

Following Edward Bennett Williams' discovery of a bug in Levinson's telephone and his subsequent blast at what he considered to be an invasion of Bobby Baker's privacy, Levinson filed two suits—one for $1,500,000 against the Central Telephone Company and, later, one for $2,000,000 against four FBI agents. The phone company suit was dismissed in 1965, but the FBI suit remained a source of increasing embarrassment to the FBI. Senator Long had carefully avoided attacking the FBI; in fact, in his speeches he quoted a letter from J. Edgar Hoover that praised his crusade. Yet the Las Vegas gamblers seemed ready to prove that where wiretapping was concerned, the much-abused IRS was an amateur compared to the FBI.

The whole truth was about to come out—that in 1961 when Robert Kennedy, using the power of the President, forced the FBI into the coordinated war on crime, Hoover's boys had to start from scratch. They had used electronic devices in the name of national security to keep tabs on suspected Communists for many years. Why not use them to collect information on gangsters? The decision was made, and the FBI started bugging every gangster in sight.

Until 1961 the tiny FBI office in Las Vegas had been chiefly concerned with recovering stolen cars. Suddenly it expanded tremendously, and the principal occupation became planting bugs in casino counting rooms and executive offices. Much useful information was obtained.

Meanwhile, the Intelligence Division proceeded along traditional paths. One of their chief targets was Moe Dalitz, a charter member of the Cleveland Syndicate. Thirty years before, they had convicted Dalitz's partner, Morris Kleinman, for tax evasion in connection with the huge profits the syndicate made in rum-running. Kleinman served his time and rejoined the syndicate, which grew and grew and grew. It expanded over Ohio, captured Newport, operated in Miami Beach, built the Desert Inn in Las Vegas, and controlled the Nacional in Havana during Lansky's last hurrah there. In Las Vegas the DI Complex, whose growth had been aided by Teamster loans, was a huge affair encompassing two casinos, hospitals, farms, and a dozen other operations. Throughout the years, Dalitz and his partners had worked closely with Meyer Lansky in a variety of joint ventures.

The Intelligence Division probe paid off on October 14, 1965, when Dalitz and his accountant, Eli Boyer, were indicted in Los Angeles. They were charged with illegally listing $14,-933, in "an intricate and confusing" series of financial transactions, as a capital gain instead of as regular income. In view of Dalitz's multimillion-dollar deals, it seemed small potatoes, but conviction would have resulted in Dalitz's losing his Nevada gaming license.

Levinson, meanwhile, was under investigation by specially trained special agents. Chicago-born, Ed had operated as an illegal but protected gambler in Detroit, Newport, and Miami Beach until coming to Las Vegas in 1952. He had been arrested several times for gambling but had paid only one $25 fine. In Vegas, he had a piece of the Sands, then the Flamingo, before moving to the Fremont in downtown "Glitter Gulch." With the help of a Teamster loan, he greatly enlarged the Fremont to the point where it could compete with the newer hotels on the Strip.

The casino operated much as others everywhere on a twenty-four-hour basis with three shifts. Depending on the activity, from four to ten crap tables were in use. Gambling was done with chips ranging in value from $1 to $100. A player entering the game could either buy chips at the cashier's window or purchase them at the tables from the dealer. In the latter case, he would give the dealer currency and receive chips. The dealer handed the money to the boxman, who checked it against the amount of chips, then put the currency across a small slot on the top of the table. Using a plastic paddle he pushed the money through the slot and into the drop box beneath the table. Eventually the drop box would be removed from the table and taken to the counting room and its contents counted. The casino management took elaborate precautions to avoid cheating by its staff, yet Nevada and United States tax officials had no choice but to accept the count supplied by the management. Everyone knew that large sums were skimmed off the top and not recorded for tax purposes. The problem was proving it. The FBI attempted to do so by bugging; the IRS used different methods.

Selected special agents were given a crash course in casino operations and assigned to pose as bettors at the crap tables. They were given floor plans of the casino and the hours when the drop boxes were changed. They began their observation at the moment a new box was installed beneath the table. Twelve special agents were used. They were divided into two six-man teams, working independently of one another. Each team was divided into two three-man squads, which worked independently while counting the same table at the same time.

Accuracy was stressed. The special agents were told that if there was any doubt about the denomination of a bill—whether it was $1 or $100—to count it at the lowest figure. If action became so slow as to make the undercover men conspicuous, they were instructed to leave the table and ignore any drops made while they were away. Signals were used when one team relieved another to avoid duplicating any drops. Each special agent kept copious notes and used mechanical unit counters to keep score.

When the results were tallied, it was found that two squads working the same table independently often had less than one percent difference in their tallies.

The undercover agents checked the play in March, 1962,

and returned to check it again in the months of April, May, and June, 1963. When all results were in, it was found that the casino understated the gambling handle by 12.07 percent in 1962 and 1963 and by 13.03 percent in 1964. When applied to the total handle for the years involved, the understatement amounted to $1,508,581 in 1962; $1,629,994 in 1963; and $2,185,368 in 1964. The estimates were confirmed by similar checks of the tables made by Nevada gaming authorities and were based on fiscal years ending March 31.

When the skim was added to the reported handle, the totals became $14,007,180 for 1962; $15,134,504 for 1963; and $18,-959,528 for 1964. The net casino profit rose from $2,007,249 to $3,515,830 in 1962; from $1,731,815 to $3,361,808 in 1963; and from $3,030,390 to $5,216,018 in 1964.

Not bad for skimming.

Investigation revealed that cash withheld from the count had to be secreted on the person of one of the counters with the knowledge of the other two counters present. Levinson, as president of the Fremont, participated in twenty-three of twenty-nine understated counts checked by Intelligence.

On May 11, 1967, a federal grand jury indicted Levinson and three of his associates on charges of corporate income tax evasion. Similar charges were brought against owners of the Riviera—the casino Sam and Ben Cohen had built. The Intelligence Division had conducted a check there similar to the one at the Fremont.

The pot began to boil over. Levinson pressed his suit against the FBI, charging the income tax case was based on wiretap evidence. It wasn't, but of course, the FBI had tapped the Fremont phones, as attorney Williams discovered in 1964. FBI special agents were forced to testify, and they admitted they were acting on J. Edgar Hoover's orders. The full extent of the FBI's electronic activity was about to become public knowledge.

Suddenly a deal was made.

Eli Boyer, the accountant who had been indicted with Dalitz, went into court and pleaded guilty to a lesser charge. He was fined $1,000.

Shortly thereafter, on March 9, 1968, the charges against

Dalitz were dismissed at the request of United States Attorney Joseph Ward.

On March 27, 1968, Levinson of the Fremont and Joe Rosenberg of the Riviera marched into court and changed their pleas to *nolo contendere*. Levinson was fined $5,000, and Rosenberg $3,000. Charges against remaining defendants in the two cases were dropped at the request of the government.

On the same day, Levinson dropped his $2,000,000 suit against the FBI.

Everybody was suddenly off the hook. Everybody was happy but the Organized Crime Section of Justice and the men of the Intelligence Division of IRS.

Henry E. Petersen, chief of the Organized Crime Section, said he knew nothing about the decision to drop the cases. Mitchell Rogovin, an Assistant Attorney General who did know of the decision, held a special meeting with the Intelligence men to explain the situation. He was quoted as saying "they felt a lot better" after listening to him.

Privately, a lot of Intelligence Division people said they were sick to their stomachs. Their feelings weren't aided any when they remembered the dozens of other cases that had gone out the window because the evidence was considered "tainted" by FBI bugs.

Meanwhile, J. Edgar Hoover warned the country that danger from "the international Communist conspiracy" still existed.

And the war on organized crime became forgotten as "law and order" became the campaign slogan of 1968.

The men of the Intelligence Division—syndicate fighters since 1919—slowly adjusted to the situation. There had been ups and downs before. Inevitably, the battle would be resumed, and when it did, the silent investigators would lead the attack as usual.

Meanwhile, there was more than enough work to do. As the fiftieth anniversary of the Intelligence Division approached, the major project occupying special agents from coast to coast involved politics. Investigation disclosed that both political parties had devised ways to channel contributions totaling many millions through third parties and so permit the contributors to write off their gifts as business expenses.

Some of the biggest names in American business were said to be involved.

Commissioner Cohen commented in 1968: "Every major gangster case has political overtones."

The year 1969 may prove that the reverse is also true.

EPILOGUE

"MYSTERIOUS Mike Malone" was buried at Arlington Cemetery on November 11, 1960. Only a few friends who knew of Mike's long career as an undercover man were present. The Associated Press, which carried a short story about the funeral, quoted Frank J. Wilson, as saying: "Mike was the best undercover agent we ever had."

To the end, Mike's name and activities were known only to a handful of top officials in the Intelligence Division. In preparation for his final assignment, he stopped in Washington to be equipped with a roll of cash and a Cadillac. His destination was Miami Beach, where he was to pose as a big spender among the big spenders of the syndicate. His objective—to get information about a nationwide abortion ring.

As usual, he succeeded.

Times had changed by 1960 from the days when Mike attended Al Capone's going-away banquet. They were to continue to change. In 1962 the IRS began operating its National Computer Center at Martinsburg, West Virginia. By 1967 seven regional data centers were in operation around the country. One was in Covington, Kentucky, across the Licking River from Newport. Many of its employees were ex-bookies thrown out of work when Newport closed down in 1961.

The Intelligence Division found the computers of great value in catching multiple filers—persons who file many returns from all parts of the country with each return requesting a refund. Forged W-2 forms are used, as well as fake names, addresses, and Social Security numbers. Computers made it easy to detect multiple filers.

But as Mysterious Mike could have predicted, men are still needed to supplement the machines—dedicated, determined men such as Special Agent Tom Harrison.

In November, 1966, a computer identified one James Blivin as a multiple filer. He was indicted for filing false claims for refunds but fled New York to escape prosecution. The only clue to his possible location was an address on a prior return —"in care of Lawson, 6513 Pines Parkway, West Hollywood, Florida."

Harrison, a special agent since 1961, was given the assignment. It seemed easy. At the address given, Harrison found an old man who answered to the name of Lawson. The man refused to talk at first, but Tom was persistent. Finally, Lawson admitted that Bliven was living in an apartment building about two blocks away.

It still seemed easy. Harrison went to 6631 Southwest Eighteenth Street. A late-model gray Chrysler Imperial was parked in front of the building, and a man with a crew cut was hurrying out to it.

"Hi, Jim," said the special agent.

It was Bliven. Harrison put handcuffs on him and took him before the United States Commissioner. An impatient Assistant United States Attorney permitted the fugitive to be released on his own recognizance.

It no longer looked easy. Harrison bet the Assistant U.S. Attorney $5 that Bliven wouldn't show up for trial. He won the bet. A bench warrant was issued. Harrison was told to forget the episode—he had done his best.

Tom wasn't satisfied, however. "It kept eating on me," he said later. On his own time he began a new investigation. He located the woman with whom Bliven had been living at the time of his first arrest. She was sore. Bliven, she said, had talked her into leaving her husband up North to go South with him. Now he had gone off with another woman. What's more, he had taken the Chrysler Imperial with him. She promised to help the special agent locate the rogue.

Now Harrison paid the penalty. Every night the woman called with a possible lead. All had to be checked out. Tom was married and the father of two children, yet hardly knowing why, he found himself devoting all his spare time to the hunt for Bliven. Six months passed.

A good tip finally proved out. The woman's brother spotted Bliven in an Italian restaurant in North Miami. His appearance was not the same, but the brother felt sure it was the same man.

Harrison drove to the restaurant. No Bliven. He began driving in circles around the restaurant, taking each block as it came. Parked on a dead-end street he found a Chrysler convertible of the same model Bliven had used. Only this car was green, not gray. Nearby was a car wash. Tom pulled into a vacant stall and waited. Hours passed.

Suddenly a pickup truck came along and stopped beside the Chrysler. A man got out. He wore a suit, his hair was beatnik long, but it was Bliven.

Harrison gunned his motor, dashed down the road, and cut off the Chrysler. Bliven sighed. "I knew you'd get me," he said.

The fugitive was not released on bond this time. Ultimately, he was sentenced to five years in prison. Meanwhile, Tom traced the ownership of the Chrysler, which had been repainted, to the people it had been stolen from. They were delighted.

"When I left them," said the special agent, "they told me: 'We're sure glad the FBI was on the job.' "

Mike Malone would have understood Tom's feelings.

INDEX

371